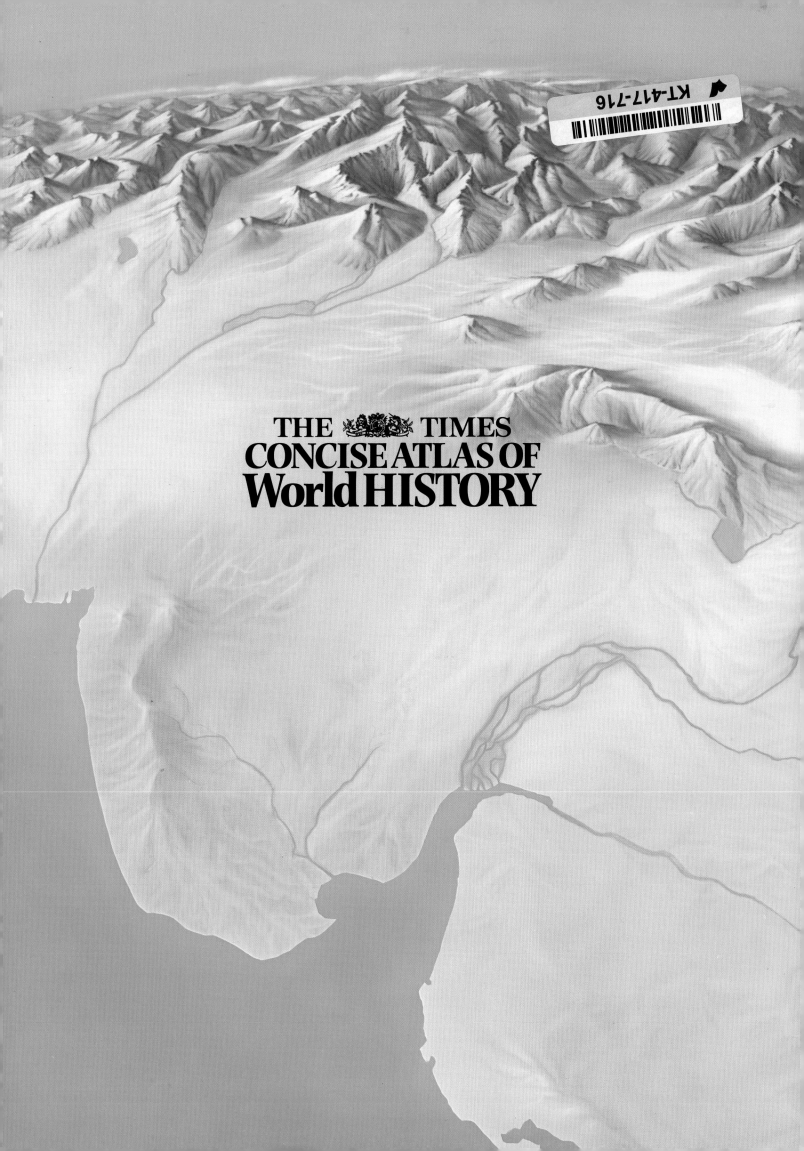

THE ❧❧ TIMES
CONCISE ATLAS OF
World HISTORY

THE ![crest] TIMES CONCISE ATLAS OF World HISTORY

Edited by
GEOFFREY BARRACLOUGH

TIMES BOOKS
A division of HarperCollins*Publishers*

Fourth edition first published in 1992 by
Times Books, a division of
HarperCollins*Publishers*
77–85 Fulham Palace Road
Hammersmith
London W6 8JB

First published in 1982
Revised editions 1986, 1988
Reprinted 1991
© Times Books
1982, 1986, 1988, 1991, 1992

British Library Cataloguing
in Publication Data
The Times concise atlas of world history
  4th ed
  911

ISBN 0 7230 0386 6

EDITORIAL DIRECTION	Barry Winkleman Ailsa Heritage
DESIGN & ART DIRECTION	Ivan and Robin Dodd
MAP DESIGN AND ARTWORK	Swanston Graphics Ltd., Derby P.S.G. Ltd., Derby Peter Sullivan Ivan and Robin Dodd
PLACE NAMES AND INDEX	P.J.M. Geelan
COLOUR SEPARATION	City Ensign Ltd., Hull D.S. Colour International Ltd., London
PRINTED AND BOUND	Hong Kong
EDITORIAL CONSULTANTS *(Fourth Edition)*	Dr Chris Scarre, *McDonald Institute,* *University of Cambridge* Geoffrey Parker, *Charles E. Nowell* *Distinguished Professor of History, University of* *Illinois at Urbana-Champaign* Dr Richard Overy, *Reader in History, King's* *College, London*

ACKNOWLEDGEMENTS — This atlas contains the work of many of the contributors to THE TIMES ATLAS OF WORLD HISTORY (Third edition, 1990) who are listed in that volume. We also wish to thank:
Christopher Bayly, *Professor of Modern Indian History, University of Cambridge*
Frederick W. Boal, *Professor of Human Geography, Queens University, Belfast*
Professor Michael Crowder, late of the *University of Botswana*
Dr Elizabeth Dunstan, *International African Institute*
Norman Hammond, *Professor of Archaeology, Boston University, USA*
David Hickman
Sinclair Hood, *formerly Director, British School of Archaeology, Athens*
Raymond Hutchings, *Senior Editor, Abstract, Soviet and Eastern European Series*
Morton Keller, *Spector Professor of History, Brandeis University, Massachusetts*
John Lynch, *Professor of Latin American History and Director, Institute of Latin American Studies, University of London*
W.H. McNeill, *Robert A. Millitin Distinguished Services Professor of History, University of Chicago*
W.H. Parker, *formerly Lecturer of the Geography of the USSR, University of Oxford*
H.W.F. Saggs, *Professor of Semitic languages, University College, Cardiff*
H.H. Scullard, *Late Emeritus Professor of Ancient History, King's College, London*
R.L. Sims, *Lecturer in the History of the Far East, School of Oriental and African Studies, University of London*
Peter Sluglett, *Lecturer in Modern Middle Eastern History, Durham University, Visiting Professor of History, Harvard University, USA*
Norman Stone, *Professor of Modern History, University of Oxford*
H.P. Willmott, *Senior Lecturer in War Studies, Royal Military Academy, Sandhurst*

CONTENTS

INTRODUCTION

The welcome given to THE TIMES ATLAS OF WORLD HISTORY, first published in English in September 1978, and now available in nine languages, shows how widespread an interest there is today in the human story. It also led us to think that there might be a place for a shorter, less elaborate atlas on a reduced scale.

The present volume is the result. Nevertheless THE TIMES CONCISE ATLAS OF WORLD HISTORY is not merely a condensed and abbreviated version of the earlier work. No fewer than 70 of the 320 maps here presented are entirely new or radically changed, and many others have been revised and redesigned. THE TIMES CONCISE ATLAS is intended to stand on its own feet as a compact, easily available reference book covering the whole story of mankind from the earliest beginnings, when man's ancestors first emerged from the tropical forests of Africa, to the complex, highly articulated world in which we live.

Although the present volume incorporates new material and differs in a number of other ways from the larger work on which it is based, the principles which have guided us are the same. As in THE TIMES ATLAS OF WORLD HISTORY, we have endeavoured to make the coverage as universal as is possible in the present state of knowledge, and in particular to provide full and clear accounts of the civilisations of Asia, Africa and the Americas, both before and after the coming of the Europeans. We have paid close attention to the relations and interactions between these different regions in all their manifestations – cultural and economic, peaceful and warlike, including invasions and migrations, the spread of agriculture and the diffusion of technologies – because we believe these to be some of the main threads of world history. Although we have given more space in this volume to the intricate web of politics (wars, treaties, frontier changes) and to the internal development of particular countries (e.g. England, Russia, Japan, and the U.S.A.), it is our view that world history is more than a combination of national histories, and we have planned this work accordingly.

A long view and a wide historical perspective are vitally important in the world as it is constituted today. If THE TIMES CONCISE ATLAS OF WORLD HISTORY has succeeded in providing such a view, it will have fulfilled one of its objectives. Nevertheless it is important to emphasise that this is not an atlas of current affairs. We have sought, in the concluding plates, to pick out and illustrate some of the more significant trends and movements in the contemporary world, but no attempt has been made to cover the years between 1945 and 1980 in detail. That was not our purpose; but we believe that informed knowledge of the past is a key to the understanding of the present and – as the great Victorian historian, Lord Acton, said it should be – 'a power that goes to the making of the future.'

GEOFFREY BARRACLOUGH
Oxford, March 1982

This fourth edition brings many changes and updates to Professor Barraclough's first edition and to the third edition overseen by Professor Norman Stone. The world order is changing so fast that Professor Barraclough's warning that this is not an atlas of current affairs must be repeated. Nonetheless the final plates have been updated extensively. The earlier plates in the atlas have undergone equally substantial revision in the wake of advances in archaeology.

TIMES BOOKS
January 1992

Human origins

In the vast time perspective of earth history the human species is a relative newcomer. The first life on earth of which we have any trace, simple single-celled organisms, date back some 4600 million years (diagram 1). In contrast, fully modern *Homo sapiens* originated a mere 120,000 years ago. Yet within that short period of time we have become one of the most successful species ever, colonising virtually every corner of the globe, increasing enormously in numbers and manipulating the earth's resources and environment in a way never attempted by any other organism on our planet.

Study of chromosomes shows that our nearest relatives in the animal kingdom are the African apes (gorillas and chimpanzees). With them we share a common descent from various ape-like species such as the *Dryopithecines* which lived in Africa, Europe and south Asia some 20–15 million years ago. The parting of the ways, when the human line diverged from that of the chimpanzees and gorillas (diagram), may have come as recently as 8 million years ago, a tiny interval in the 4600 million years of life on earth.

The origins of the earliest hominids lie in equatorial Africa, and it is here that the oldest remains have been found (map 3). These are of a small creature known as *Australopithecus* or 'southern ape', from the first dis-

covery at Taung in South Africa in 1924. No fewer than four separate species of *Australopithecus* have now been distinguished in the fossil record, all restricted to Africa and living in the period from 5 million to 1 million years ago. We know that they walked upright on two legs from footsteps left in the mud at Laetoli in east Africa.

These *Australopithecines* were small agile creatures, only around four feet tall, and they lived almost exclusively on nuts, fruits and berries. But they already displayed some of the trends which were to lead to modern humans. The bipedal posture freed the hands for other tasks, in turn stimulating the development of a larger brain. At the same time, the jaw and snout became less prominent as hands could be used to break off foods

2 The spread of Homo sapiens

35,000 years ago
50,000 years ago
100,000 years ago

1 The origin and development of life

● first appearance
▬ mass extinction of land life
● mass extinction of marine life
✳ glaciation

and bring them to the mouth.

A crucial stage in the development of modern man was the appearance of a new species, *Homo habilis* or 'handy man', in East Africa around 2 million years ago. These may have been the first hominids to make and use stone tools, and probably the first to scavenge for meat as a regular part of their diet. They were followed around 1.5 million years ago by *Homo erectus*, a larger and more intelligent creature, and the first human ancestor to spread beyond the confines of Africa to Europe, China and South-East Asia.

The colonisation of the Old World by *Homo erectus* was a considerable achievement given the environmental conditions of the period. *Homo erectus* and his descendants were able to make use of clothes and artificial shelters. They may also have started to hunt. Most important, however, was their mastery of fire. With more sophisticated tools, a larger brain, and command of fire, *Homo erectus* was able to survive north of the frost line at sites such as Chou-k'ou-tien (Zhoukoudian) near Peking around half a million years ago.

Homo erectus survived for a million years or more, but some time after 500,000 years ago new types of hominid began to develop in Europe and Africa. In Europe, these changes led c.100,000 BC to the appearance of Neanderthal man, named after a skull found in the Neander valley in Germany in 1856. The line of development leading to modern humans, however, was based in Africa. Here, a little over 100,000 years ago, developed the first members of our own species, *Homo sapiens sapiens*: larger-brained creatures, able hunters and gatherers, equipped with sophisticated language and technology. From Africa the new species spread throughout the whole of the territory which had been occupied by *Homo erectus* and its descendants (map 2), and beyond into the hitherto unsettled regions of Australia and the Americas. For a while, Neanderthals hung on in parts of Europe, as the last Ice Age gathered pace; but their days were numbered. By 30,000 years ago, of the many species of hominid which had walked the earth during the past 5 million years of human development, only one, *Homo sapiens sapiens*, was left.

3 Traces of human origins

- Australopithecus
- Homo habilis
- Homo erectus
- Homo sapiens (archaic)
- Homo sapiens (Neanderthal)
- Homo sapiens (modern)

The Ice Ages

We are well aware today that the earth's climate is not a stable, static phenomenon. Indeed, for at least 14 million years world climate has gradually been cooling. Around 2 million years ago this process intensified, and by 800,000 years ago the earth was in the grip of the first of the great ice ages which were to come and go roughly every 100,000 years, and to dominate human history until the last of them receded only 10,000 years ago.

The ice ages were periods of intense cold in northern and southern latitudes away from the equator. Temperatures fell by up to 15°C, and ice sheets advanced across the frozen wastes of northern Eurasia and North America. As more and more of the earth's water became locked into the growing ice sheets, sea levels fell, and even equatorial regions did not escape the effects of climatic adversity as rainfall diminished, turning half of all the land area between the tropics into desert.

The glaciers advanced and retreated several times, reaching a climax every 100,000 years but also giving way for short periods of 10,000 years or so to more temperate regimes. With each ice advance the plants and animals of the northern hemisphere withdrew before them to warmer latitudes waiting, perhaps several thousand years, for the ice to retreat and allow them to move northwards again. Hominids too such as *Homo erectus* must have migrated with the changing climate.

Yet despite the harshness of the coldest periods, the human species continued to develop during these millennia. It was indeed at this time that the human species spread from its original African homeland to east and south-east Asia and Europe. The mastery of fire and the invention of clothing and shelter were crucial to this achievement, but so were new social and communication skills. The human species as we know it today is the product of the long process of adaptation to the harsh conditions of the ice age.

The final phase of the ice ages began 75,000 years ago with the advance of the Würm glaciers in central Europe and the associated Weichsel and Wisconsin glacier fields in northern Europe and North America. By tying up water on a grand scale these reduced sea levels, and land bridges appeared, linking most of the major land areas and many present-day islands (including the British Isles) into one single continental mass. It was at this time, too, that a new species of human, fully modern *Homo sapiens sapiens*, began to spread from Africa, replacing or interbreeding with existing hominid populations in Europe and Asia. It was thus modern humans that were able to take advantage of the short sea crossing caused by sea-level fall and colonise Australasia in about 50,000 BC. A little later, perhaps as early as 40,000 BC, humans also colonised America (map 2), either by crossing the land bridge which joined the two sides of the Bering Straits at certain periods or by use of boats. With the onset of warmer conditions some 10,000 years ago

rising sea levels cut off these human communities in Australia and the Americas from further contact with Eurasia. Henceforward, these regions pursued their own independent lines of development.

Modern humans were relatively late arrivals in western Europe, replacing earlier Neanderthal populations only around 35,000 years ago. Yet here, as in Australia and South America, the new communities soon developed new levels of cultural expression which still impress us today (map 3). In the Dordogne area of south-west France, in the Pyrenees and in the Cantabrian region of northern Spain, hundreds of caves were decorated with paintings of symbols and animals, sometimes in rich polychrome style.

As hunting techniques and tool technology became more sophisticated, human communities became more and more able to cope with their environment. It was, however, change in the environment itself which was most important in opening up new opportunities. Around 20,000 years ago, the last ice age was at its peak (map 1); ten thousand years later, it was in its closing stages. As temperatures rose, vegetation spread and animals began to recolonise the cold northern wastes. With them went the human hunters and gatherers. By 8000 BC, in certain crucial corners of the world such as Central America and the Near East, people had begun to move beyond their existing resources to investigate new ways of producing food, manipulating plants and animals in the first experiments in farming.

1 The world 20,000 years ago

— coastline 20,000 years ago
— modern coastline

glacier
sea ice

tundra
temperate steppe

temperate forest
tropical forest

desert
tropical glacier

FENNOSCANDIAN ICE SHEET

BERINGIA *early settlements in Alaska*

CORDILLERAN ICE SHEET

North Sea Lake

mammoth-hunters of S Russian plain
Black Sea Lake

Caspian Sea Lake

painted caves of SW France and N Spain

Mediterranean

Sea of Japan

early settlements of E Japan

Lake Bonneville

arid Sahara

Red Sea

TIBET

Lake Chad

Lake Makgadikgadi

SUNDA

SAHEL

painted rock shelters of S Namibia

GREATER AUSTRALIA

Koonalda Cave flint mine

settlements and painted rock-shelters of SE Australia and Tasmania

TASMANIA

Magnetic pole reversals
epochs   *events*

Temperature fluctuations based on analysis of deep sea cores

BRUNCHES NORMAL

Jaramillo

MATUYAMA REVERSED

Olduvai

0.5

1.0

1.5

2.0

million years ago

no further data available

Climatic changes of the Pleistocene

2 The colonisation of the Americas

- land bridge
- route of colonisation
- ▲ major site

Arctic Ocean

Bluefish Cave
c.40,000 BC?

NORTH AMERICA

Calico Hills ▲
Meadowcroft ▲
Clovis ▲

Pacific Ocean
Atlantic Ocean
Caribbean Sea

SOUTH AMERICA

Pedra Furada ▲
Monte Verde ▲

GREENLAND ICE SHEET

LAURENTIDE ICE SHEET

t Salt

painted rock-shelters of Brazil

ANDES ICE SHEET

3 Palaeolithic art in Europe

- ○ site location

finds of:
- ● mural art
- ■ portable art
- ▲ female figurines

Arctic Ocean

R. Lena
Bérelekh

L. Baikal
Buret ▲
Mal'ta ▲
Maininskaya ▲

R. Yenisey
R. Ob'
R. Irtysh
R. Tobol

SIBERIA

Kara Sea
Ural Mts

Barents Sea

R. Ural

Kapovaya

Caspian Sea

Sungir

L. Ladoga

R. Volga
R. Don

SCANDINAVIA

Gagarino ▲
Kostienki ▲

Khotylevo ▲
Yeliseyevichi
Yudinovo
Kirillovskaya

Avdeyevo
Mezin
Mezhirich'

Caucasus Mts

Baltic Sea

R. Vistula
R. Dniester

Black Sea

North Sea

R. Oder

Maszycka

Molodovo

ANATOLIA

R. Elbe
Petřkovice
Předmosti
Brno
Moravany
Dolní Věstonice
Pavlov
Willendorf ▲

BALKANS

R. Drava
R. Danube

Taurus Mts

Oberkassel
Goyet
Trou Magrite
Gough's Cave
Gouy

Gönnersdorf
Andernach
Verlaine
Vogelherd
Petersfels
Mauern
Kesslerloch
Schweizersbild

Cyprus

BRITISH ISLES

Mayenne Sciences
Chiozza
Savignano
Trasimeno

Arene Candide
Grimaldi

Crete

R. Loire

see below

Corsica

Romanelli

ALPS

R. Rhône

Sardinia

Levanzo
Sicily

Pyrenees

R. Ebro

Los Casares
La Hoz
Parpalló

Mediterranean Sea

Mazouco
El Reguerillo

R. Tagus

Escoural
Ardales
La Pileta
Nerja
Las Palomas

NORTH AFRICA

Atlas Mts

R. Loire

Angles-sur-l'Anglin

La Marche

FRANCE

La Marche
Teyjat
Roc de Sers
Fourneau du Diable
Rouffignac
Le Gabillou
Pair-non-Pair
Laugerie Basse
Bara-Bahau
St-Cirq
Le Poisson
La Mouthe
Font de Gaume

Le Placard
Montgaudier
Badegoule
Laugerie Haute
La Madeleine
Lascaux
Combarelles
Laussel
Cap Blanc
Bernifal
Pech-Merle
La Magdeleine
Cougnac
Bruniquel

Ebbou

L'Aldène

La Baume-Latrone

Bay of Biscay

R. Adour

Brassempouy
Isturits

R. Rhône

Tito Bustillo
Candamo
Pindal
Altamira
Castillo

Herrerías
Chufín
Ekain
Cullalvera

Altxerri

Santimamiñe

Lespugue ▲
Labastide
Gargas
Les Trois Frères
Le Tuc d'Audoubert

Ganties-Montespan
Le Mas-d'Azil
Bédeilhac
Niaux

Gulf of Lions

From hunting to farming

Somewhere around 8000 BC human communities began to select, breed, domesticate and cultivate various species of plant and animal. This was the beginning of agriculture and is sometimes called the Neolithic or agricultural revolution. In fact, it was a slow and partial process which occurred at different times and speeds in different parts of the world and was never complete, if only because climatic and soil variations precluded agriculture in many areas. The arid zones were the home of mobile pastoralists, who domesticated sheep and horses and colonised the grazing grounds of the steppes, while the densely afforested areas, in northern Europe and elsewhere, were inhabited, as earlier, by hunters. The result, following the spread of agriculture, was a differentiated world economy, with well defined zones, cereal and root-crop cultivation being characteristic of the temperate and tropical regions respectively (map 1).

The transformation from a hunter and fisher to an agriculturalist, and from a migratory to a sedentary life, was a decisive event in world history. The increase in food resources which followed made possible a spectacular growth of human population calculated to have multiplied sixteen times between 8000 and 4000 BC. It also required co-operative effort, particularly after the introduction of irrigation c.5000 BC, leading to the establishment of settled, organised societies, at first villages, then towns and cities. Urban civilisation dates from c.3500 BC, but already before 6000 BC there were 'proto-cities' covering extensive sites (up to 30 acres) at Jericho in the Jordan valley and Çatal Hüyük in Anatolia. Here also there is evidence of long-distance trade.

There is no doubt that agriculture developed independently in different parts of the world, presumably in response to similar stimuli, but the beginnings of cereal cultivation are clearly associated with the Near East. Here, on the remote mountain uplands, were found the wild ancestors of wheat and barley, and the villages where they were first cultivated (c.8000 BC) grew up on the edge of this zone, within the critical rainfall limit of 300 mm (12 ins) a year (map 4). Only with the introduction of irrigation was it possible to extend cultivation into the adjacent dry plains. This occurred during the fifth and fourth millennia BC. At about the same time the ox-drawn plough began to be adopted throughout much of Eurasia, enlisting animal traction to increase the efficiency of farming (map 2). In much of the world, however, hoe agriculture persisted and human muscle power remained the basis of farming until relatively recent times.

Many other parts of the globe contributed their quota at different times to the supply of domesticated plants and animals (map 4). Their diffusion from their original habitat not only supplemented native food resources, but also affected human diet. Rice, which originated in South-East Asia and southern China, passed into the Near East and Mediterranean Europe, where it became a staple foodstuff. The yam and banana, later to be major African food crops, were introduced from Asia during the first millennium BC.

As farming spread, hunting and gathering was increasingly relegated to the more marginal world environments where agriculture was unable to secure a foothold (map 3). The gradual decline of hunters and gatherers can be traced across the centuries, until in recent times their sole surviving representatives have been found only in hot deserts such as the Kalahari and Australia, in the dense rain forests of the Amazon basin, central Africa and South-East Asia, and in the frozen wastes of the Arctic.

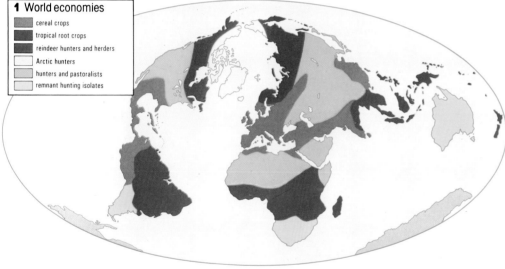

1 World economies
- cereal crops
- tropical root crops
- reindeer hunters and herders
- Arctic hunters
- hunters and pastoralists
- remnant hunting isolates

3 The decline of hunter-gathering

world distribution of hunter-gathering peoples

AD 1500

world population: 350 million
% hunters: 1.0

15,000 BC

world population: 10 million
% hunters: 100

1960

world population: 3 billion
% hunters: 0.001

5 Centres of animal and plant domestication

alfalfa		oats
avocado		olive
banana		peas
barley		peanuts
breadfruit		peppers
cocoa		pineapple
coconut		potato
cotton		rice
cucumber		runner bean
cucurbits		rye
dates		sorghum
finger millet		soya bean
foxtail millet		sunflower
grapes		sweet potato
hemp		tepary bean
lentil		tomato
lima bean		watermelon
maize		wheat
manioc		yam

Indus Valley (Kalibangan):
plough marks c.2600 BC

China (Hangchow area):
stone objects thought to be
plough shares c.3000 BC

northern Thailand
(Ban Chiang):
bones of water buffalo
suggest use as plough
animals c.300 BC

limit of plough agriculture

L. Baikal

L. Balkhash

R. Amur

Yellow R.

CHINA

Yangtze R.

R. Ganges

INDIA

R. Mekong

Bay of
Bengal

USSIA

Sea of
Okhotsk

Sea of
Japan

Pacific
Ocean

South
China
Sea

2 Adoption of
the plough

△ before 4000 BC
▲ 4000–2000 BC
▲ after 2000 BC

Black Sea

Caspian Sea

ANATOLIA

Taurus Mts

L. Van
L. Urmia

Zawi Chemi

Çayönü
Nineveh
Arpachiyah

Tell Brak
Hassuna
Jarmo

Hacilar

Tell Halaf
Samarra
Tell es-Sawwan
Choga Mami

Zagros Mts

Ali Kosh

SYRIA

Cyprus

Khirokitia

Tell Abu Hureira

MESOPOTAMIA

R. Tigris

Mediterranean Sea

Tell Ramad

R. Euphrates

Uruk

Jericho
Dead Sea
S y r i a n   D e s e r t

Eridu
Ur

30°

EGYPT

R. Nile

30°

40°

4 The agricultural revolution in the Near East

◯ natural distribution of wheat and barley

⎯ southern limit of rain-fed agriculture

● early farming sites 9000–6000 BC

◉ farming villages 6000–4000 BC

80°

NORTH-
WEST
EURASIA

Reindeer

CENTRAL ASIA

Cattle

Pig

SOUTHERN EUROPE

Horse

SOUTH-WESTERN
STEPPES

Bactrian Camel

Yak

CHINA

40°

Atlantic
Ocean

NEAR EAST

HIMALAYAS

Pacific
Ocean

Ass

Goose
Goat
Sheep

INDUS

SOUTH-EAST ASIA

Zebu

Pig

Water
Buffalo

WEST AFRICA

NORTH-EAST
AFRICA

Chicken

Indian

SOUTH PACIFIC

0°

LOWLAND
SOUTH
AMERICA

Ocean

60°

0°

60°

120°

60°

7

Early cultures of Asia

From an origin in Africa, *Homo erectus* or its close relatives had spread widely through Asia by the Middle Pleistocene period (400–200,000 years ago). It is not possible to establish the precise history of this colonisation process, but it is reasonable to assume that these hominids first reached India, where hand-axes, chopping tools and flakes of the early Stone Age are found not only in the foothills of the Punjab but as far east as southern Bihar and northern Orissa and as far south as Madras (map 1). It was not long before *Homo erectus* also became established in both East and South-East Asia, as shown by skeletal remains from Java and China. Here they remained until replaced some 60,000 years ago by our own fully modern species, *Homo sapiens sapiens*.

Little is known of the development of human societies in this part of the world until the advent of agriculture. At about the same time as farming communities were getting under way in western Asia, the first experiments in agriculture were also being made in East and South Asia. In China, the most important centre of early farming was the Yellow River valley in the north, where crops of millet were raised on the well-drained loess terraces of the river valleys from around 6000 BC (map 2). A little later, rice cultivation spread northwards from its original heartland in South-East Asia, giving a second productive staple crop. The early villages grew and prospered, and new technologies made their appearance: jade-carving, silk-weaving and very high quality pottery production using the fast wheel.

In about 1800 BC the thriving villages and small towns which had developed in northern China gave rise to the first Chinese civilisation. Early dynasties soon gave way to the Shang, who ruled much of the North China plain and parts of the Yangtze valley from the 16th to the 11th century BC (map 4). Great cities developed, notably at Cheng-chou and An-yang, and rulers were given lavish burial in royal tombs.

The first civilisation of South Asia developed in the valley of the Indus river. Again, this was founded on a secure agricultural base which had been developing since c.6000 BC or earlier. Large-scale settlement of the fertile river plain seems to have occurred in the 4th millennium BC, and soon afterwards the first cities appear, notably those of Harappa and Mohenjo-daro (map 5). These were highly-developed cities covering nearly 1,295,000 sq.kms, and surviving for over 1000 years. A standardised system of weights and measures was devised, and trade with the Persian Gulf brought Indus products to the great cities of southern Mesopotamia. Influences from South Asia also reached South-East Asia, where the distinctive Dong Son drums were produced by communities of village farmers from 1500–500 BC (map 3).

The Indus cities were abandoned soon after 2000 BC, overtaken perhaps by environmental change or natural disaster, and it was over 1000 years before cities reappeared in the sub-continent. The focus had by this time shifted to the Ganges, where the historic cities and states of northern India began to form in about 500 BC. By that time China too was divided between a number of major kingdoms, as the unified rule of the Shang and their successors the Chou broke down and fragmented (map 6). Yet despite the divisions, the basic foundations of Chinese and Indian civilisation had been laid.

2 Early Chinese agriculture

- area of loess soil
- redeposited loess
- early millet cultivation
- approximate northern limit of wild rice distribution
- early wet rice cultivation

Chinese settlement:
- ▲ 6000-5000 BC
- ■ 6000-4000 BC
- ● 5000-2500 BC

4 Shang China

- ● cities
- ▬ rich burials
- ▲ oracle bones
- ancient coastline
- ancient river course

8

6 China under the Western Chou, c.1027-771 BC
- Chou capitals
- the royal domain
- fiefs allocated to Chou royal family
- Shang royal family
- fiefs allocated to other families
- major excavated sites

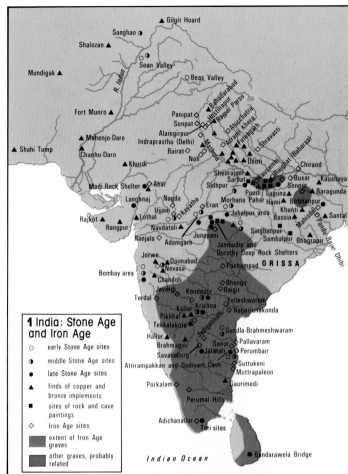

1 India: Stone Age and Iron Age
- early Stone Age sites
- middle Stone Age sites
- late Stone Age sites
- finds of copper and bronze implements
- sites of rock and cave paintings
- Iron Age sites
- extent of Iron Age graves
- other graves, probably related

3 Prehistoric sites in South-East Asia
- Neolithic/Bronze Age settlements
- Dong Son drums
- Early Iron Age and urn burial sites

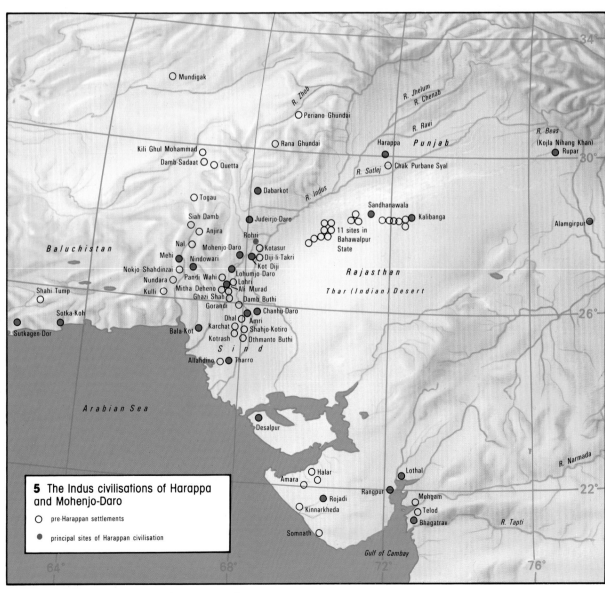

5 The Indus civilisations of Harappa and Mohenjo-Daro
- pre-Harappan settlements
- principal sites of Harappan civilisation

Prehistoric Africa and Australasia

Climatic change, between 5–6000 years ago, profoundly influenced the early history of Africa and Australasia. North Africa developed in close association with western Asia, and by 3000 BC an advanced civilisation was established in Egypt. But Africa south of the equator, almost certainly the original home of humans, was cut off from the mainstream for centuries by the desiccation of the Sahara. Similar changes occurred in Australia which had been populated during the late Pleistocene ice age via the land bridge from New Guinea (page 4). Here the rise of the sea level drowned large areas of coastal lowland and severed the land link with New Guinea. The Australasian continent developed thenceforth in geographical isolation. The colonisation of the islands of Melanesia occurred considerably later, when settlers from New Guinea, associated with the distinctive Lapita pottery, reached Fiji (c.1300 BC) and then made their way into Polynesia via Tonga and Samoa, reaching the Marquesas Islands c.AD 300 (map 2). From here they spread north to Hawaii (c.AD 800) and south-west via the Cook Islands to New Zealand between 850 and 1100 (map 3).

Geographical isolation was an important factor in shaping the cultures of southern Africa and of Oceania. In much of Australia the aborigines remained hunters and gatherers and there was no use of iron, but they were prolific in their decoration of rock shelters with deeply symbolic designs. Elsewhere in Oceania, notably in New Zealand, a mixed hunting-farming society developed and settlement spread inland. But population remained small, about 300,000 in Australia and 100,000 in New Zealand when the Europeans arrived. The isolation of southern Africa was never so complete. In East Africa settlers spread down the Rift Valley during the first millennium BC, and trans-Saharan trade increased in importance after the introduction of the camel from Asia c.100 BC (map 1).This facilitated the spread of iron tools and weapons, introduced in the north by Greeks and Carthaginians in the eighth and seventh centuries. Aided by the new iron technology, Bantu-speaking farmers and cattle-herdsmen began to colonise southern Africa in the early centuries AD. By the thirteenth century powerful Bantu chiefdoms had emerged, such as that centred on the Great Zimbabwe enclosure, cattle-raising communities already engaged in trade when the Portuguese arrived at the close of the fifteenth century.

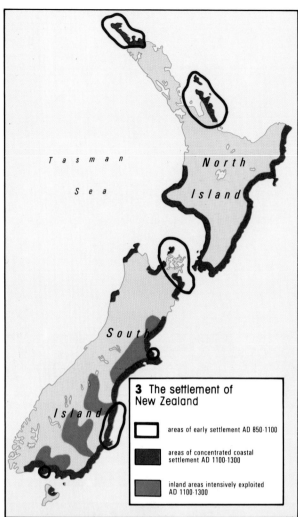

3 The settlement of New Zealand

□ areas of early settlement AD 850-1100

■ areas of concentrated coastal settlement AD 1100-1300

■ inland areas intensively exploited AD 1100-1300

Atlantic Ocean

Zemmour

Akjoujt
○ copper mining
5th century BC

Adrar

R. Senega/

KINGD
OF GHA
1st MILLENNI

megalithic graves
1st millennium AD

Mediterranean Sea

N. African megaliths
2nd and 1st millennium BC

Utica
Carthage
Capeletti

PHOENICIA

Cyrene

Leptis
(Homs)

Greek and Phoenician colonists

Atlas Mts

4500 BC

Sahara Desert

Naucratis Sais
Merimbe 4200 BC
Memphis
Fayum 4300 BC

EGYPT

Thebes

Red Sea

3000 BC

Meniet
Adrar Tiouiyne
Uan Muhaggiag
Immidir
Adrar Bous
Arlit
Hoggar
Massif
Tassili
Massif

*Jebel
'Uweinat*

Tibesti Massif

NUBIA

iron

Nuri
Napata
Shaheinab
3200 BC
Meroe 500 BC

**KINGDOM OF MEROE
900 BC-AD 400**

Kadero

Adulis

Axum

**KINGDOM
OF AXUM
AD 100-1000**

Air

2000 BC

Ennedi

Darfur

Jebel Moya

Blue Nile
White Nile

Karkarchinkat

Gao

iron

1500 BC

Agadez
copper working in 2nd millennium BC

1500 BC

Daima

500 BC

*Ethiopian
Highlands*

Ethiopian megaliths
1st and 2nd millennium AD
fleret

Jenne-jeno
proto-urban settlement
by 1st century AD

R. Niger

Kintampo Nteroso 1400 BC

Jos Plateau
Nok
Taruga 440 BC
R. Benue
Ife

Igbo Ukwu
shrines AD 840

possible spread of
cultivation to lower
Congo Basin
1st millennium BC

iron and cattle

Arab traders and colonists

Indian Ocean

Atwetwebooso

R. Congo

Western Stream Iron Age sites

Urewe Iron Age groups

Rift Valley

Urewe
Elmenteita
Crescent Is.   Manda

Kaduruka 5th
century BC
Narosura

East African 'pastoral neolithic' sites

*Lake
Victoria*

Eastern Stream Iron Age sites

Kwale

ports involved in Indian
Ocean trade by 8th
century AD. SE Asian
foodstuffs (bananas,
taro) introduced

Kilwa

iron and cattle

Funa River 270 BC

*Lake
Tanganyika*

*Lake
Nyasa*

R. Ruvuma

Kamnama

Kalambo

Sanga
late 1st millennium AD
cemetery of 144 graves

AD 500
Lubusi

iron and cattle

Nkope

R. Zambezi

AD 1000

Kapwirimbe
Kalundu

Ziwa

Gokomere
Zimbabwe
Malapati
Mabueni

Phalaborwa

Madagascar

Indonesian colonists

Kalahari Desert

Castle
Cavern

Shongweni

domestic sheep obtained
by 1st century AD, perhaps
from Iron Age source

R. Orange

Blackburn

Zaayfontein

Drakensberg Mts

Wilton

Bonteberg

Nelson Bay

Die Kelders

tu Archipelago

Pitcairn I.

Easter I.

Peoples and cultures of the Americas

America, like Australia (page 10), was colonised from Asia during the last Ice Age more than 10,000 years ago, and like Australia was later cut off from the Old World by the melting of the ice and the rise of the sea level which submerged the land bridge across the Bering Strait (page 4). Unlike the Australian aborigines, however, who never progressed beyond a Stone Age hunting and gathering culture, geographic isolation did not prevent the American Indians from developing independently a high level of civilisation, based on agriculture (particularly the cultivation of maize), mining (particularly obsidian for tools and weapons), pottery manufacture and gold, silver and copper working. It was a civilisation distinguished not only by magnificent art and remarkable mathematical and astronomical skills, but also by monumental building on a grand scale. In its prime, around AD 600, the city of Teotihuacán in the basin of Mexico covered 20 sq. km (8 sq. miles) and had a population of 125,000.

The first civilisations arose in the climatically favourable regions of Mesoamerica and the central Andes, where maize farming, permitting a rapid increase in population, became widespread from c. 1500 BC. Between 800 and 500 BC the Olmecs on the Gulf of Mexico, the Zapotecs at Monte Albán, and the inhabitants of Chavín in Peru had developed complex societies with populations numbering tens of thousands, possibly a professional priesthood, and several social ranks including craftsmen and traders. Mesoamerica and the central Andes remained the main centres of civilisation, but the diffusion of agriculture and growing commercial exchanges soon affected other regions. In North America the introduction of maize, beans and squashes from Mexico initiated a period of rapid development between 300 BC and AD 550. Its centre was the Hopewell territory in Illinois and Ohio, but trading contacts (mainly for precious metals) extended its influence as far as Florida and the Rockies (map 3). In South America a number of separate centres, each with its own distinctive artistic style, developed in the Andes (map 4), and were fused after AD 600 into the empires of Tiahuanaco and Huari (map 5). But this precarious unity broke down after AD 800 and it was not until the fifteenth century under the Incas that Peru was once again united (page 62).

In Mesoamerica, the early Olmec and Zapotec civilisations were complemented by new influences, including the Maya in Yucatán from the fourth century BC, then the Toltecs in the ninth century and finally the Aztecs in the thirteenth century. The classic period of Maya civilisation falls between AD 300 and AD 900; but influences radiating from Teotihuacán were strong (map 2), and Maya civilisation, like all the other civilisations of the classical period, was essentially a variant of a common Mesoamerican culture pattern. Internecine warfare appears to have weakened these civilisations and left them prey to invaders or local instability. Teotihuacán was destroyed c. 750, Monte Albán allowed to go to ruin during the tenth century, and Maya civilisation collapsed between AD 800 and 900.

For all their brilliant architectural and artistic achievements, the civilisations of Mesoamerica and the Andes account for only a small area of the Americas taken as a whole (map 1). Climatic variation alone dictated disparate ways of life. Particularly in the far north and far south, where conditions were too harsh for farming, the small nomadic populations depended on hunting and fishing. Climate was also a determining factor for the desert gatherers in the interior. The continent the Europeans encountered when they arrived in the sixteenth century was at widely different levels of development; but even the simpler societies had adapted themselves to the environment and its requirements.

Asia

Bering Strait

ARCTIC LITTORAL HUNTERS

HUNTERS OF THE SUB-ARCTIC FOREST

(ESKIMO)

L'Anse aux Meadows
(Norse colony, founded by
Icelanders AD 1001
but soon abandoned)

PLATEAU
FISHERMEN
PLANT GATHERERS
HUNTERS

Huff Village

PLAINS HUNTERS
farming introduced
along river valleys
from eastern
woodlands

Simonsen

FISHERMEN
MONTANE
GATHERERS

Hogup Cave
Danger Cave

DESERT
GATHERERS

Hopewell

S.W.
FARMERS

PUEBLO
INDIANS

Tyuonyi

WOODLAND
FARMERS

Pueblo Bonito

DESERT
GATHERERS
FISHERMEN
SHELLFISH
COLLECTORS

DESERT
GATHERERS

Poverty Point

Hardaway

Etowah

Atlantic Ocean

Gulf of Mexico

El Tajin

CARIBBEAN

Teotihuacán

Monte Albán

Tikal

FARMERS

MESOAMERICAN
CIVILISATION

MAYA

Caribbean Sea

MAIZE AND MANIOC
CULTIVATORS OF
CARIBBEAN LOWLANDS

WARU

Lake
Titicaca

TIAHUANACO

Tiahuanaco

SAVANNAH
FARMERS

ATACAMEÑO

Lake
Poopó

NORTH
ANDEAN
CHIEFDOMS

San Agustín

FARMING TRIBES
(manioc cultivators)
of the Amazon Rain Forest

Teso dos Bichos

Pacific Ocean

Moche

Chavin

CENTRAL
ANDEAN
CIVILISATION

Las Haldas
La Florida
Huari

Pedra Furada

Nasca

SAVANNAH
FARMERS

Tiahuanaco

about AD 500
farming introduced
from Amazon Basin
into Brazilian forest
and savannah

Piquillacta

immigration of
Tupi-Guaraní tribes

Lake
Titicaca

Tiahuanaco

HUNTERS
OF THE
CHACO
SAVANNAH

TIAHUANACO EMPIRE

Lake
Poopó

1 American peoples
and cultures, c. AD 500

farming peoples

chiefdoms

civilised states

hunters and gatherers

■ archaeological site

GRASSLAND,
STEPPE HUNTERS

Monte Verde

MARITIME
HUNTERS

SHELLFISH
COLLECTORS

The development of Europe, 6000-300BC

It was only after farming had been established in the Near East for several hundred years that it first spread westwards to Europe. The earliest European agriculturalists settled in farming villages on the plains of Thessaly and Crete c.6000 BC (map 1). The crops of wheat and barley which these communities grew were of Near Eastern type, and they relied heavily on the Near Eastern animal domesticates sheep and goat. As farming spread north and west into temperate Europe, however, major adjustments were necessary. New types of wheat and barley replaced those of Greece and the Near East, and cattle and pig became the dominant species of livestock in forested parts of central, western and northern Europe in place of sheep and goat.

The new farming technology, including not only domesticated species of plants and animals but also pottery and polished stone tools, spread rapidly across Europe in the 6th and 5th millennia BC, reaching Britain and Denmark by 4000 BC. In the centuries of consolidation which followed, the early farmers of western and northern Europe built great burial mounds with megalithic chambers in which dozens if not hundreds of dead bodies were deposited. They also raised circles of standing stones (map 3).

By this time a new technology was spreading across Europe, supplementing the stone tools of the previous centuries: metallurgy (map 2). South-east Europe became an important centre of gold and copper-working as early as 4500 BC. By 2500 BC it had become common to alloy the copper with tin to produce bronze, an alloy of greater hardness, thus initiating the period known as the Bronze Age. The need to obtain access to the raw materials copper and tin led to the development of extensive trade networks along which other materials also travelled, such as the Baltic amber which is found as far afield as Mycenae (map 4).

Around 1200 BC a more closely articulated political organisation began to emerge, centred upon hillforts built to house and defend a warrior-aristocracy. The upper Rhine/upper Danube became an important core area where a distinctive Celtic culture emerged in the 1st millennium BC (map 5). Ironworking was introduced c.1000–700 BC, which together with population growth fuelled a period of Celtic expansion in the La Tène period (from 480 BC). Contact with the Mediterranean world stimulated Celtic civilisation, but it also prepared the way for Caesar's campaigns. Thus it was that by 50 BC most of the western Celtic world was under Roman control.

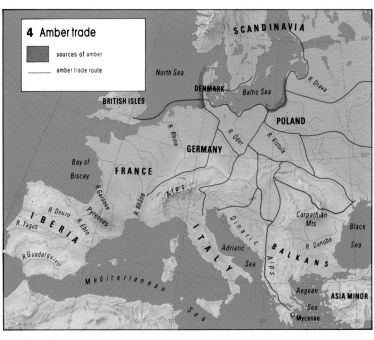

4 Amber trade
- sources of amber
- amber trade route

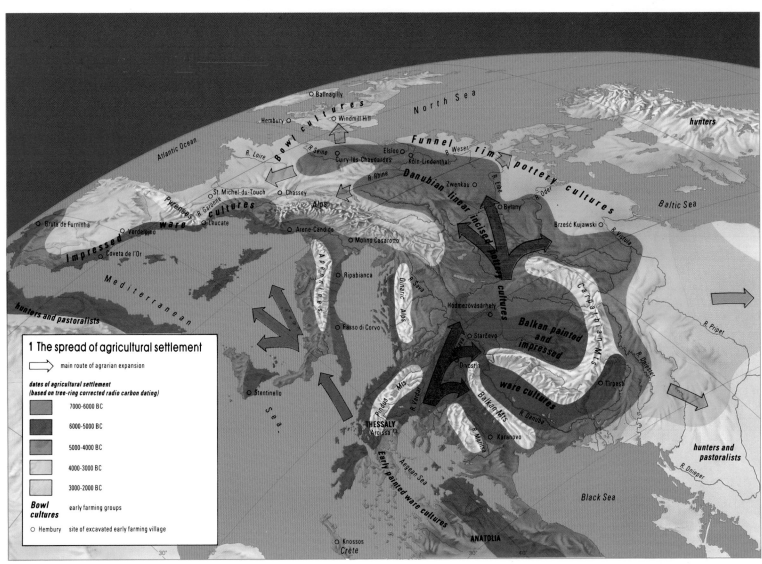

1 The spread of agricultural settlement

→ main route of agrarian expansion

dates of agricultural settlement
(based on tree-ring corrected radio carbon dating)
- 7000-6000 BC
- 6000-5000 BC
- 5000-4000 BC
- 4000-3000 BC
- 3000-2000 BC

Bowl cultures early farming groups

○ Hembury site of excavated early farming village

3 Megalithic monuments

○ chambered tombs

▲ axe factories

□ flint mines

■ areas of megalithic chambered tombs

5 The expansion of the Celts

■ area of major Celtic settlement and influence by 200 BC (early to middle La Tène culture)

→ principal inroads for plunder and partial settlement

⇢ penetration of Celtic-speaking peoples to the Iberian Peninsula 7th-6th centuries BC

⇨ Celtic introduction to Britain and Ireland

North Sea

R. Elbe

R. Vistula

R. Rhine

R. Seine

○ La Tène

R. Danube

R. Dnieper

R. Garonne

R. Rhône

R. Dniester

R. Ebro

Black Sea

R. Po

R. Tiber

○ Rome *390 BC*

Galatia *276 BC*

Mediterranean Sea

○ Delphi *279 BC*

2 The introduction of metallurgy to Europe

main periods of activity of local schools of metal production

◯ 4500-3500 BC – early copper age

◯ 3500-2500 BC – later copper age

◯ 2500-1500 BC – early Bronze Age

Hesse centres of prehistoric copper and bronze working

◼ main tin sources used in the 2nd millennium BC

■ settlement ◖ burial

Scottish

North Sea

Irish *North Welsh*

Eynsham

Roundway

CORNWALL

Exloo ◖

Major metal-importing area

Central European school

Harz

Vikletice ◼

Little Carpathian

Hesse BOHEMIA

Slovakian

Tiszapolgár

Salzkamm-ergut

Branč ◖

Auvernier ■

Gornja Tuzla

Transylvanian

Tărtăria ■

Vinča

Balkan-Carpathian school

Varna ◖

Remedello ◖

Cambous ▲ Grotte des Fées

Boussargues ■ ■

Pločnik ◼ *West Balkan*

East Balkan

Kalanovo

Rinaldone ◖

NORTH WEST IBERIA ◼

Sitagroi-Fotolivos ■

Anatolian school

Praia das Maçãs ○

Vila Nova de São Pedro ○

Anghelu Ruju ◖

South west Iberian

Iberian school

South east Iberian

Mecas de Asta

Los Millares ○

Mediterranean Sea

Lipari ■

Kastri ■

Phylakopi ■ Karos ◖

Egypt and Mesopotamia
3500-1600BC

The rise of the great riverine civilisations in the fertile valleys of the Nile in Egypt, the Euphrates and Tigris in Mesopotamia, and the Indus valley in north-west India (map 1), was a decisive stage in the development of human society. The springboard for this development was provided by the prosperous farming communities which had grown up in the hill country around the foothills of the Fertile Crescent from 8000 BC. Some of these settlements, such as Jericho and Catal Hüyük, had been of considerable size and were already small towns rather than mere villages. But the alluvial valleys of Egypt and Mesopotamia offered far greater potential, and it was here, around 3500 BC, that cities and city-states distinguished by size, planning, architecture and fortifications first appeared. It was here also, because of the need for accounting procedures in the collection and distribution of agricultural produce, that writing was first invented.

The early cities of Egypt and Mesopotamia were entirely dependent on the agricultural productivity of the alluvial plains. Water was the key to life in these semi-arid environments. In Egypt, the River Nile did most of the work, its annual flood bringing not only water but a deposit of rich alluvial silt to the farmlands of the valley and delta. In Mesopotamia, the rivers Tigris and Euphrates provided the water but to bring it to the fields an extensive network of irrigation canals was created.

Because of geographical factors political unification came early to Egypt. It was King Menes of Upper (southern) Egypt who in c.3100 BC conquered the delta kingdoms and founded a new capital at Memphis, which remained the administrative centre of Egypt for almost 2000 years. During the Old Kingdom period (map 3) (2685–2180 BC) Egyptian rulers built a series of massive pyramid-tombs along the desert edge opposite Memphis which emphasised their power and prestige and are among the greatest constructions of their age. Despite a period of setback in the political anarchy of the First Intermediate Period, the Egyptian state was sufficiently firmly established to recover and entered a second period of impressive cultural achievement under the able rulers of the Middle Kingdom (2040–1783 BC).

In Mesopotamia the basic political pattern until the second half of the third millennium BC remained one of city states, with a shifting hegemony between them but no centralised control. The Sumerians who built these cities (map 2) were also responsible for the invention of writing, at first pictographic but soon developing into the cuneiform script used on clay tablets and in inscriptions on stone. An important factor in Mesopotamian economic organisation was the need to acquire scarce resources. Southern Mesopotamia lacked stone, metals and timber, which led the Sumerians to exploit the Zagros mountains and to develop trading relations with Iran and Asia Minor. Egypt was more self-sufficient, but here also the need for timber stimulated trade with Syria, and Syria served as a link between Egypt and Mesopotamia.

The first significant attempt at empire in Mesopotamia came when Sargon (2371–16 BC), of Akkadian immigrant descent, founded the city of Agade (site uncertain) and made it his task to bring the old Sumerian city states under centralised control (map 4). From this base he and his successors, notably his grandson, Naram-Sin (2291–55 BC), undertook conquests from Elam in south-west Iran to Syria, including the recently excavated city of Ebla, and possibly also into south-eastern Asia Minor. Motivated by trade, this expansion extended sea-links which reached as far east as the Indus valley.

Sargon's empire collapsed as a result of internal stresses and the invasion of hillmen from the central Zagros, and was followed by a revival of the Sumerian city-state system, in which Ur emerged as the dominant element. This was a highly bureaucratic empire, more stable than that of Agade; but it collapsed in turn (c.2000 BC) under the pressure of a new wave of Semitic invaders, the Amorites from the Syrian desert, who established control over the whole region from Syria to southern Mesopotamia, where they set up a number of small kingdoms, among which Assyria and Babylon eventually won pre-eminence. The former emerged under the Amorite Shamshi-Adad I (1813–1781 BC), who annexed the kingdom of Mari on the middle Euphrates and formed a powerful state extending from the Zagros mountains to the border of the Anatolian plateau. But the pre-eminence of Assyria was short-lived, and after Shamshi-Adad's death its place was taken by Babylon under Hammurabi (1792–50 BC). By the seventeenth century BC a new power centre was developing further north, in Anatolia, where the Hittites set up a kingdom with its capital at Hattushash. After 1650 BC they began to spread southwards and in 1595 they sacked Babylon. In the dislocation which ensued the first Babylonian dynasty collapsed; but the ideal of a single south Mesopotamian kingdom with Babylon as its capital, survived as Hammurabi's enduring legacy.

1 The spread of civilisation

centres of urban life

main trade routes of urban zone

trading area with secondary urban centres   ○ early cities

principal traded commodities

copper	obsidian	ivory
grain	pearls	textiles
lapis lazuli	tin	silver
carnelian	timber	gold

2 Sumerian Mesopotamia 2500-2000 BC

fertile area

marsh area

- - - irrigation and ancient water courses
- city or other important site
- important temple
- trade route

3 Old Kingdom Egypt c.3000-2000 BC

● town or city c.3250-2000 BC

■ royal tomb c.3250-2650 BC

▲ pyramid c.2650-2000 BC

cultivable land

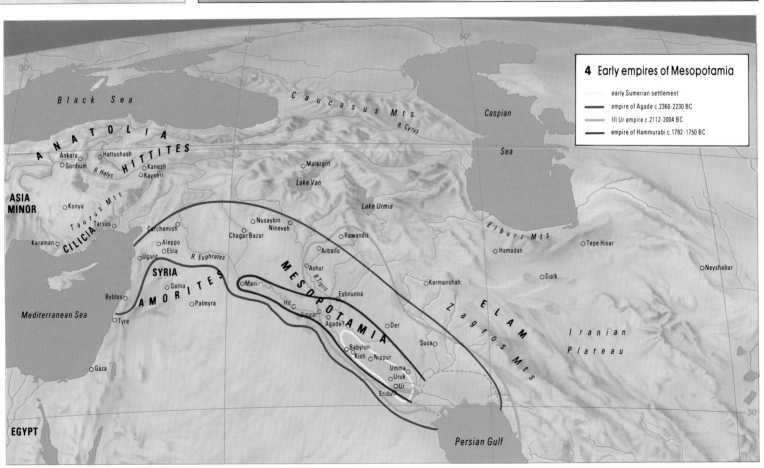

4 Early empires of Mesopotamia

early Sumerian settlement

empire of Agade c.2360-2230 BC

III Ur empire c.2112-2004 BC

empire of Hammurabi c.1792-1750 BC

The first civilisations of Europe
3000-600BC

The earliest civilisations in the western world arose in western Asia and the Nile valley in the fourth millennium BC, but within two thousand years new civilisations, distinctively different in character, had appeared around the shores of the Aegean in Crete, Greece, and western Asia Minor.

The first European civilisation was that of Minoan Crete, based on elaborate palaces which were both the seats of rulers and the centres of a bureaucratic administration. The most famous of the Minoan palaces is that of Knossos in northern Crete, in later Greek legend the home of King Minos. Cretan civilisation reached a level of considerable sophistication in the middle of the second millennium BC. The palaces were decorated with colourful frescoes and equipped with elaborate sanitary and drainage systems. Cretan traders visited Egypt, and spread Minoan influence among the Aegean islands. Bureaucracy flourished with the adoption of writing in around 1600 BC, using the locally-invented Linear A script. With a powerful fleet giving security at sea, the development of Minoan civilisation appears to have been interrupted only by the recurrent earthquakes of the region.

The development of civilisation on the Greek mainland owed something to contact with Crete but was nonetheless a largely independent process. Soon after 1600 BC rich graves make their appearance at important centres such as Mycenae, with sumptuous offerings of gold and jewellery, testifying to the rise of a wealthy and powerful artistocracy. These warlike rulers built themselves fortified palaces and drove to battle in horse-drawn chariots. The Mycenaeans

were not only warriors, however, but also cultivated the arts and became successful traders whose products are found throughout the east and central Mediterranean (map 2).

In the fifteenth century BC the Mycenaeans conquered Minoan Crete and became the principal political and military power in the Aegean (map 1). They adapted the Minoan Linear A script and carried their modified version, Linear B, back to the mainland where it was used in the administration of their own kingdoms. Within two hundred years their ambitions had stretched still further to the coast of Asia Minor. The legend of the Trojan war is generally thought to be a memory of a successful Mycenaean campaign of c.1250 BC against a rival power, the city of Troy, strategically situated at the mouth of the Dardenelles, controlling access to the Black Sea.

The Trojan war, if indeed it really happened, must have been the final fling of the Mycenaean warlords. By 1200 BC, most of their palaces were in ruins, overthrown perhaps by civil strife, perhaps by piracy and a rebellious peasantry. With the demise of the Mycenaean kingdoms Greece entered a Dark Age which lasted some 400 years. It was only in the eighth century BC that trade and city life began to recover. The recovery was rapid, however, and two centuries later Greek colonies had been established all along the northern Mediterranean and Black Sea coasts (map 4). Writing was reintroduced, using an alphabetic script adapted from the Phoenician, and new styles of sculpture, architecture and vase-painting developed. Yet while sharing a common language and culture the Greek world of the eighth century was divided between hundreds of independent city-states, and was to remain so throughout the Classical age of the fifth and fourth centuries BC until conquered and united by Philip of Macedon in 338 BC.

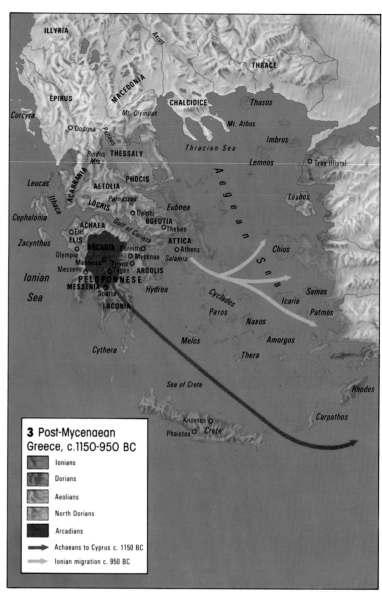

3 Post-Mycenaean Greece, c.1150-950 BC

- Ionians
- Dorians
- Aeolians
- North Dorians
- Arcadians
- → Achaeans to Cyprus c. 1150 BC
- → Ionian migration c. 950 BC

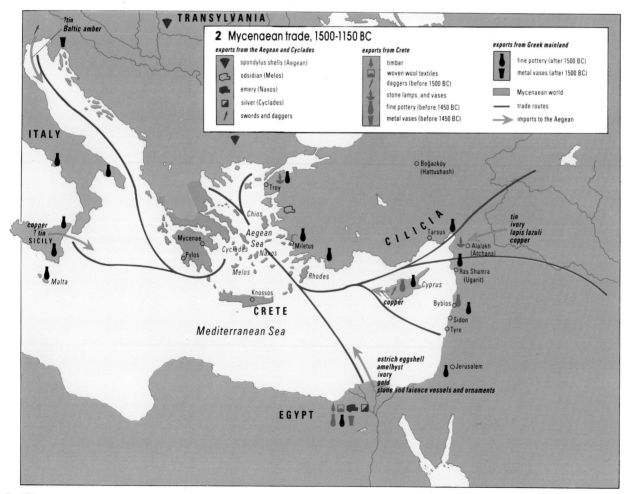

2 Mycenaean trade, 1500-1150 BC

exports from the Aegean and Cyclades
- spondylus shells (Aegean)
- odsidian (Melos)
- emery (Naxos)
- silver (Cyclades)
- swords and daggers

exports from Crete
- timber
- woven wool textiles
- daggers (before 1500 BC)
- stone lamps, and vases
- fine pottery (before 1450 BC)
- metal vases (before 1450 BC)

exports from Greek mainland
- fine pottery (after 1500 BC)
- metal vases (after 1500 BC)
- Mycenaean world
- — trade routes
- → imports to the Aegean

Near Eastern empires, 1600-330BC

Since the third millennium BC the rich lands of the Fertile Crescent had been subject to periodic invasion by warlike but less prosperous peoples from adjoining steppes and mountains, jealous of their civilisation and greedy for their riches. Egypt alone was sheltered by the desert; but even Egypt fell prey about 1730 BC to an Asiatic people known as the Hyksos, who conquered the Delta and the Nile valley as far as Cusae, and ruled there until 1567 BC. But the Hyksos occupation stimulated a great revival and, under the XVIIIth dynasty (1570-1320 BC), a policy of expansion was initiated to preclude any further occupation. Egypt advanced through Palestine into Syria and created an empire which extended almost to the Euphrates for the next four hundred years.

Egyptian control over Syria and Palestine may in part have been an attempt to shield the Nile valley from further invasions, but it in fact brought it directly into conflict with the Hittites of Asia Minor and the Mitannians of north-central Syria (map 1). In the fourteenth century BC the Hittites defeated Mitanni, which ceased to be a major actor in the struggle for the Levant. Egyptian power remained strong, however, and after the drawn battle of Kadesh in 1279 BC Hittites and Egyptians agreed to respect each other's sphere of influence.

The Egyptian pharaohs channelled the profits of empire into vast building programmes, such as the so-called 'Colossi of Memnon' built by Amenhotep III at Thebes (1391-1353 BC) or the massive rock-cut temple at Abu Simbel created by Ramesses II (1290-1224 BC). Memphis remained the administrative capital, but the power of Thebes as the religious centre of Egypt steadily grew.

The balance of power between Egyptians and Hittites in the Levant did not last long after Kadesh, since the Hittite empire collapsed around 1200 BC under internal pressure and attacks by their northern neighbours and by seaborne invaders – the so-called 'peoples of the sea'. Egypt successfully fought off similar attacks, but only with the loss of its Levantine possessions. Into the gap created by the decline of the Hittites and Egyptian empires new peoples entered; Phrygians in Asia Minor, Hebrews and Philistines in Palestine. The power vacuum enabled the Israelites under King David (c.1006-966 BC) to create a kingdom briefly controlling Palestine and Syria (map 2); but after Solomon (966-926 BC) the kingdom, inherently unstable because of its disparate tribal origins, quickly disintegrated. But change and fluidity had the effect of breaking down old geographical and cultural barriers and fusing the whole region into a single cosmopolitan society, over which, after 539 BC, Persia established hegemony.

The immediate beneficiary was Assyria, the political successor of Mitanni (map 3). Already in the thirteenth century this city-state had joined the ranks of the great powers of the ancient Near East. Early in the ninth century, the Assyrian kings again began to flex their military muscle, embarking on a policy of conquest which soon brought them to the shores of the Mediterranean (map 3). The profits were ploughed back into the construction of the successive capitals of the Assyrian empire: Nimrud, Khorsabad and Nineveh. At its greatest extent, in the seventh century BC, the empire stretched from the Nile valley to the Persian Gulf and northwards into Armenia and eastern Turkey. But during the long reign of Ashurbanipal (668–627 BC) Assyria began to lose its military dominance and soon afterwards the assault of Medes and Scythians, combined with the secession of Babylonia, brought Assyrian power to ruin. The capital Nineveh was destroyed in 612 BC, and Assyria disappeared for ever in 605 BC. After an interlude in which Medes, Chaldeans and Egyptians divided the legacy, another semi-barbarian conqueror, Cyrus the Persian, rebelled against his Median overlord, captured the Median capital Ecbatana in 550 BC, and quickly overran most of the Middle East. When his son Cambyses (529–522 BC) conquered Egypt (525 BC), the Persian empire extended from the Nile to the Oxus (map 5). The ancient world was for the first time united under one administration. Persian attempts to extend their power to the west, however, met with resistance from the Greeks and defeat at Marathon (490 BC), Salamis (480 BC) and Plataea (479 BC), and the Persian empire entered a period of slow decline. The way was opened for the ultimate triumph of Hellenism and the conquest of Persia by Alexander the Great a century and a half later.

4 The Babylonian Kingdom 604-539 BC

→ campaigns of Nebuchadnezzar

— maximum extent under Nabonidus

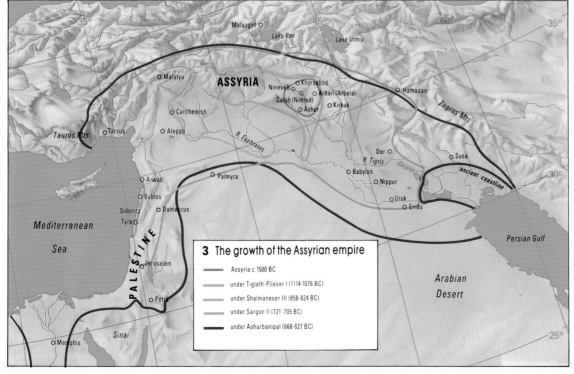

3 The growth of the Assyrian empire

- - - - Assyria c.1500 BC
──── under Tiglath-Pileser I (1114-1076 BC)
──── under Shalmaneser III (858-824 BC)
──── under Sargon II (721-705 BC)
──── under Ashurbanipal (668-627 BC)

2 Palestine at the time of David c.980 BC

- empire of King David c 980 BC
- division of the kingdoms 931 BC
- ■ state capital
- campaign of Shishak, King of Egypt, 924 BC

5 The Persian Empire, 550-331 BC

- Achaemenid empire at greatest extent
- **MADA** satrapy of Achaemenid empire
- route of march of Cyrus the Younger
- return route of the 'Ten Thousand'
- campaigns of war with Greece
- the Persian Royal Road

1 Kingdoms and empires of the Near East, c.1500-1200 BC

Hittite:
- city
- heartland
- area of influence

Egyptian:
- city
- New Kingdom temple
- fortress or garrison
- state
- area of influence

Levantine:
- ● city
- ⚓ port

Mitannian:
- ● city
- heartland
- area of influence
- Nubian gold resources
- trade route

21

The Greek world
497-185 BC

The fifth century BC was the great age of Greece – the age of Pericles and Socrates, of Sophocles and Euripides, of the Parthenon and the sculptures of Phidias. It was also the century when internal strains (the growing conflict between oligarchy and democracy) and internecine war undermined the stability of the Greek city states and their ability to withstand external pressures. Colonisation had already carried Greek civilisation and Greek city life to Asia Minor (page 18). But here it came up against the Persian empire under Darius and Xerxes (page 20). Persian attempts to subdue Athens, which had been supporting the rebellious Ionians, were almost miraculously defeated at Marathon (490) and Salamis (480), (map 1). But thereafter the cities which had united against Persia fell apart, and the Peloponnesian war between Athens and Sparta and their allies (map 2) permanently weakened Greek resistance, and ensured the victory of Philip of Macedon (338). Under Philip's son, Alexander the Great, Macedonia became a world power, its dominion stretching from the Adriatic to India (map 3). Alexander's death in 323 BC at the age of 32 prevented the consolidation of his empire. In the succeeding struggles between his generals three major powers arose: Macedonia, shorn of its Asiatic conquests but still dominant in northern Greece; Egypt under the Ptolemies, with its capital at Alexander's newly founded city of Alexandria; and

the Seleucid kingdom comprising the bulk of the Persian empire (map 4). To these were added in the east the Bactrian kingdom, extending over Afghanistan into northern India, and the Parthian empire, founded in 247 BC when a dissident provincial governor broke away from the Bactrian Greeks. This Parthian state eventually stretched from the Euphrates to the Indus and successfully withstood Roman expansion until it was displaced in AD 224 by a resurgent Persia under the Sasanian dynasty.

Although politically the empire of Alexander the Great proved ephemeral, in other respects its consequences were epoch-making. Alexander himself founded some 70 cities, not merely as military strongholds but as cultural centres – a policy continued by his Seleucid successors – and thus carried Greek civilisation far to the east. Greek culture was now no longer the preserve of separate city-states but infused and Hellenised the whole civilised world (*oikoumene*) as far as India and China. Greek itself became the *lingua franca* of the whole region, though more subtly the Greek world itself was permeated by oriental influences as its contacts with the ancient civilisations of the Near East intensified. When Rome asserted control over the Hellenistic world after its defeat of Macedon at Cynoscephalae in 197 and of the Seleucids at Magnesia in 190 BC, this was its inheritance; and the longer the Roman empire existed, the greater was the part played by the Hellenic and oriental elements in its civilisation.

1 The Persian wars 490 – 479 BC
- Persian Empire in 497 BC
- Ionian rebel territory reconquered by Persia 496-493 BC
- Persian conquest 492 BC
- neutral and pro-Persian states
- Greek allies
- ✕ Persian victory
- ✕ Greek victory
- ✕ indecisive battle

3 The empire of Alexander the Great
- — empire of Alexander
- — states federated to the empire
- — independent states
- → route of Alexander the Great
- ⇢ route of Nearchus
- → return route of Craterus
- ✕ Alexander's major battles

4 The Hellenistic world in 185 BC
- independent Greek states
- Antigonid kingdom (and dependencies 240BC)
- Kingdom of Pergamum
- Hellenised non-Greek kingdoms

Trading links of the ancient world

Trade is as old as the beginning of settled urban life. Though ordinary needs were met by local agriculture and local manufacture, even the earliest cities had requirements that could not be satisfied locally. Jericho imported stone for tools from Anatolia (page 6); the Sumerians, who lacked timber, stone and minerals, developed trading links with Asia Minor and by sea with Dilmun on the Persian Gulf. But the formation of an intensive trading network spanning the whole Eurasian world only became possible after the rise of empires which could provide peace and security, build roads and maintain harbours. The Achaemenids made a beginning in sixth-century Persia, where Darius's Royal Road ran 1420 well-garrisoned miles (2300 km) from Sardis to Susa (page 20). But the decisive step forward was the rise, after 202 BC, of the Roman empire in the west and the Han empire in China. By the close of the first century BC Rome's conquests from the Atlantic to Syria formed a single vast trading area, gathered round a Mediterranean axis (map 2), and the expansion of Han China under Wu-ti (140–87 BC) created an economic bloc of similar

dimensions in the east (page 28). Both possessed an elaborate network of roads and a highly organised system of transport and marketing, which encouraged regional specialisation and an unprecedented interchange of goods and manufactures. In the west the requirements of the legions in the frontier provinces of Gaul and the Balkans were a further stimulus. Spain became a large-scale producer and exporter of wine and olive oil; but the most important export of all was grain from Egypt, North Africa and the Pontine provinces, upon which Rome itself and many cities of Greece and Asia Minor were dependent.

Nor did trade halt at the frontier. China sent a mission to Ferghana, Bukhara and Bactria in 128 BC, and shortly afterwards the famous Silk Route came into operation (map 1). It started at Tunhwang on China's far western boundary, and skirted north or south of the Takla Makan Desert to Kashgar, before crossing the Pamirs and debouching into Bactria, Persia and the Mediterranean coastal belt. But the Silk Route, spectacular though it was, was less important in economic terms than the sea route to India and the Far East, traffic along which increased greatly after the discovery of the monsoon around 100 BC. Previously there had been coastal traffic, mainly in Arab or Indian hands. Now up to 120 Greek vessels a year, some with a carry-

ing capacity of up to 500 tons, plied direct to the Indian ports of Barbaricum, Barygaza and Muziris, where they picked up eastern cargoes shipped by Indian merchants from Go Oc Eo in southern Cambodia, and carried them to Berenice and other Red Sea ports for transport on to Alexandria and thence to all parts of the Roman empire.

These far-flung trading links are impressive, but their economic importance should not be exaggerated. Both the Roman and the Han empires were self-sufficient in all essential commodities, and foreign trade was essentially a luxury trade, marginal to everyday needs. On the other hand, there is no doubt that foreign trade contributed directly to cultural interchange and to the spread of the great world religions (page 26). However, it also had other less happy consequences, particularly the spread of disease and pestilence (map 3). Earlier epidemics, like that which smote Athens in 430–29 BC, may have been transmitted by armies; but their incidence after about 100 BC leaves little doubt that, both in east and west, they were carried by caravans or merchant shipping from India or tropical Africa. Their precise character is not easily determined, though they seem to fall into two main groups, smallpox or measles, and bubonic plague; but there is no doubt about their devastating effects on vulnerable populations. 'One or two out of a hundred survived,' wrote the Chinese historian Ssu-ma Kuang of the epidemic of AD 317, and some later historians have attributed the failure both of China and of Rome to withstand the barbarian onslaughts of the fourth and fifth centuries to the sharp fall in manpower caused by imported pestilences.

1 Eurasian trade routes, c.AD200

- ▬▬ Silk Road
- ── trade route
- ■ trading capital
- ● trading centre

distribution of:
- ◗ Han mirrors
- ◆ Chinese silks
- ▲ Graeco-Roman objects in East AD1-300

2 The economy of the Roman Empire, c. AD 200

- ▬▬ boundary of Roman Empire c. AD 200
- ── sea routes
- → land trade routes in Germany
- ── caravan routes
- ⌄ lighthouse
- ∿ navigable rivers (named)
- XIV Roman legion
- ∿ fossatum Africae, fortifications
- ▨ olive-growing areas in N. Africa
- ● provincial colonial settlements
- ◉ important pottery, (modern name in brackets)
- ── road

- ◈ amber
- ◉ bitumen
- ◆ brass objects
- ▭ bronzeware
- ⋈ cinnabar
- C copper
- ∥ corn
- ▯ garum
- ▢ glass
- ▰ gold
- ◆ horses
- ▲ iron
- ▬ lead
- + linen
- ◆ marble
- ⊕ olives
- ▽ papyrus
- ⬤ pottery
- ◐ purple dye
- ◀ silk
- ⚡ silphium
- ▣ silver
- ⊍ slave market
- ⌣ source of slaves
- ▲ timber
- ▣ tin
- ⊻ wine
- ▭ woollen textiles
- Z zinc

3 The spread of epidemics

AD 542-3 Plague of Justinian
AD 165-80 Antonine Plague
AD 251-66
AD 312-22
AD 162
AD 552
AD 610
AD 808
AD 16 malaria?
SHENSI 243 BC
430-429 BC
malaria?
measles?
malaria?
malaria?
silk route

- → probably smallpox or measles
- → bubonic plague
- → nature of epidemic unknown

The world religions
c.500BC-AD500

The period 550–500 BC saw the birth of great world religions in all the main centres of civilisation. Their appearance perhaps reflected a need in the rising empires of the old world for more universal creeds than the local tribal deities could provide, and their diffusion – particularly the spread of the great missionary religions, Buddhism and Christianity – was an important factor in linking together the different areas of civilisation (map 1). Their other major contribution – seen, for example, in the work of Anglo-Saxon missionaries in Germany or of Russian missionaries among the heathen tribes of the Urals (page 38) – was to carry civilisation to peoples outside the frontiers of the civilised world.

All the great religions shared, to one degree or another, a belief in a single spiritual reality. Not all were inspired by a missionary spirit. Hinduism, the oldest, was essentially the religion of the people of India, and Judaism, the religion of 'the chosen people of the Lord', was also exclusive. But Buddhism, originally a reformist movement within Hinduism, became perhaps the greatest of all missionary religions when it assumed its universalist, or Mahayana, form some 500 years after the death of its founder, Gautama (c.563–483 BC). Judaism also spread as a result of the persecution of the Jews by more formidable neighbours, beginning with the Babylonian exile (586 BC). After the Roman destruction of the temple in Jerusalem in AD 70 (map 3) the Jewish diaspora carried Judaism far and wide from its home in Palestine, until in time it became a worldwide religion. It also gave birth, directly or indirectly, to two of the world's great missionary religions, Christianity and Islam.

In the Far East the same period saw the rise of the ethical system of Kung Fu-tzu or Confucius (551–479 BC) and the mystical religion of the Tao, or 'the Way', associated with the shadowy figure of Lao-tzu. Later Buddhism spread eastward along the Silk Route through central Asia and with Taoism and Confucianism became one of the 'three religions' of traditional China. Buddhism also reached Japan in the sixth century AD, where it effectively displaced spirit-worship and traditional Shinto until the revival of the latter in the nineteenth century.

The other great religion of the period was Zoroastrianism, which originated in Persia and is associated with another shadowy figure, Zarathustra. Zoroastrianism, which sees life as a battleground between the forces of good and the forces of evil, spread rapidly through the Roman world in the form of Mithraism, with shrines as far afield as northern Britain. It was one of the many oriental cults which permeated the Roman empire when, after the beginning of the Christian era, belief in the Greek pantheon and the household deities broke down. Until the end of the third century AD it was undecided which of the oriental mystery cults would prevail; but with the conversion of the emperor Constantine to Christianity and its recognition by the Edict of Milan (AD 313), still more after it became the official religion of the Roman empire under Theodosius (374–95), the die was cast. Heathen temples were uprooted; rival cults were condemned.

Christianity had begun as a Jewish splinter-movement; its founder, Jesus of Nazareth, saw himself as the Messiah, or Saviour, sent to liberate the Jews from the Roman yoke. But when, after Jesus's condemnation and crucifixion (AD 29), Jewish orthodoxy rejected his message, his disciples, notably Paul of Tarsus, turned instead to the conversion of the 'gentiles', or people outside the law. Paul's journeys (map 2) were a turning point. Thereafter Christianity spread rapidly, both in the Roman empire and also further east. Here the great Christian centres were Antioch and Edessa, the home of the Nestorian church which carried Christ's teaching to Persia and from there to China and India (page 38). This was the situation until the rise of Islam (page 40) changed the scene.

3 Judaea 63 BC-AD 73

area of Roman procuratorial rule in Judaea

Agrippa II's kingdom AD 61

area of major revolt at start of AD 66

area of revolt at end of AD 69

Roman armies

1 The diffusion of religions

dispersion of Jews up to AD 500

spread of Christianity

area converted to Christianity by AD 600

spread of Buddhism

area of Buddhist missionary activity

area of rise of Mahayana Buddhism

Buddhist sites

area embracing Hinduism

area embracing Taoism

area embracing Shintoism

area converted to Zoroastrianism

spread of Mithraism

Mithraic sites

India and China: the first empires

The fifth and sixth centuries BC were a period of consolidation in India and China. In India by the end of the fifth century the 16 political units in existence in 600 BC had been reduced to four. In China, by 400 BC, instead of the multiple feudal principalities of the Chou period (page 8) seven major states were contending for supremacy. In both countries iron tools increased both agricultural productivity and the resources of the rising states. In China the area of civilisation had expanded from the Yellow river to the Yangtze valley and beyond. In India the deforestation of the north shifted the centre of power from the Indus, the seat of the earliest civilisations (page 8), to the fertile plain of the Ganges. Here the kingdom of Magadha emerged as the nucleus of the first Indian empire.

Politically, nevertheless, it was a period of continuous strife, and the resulting social tensions were a major factor in the emergence of the great religious and ethical systems, Buddhism, Taoism, Confucianism and Jainism (page 26), which, in various ways, expressed a yearning for a more stable world order. In India the turning point came in 320 BC when Chandragupta Maurya seized the Magadhan throne, annexed the lands east of the Indus, occupied large parts of central India north of the Narmada river, and in 303 BC annexed the Seleucid province of Trans-Indus. Chandragupta's grandson, Asoka (273–236), conquered Kalinga on the Bay of Bengal, and the greater part of the subcontinent was brought under one rule. His edicts, inscribed on pillars and rocks, evidence Asoka's conversion to Buddhism (map 4).

In China the turning point came with the rise of the state of Ch'in (328–308), which finally dominated China in 221 BC (map 1). But the ruthless centralising policy of the first Ch'in emperor, Shih Huang-ti (221–206), provoked a reaction, and after his death his empire collapsed. It was revived, after a period of civil war, by the Han dynasty, which compromised between centralising policies and the feudal principalities. In India, also, the death of Asoka introduced a long period of decentralisation, punctuated by invasion from the north, which was not overcome until AD 320 when the Guptas, based again on Magadha, imposed a new imperial rule (map 5). This classical age of Indian civilisation survived beyond the collapse of the Gupta empire caused by the barbarian invasions of the fifth century (page 32).

The barbarian invasions were also a turning point in China. The Ch'in and the Han built and extended the Great Wall against the nomad Hsiungnu in the north. Under the emperor Wu-ti (140–87) the Han extended their power to central Asia (map 2). With its efficient administration, a large export trade, and an extensive network of roads and canals, Han China, with its capital at Changan was extremely prosperous (map 3). But control over south China was tenuous, while in the north feudal magnates still exercised great power, which grew with the threat of war. Crisis came in AD 9, and although Han rule was restored, disintegration set in after c.AD 160. When in 304 the Hsiungnu broke through the Great Wall, China remained divided until 589.

2 The expansion of the Han Empire

- China in 206 BC
- boundary of Former Han Empire
- territory added under Former Han
- boundary of Chinese protectorate of Western Regions
- journey of Chang Chien, envoy of Han Emperor 138-126 BC

1 The unification of China 328-221 BC

- defensive walls with dates of first construction; rebuilt and unified by Ch'in after 220 BC
- original Ch'in territory
- Ch'in expansion before 300 BC
- other major states with dates of conquest by Ch'in
- new areas conquered by Ch'in after unification

4 India's first empires, 297 BC – AD 150

(approximate limits shown)

- Chandragupta Maurya's Empire 297 BC
- Bindusara's Empire 272 BC
- Asoka's Empire 232 BC
- ▲ rock and pillar edicts
- Western Satraps AD 150
- Kushan Empire AD 150 (eastern limit)
- Satavahana Kingdom AD 150

Legend (top left):
- routes opened to trade by Former Han
- ⊞ administrative centres under Later Han
- ⊡ centre of Later Han protectorate, 73-127 AD
- territory added under Later Han
- new route opened by General Pan Ch'ao for Later Han
- expeditions against Hsiungnu (Huns)
- conquered and put under Chinese administration 109 /06 BC

3 Han China in AD 2

- ⊞ imperial capital
- enfiefed principalities
- commanderies
- highways
- canals

5 Gupta India

- Empire of Chandragupta I
- added by Samudragupta
- temporarily tributary to Samudragupta
- added by Chandragupta II
- tributary tribes and states
- under Gupta influence (c. AD 380-410)

The Roman Empire
264 BC-AD 565

The rise of Rome from a collection of shepherds' huts on the hills overlooking the Tiber to a great world empire is a story of seven centuries of constant warfare. According to tradition, the city of Rome was founded in 754 BC by descendants of Aeneas, the legendary hero who had fled to Italy after the sack of Troy. Archaeology shows that it was only in the sixth century that it began to take on the trappings of a city.

In 510 BC the citizens of Rome expelled the last of the Etruscan kings and formed a republic. Over the next 300 years victories over Etruscans, Greeks and Celts gradually extended Roman control over the whole of Italy (map 1), but this expansion brought her into direct conflict with the imperialist ambitions of Carthage on the North African coast. Three fierce Punic Wars were fought for supremacy between the two powers (map 2). In the second (218–201 BC), the Carthaginians under the brilliant generalship of Hannibal inflicted a series of crushing defeats on the Romans. But Roman resolve held, Hannibal was ultimately defeated, and some fifty years later Carthage itself was destroyed in the Third Punic War (146 BC).

The Punic Wars gave Rome control over Sicily (241 BC), Spain (206 BC), and North Africa (146 BC). At the same time, conflict with the Hellenistic kingdoms of the East Mediterranean resulted in the conquest of Macedon, Greece and western Asia Minor. In this way, almost by accident, Rome

became an imperial power with far-flung possessions. In the first century BC the growing power of successful war-leaders led to fierce rivalries and civil wars, culminating in the struggle between Caesar and Pompey (49–45 BC), from which Caesar emerged victorious. His assassination in 44 BC, however, initiated a further thirteen years of conflict, only ending with Augustus' victory over Antony and Cleopatra at Actium in 31 BC.

Augustus' rule initiated a period of two centuries of unprecedented peace and prosperity in the extensive lands of the Roman empire (map 3). Population increased, trade flourished, and cities grew. Civic authorities and wealthy individuals embellished their cities with theatres, baths and temples, while roads, aqueducts and harbours brought in essential supplies from outside. This vast common market was further united by Roman law and by the use of Latin.

This peace was broken in the middle of the third century AD by Germanic invasions in the west and Persian victories in the east which brought the empire temporarily to its knees (map 4). Reform and reorganisation under Diocletian (AD 284–305) and Constantine (306–337) ensured the continued survival of the eastern half of the empire, with its new capital at Constantinople (Byzantium), but Rome itself fell to the Goths in AD 410 and Justinian's abortive efforts to recover the western provinces in the mid-sixth century showed clearly that the unified empire was a thing of the past. The ghost of the Roman empire lived on in the west, however, in the continued importance of Roman law and the continued use of Latin by the Christian church.

2 The Punic Wars, 264-146 BC

- Carthaginian territory 264 BC
- Roman territory 264 BC
- conquered by Carthage 237-218 BC
- 206 date of Roman conquests
- Hannibal's expeditions 220-203 BC
- Roman expedition 256 BC
- Hasdrubal's expedition 208-207 BC
- Roman expeditions 218-206 BC
- Roman expeditions 204,149 BC

1 Roman expansion in Italy

- Roman territory by 264 BC
- ■ Roman colonies before the Gracchi (133 BC)
- ● Latin colonies before the Gracchi
- allied states or tribal areas
- *VENETI* peoples

The barbarian invasions

In the fourth and fifth centuries AD the irruption of nomadic peoples from central Asia threw the civilised world into disarray. The invading nomads were under no form of central control though their movements radiated from a common centre. They were mostly Mongoloid and their languages mostly of the Turkish family; they were largely pastoralists with mobile encampments of tents and their success in war owed much to their mounted archers. All the established centres of civilisation were affected by them: China, the Gupta empire in India, Sasanian Persia and the Roman empire in the west (map 1). In 304 the Great Wall of China was breached by the Hsiung-nu, forbears of the Huns; in 367, Picts and Scots broke through Hadrian's Wall into Britain. The setbacks were lasting. China remained disunited until 589, and western Europe (if we except the short-lived Carolingian revival) only began to recover from invasion around the middle of the eleventh century (page 36).

The appearance of the Huns in Europe c.370 immediately caused a great involuntary movement among the Germanic peoples who had long been settled in northern and central Europe beyond the confines of the Roman empire. The details, beginning with the Visigoths, who defeated the Roman emperor at Adrianople in 378, sacked Rome in 410 and were settled in Aquitaine in 418, can be followed on map 2. Behind the Visigoths followed other east and west Germanic peoples: Alans, Vandals, Sueves, Alemans, Franks, and finally the Ostrogoths who, having earlier been forced into subjection, liberated themselves after the defeat of the Huns in 451, and descended into Italy, where they were in control by 493. Only the Anglo-Saxon invasion of Britain, beginning c.440, followed a different course. Here scattered bands of warriors and settlers, moving by ship up the estuaries of the Humber, Thames and the Wash, met with stubborn resistance. It was to be almost two centuries before the invaders, following their victories at Deorham (577) and Chester (616), established control of Britain (map 3). Here continuity with the Roman past was at a modest level at best.

In continental Europe continuity was more evident. Political control passed from Roman officials to German kings; but, except for the Anglo-Saxons and Franks, who could draw manpower from their homeland, the invaders were too few in number to change decisively the character of Roman society. Hence the success of the counter-offensive which Justinian launched in 533 (page 30). But Justinian's wars, and the havoc they wrought, left the way open for another wave of invasion from Asia, this time the Avars, and it was their onslaught, beginning c.560, that drove the Lombards into Italy (568). But they were too few in number to occupy the whole peninsula, and Italy remained divided between the Lombards, the Byzantine emperor and the Papacy (map 4). When the Lombard ruler Aistulf advanced south, seeking to establish his authority over the Lombard dukes of Spoleto and Benevento, occupied Ravenna in 751 and drove out the Byzantine exarch, the Pope, fearing for his independence, called on the Franks for aid. Thus was sealed the momentous alliance of the Carolingians and the Papacy, which resulted in Charles the Great's invasion, conquest and annexation of the Lombard kingdom in 774.

The appearance of the Avars also unsettled the Slav peoples who had greatly extended their settlement in eastern Europe following the Germanic migration westwards. Beginning c.600 Slav warbands descended into Greece and the Balkans, while the Bulgars took control of the western shore of the Black Sea (map 5). The arrival of the Slavs, cutting the landbridge between Byzantium and the west, was a cardinal fact in European history. The rise of the Bulgarian Empire and the gradual consolidation of Serbia and Croatia left a permanent imprint on the demography and historical geography of Europe.

2 Germanic invasions of Europe

- → Huns and campaigns of Attila
- → Vandals, Alans, Sueves
- → Visigoths
- → Ostrogoths
- → other Germanic peoples
- → Scots and Britons
- → Slavs
- ∼ boundary of Roman Empire AD395
- ▭ Anglo-Saxon settlement in England to AD626

5 The expansion of the Slavs to c.700

→ expansion of Slavs
〰 western limit of Slav expansion in 8th century AD
Sorbs Slav people
AVARS non-Slav people

North Sea

FINNISH PEOPLES
LITHUANIANS c.500-700
SAXONS
Abodrites c.500
Sorbs
Bohemians c.500
Slavs 1st century AD
Pripet Marshes
Kiev
R. Danube
Slovenes c.600
AVARS c.400-500
Croats
Serbs c.640
BULGARS
THRACE
MACEDONIA c.600-700
Salonika
Black Sea

3 Anglo-Saxon invasions of Britain, c.440-650

→ lines of Anglo-Saxon advance
forest
fenland, swamp
· Anglo-Saxon burial places c.450-650
〃 British fortifications

North Sea

LOTHIAN
STRATHCLYDE
BERNICIA — Bamburgh 547
REGED
Hexham 633
DEIRÃ — York
ELMEDSAETE (ELMET)
R. Ribble
Humber
LINDSEY
The Wash
GWYNEDD — Chester 616
R. Dee
PECSAETE
MERCIANS
POWYS
WREOCENSAETE
EAST ANGLES
MIDDLE ANGLES
R. Wye
R. Severn
DYFED
BRYCHEINIOG
GWYNLLWG
R. Thames
Bedcanford 571
London
EAST SAXONS
Chiltern Hills
Crayford 457
Ebbsfleet 449
KENT
HÆSTINGAS
Deorham 577
WEST SAXONS
Old Sarum 552
ANDREDESWEALD
Cerdicesford 519
SOUTH SAXONS
Andredescester 491
WIHT
WEST WALES
Bindon 614
GAUL

Cividale
LOMBARDY — Verona — Pavia
ISTRIA
LIGURIA — Parma — Ravenna — Bologna — Rimini
TUSCANY
EXARCHATE OF RAVENNA
Siena
Adriatic Sea
DUCHY OF SPOLETO
DUCHY OF ROME — Rome
DUCHY OF BENEVENTO
Brindisi
CAMPANIA
CALABRIA
Naples
Amalfi
Tyrrhenian Sea
SICILY
Syracuse

4 The Lombards in Italy
Lombard Kingdom and duchies c.600
Imperial territory c.600

1 Barbarian invasions of the ancient world

→ Hsiung-nu and Huns
→ Juan-Juan (Avars)
→ Goths and Vandals
— boundary of Roman Empire in AD454
— other frontiers as marked on map
···· frontiers of Sasanian Empire

approximate limits of nomad belt
areas of good pasture

border of western Turkish Empire of AD600
L. Balkhash
Syr Darya
Amu Darya (Oxus)
R. Irtysh
Altai Mts
L. Baikal
R. Yenisei
R. Selenga
MONGOLIA
Gobi Desert
R. Amur
MANCHURIA
border of eastern Turkish Empire of AD600
550 Juan-juan (Avars) driven westwards out of Mongolia by the Blue (Celestial) Turks
Toba Wei Empire c.AD500
Great Wall of China at AD220
R. Tarim
KANSU
Ordos Desert
Takla Makan Desert
SINKIANG
Hsien-pi invade
Pamirs
Hindu Kush
R. Indus
TIBET
expansion of Tibetans
Himalayas
480 White Huns destroy Gupta Empire of India
INDIA
1st century AD Hsiung-nu broken by Han China and move westwards
Changan
Loyang
re-unified north China under Toba (northern) Wei control
315 Hsiung-nu renew attacks on China and sack capital, Loyang
Yellow River
R. Yangtze
CHINA

Germanic kingdoms of Western Europe

Within a century of the Germanic invasions there were settled kingdoms in western Europe, except in Britain where invaders still met resistance. Among these (map 1) the Ostrogothic kingdom of Theodoric the Great (493–526) was outstanding. In Spain, the kingdom of the Visigoths was to endure from the late fifth century until the Arab conquest in 711. But monarchical institutions were still weak and religious differences divided the Arian rulers from their Catholic subjects. Justinian's attack on the Ostrogothic kingdom (page 30) destroyed equilibrium in the west and opened the way for the advance of the Franks (map 2).

The Franks also had appeared on the scene as scattered warbands, but Clovis (486–511) ruthlessly eliminated his rivals, made himself sole king, and reconciled the Gallo-Roman population by embracing the Catholic faith (497). He then turned against the neighbouring peoples, the Alemanni and Burgundians, defeated the Visigoths at Vouillé (507), near Poitiers, and forced them to withdraw to Spain and Septimania. But Theodoric's support for the other Germanic kingdoms checked further advance, and only after his death was a new phase of Frankish expansion possible. Deprived of Ostrogothic support, the Thuringians (531), Burgundians (532–4), and Alemanni (535) succumbed, and in 537 the Franks seized Provence.

Once the initial wave of conquest was spent, however, decline set in. Division of the royal patrimony, dynastic quarrels and alienation of the royal estates to buy aristocratic and ecclesiastical support, seemed after the death of Dagobert I (629–39) to presage the break-up of the kingdom. In Britain, on the other hand, the seventh century saw the emergence and consolidation of the kingdoms known as the Heptarchy. It seems that the kingdoms of the south-east (Sussex, Kent, Essex, East Anglia) were prevented from expanding by geographical obstacles, and leadership passed first to Northumbria and then to Mercia. The progress of Northumbria was helped by its early conversion to Christianity, but it was resisted by pagan Mercia under Penda (632–54), sometimes in alliance with the Britons, and by the time of Offa (757–96) the pre-eminence of Mercia, now Christian, was unquestionable. It controlled the four eastern kingdoms (map 3), and even Wessex recognised Mercian overlordship.

In the Frankish lands the turning point came with the battle of Tertry (687), when the leaders of the Austrasian aristocracy established their preponderance. This was the beginning of the rise of the Carolingian dynasty. Ruling at first indirectly, but after 751 with the royal title, the Carolingians restored Frankish fortunes and inaugurated a great surge of territorial expansion (map 4). Charles Martel (714–41) won a famous victory over the Arabs at Poitiers (732). His son Pepin (751–68) expelled them from Aquitania (752). Charles the Great, or Charlemagne (768–814), conquered Lombardy (774) and established Frankish rule in Italy. But his greatest victories were in the east, against the Bavarians (788), the Avars (796), and the Saxons (finally subdued in 804). His coronation as emperor by Pope Leo III in 800 marked the apogee of Frankish success.

However, Charlemagne's last ten years were beset by problems, the frontier marches never safe from attack; and after his death the inherent institutional weaknesses quickly became apparent. Civil war led to a first partition in 843. But the famous treaty of Verdun (map 5) was only a first step, and at Meersen (870) the 'Middle Kingdom' was eliminated (map 6) and the familiar outlines of Europe began to take shape. In 888 the Carolingian empire collapsed but its legacy to European civilisation remained.

1 Germanic kingdoms in AD 493

4 The Frankish Empire, 714-814

- Frankish realm 714
- extent of empire 814
- marches in 814 (with date of formation)
- Frankish royal residencies
- archbishoprics
- important monasteries

GASCONY 769 province with date of acquisition

2 Early Frankish expansion

Cologne
HESSE
THURINGIA
Tournai
Cambrai
Trier
Worms
Rouen
Soissons
Verdun
Strasbourg
BRETONS
Le Mans
ALEMANNIA
BAVARIA
Tours
RHAETIA
Vouillé 507
Poitiers
OSTROGOTHS
ITALY
BURGUNDIAN
KINGDOM
VISIGOTHIC
AQUITANIA
Bordeaux
PROVENCE
(ACQUIRED 537)
BASQUES
SEPTIMANIA
Narbonne
VISIGOTHS

- Frankish territory at the accession of Clovis 486
- Merovingian territory before the battle of Vouillé 507
- Merovingian territory in 560
- area of Merovingian overlordship in Germany

5 Treaty of Verdun, 843

KINGDOM OF LOUIS THE GERMAN
(tributary territories)
KINGDOM OF CHARLES II THE BALD
KINGDOM OF LOTHAR I

6 Partition of Meersen, 870

KINGDOM OF LOUIS THE GERMAN
(tributary territories)
KINGDOM OF CHARLES II THE BALD
KINGDOM OF LOUIS II

SAXON MARCH 808-810
WILZI
ABODRITES
Magdeburg
R. Elbe
SORBS
R. Oder
R. Saale
THURINGIAN MARCH 806
BOHEMIA
Regensburg
Altaich
R. Danube
Passau
OSTMARK 803
Kremsmünster
Salzburg
BAVARIA 788
CARINTHIA 788
PANNONIA 795-6
AVAR KINGDOM
(destroyed 796)
FRIULI 776
Aquileia
VENICE
under Frankish control 806-12
ISTRIA
conquered by Franks 788
Ravenna
Spoleto
Adriatic Sea
Rome
Monte Cassino

3 Anglo-Saxon England c.AD 800

LOTHIAN
STRATHCLYDE
BERNICIA
GALLOWAY
NORTHUMBRIA
Irish Sea
York
DEIRA
North Sea
R. Humber
GWYNEDD
R. Dee
Chester
PECSAETE
LINDSEY
POWYS
WREOCENSAETE
Offa's Dyke
Lichfield
Tamworth
MERCIA
R. Severn
DYFED
Hereford
EAST ANGLIA
HWICCE
GWENT
Bensington 779
Dorchester-on-Thames
ESSEX
London
SURREY
R. Thames
Otford 776
WESSEX
Winchester
KENT
SUSSEX
WEST WALES
Hastings
English Channel

- Mercia and subordinate kingdoms under Offa (757 - 796)
- allied with Mercia
- British kingdoms

35

Invasion and recovery: Europe, 814-1149

The relative stability of western Europe under Charles the Great (Charlemagne) and of England under Offa of Mercia (page 34) was shattered in the ninth century by attacks by Saracens in the south, Magyars in the east, and Norwegians and Danes in the north and west (map 1). The Saracens pillaged Rome in 846, and after establishing a base at Fraxinetum in 890 raided deep into southern Gaul. Northern Italy and Germany were a prey to the Magyars who had moved into the Hungarian plain after Charlemagne's destruction of Avar power. The Vikings of Norway and Denmark also began as raiders; but in their case an initial phase of plunder was followed by settlement and colonisation, first in Orkney and Shetland, then in Ireland where Dublin was founded c.841, later (c.870) in Iceland and in England, where the Danish armies occupied the countryside round the Five Boroughs of the Midlands after 876. In France the West Frankish king conferred the lands at the mouth of the Seine – the later duchy of Normandy – on the Danish leader Rollo in 911.

The invasions were accompanied by widespread devastation and depopulation. Inevitably recovery was slow. In Germany (page 54) Otto I's defeat of the Magyars at the river Lech (955) was a turning point. In England only determined resistance by Alfred the Great of Wessex (871–99) held the Danes at bay. After 909 his successors went over to the offensive and by 939 Scandinavian England had been subjugated. But after the death of Edgar (959–75) a second wave of Danish invasion began.

In southern Europe, where most of Spain had been in Arab hands for over two centuries, the Mediterranean was by 950 virtually a 'Muslim lake'. But the collapse of Arab unity after 936 (page 40) facilitated a Christian revival. After the fall of Fraxinetum in 972 the fleets of Pisa and Genoa went over to the offensive, attacking Muslim bases in North Africa, while Venice cleared the Adriatic (map 2). After the First Crusade (1096–99) and

the great Venetian naval victory off Ascalon in 1123, the Italian cities dominated Mediterranean trade. The period of the First Crusade also saw the beginning of the Christian reconquest of Spain under Alfonso VI (1065–1109), king of León and Castile, who actually advanced as far as Toledo in 1084 (map 4). But the first wave of reconquest was halted by the great Islamic revival under the Almoravid and Almohad dynasties. The Christian advance only resumed in the thirteenth century after the decisive victory at Las Navas de Tolosa (1212) which led to the conquest of Córdoba (1236), Valencia (1238), Murcia (1243), Seville (1248) and Cádiz (1262).

The ninth and tenth century invasions also disrupted royal authority and created political fragmentation. In Gaul the Frankish rulers virtually capitulated to the Vikings, leaving defence to the local magnates. The result was a great upsurge of feudalism. Peasant freemen virtually disappeared and society was polarised between nobles and serfs. In Germany power devolved into the hands of dukes and margraves who defended the frontiers, and in Italy only the walled cities could withstand the Magyar onslaught. The kingdom of Wessex was the exception, unique in tenth century Europe beyond the borders of Muslim Spain and Byzantium. Here the monarchy took control, creating during the reconquest of the Danelaw a system of shires and hundreds administered by sheriffs who were officials, not feudatories. But this royal government could not withstand the renewal of Danish attacks during the reign of Aethelred II (978–1016). By the beginning of the eleventh century England seemed destined to pass into a Scandinavian orbit (page 52). The Norman Conquest (map 3) decisively halted this development. William the Conqueror quickly established control in the south; but in the north, where Danish and Scottish intervention underpinned resistance, he only made his authority secure by systematic devastation (1069). Danish reconquest was still a threat until 1085; but after 1066 England was permanently aligned with the Christian and feudal civilisation of western Europe. The period of invasions had irrevocably changed the structure of Western society.

2 The Western reconquest of the Mediterranean

- Muslim areas in 950
- Byzantine Empire
- Western Christendom
- Byzantine reconquests
- Pisan and Genoese raids and conquests
- Norman conquests
- Venetian expansion

Mediterranean trade routes:
- Venice
- Amalfi
- Pisa
- Genoa

1 Viking, Magyar and Saracen invasions

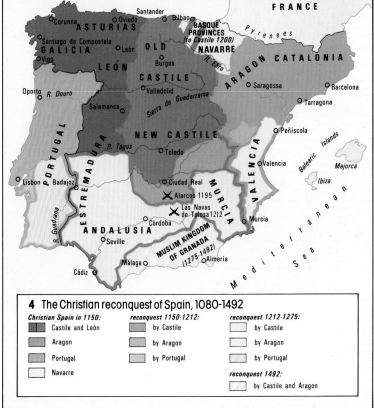

4 The Christian reconquest of Spain, 1080-1492

Christianity and Judaism, c.600-1500

By the time of Pope Leo I (440–461) an organised Christian church existed with a hierarchy of bishops and a full-scale framework of patriarchates, provinces and dioceses. But the attempt to enforce orthodoxy, particularly at the Council of Chalcedon (451), caused serious internal conflict. The Monophysite or Coptic Christians of Egypt were alienated, the Nestorians driven into exile in Persia. Here they carried on great missionary work (map 1), only halted centuries later by the advance of Islam (page 40). In the west, however, where Christianity was the official religion of the Roman empire, the church suffered from the setbacks inflicted by the Germanic invasions of the western provinces (page 32), and subsequent rivalry between Rome and Constantinople resulted after 1054 in schism between Catholicism and Orthodoxy. A period of stagnation had set in, only ended by the Irish and later Anglo-Saxon missionaries (map 3), who converted the heathen tribes of Germany, reformed the Frankish church, and inaugurated a great missionary drive to Scandinavia and eastern Europe. In addition a counter-offensive against Islam was launched in a series of Crusades beginning in 1096. The general outline of the Christian thrust, north and east from the Rhine and Danube, can be followed on map 2.

The resurgence of Christianity, particularly marked after the pontificate of

Leo IX (1048–54) was a disaster for the Jewish communities which had spread throughout Europe before and after the suppression of the Jewish revolts in Palestine by the Romans in AD 66 and 132. The Jews suffered no restrictions in the Roman empire and, with their widespread international connections, were welcomed as traders by the Carolingians and other early medieval kings. But the Crusades inaugurated a wave of intolerance, and the third and fourth Lateran Councils (1179, 1215) passed discriminatory legislation. The rise of a native merchant class also made Jews less indis-

pensable to Christian rulers, and later they became the scapegoats for the economic setbacks of the fourteenth century (page 56). The result was the series of expulsions, beginning in England in 1290. In 1492 the Sephardic Jews were expelled from Spain, in 1497 from Portugal. The Ashkenazi in the German lands took refuge in Poland and Lithuania, where they formed tight communities in what later was called 'the Pale'. Only the eighteenth-century Enlightenment brought a beginning of reconciliation, but the Nazi experience was to show that it was far from complete.

2 **Christianity in Europe**

- Monophysite Christians
- Orthodox Christians
- Catholic Christians
- original Catholic core
- Celtic churches
- Islam
- heathen peoples
- metropolitan see
- bishopric
- monastery/hermitage
- other churches
- routes of missionaries

38

4 The Jews in medieval Europe

cultural areas:

- Ashkenazi
- South Italian
- Islamic
- homeland of Spanish culture (Sephardi)
- → migrations
- → expulsions

ENGLAND
Oxford   London
Southampton
Amsterdam
Cologne
Antwerp   Marburg
Frankfurt
1290   Trier   Mainz
Paris   Worms
Troyes   Speyer   Augsburg
FRANCE *1394*   Nuremberg   Regensburg
1394   Lyons   Munich
Montpellier   Arles
Narbonne   Venice
Perpignan   Marseilles   Ferrara
Barcelona   Florence   *c.500-800*
ossa   Rome
Naples   Taranto

POLAND   *R. Vistula*   LITHUANIA
Poznań   Brest-Litovsk   Minsk   *c.1450-1500*   RUSSIA
c.1100-1400   Breslau   Lublin
GERMANIC   Prague   Cracow   Lemberg   Kiev
Nuremberg   Vienna   *c.1150-1350*   *R. Dnieper*
LANDS   Budapest   *c.1350-1450*   *c.1450-1500*
R. Danube   *c.700-900*
Adrianople
Salonika   Constantinople   *Black Sea*

Algiers   TUNISIA   Tunis
Mediterranean   Sea
Smyrna
Caspian Sea
40°
Aleppo
R. Euphrates   *R. Tigris*   PERSIA
Tyre   Damascus
Safed
Tripoli   Alexandria   Jerusalem   Baghdad
Cairo   ARABIA
EGYPT
20°   *40°*

menians
orians
Arbela   Bardaa   *Caspian*   Aral Sea   Lake Balkhash   MONGOLIA   Khanbalik (Peking)   KOREA
Tabriz   *Sea*   TRANSOXIANA   ONGUTS   *Yellow Sea*
Karkh   Halwan
Baghdad (from 800)   Rai   Nishapur   Merv   Bukhara   Samarkand   TURKESTAN   Almalyk   Cambaluc   Kumul   Tatung Hira   Yangchow
Seleucia-Ctesiphon   UIGHURS   Khara-Khoja   Tunhwang   Ningsia   Chinkiang
(to 800)   Jund-i Shapur   Herat   Balkh   Kashgar   Kucha   Kanchow   Sianfu   CHINA   Hangchow
a   Rewardashur   Isfahan
PERSIA   Sining   Chengtu   Chuanchow
TIBET
Beth Katraye
Dhofar   Arabian   Sea
Socotra   INDIA   Canton
Bay of   Bengal   South China   Sea
Cranganore   MALABAR
Kottayam
Quilon
CEYLON
Indian Ocean

Christianity in Asia

ian churches:

- Nestorian churches
- Coptic (Monophysite) missionary activity
- Jacobite/Nestorian missions (the St Thomas church)
- etropolitan   ⊙ bishopric   ⊕ monastery   o other churches

bution of non-Christian religions:

- Islam
- Buddhism
- Hinduism
- *GUTS*   pagan peoples

The rise and expansion of Islam was one of the most significant and far-reaching events in modern history. 'Islam' means 'submission to the will of God'; God's message has been conveyed to mankind through a series of prophets, culminating in Mohammed. The Koran is the Word of God; Mohammed is the Seal of the Prophets, and no others will come after him. Mohammed was born in Mecca about AD 570, and received his first revelations in 610. As his followers grew in number they aroused the hostility of the merchant aristocracy of Mecca, and the group was eventually obliged to withdraw to Medina, some 280 miles north-east of Mecca. This migration, *hijra* in Arabic, marks the beginning of the Islamic era and of the Muslim calendar. Mohammed eventually returned to Mecca in triumph in 630. He died in 632, but Islam expanded rapidly; over the next century Arab armies brought the new religion as far west as Spain and the Mediterranean islands and as far east as northern India (map 1).

In 661 the political control of the Arab-Islamic empire passed to the Umayyads, a dynasty originating from the pre-Islamic Meccan aristocracy, whose power was now centred on Damascus. In 750 the Umayyads were replaced by the Abbasids, a family claiming direct descent from Mohammed. The capital now shifted from Syria to Baghdad, and power began to pass from the Arab minority to the non-Arab Muslims, who had always formed the numerical majority in the Muslim Empire. The Abbasid period was a time of great prosperity and cultural and intellectual achievement, although the Muslim world gradually lost its political unity and split into a number of local dynastic entities (map 2). Among these were the Umayyads and Almoravids of Spain and North Africa, the Fatimids of Egypt and the Ghaznavids of north India.

In 945, the centre of the empire itself was captured by the Buyids, who ruled in the Abbasids' name for over a century. These were displaced in their turn by the Seljuks, Turks from central Asia, who gradually expanded into Anatolia. Their defeat of the Byzantine army at Manzikert in 1071 caused the Byzantines to seek the aid of Western Christendom which was to materialise in the form of the Crusades, principally in the late eleventh and twelfth centuries (map 3). The Crusades had little impact upon Arab society, but

the Norman conquest of southern Italy and the southward expansion of the Christian states of northern Spain combined to push the Muslims out of Europe by the end of the fifteenth century, and to move the centre of gravity of the Muslim world permanently further east.

In the twelfth and thirteenth centuries the Islamic world was disrupted by a new wave of invaders, the Mongols, who founded states in Iran, central Asia and south Russia (page 46). The Mongols defeated the Seljuk Turks in 1243 and sacked Baghdad in 1258, bringing about the end of the Abbasid Empire, but their defeat by the Mamelukes of Egypt at Ain Jalut in Palestine in 1260 marked their furthest westward advance. The Mongols' retreat created a vacuum which was

filled by the rise of a number of Turcoman dynasties, one of which, the Ottomans, had risen to pre-eminence by the beginning of the fourteenth century. Islam continued to expand in India (map 4), Indonesia (map 5) and in sub-Saharan Africa (page 60); today there are about 400 million Muslims, forming about one seventh of the population of the world.

5 Islam in S.E. Asia
→ spread of Islam
13th/14th centuries
15th century
16th century

2 The Middle East and North Africa, 786-1260
Abbasid Caliphate at greatest extent 786-809
countries recognising Abbasid suzerainty c.1090
territory disputed between Seljuks and Byzantine Empire
Zaidi Imams
Almohads 1130-1269
→ line of Turkish advance
Seljuks Muslim dynasties with dates

3 The Muslim reconquest of Palestine
— boundary of Crusader states
Byzantine Empire
conquests of Saladin:
before 1171
before 1187
1187 to 1189

Map 1 — The expansion of Islam, 632-936

Urgench
KHWARIZM
Karakhanids (992-1211)
Bukhara
Samarkand
TRANSOXIANA
R. Jaxartes (Syr Darya)
Kashgar
R. Oxus (Amu Darya)
Merv
Balkh
Nishapur
Hindu Kush
Kabul
Herat
Ghazni
KHURASAN
AFGHANISTAN
Manzikert 1071
Tabriz
AZERBAIJAN
Turks
Seljuks (1038-1194)
IRAN
SEISTAN
Ghaznavids (977-1186)
Kandahar
Lahore
Tiflis
Derbent
Caspian Sea
Mosul
R. Tigris
Hamadan
Kermanshah
Isfahan
Yazd
Multan
R. Indus
ghdad
R. Euphrates
Basra
Shiraz
Persian Gulf
INDIA
ARABIA
Muscat
OMAN
Arabian Sea
cca
YEMEN
Sana
Aden

4 Islam in India

PUNJAB
Himalayas
Lahore
Multan 711-713
713 Multan
Delhi 1295
R. Indus
R. Brahmaputra
R. Ganges
SIND
c.1024
1304-11
BENGAL
Broach
Surat
R. Godavari
ORISSA
Arabian Sea
1304-11
DECCAN
Bay of Bengal
Laccadive Is. converted 13th century
Calicut
Tanjore
Maldive Is. converted 12th century
Madura
Quilon
1304
CEYLON

- → spread of Islam
- ▅ Islamic area by 1200
- ▅ Delhi Sultanate under the Khaljis, 1306
- ▅ Islamic area by 1400
- ━ Mughal Empire, c.1690

1 The expansion of Islam, 632-936

- empire under Mohammed
- growth under Abu Bakr (632-634)
- growth under Omar (634-644)
- growth under Othman (644-656) and Ali (656-661)
- expansion of the Umayyad Caliphate (661-750)
- expansion 750-850
- → routes of advance
- ✕ battles

Aral Sea
TRANSOXIANA
FERGHANA
Talas 751
R. Oxus
Samarkand 710
Bukhara 710
KHAZAR EMPIRE
R. Don
Merv
Balkh 651
R. Dnieper
Caucasus Mts
Tiflis
Derbent
Caspian Sea
Ardabil
GURGAN
Nishapur
Herat
KHURASAN
Hindu Kush
Kabul 664
PUNJAB
R. Dnieper
Black Sea
Erzurum
ARMENIA
AZERBAIJAN
Tabriz
Rai
PERSIA
Multan 711
R. Indus
Sulaiman Range
SEISTAN
SIND
Asia Minor
Tarsus
Taurus Mts
Antioch
Edessa
MESOPOTAMIA
R. Tigris
Mosul 641
Jalula
Nehavend 642
Isfahan
Sus
Zagros Mts
KIRMAN
Cyprus 648
Damascus 635
Yarmuk 636
Fihl
SYRIA
Ramla
R. Euphrates
Kerbela 680
Baghdad
Ctesiphon
Kufa
Qadisiya 636
Basra 656
Persepolis (Istakhr) 648
FARS
MAKRAN
Jerusalem 638
Ajnadain 634
a 646
Heliopolis 640
Fustat (Cairo) 670
BAHRAIN
Persian Gulf
Suhar
OMAN
Arabian Sea
EGYPT 640
R. Nile
Tabuk
YAMAMA
Hijr
HEJAZ
Medina
Badr 624
Mecca
Red Sea
NUBIANS
Dongola
YEMEN
HADHRAMAUT
KINGDOM OF AXUM

The Byzantine world, 610-1453

The history of the Roman empire was marked almost from the outset by a shift of focus to the east. The original cause was the lure of the wealth of the older oriental civilisations and the economic strength of the great commercial centres of Egypt and western Asia (page 24). Later, the loss of the western provinces to Germanic invaders (page 34) hastened the trend. Simultaneously the great Persian revival under the Sasanians forced Rome to concentrate its efforts on defence of its eastern frontier. After Justinian (page 30) the west was neglected, the Roman empire became an eastern, Greek-speaking dominion. The change is conventionally placed in the reign of Heraclius (610–641). From this time it is customary to speak of a Byzantine rather than a Roman empire.

Heraclius brought the long contest with Persia to a victorious close at Nineveh (628), but almost immediately was confronted by an even more redoubtable foe: Islam. The struggle with Islam (page 40) and with the Slavs, pressing against the European frontier in the Balkans (page 32), now became the dominant fact in Byzantine history. What is remarkable is Byzantine resilience. To meet the Arab threat, Asia Minor was reorganised into military districts, or 'themes', manned by a peasant militia (map 2). After two long Arab sieges of Constantinople had been repelled (674–8, 717–8), the new Macedonian dynasty (867–1056) launched a vigorous counter-offensive. By the death of Basil II (976–1025) the frontiers had been pushed back almost to their earlier limits. The Arabs were driven back to Jerusalem (976), and Bulgaria was finally reduced to a group of Christian provinces. Even later Manuel I (1143–80) still planned to recover the former Byzantine territories in Italy. But constant war imposed heavy financial strains, as well as profound and debilitating social change, and in spite of phases of aggressive counter-offensive

and expansion, the frontiers steadily shrank (map 1).

After Basil I, the decisive fact was the appearance of a new foe, the Seljuk Turks (page 40). The crushing Seljuk victory at Manzikert (1071) induced Alexios I (1081–1118) to call on the west for help, thus initiating the sequence of events that led to the First Crusade. In retrospect, it was a disastrous move. The Franks were less concerned to aid Byzantium than to set up their own principalities in Palestine and Asia Minor. The Normans, by now in control of Sicily and Byzantine Italy, were greedy for Byzantine territory in the Morea (Peloponnese) and further east. The Italian cities, Venice to the fore, were striving to engross the oriental trade (page 36). The outcome, after a century of vicissitudes, was the Fourth Crusade (1202–4), the conquest and pillage of Constantinople, the partition of the Byzantine empire, and the establishment in its place of a Latin empire (map 3). But the Latin empire proved short-lived. The Greek-speaking population resented it, and a new dynasty, the Palaeologi, restored the Greek empire in 1261.

It was, nevertheless, only a shadow of the former Byzantine empire; and when a new Turkish people, the Ottomans, established itself in Anatolia, and then, outflanking Constantinople, advanced into Byzantium's European territories (page 48), its fate was sealed (map 4). The rest of the story is an epilogue, ending with the fall of Constantinople in 1453. Nevertheless the story of Byzantium is not without greatness and lasting achievements. For centuries it was ahead of the west in government and in the arts of civilisation. It also passed on its culture and its religion to the Balkan peoples and to Russia. 'Two Romes have fallen,' a Russian monk wrote shortly after 1453, 'but the third is standing, and there shall be no fourth.' He was speaking of Moscow. Russia, gradually consolidated under its Varangian rulers and their Muscovite successors (page 44), now emerged as heir to the Byzantine inheritance. This was to be a fact of lasting importance in world history.

2 The "themes" and the Arab invasions

- final organisation of themes

first four themes:
- Opsician
- Anatolic
- Armeniac
- theme of the Carabisiani

Arab invasion routes:
- → by land
- → by sea
- ● invasion bases

4 The Muslim conquest of Anatolia

- Byzantine eastern frontier c. 930
- the frontier c.1070
- controlled by Seljuk Turks c. 1080
- Seljuk control early 13th century

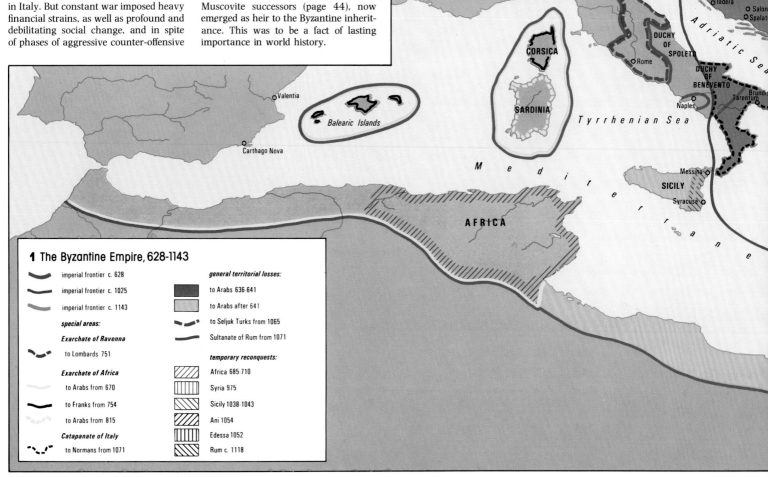

1 The Byzantine Empire, 628-1143

- imperial frontier c. 628
- imperial frontier c. 1025
- imperial frontier c. 1143

special areas:

Exarchate of Ravenna
- to Lombards 751

Exarchate of Africa
- to Arabs from 670
- to Franks from 754
- to Arabs from 815

Catapanate of Italy
- to Normans from 1071

general territorial losses:
- to Arabs 636-641
- to Arabs after 641
- to Seljuk Turks from 1065
- Sultanate of Rum from 1071

temporary reconquests:
- Africa 685-710
- Syria 975
- Sicily 1038-1043
- Ani 1054
- Edessa 1052
- Rum c. 1118

3 The Crusades and the decline of Byzantium

- → the Norman attack 1084-5
- → routes of the First Crusade 1096-7
- ●●●→ the Norman attack 1147
- ----→ the Norman attack 1185
- – – → route of Fourth Crusade 1202-4
- ▬▬ imperial frontier 1180
- ▮▮ imperial territory in 1214
- ▮▮ Despotate of Epirus
- ▮▮ Latin Empire in 1204
- ▮▮ Venetian territory in 1214

PECHENEGS

Black Sea

WALLACHIA

SERBIA

DALMATIA

Adriatic Sea

R. Drina

R. Danube

Vidin

Mesembria

Sinope

Theodosiopolis

Ragusa

Serdica

Philippopolis

Adrianople

Constantinople

Kastamuni

Manzikert

Ochrida

Prilep

Vodena

Tzurulum

Nicomedia

Ancyra

Sebastea

SELJUKS OF RUM

Durrhachium

Bari

Brundisium

Avlona

Castoria

Berrhoea

Thessalonica

Cyzicus

Prusa

EMPIRE OF NICAEA

Nicaea

Dorylaeum

R. Halys

Caesarea

L. Van

Corfu

Larissa

Nicopolis

Aegean Sea

Lemnos

Lesbos

Adramyttium

Pergamum

Sardis

Amorium

Philomelium

Sozopolis

Iconium

Heraclea

Tyana

Marash

Samosata

Edessa

NORMANS

Cephalonia

Athens

MOREA

Zacynthus

Corinth

Modon

Monemvasia

Cerigo

Negroponte

Chios

Smyrna

R. Meander

Chonae

Attalia

RHODES

Cos

Tarsus

Antioch

Aleppo

R. Euphrates

Carrhae

CYPRUS

R. Orontes

Homs

Tripoli

Tyre

Acre

CRETE

Mediterranean Sea

Caspian Sea

ABASGIA

IBERIA

Tiflis

ALBANIA

Bosporus

Cherson

Black Sea

Phasis

LAZICA

Kars

Ani

R. Araxes

ASIA

Singidunum

R. Danube

Dorostolon

Nicopolis

Marcianopolis

Sinope

Trebizond

PONTUS

Manzikert 1071

DACIA

Serdica

Anchialus

PAPHLAGONIA

Neocaesarea

L. Van

Bitlis

L. Urmia

PERSIA

Philippopolis

THRACE

Arcadiopolis

Scupi

Adrianople

Constantinople

Ancyra

Sebastea

GALATIA

Caesarea

Arabissos

Samosata

R. Tigris

Dyrrhachium

Melantias

Heraclea

Pylae

Nicomedia

Helenopolis

NEW EPIRUS

Avlona

MACEDONIA

Thessalonica

Gallipoli

Prusa

BITHYNIA

Malagina

Cotiaeum

CAPPADOCIA

Germaniceia

Edessa

Carrhae

Zeugma

Callinicum

Mosul

Kirkuk

Nineveh

Larissa

Demetrias

Troy

Abydus

LYDIA

ANCIENT EPIRUS

THESSALY

Nicopolis

Thebes

Aegean Sea

Sardis

PHRYGIA

PISIDIA

Iconium

CILICIA

Hieropolis

Zenobia

Dastagord

Ionian Sea

Patras

Athens

Corinth

Lacedaemon

Ephesus

Miletus

Halicarnassus

PAMPHYLIA

Attalia

ISAURIA

Adana

Tarsus

Antioch

Aleppo

Circesium

R. Euphrates

Ctesiphon

Seleucia

Rhodes

Laodicea

Emesa

Palmyra

Hira

CYPRUS

Tripoli

Damascus

CRETE

Tiberias

Apollonia

Sea

PALESTINE

Bostra

Maan

Gaza

Jerusalem

Hebron

Petra

PENTAPOLIS

Damietta

Pelusium

TRIPOLITANIA

Alexandria

Mareotis

Memphis

ARABIA

Arsenoe

Tabuk

EGYPT

R. Nile

Red Sea

Early Russia
862-1245

Three factors shaped the early history of Russia: the movement eastward of Slav tribal settlers; the impact of the Vikings or Varangians, seafaring raiders and traders from Sweden who entered northern Russia c.850 (page 36) and imposed tribute on the neighbouring Slavs and Finns; the basic geography of the region, particularly the division between the forests of central and northern Russia and the treeless steppes of the south through which successive waves of invaders from Asia poured into Europe. Fierce Pechenegs controlled the fertile steppelands. To avoid them Slav colonists moved into central Russia, where they settled in the river basins, clearing the forests and living by agriculture, hunting, trapping and by the fur trade.

At first the Slavs resisted the Varangians. But in 862 they called in 'Rurik the Viking' to restore order and protect them from Pecheneg raiders. Rurik occupied Novgorod, but the Varangians immediately pushed south to Smolensk and then along the Dnieper to Kiev (882). They thus controlled the trade route from the Baltic to the Black Sea. At the same time they imposed their rule over the Slav tribes on both sides of the river (map 1). It was nevertheless only a loose tributary overlordship, and it was not until the time of Vladimir I of Kiev (980–1015)

that the tribal regions were welded together into a single state.

The reign of Vladimir's son, Yaroslav I (1019–54) was the high point of Kievan Russia. Converted to Christianity under Vladimir and in close contact with Constantinople, Kiev ranked high among European cities. But the new state had grown too quickly and after 1054 its decline was rapid. Dynastic conflict was incessant, and the administration ineffective. At the same time the destruction of the Khazar empire by Svyatoslav (965) opened the way for a new wave of Asiatic nomads, the Polovtsy, who broke through the defences erected by Vladimir I and sacked Kiev in 1093. The result was a great exodus of peasants northwards to the region between the Oka and the Volga, where many new towns were founded including Vladimir, Suzdal, Rostov, Moscow and Tver. Novgorod-Seversk, and in the west, Galich and Vladimir-Volynsk broke away from Kiev. After 1125 the axis of Russian life shifted north and the state broke up into warring principalities (map 2), among which Vladimir-Suzdal was outstanding.

The final blow to the old order was the Mongol invasions, which fell upon the Volga region before turning south against Kiev which was sacked in 1240 (map 3), while Novgorod was exposed simultaneously to German and Swedish attack. Mongol control was only indirect, but its results were far-reaching. Kievan Russia, already debilitated, disappeared for ever, and the way was open for the rise of Moscow.

1 Varangian Russia, 862-1054

Varangian territory c.980

Ulichi East Slav tribes

KHAZARS Finno-Ugrian and Asiatic peoples

Varangian (Viking) trade routes

Varangian raids on Constantinople 907, 944

Svyatoslav's campaigns 964-71

Pecheneg raids

3 Mongol invasions, 1223-40

Russian principalities

Mongol incursion of Dzhebe and Subedeya

route of Batya's conquering horde

movement of Russian forces

movement of Polovtsian forces

movement of Volga Bulgar forces

2 Kievan Russia, 1054-1242

- ○ towns and places of significance 1054
- □ towns and places of significance 1054-1200
- *MARI* tribes
- ➤ movement of steppe nomads in 11th century
- defensive works built against nomads
- boundaries of Russian principalities c. 1200
- Prince Igor Svyatoslavich's campaign against Polovtsy 1185
- waterway trade routes
- tundra
- coniferous and deciduous forest
- steppe and desert
- mountain vegetation

Arctic Circle

70°

R. Pechora

Ural Mrs

S A M O Y E D

White Sea

R. Mezen □ Pinega

Northern Dvina

N O V G O R O D   E M P I R E

C H U D

Y U G R A

P E R M

R. Onega

R. Vychegda

L. Onega

R. Sukhona

L. Ladoga

60°

60°

Gulf of Finland

○ Beloozero

VYATKA TERRITORY

Baltic Sea

ESTS

Ladoga

R. Neva 1240 ✗

R. Volkhov

L. Peipus 1242 ✗

Yuriev ○

Novgorod ○

L. Ilmen

□ Galich

M A R I

KURS

Riga ○

○ Pskov

○ Izborsk

R. Lovat

LIVONIAN

ORDER

Kukeynoys ○

○ Gertsike

Western Dvina

Torzhok ○

Toropets □

Yaroslavl ○

□ Kostroma

Rostov ○

VLADIMIR-SUZDAL

♛

Tver ○

○ Suzdal

ZHMUD

Volok-Lamsky □ Pereyaslavl □

□ Dmitrov

○ Nizhniy Novgorod

R. Kama

TEUTONIC ORDER

○ Polotsk

Vitebsk ○

SMOLENSK

♛

Moscow ○ Vladimir ○

R. Klyazma

LITVA

POLOTSK

♛

Orsha ○

Smolensk ○

R. Moskva

○ Murom

Gorodno □

□ Kopys

Kolomna ○

○ Bolgar

○ Bilyar

Minsk □

Koselsk ○

Ryazan ○

Suvar ○

VOLGA BULGARS

Nesvizh □

MUROM-RYAZAN

♛

R. Oka

Berestye ○ Klechesk □

Drogochin □

CHERNIGOV

♛

Bryansk ○

M O R D V A

VLADIMIR-VOLYNSK

♛

TUROV-PINSK

♛

Pinsk □

R. Desna

□ Karachev

○ Novosil

Kholm ○

Turov □

Rechitsa ○

NOVGOROD-SEVERSK

♛

Vladimir ○

Vruchy ○

○ Listem

Cherven ○

Lyubech ○

Novgorod-Severskiy □

○ Belz

○ Chernigov

Rylsk □ □ Kursk

Peremyshl ○

Terebovl ○

Korosten ○

R. Ural

□ Gorodets

KIEV

♛

✗

R. Don

Galich ○

GALICH

♛

Kiev 1093 ○

PEREYASLAVL

♛

Kolomyya ○

Kamenets ○

Pereyaslavl ○

R. Donets

○ Rodnya

Donets □

50°

50°

P O L O V T S Y

(in 1054)

Poltava □

R. Volga

HUNGARIAN KINGDOM

R. Prut

Peresechen ○

P E C H E N E G S

P O L O V T S Y

T O R K I

Southern Bug

in 1200

R. Donets

S A K S I N Y

Carpathian Mts

Belgorod ○

R. Dniester

R. Dniester

R. Dnieper

○ Sarkel

Oleshe ○

○ Itil

Pereslavets ○

Sea of Azov

B U L G A R I A

R. Danube

○ Dristov

Black Sea

Khersones ○ ○ Sugdeya

○ Tmutarakan

K A S O G I

R. Kuban

Caspian Sea

Y A S I

R. Kuma

60°

R. Terek

45

The Mongol Empire, 1206-1696

The Mongols, a primitive nomadic people from the depths of Asia, had tremendous influence on the course of world history. Few in number, but augmented by Turcoman auxiliaries, they threw themselves against the old centres of civilisation in east and west (map 1). After overrunning the Ch'in empire in north China between 1211 and 1234, they defeated the Sung army and ruled over the whole of China from 1280 to 1367 (page 50). They even launched seaborne expeditions against Java and Japan, though neither was successful. In the west their first victim was the Muslim empire of Khwarizm (1220), after which they turned against the Abbasid caliphate, sacking Baghdad in 1258. But the decisive Mameluke victory at Ain Jalut (1260) halted their advance in this direction. Meanwhile, they had thrown themselves against Christian Europe, overrunning the northern Russian principalities in 1237-8 and sacking Kiev in 1240 (page 44), before advancing into Hungary and Poland and destroying a German-Polish army at Legnica in 1241 (map 2).

The architect of these amazing victories was a certain Temujin, known to history as Genghis Khan, son of a Mongol chief, who united the different Mongol tribes under his leadership (1206) and subdued other neighbouring, mainly Turcoman, tribes, before turning against China in 1211. Genghis died in 1227, but his wars of conquest were continued by his sons and grandsons, among whom Ogedei, elected Great Khan in 1229, and Möngke, who succeeded in 1251, were outstanding. But the vast empire lacked coherence and stability, and the Mongols failed to develop appropriate institutions. Genghis himself divided his empire among his four sons, like earlier Frankish rulers in the west (page 34), and with similar results. Already on the death of Ogedei (1241), Genghis' grandson Batu, commander-in-chief in the west, withdrew his army from Poland to the base on the lower Volga, in order to take part in the choice of a successor. It never returned and western Europe was spared, though Russia remained a Mongol tributary for over two centuries. Finally, on the death of Möngke (1259), the brittle unity dissolved. Kublai (d. 1294) was elected Great Khan, but instead of a general overlordship, his authority was confined to the east, and the western khanates (Chagatai, Il-Khan and the Golden Horde) went their own way (map 3). By the sixteenth century only the eastern khanate survived: in Persia the Ilkhanids were displaced by a local Turcoman dynasty in 1353, and later the successors of the Golden Horde, which had broken up into a number of smaller khanates at the time of Tamerlane the Great, were mopped up by a resurgent Russia.

It was, paradoxically, Timur, or Tamerlane (1336-1405), traditionally the last great Mongol conqueror (though he was in fact a Turcoman from Transoxiana), whose victorious career initiated the decline. Timur's vast empire (map 4) fell apart rapidly after his death while leading an expedition against China; but in the course of his conquests he destroyed the Chagatai khanate, which ceased to exist in 1405, and dislocated the

Golden Horde. Henceforward the Mongols were under attack from all sides, increasingly at a disadvantage as the introduction of firearms weighed the balance on their adversaries' side. In the west Russia absorbed the former territories of the Golden Horde (page 84). In the east, the Mongols threw back a major Chinese assault in 1449 (page 50) and resumed their offensive under Altan Khan (1507-82); but in the end Mongolia itself was brought under Chinese dominion in 1696 by the new Ch'ing dynasty (page 106). Nevertheless the Mongol impact had lasting results. All the older civilisations were affected; faced by the Mongol challenge, their history took a new course.

1 The Mongol Empire before 1259

   the Mongol Empire before 1259

   campaigns under Genghis Khan

   campaigns of his successors

   incursions and loose Mongol control

OIROTS   Mongol tribes around 1220

2 The Mongol invasion of Europe, 1237-42

3 The break-up of the Mongol Empire after 1259

   successor states to the Mongol Empire

4 The conquests of Timur, 1370-1405

→ Timur's campaigns

The Muslim resurgence
1301-1639

The revival of Islam after 1300 and the great wave of Muslim expansion that followed, dominated the next four centuries, far more so than European expansion, which had only marginal effects before 1700. After 1354 the Christian west stood on the defensive, while the Turks conquered the whole of Europe east of the Adriatic and south of the Danube. The progress of Islam in the east was equally remarkable. By 1500 northern India was under Muslim rule, and most of the south after 1565 when the last surviving Hindu state, Vijayanagar, succumbed. It prevailed also in the oases of central Asia, in the outlying provinces of Ming China, and was making rapid headway in Java.

This amazing revival was the more remarkable because in 1258, when the Mongols sacked Baghdad and overthrew the caliphate (page 46), the Muslim world was in disarray. The Seljuk sultanate (page 40) had broken up after half a century, and only the Mamelukes of Egypt and Syria maintained any sort of political stability. Two factors transformed the situation. One was the revitalisation of Islam itself under the impact of Sufi mysticism. The other was the infiltration, with or in the wake of the Mongols, of Turkic peoples from central Asia, who, after conversion and assimilation, became the spearhead of Muslim advance. It was they who, in 1206, set up the Delhi Sultanate, the leading Indian state until the appearance in 1526 of Babur, another warrior from inner Asia. In the west Turkish warriors settled around 1265 in north-west Anatolia, and here in 1301 their leader, Osman, founded a state which became the core of the future Ottoman empire (map 1). By 1354 the Turks had crossed the Dardanelles to Gallipoli, and their victory at Kosovo (1389) and repulse of a Christian counter-offensive at Nicopolis (1396) left them masters of the Balkans. Only the invasion of Timur (page 46) and his destruction of the Turkish army at Ankara (1402) gave hard-pressed Byzantium respite. But the renewal of expansion under Murad II (1421–51) and Mehemmed II (1451–81) sealed its fate. In 1453 Constantinople fell, and Mehemmed went on to extend control over Moldavia, the Crimea and Trebizond, turning the Black Sea into an Ottoman lake.

By the time that Suleiman the Magnificent (1520–66) succeeded to the throne, the Ottoman empire was one of the world's leading powers, comparable with Ming China or Charles V's empire in the west. But now two other empires arose to share pre-eminence in the Muslim world. The one was the Mughal empire, founded by Babur in 1526, but only consolidated by his grandson, Akbar (1556–1605). The other was Persia, which had been in a state of chaos ever since it was overrun by Timur. Here, in 1500, the leader of a fanatical Shi'i sect, Ismail Safavi, seized Tabriz, crowned himself shah as Ismail I (1500–24), and quickly reunited the country. Safavid Persia reached its peak under Abbas I (1587–1629), by which time the three Muslim empires controlled a wide belt of territory from the frontiers of Austria and Morocco to the borders of China, the foothills of the Himalayas and the Bay of Bengal (map 2). But their divisions and rivalries, particularly the clash between Sunni Turkey and Shi'i Persia, drove a wedge into the Muslim world, comparable to the conflict between Catholics and Protestants in western Europe. Shi'ism had originated centuries earlier over the question of the true succession to the Prophet Mohammed; but wider issues, religious and political, were involved. In Persia a resurgent nationalism certainly played a part. The Safavids were the first native Persian dynasty since Sasanian times, and Ismail I's decision to make Shi'ism the Persian state religion was a challenge to the Sunni Turkish sultan. The Ottoman reaction was swift. In 1514 Ismail's armies were defeated at Çaldiran, and in 1516–17 the Ottomans captured Syria and Egypt from the Mamelukes. These successes enabled Suleiman to resume the Ottoman advance in Europe. After the battle of Mohács (1526) Hungary was overrun and Vienna was besieged (1529). But Persia remained a thorn in the Ottoman side. The long wars against the Safavids (1534–35, 1554–55, 1577–90, 1603–19) were not the only reason for the Muslim decline which became apparent after 1560, but they certainly hastened it. This was a great age of Islamic art and architecture, particularly in Persia and India. But in a changing world Islam remained static. All three Muslim empires were essentially land-based; but now hegemony was passing to the sea, and to the peoples on the fringe – the Dutch, the French, the English – who knew how to master and exploit it.

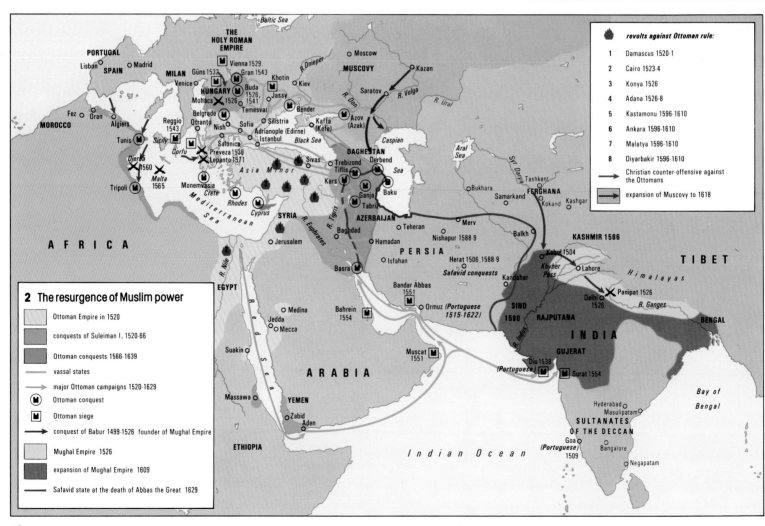

2 The resurgence of Muslim power

- Ottoman Empire in 1520
- conquests of Suleiman I, 1520-66
- Ottoman conquests 1566-1639
- vassal states
- major Ottoman campaigns 1520-1629
- Ottoman conquest
- Ottoman siege
- conquest of Babur 1499-1526 founder of Mughal Empire
- Mughal Empire 1526
- expansion of Mughal Empire 1609
- Safavid state at the death of Abbas the Great 1629

revolts against Ottoman rule:

1 Damascus 1520-1
2 Cairo 1523-4
3 Konya 1526
4 Adana 1526-8
5 Kastamonu 1596-1610
6 Ankara 1596-1610
7 Malatya 1596-1610
8 Diyarbakir 1596-1610

Christian counter-offensive against the Ottomans

expansion of Muscovy to 1618

A R Y

TRANSYLVANIA

Carpathian Mts.

o Suczawa

o Jassy (Yaş)

MOLDAVIA (1455)
(BOĞDAN)

R. Dniester (Turla)

R. Prut

(1484)

o Akkerman

BUJAK

WALLACHIA (1396)
(EFLÂK)

Targoviste

o Bucharest (Bükreş)

Giurgiu (Yergöğü) o

Silistria

Kilia

DOBRUJA

o Vidin

Nicopolis
1396

1444 o
Varna

o Sofia

o Trnovo

ELIA (1393)

LGARIA)

o Philippopolis
(Filibe)

o Adrianople (Edirne)
1361

Gallipoli
(Gelibolu)
1354

Dardanelles

KARASI 1345

o Bursa
1326

Söğüt 1265

Eskişehir 1289

Manisa o

A N A T O L I A

SARUHAN 1390
[1405]

Smyrna
(İzmir)

Chios
Genoa

Samos

AYDIN
1396
[1426]

MENTEŞE
1396
[1426]

TEKE 1391
[1427]

Rhodes

KNIGHTS OF ST JOHN

GERMIYAN 1380
[1428]

o Konya

HAMID
1381-90

o Kayseri

KARAMAN
1390 [1468]

Taurus Mts

o Adana

DHU'L-KADR
1398 [1515]

Marj Dabik 1516

Aleppo 1516

Cyprus
(Venetian 1489,
Ottoman tributary 1517)

M e d i t e r r a n e a n   S e a

o Tripoli

o Beirut

Damascus 1516

o Alexandria

Ar-Raydaniyya

o Cairo 1517

M A M E L U K E   E M P I R E   (1517)

R. Nile

to 3rd cataract
of the R. Nile

SHARIFS OF MECCA

R e d   S e a

o Jerusalem

COSSACK SETTLEMENTS   R U S S I A

R. Dnieper (Ak Su)

KHANATE OF THE CRIMEA (VASSAL 1475)

R. Don

Sea of Azov

Azov (Azak) o

Bakhchesaray
(Bahçesaray) o

Kerch (Kerç) o

Kaffa
(Kefe) o

CIRCASSIA
(ÇERKES)

B l a c k   S e a

o Sinop

ÇANDAR
(KASTAMONU) 1393 [1461]

o Kastamonu

o Samsun

nucleus of
Ottoman state c. 1281

Bosporus
Istanbul (Constantinople)
1453

Ankara
1402

Amasya o

Trebizond
(Trabzon)
1461

EMPIRE OF TREBIZOND

o Tiflis

C a u c a s u s   M t s

Sivas o

SIVAS 1398

Otluk-Beli 1473

Erzurum o

KARAKOYUNLU

AKKOYUNLU

Diyarbakir o

R. Tigris

Lake Van

K u r d i s t a n

Çaldiran
1514

Lake Urmia

Tabriz
1514

o Mosul

R. Euphrates

SAFAVID   EMPIRE

(f r o m   1 5 0 1)

Baghdad o

1 The Ottoman advance, 1300-1520

☐ probable extent of Ottoman state c. 1300

← main routes of Ottoman advance

⌐⌐⌐ conquests of Osman c. 1300-26

☐ conquests of Orkhan 1326-62

☐ conquests of Murad I, 1362-89

1390 absorbed Emirates with date of first absorption

☐ conquests of Bayezid 1389-1402

(1389) other places and dates of Ottoman conquest

☐ vassal states of Bayezid 1402

■ Venetian territories

← invasion of Timur (Tamerlane) 1402

◉ successive centres of Ottoman state, with dates of conquest

☐ reduced frontiers of Ottoman state after Timur's invasion and civil war of 1403-13

● Emirates restored by Timur in 1402

1468 date of final reincorporation into Ottoman Empire

✕ European counter-offensive against the Ottomans

///// conquests and re-conquests 1413-51 (Mehemmed I, 1413-21, Murad II, 1421-51)

☐ boundary of Ottoman state at the accession of Mehemmed II, 1451

☐ vassal states 1451

■ vassal states 1512

☐ Ottoman empire in 1512

☐ western frontiers of Safavid state in c. 1512 including tributary states

← major campaigns of Selim I, 1512-1520

☐ Ottoman sphere of influence c. 1520

China and its neighbours
618-1644

The recovery of China from the barbarian invasions of the fourth and fifth centuries (page 32) was the work of the Sui dynasty (581–617). But it was the T'ang (618–907) who ushered in one of the great ages of Chinese history. Under the T'ang and their successors, the Sung (960–1279), China attained a level of prosperity, social stability and civilisation far ahead of contemporary Europe; and it was only another wave of invasion from inner Asia, this time the Mongols (page 46), that brought this era of wellbeing to a temporary halt. During the period of Mongol domination (1280–1368) much of the land was devastated, particularly in the north, and the population, which in 1280 probably topped 100 million, was reduced by 1393 to 60 million. The Ming dynasty (1368–1644) reversed these setbacks and put China back on the course charted by its T'ang predecessors.

T'ang China (map 1) was a centralised empire with a uniform administrative organisation of prefectures, in which the old ruling aristocracy was replaced by officials recruited by an examination system which lasted into the twentieth century. A massive movement of popu-lation into the fertile Yangtze valley and southern China produced large agricultural surpluses which stimulated trade and urban development. The T'ang also embarked on an ambitious programme of external expansion which carried them in the north-west to the Tarim Basin before they were halted by the Arabs at the Talas river in 751. By 649, the end of the reign of T'ai-tsung, 88 Asiatic peoples recognised Chinese overlordship. But the widespread military expeditions over-extended the empire's resources, many of the gains proved only tem-porary, and after 1127 even north China was lost and only recovered after the fall of the Mongol dynasty in 1386. Their successors, the Ming, also engaged in an active foreign policy, particularly against the Mongols in the north (map 4), but these ventures proved too costly and sparked off a series of rebellions which, coupled with external pressures from the Manchus in Liaotung and Japanese raiders, toppled the dynasty.

Military and political reverses did not impede the expansion of Chinese culture and political institutions to all her neighbouring states. Those most directly affected were Korea, under Chinese rule from 668 to 676 and a vassal state after 1392, Japan and South-East Asia, though in the latter region, where they came into contact with Indian and (from about AD 1300) Islamic influences, they were largely confined to north Vietnam. In South-East Asia the small temple states of the ninth to twelfth centuries (Prambanan, Angkor, Pagan), established under Hindu and Buddhist influ-ence, gave way after the thirteenth century to new political centres (Ava, Pegu, Phnom Penh), while in Vietnam, where Chinese attempts at reconquest failed, a new kingdom of Dai Viet arose. But behind the fluctu-ating political fortunes the outstanding fact was the formative influence of Hinduism, Buddhism and Con-fucianism; their assimilation defined the distinctive character of South-East Asian civilisation (map 2).

In Japan Chinese influence was more direct. As early as AD 645 the whole administration had been re-modelled on the pattern of T'ang China. The two capitals, Nara (710) and Kyoto (794), were copied from the T'ang capital of Changan, and Buddhism was intro-duced from China. But after 1192 the bureaucratic state was displaced by a feudalised society, until finally, be-tween 1467 and 1590, the country broke up into a series of warring Daimyo clans (map 3). It was the work of Oda Nobunaga (1534–82) and Hideyoshi Toyotomi (1535–98) to bring the anarchy under control, and prepare the way for the Tokugawa shogunate which gave Japan 250 years of internal peace and prosperity until, in the middle of the nineteenth century the western powers forced Japan into the modern world (page 126).

3 Civil war in Japan 1467-1590

Uesugi
Hojo
Takeda
Oda
Imagawa
Kyoto
Nara
Mori
Sogabe
Otomo
Shimazu

Sea of Japan

spheres of influence of the most powerful Daimyo clans
— boundaries of Daimyo domains

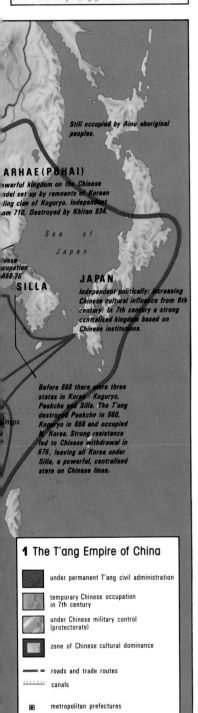

Still occupied by Ainu aboriginal peoples.

ARHAE (POHAI)
...owerful kingdom on the Chinese ...del set up by remnants of Korean ...ling clan of Koguryo. Independent ...om 710. Destroyed by Khitan 934.

Sea of Japan

...nese ...cupation ...68-76

SILLA

JAPAN
Independent politically: increasing Chinese cultural influence from 6th century. In 7th century a strong centralised kingdom based on Chinese institutions.

...ngpo

Before 660 there were three states in Korea - Koguryo, Paekche and Silla. The T'ang destroyed Paekche in 660, Koguryo in 668 and occupied N. Korea. Strong resistance led to Chinese withdrawal in 676, leaving all Korea under Silla, a powerful, centralised state on Chinese lines.

1 The T'ang Empire of China

under permanent T'ang civil administration
temporary Chinese occupation in 7th century
under Chinese military control (protectorate)
zone of Chinese cultural dominance
— — roads and trade routes
canals
metropolitan prefectures
principal prefectures

2 South-East Asia, AD 500-1500

▲ Hindu-Buddhist remains and temples AD 500-1300
⊡ major political centres of c.AD 1200-c.1300
← Mongol attacks 1257-92

Dai Viet Kingdom: independent from 10th century

Champa Kingdom: gradually absorbed by Dai Viet (11th-15th centuries).

Khmers: their temple kingdoms united under Angkor (9th-14th centuries).

Thai-Lao-Shan region: the Thai peoples expanded southwards from the 12th century, conquering the Mons of Dvaravati. Shan states later fell under Burmese domination.

Mons: their kingdoms of Thaton (11th century) and Pegu (14th-16th centuries) were later absorbed by the Burmese, and their kingdom of Dvaravati (7th-13th centuries) by the Thais.

Burmese: their empire of Pagan (11th-13th centuries) was succeeded by Ava and other states (14th-16th centuries)

Arakanese: their Muslim kingdom independent in 14th and 15th centuries; later absorbed by Burma.

In maritime S.E. Asia temple kingdoms are found in Java and seafaring trading states flourished, notably the Srivijayan empire of Sumatra and the Malay Peninsula (7th-13th centuries).

CHINA
BURMA
KINGDOM OF NANCHAO
R. Chindwin
Mogaung
Halin
Vaisali
ARAKAN
Pagan
Ava
Sri Ksetra (Prome)
Toungoo
Chiengmai
Luang Prabang
Thang Long (Hanoi)
LAOS
DAI VIET
Bassein
Pegu
Thaton
Vienliane
Sukhothai
Korat
SIAM
Ayutthaya
Sitep
Tra Kieu
DVARAVATI
U Tong
Nakhon Pathom
Mison
Dong Duong
Wat Phu
CAMBODIA
Angkor
Sambor
Prei Kuk
CHAMPA
Nha Trang
Phnom Penh
Vijaya (Binh Dinh)
Andaman Sea
Isthmus of Kra
Chaiya
Gulf of Siam
Angkor Borei
Phan Rang
Takua Pa
Ligor
Oc Eo
ATJEH
Kuala Selinsing
SULTANATE OF MALACCA
BRUNEI
R. Rajang
Celebes Sea
Malacca
Tumasik (Singapore)
Sumatra
Lingga
SRIVIJAYAN
Borneo
Makakam
Tidore
The Moluccas (Spice Islands)
R. Jambi
Jambi (Malayu)
Celebes
Palembang
EMPIRE
Java Sea
Banda Sea
Sunda Strait
Indian Ocean
PAJAJARAN
Majapahit
Borobudur
Madura
Singhasari
Prambanan
KEDIRI
Java
Bali
Sumbawa
Flores
Timor
South China Sea
R. Salween
R. Irrawaddy
R. Sittang
Black River
Red River
Mae Ping
R. Mekong
Gulf of Martaban
Malay Peninsula

4 China under the Ming, 1368-1644

major post roads
Great Wall
canals
National capital
provincial capital
the nine frontier defence areas
guard units

Japanese pirate invasions before 16th century
Japanese pirate invasions after 1550
Chinese expeditions against the Mongols

Tuul Gol
Onon Gol ✕1410
✕1414
Kerulen R.
Buyr Nuur
✕1422
✕1424
✕1410
MONGOLIA
General Chiu Fu 1409
✕1422
Gobi Desert
KHALKHA
Shachou
Kuachou
Suchow
TUMET
Shara Muren
MANCHUS
The 'Willow palisade' surrounding area of Chinese settlement in Liaotung
TSINGHAI
Kanchow
Liangchow
Ningsia
Suanfu
Tatung
Peking
Kichow
Liaotung
Mukden
Chienchou
Sining
Yulin
Taiyuan
PEI CHIHLI
Ming counter-attack to defend Korea
Kuyuan
Taochow
SHANSI
Tsingchow
Po Hai
Kinchow
KOREA
Sea of Japan
TIBET
SHENSI
Sian
Kaifeng
Tsinan
SHANTUNG
Haining
Japanese invasions of Korea under Hideyoshi Toyotomi 1582, 1592, 1597-98
HONAN
Peichow
Hwaian
NAN CHIHLI
Chengtu
SZECHWAN
R. Yangtze
Wuchang
Nanking
JAPAN
Hirado
Hakata
Shanghai
HUKWANG
Hangchow
CHEKIANG
Boten
YUNNAN
Yunnan
Kweiyang
KWEICHOW
Nanchang
KIANGSI
Ningpo
Liuchow
Kwedin
BURMA
FUKIEN
Funing
ANNAM (VIET NAM)
KWANGSI
Foochow
Kwangchow
Macao
Amoy
Chaochow
KWANGTUNG
SIAM
Limchow
Chinghua
Luichow
Tainan
HAINAN
R. Yellow River (Huang Ho)

Northern and Western Europe, 930-1314

Two features marked the period following the Viking and Magyar invasions in northern and western Europe: the emergence of settled states and the spread of Christianity. The two went hand in hand. Both in Scandinavia and in the Slavonic east the Christian church, introduced in Denmark by Harold Bluetooth in 965, in Norway by Olaf Tryggveson (995–1000), in Bohemia by Boleslav II (967–99), and in Poland by Miesko I (960–92), contributed substantially to political cohesion. The rise of powerful kingdoms in Poland and Denmark was also in part a response to German pressure. In Poland (map 1) the Piast dynasty united the tribes of Great (or northern) Poland. Boleslav Chrobry (992–1025) not only added Little Poland, Silesia and Lausitz but also temporarily Bohemia and Moravia. In Denmark Harold Bluetooth (940–86) defended Slesvig from German attack, strengthening and extending the fortified Danevirke (map 3). In Norway and Sweden development was hampered by formidable geographical obstacles (map 5). Under Sweyn I, who also became king of England in 1013, both countries were under Danish control; and Sweyn's son Canute the Great (1014–35) ruled a great but short-lived Anglo-Scandinavian empire (map 4). Following an interlude under Edward the Confessor (1042–66) England passed under Norman rule (page 36). Norway achieved independence and was united under Magnus the Good (1033–47). Sweden (except for the southern provinces which remained under Danish rule) was welded together by the kings of Uppland, and Denmark itself settled down within its frontiers after the death of Sweyn II (1047–74).

Nevertheless all countries were plagued by dynastic conflict and aristocratic resistance. In Poland Boleslav Chrobry's ambitious foreign policy provoked a sharp reaction after his death. In England William the Conqueror was faced by baronial unrest as early as 1074. But it was France that suffered most from feudal disruption. The Capetian kings, who displaced the Carolingians in 987, were confined to the Ile de France, and even here royal authority was insecure until the reign of Louis VI (1108–37). Even then the Capetians lagged behind the feudal princes. The continental possessions of Henry II of England (the so-called Angevin Empire) far outmatched the French royal domain (map 2). When Philip Augustus (1180–1223) conquered Normandy (1204) and the Angevin Empire collapsed, English rule was confined to Gascony, and the Capetians embarked on a policy of expansion which carried them to the Mediterranean by 1229.

In England expansion had begun on the morrow of the Conquest when Norman barons invaded Wales and set up extensive marcher lordships. A century later they moved on to Ireland. By 1250 two-thirds of the country had been occupied, but Ireland remained divided and rebellious. So also did Wales which had seen a remarkable national resurgence under Llewellyn the Great (1197–1240). But Edward I (1272–1307) would not brook Welsh independence. After a first campaign (1276), followed by systematic castle building to enforce English control, a second campaign in 1283 (map 7) placed the principality directly under royal administration in 1284. Edward's attempt in 1296 to repeat the process in Scotland was a costly failure, culminating in the English defeat at Bannockburn in 1314. Like his French contemporary, Philip the Fair (1285–1314), defeated by the Flemings in 1302, Edward had overreached himself. The great baronial families, still firmly ensconced (map 6), forced him in 1297 to confirm the charters wrested from King John in 1215. It was a prelude to the aristocratic reaction and the setbacks of the fourteenth century.

1 The rise of Poland

- Polish territory 960-92
- lands added by Boleslav Chrobry 992-1025
- lands temporarily in Polish occupation
- Hungarian territory
- German territory
- ⊡ bishoprics with date of foundation
- ☗ archbishoprics
- ⊟ wasteland (forest and swamp)

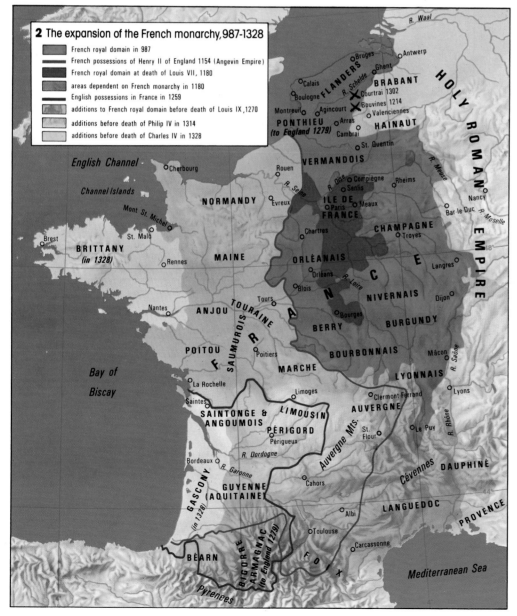

2 The expansion of the French monarchy, 987-1328

- French royal domain in 987
- French possessions of Henry II of England 1154 (Angevin Empire)
- French royal domain at death of Louis VII, 1180
- areas dependent on French monarchy in 1180
- English possessions in France in 1259
- additions to French royal domain before death of Louis IX, 1270
- additions before death of Philip IV in 1314
- additions before death of Charles IV in 1328

6 The British Isles, 1215-1307

- ⌇ boundary of England and Scotland 1157
- land claimed by Scotland 1139-57
- English Marcher lordships in Wales
- Principality of Wales 1284
- County Palatine of Chester with Flint
- → Edward I's Scottish campaign 1296
- ⊙ meetings of Edward I's Parliament
- Clare great landowners c.1307

Ireland:
- Norman conquests 1169-1215
- Norman conquests 1215-1307
- Irish lands 1307
- ♙ Norman castles

4 The empire of Canute the Great, 1014-1035

5 The Northern Kingdoms c.1035

3 The rise of Denmark

- ⌷ bishoprics
- ⚲ archbishoprics
- ▬ ▬ northern extent of Danish territory
- ⊙ circular fortifications
- Haervej - the main land route through Jutland

7 The conquest of Wales, 1283-4

- Principality of Wales in 1282
- ♙ Edward I's Welsh castles
- ← Edward I's campaigns 1283-4

The medieval German Empire
962-1356

Germany, or the eastern half of the Frankish empire, was the first country in Europe to recover from the setbacks of the ninth century invasions (page 36). This fact assured its predominance for upward of three centuries. German rulers never sought to assert control over the West Frankish lands, but, as heirs to the Carolingians, they claimed the imperial title and the right to rule over Italy and the lands of the former 'Middle Kingdom.' Germany's control of the Alpine passes between Lombardy and the Rhinelands assured not only its political preponderance but also gave it a leading place in the cultural exchange between Mediterranean and northern Europe.

There was, at first, no sense of a common German, or East Frankish, identity, and the effective control of the first German ruler, Henry I of Saxony (919–936), scarcely extended beyond Saxony and Franconia (map 1). But his son, Otto I (936–973), brought the other German duchies under royal control. Also, by defeating the Magyars at the battle of Lechfeld (955), he freed Germany from external threats and was able, in 951 and 961, to intervene effectively in Italy. His coronation as emperor (962) sealed the historic connexion between Germany and Italy. As heir to the Carolingian tradition, he also inaugurated a Christian drive against the pagan Slavs on the eastern frontier. But the great Slav revolt of 983 halted this advance until the twelfth century, and German efforts were concentrated instead on the south and south-west. The result, in 1034, was the addition of Burgundy to the imperial domains.

In spite of these successes, aristocratic resistance to royal centralisation was never overcome, and an opportunity to renew it came in 1075, when the outbreak of conflict between the emperor Henry IV (1056–1106) and the papacy, which saw imperial power in Italy as a threat to its independence, played into the German princes' hands. The ensuing civil war (1076–1122) was a turning point in German history. Although the monarchy emerged successful, its position was permanently weakened. German power was apparently restored during the reign of Frederick I (1152–1190), but it depended increasingly on the riches of Italy, and this embroiled Frederick not only with the papacy but also with the Italian cities. The marriage of his son, Henry VI, with Constance, the heiress of Sicily (1186), held out new possibilities. But the prospect of the union of Sicily and the empire alarmed the papacy, which saw itself being encircled, and led to the final struggle between Frederick II (1212–1250), and Pope Innocent IV (1243–1254).

Meanwhile Germany was being overtaken by the western monarchies (page 52). The empire under Frederick II was still the most imposing political body in Europe (map 3), but by 1200 Paris was the intellectual and cultural centre of Europe, and by comparison with England and Sicily Germany's financial organisation was antiquated. Eastward expansion had begun again after 1138 (map 2). It added two-thirds to the German territories and shifted the seat of power from Rhine to Elbe. But the beneficiaries were the princes on the eastern frontier, not the monarchy. Later, the Teutonic Knights conquered heathen Prussia (map 4), but within the empire the tendency was to fragmentation rather than expansion, and gains in the east were offset by loss of control over Italy which now went its own way (page 56). In default of royal authority local leagues were formed to resist princely encroachments and to preserve the peace. The most famous and enduring was the Swiss Confederation, formed in 1291 (map 5). The Golden Bull of 1356, formally recognising the autonomy of the princes, marked the beginning of a new era in German history; but the age of German preponderance in Europe had already ended a century earlier.

2 German eastward expansion

SORBS   west Slav tribes most affected by German expansion

expansion to 1250

expansion 1250 to 1300

expansion during 14th century

5 The rise of the Swiss Confederation

original cantons 1291-1315

cantons added to 1389

✕ battles for independence

main roads

4 The conquest of Prussia

➤ advance of Teutonic Knights

swamp and wilderness

occupied before 1309

occupied 1309-1382

occupied 1382-1411

Riga 1201   foundation date of town

1 The East Frankish Kingdom of Otto I

▲ royal mint under Otto I

← Otto's main campaigns

← main Magyar raids

North Sea

Baltic Sea

Gdansk (Danzig)

Holstein
Bornhöved 1227

Hamburg
Lübeck
Schwerin
Cammin
Stettin

Bremen
Lüneburg
Havelberg
Pomerania
Gniezno

Altmark
DUCHY OF BRUNSWICK
(after 1235)
Brandenburg
Poznań

Utrecht
S a x o n y
Magdeburg
Lusatia

Lower
Lorraine
Münster
Paderborn
Goslar
Meissen
Silesia

Dortmund
DUCHY OF
WESTPHALIA
(after 1180)
ANHALT
(After 1180)
Naumburg
Meissen
Freiberg
Wrocław (Breslau)

Bruges
Ghent
Cologne
Aachen
Thuringia
Hersfeld
Erfurt
Altenburg

Brabant
Liège
K I N G D O M
Eger
K I N G D O M

Bouvines 1214
Prague

Hainaut
Frankfurt
Gelnhausen
O F   B O H E M I A

Cambrai
Trier
Mainz
Würzburg
Bamberg

Verdun
Worms
Nuremberg
Moravia

Upper
Metz
Kaiserslautern
Speyer

Lorraine
Toul
Trifels
Regensburg
Austria

Hagenau
Strassburg
Hohenstaufen
Vienna

Alsace
O F
Ulm
Augsburg
B a v a r i a

Besancon
S w a b i a
Munich
Salzburg
Styria

Burgundy
Basel
Constance
Zurich
G E R M A N Y
Semmering

Tyrol
Brenner
Carinthia

St. Gotthard
Septimer
Brixen
Bozen
Pontebba

Lyons
St. Bernard
Trient
Verona
Friuli
Carniola

K I N G D O M
Como
Bergamo
Vicenza
Treviso
Aquileia

Mont Cenis
O F
Novara
Milan
Brescia
Verona
Padua
Venice
VENETIAN TERRITORIES

Turin
Vercelli
Pavia
Lodi
Crema
Cremona
Mantua

A R L E S
Savoy
Asti
K I N G D O M
Piacenza
Parma
Modena
Ferrara

Alessandria
Tortona
Reggio
Bologna
Imola
Ravenna

Genoa
L o m b a r d y
Faenza
Rimini

Adriatic Sea

Provence
O F
Pistoia
Lucca
Florence
expansion of Papal States under Innocent III

Arles
Pisa
I T A L Y
Arezzo
Ancona

Marseilles
Siena
Perugia
Assisi

T u s c a n y
Orvieto
Spoleto

Viterbo
Rieti
Tagliacozzo
1268

PAPAL
PATRIMONY
Tivoli
1190
Apricena

Rome
Lucera

Ostia
Anagni
Tusculum
1193
San Germano
Troia
Foggia
Barletta

1191, 1194
Benevento
Bari

Gaeta
Capua
Melfi

1194
Naples
Salerno
K I N G D O M
Brindisi

Amalfi
Taranto
Lecce

O F

Cosenza

SICILY
Messina
Reggio

Palermo
Monreale
Cefalù
Trapani
Catania

Syracuse

Baltic Sea

Hedeby
Oldenburg 948

WAGRIANS
ABODRITES
Hamburg
WARNABI
March of the Billungs
POLABII
937-82
REDARII
Pomerania

Lenzen
928
VELETIANS
Nordmark

Saxony
Havelberg 948
HEVELLI
Brandenburg 948
Gniezno 1000

Magdeburg 967
Werla
Poznań 968

Pöhlde
Quedlinburg
Lusatia

Wallhausen
Merseburg 968
LUSIZZI

Erfurt
Zeitz 968
Meissen 968
SORBS
MILIZI

Fulda
Salz
Mark
Zeitz
DALEMINZI
933
POLAND

Franconia
950
Prague 975
938

937
954

Regensburg
Bohemia
(tributary from 950)

Augsburg
955

Swabia
Lechfeld 955
Ostmark
Pressburg

Wels 943
H U N G A R Y

951
961
B a v a r i a

St. Gallen
Pitten
Styria

C a r i n t h i a
(Duchy 976)

55

Fourteenth century Europe

After the rise and consolidation of national monarchies in Spain, France and England in the thirteenth century (page 52), the fourteenth century was a period of setbacks on all fronts in western Europe. In part, this may be attributed to a sudden climatic deterioration (the onset of the 'little ice age') which brought to an end the agricultural boom that had been virtually continuous since 1150. Already in 1315–17 Europe experienced a 'great famine', and the weakening of human powers of resistance induced by inadequate nourishment may have been one factor accounting for the rapid spread of the Black Death, or bubonic plague, which first appeared in the Crimea in 1346 and spread from there first by ship to Italy and then to the west (map 1). But there were also other factors. All the western monarchies had over-extended themselves financially, and the economic setback accentuated their difficulties. Philip IV's unsuccessful attempts to subdue Flanders played after his death (1314) into the hands of the aristocracy; so also

did the involvement of Catalonia in Italy after the death of James II (1285–1327); and in England the attempt to subdue Scotland (map 4) proved to be a running sore. Ireland also virtually went its own way until Tudor times (page 72), and Wales, conquered but not subdued by Edward I (page 52), had a great national revival under Owain Glyndwr (1400–1409). Germany broke apart into rival principalities after the extermination of the Hohenstaufen dynasty (page 54), and Italy went the same way once Hohenstaufen rule was removed, breaking up into a number of local lordships or *signorie* (map 3). In the end, even the Catholic church was affected by the economic and fiscal stringency. From 1378 to 1417 it was divided by schism (map 6), which undermined its authority, while its financial extortions gave impetus to the anti-papal, reformatory movements of Hus in Bohemia and Wyclif in England.

Eastern Europe, on the other hand, was in process of recovery from the Mongol incursions of the thirteenth century (page 46). Bohemia under Charles IV (1333–78), Poland under Casimir III (1339–70), and Hungary

under Louis the Great (1342–82), all made rapid strides, helped perhaps by the fact that the impact of the Black Death was less severe in the east than in the west, and also by exploitation of their natural resources, such as the silver mines of Kutna Hora (map 2). In the west, on the other hand, the setback was lasting. Two English kings, Edward II (1327) and Richard II (1399) were murdered. The Hundred Years' War between England and France (map 5) resulted in widespread devastation. Overall, the Black Death reduced the population of Europe by roughly one-third. Further, the misery caused by economic recession and military ravages sparked off a series of popular risings, the Jacquerie in France and the Peasants' Revolt in England being best known (map 1), although urban discontent – the weavers' rising in Flanders under Artevelde, or the Ciompi in Florence – was no less significant in the long run. It was not until after c.1450 that recovery began (page 82); but even then under-currents of popular resentment persisted, which found their outlet in the Peasants' War of 1524–5 and the messianic movements of the Reformation.

3 Italy, c.1310

- Papal states
- ◑ Republican communes
- ○ cities under Signorial domination c.1310

the Signorie:

1 Avvocati	5 Da Camino	9 Este	13 Malatesta
2 Bonacolsi	6 Da Correggio	10 Fissiraga	14 Robert of Anjou
3 Brusati	7 Da Polenta	11 Langosco	15 Scotti
4 Cavalcabo	8 Della Scala	12 Maggi	16 Visconti

2 Eastern Europe 1278-1389

growth of Lithuania 1300-1377:

- to 1300
- under Gedymin 1316-41
- under Olgierd 1345-77
- Lithuania under Jagiello and Witold from 1377
- Poland-Lithuania after union of 1386
- Habsburg lands
- Bohemian lands

5 The Hundred Years' War

- ● English bases in 1380
- acquired for Burgundy 1363-1404
- acquired for Burgundy 1419-67

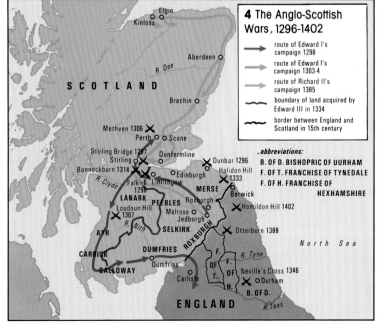

4 The Anglo-Scottish Wars, 1296-1402

- → route of Edward I's campaign 1298
- → route of Edward I's campaign 1303-4
- → route of Richard II's campaign 1385
- — boundary of land acquired by Edward III in 1334
- — border between England and Scotland in 15th century

. abbreviations:

B. OF D. BISHOPRIC OF DURHAM
F. OF T. FRANCHISE OF TYNEDALE
F. OF H. FRANCHISE OF HEXHAMSHIRE

1 Europe at the time of the Black Death

extent of spread of Black Death:

1346

1347

mid 1348

end 1348

mid 1349

end 1349

1350

c. 1351

c. 1353

little or no plague mortality

political change:

union of Kalmar 1397

Milanese territory under Giangaleazzo Visconti 1378-1402

territory under Florentine control, end 14th century

Luxembourg lands

Wittelsbach lands

Habsburg lands

social unrest:

areas of disturbance during Great Peasant Revolt in England 1381

centre of urban revolt

rural uprisings

defeats in battle of lower class   ✕ battle

religious unrest:

spread of Lollardry in England to death of Richard II, 1399

area of Hussite influence

Hussite centre

the Western Schism (inset map right):

areas giving allegiance to Pope in Rome

areas giving allegiance to Pope in Avignon

allegiance officially to Rome but shifting local allegiances

6 The Western Schism, 1378-1417

Avignon

Rome

*Map labels:*

Hebrides, Orkneys, NORWAY, S W E D E N, Oslo, Uppsala, Stockholm, RUSSIAN STATES, Novgorod, SCOTLAND, Edinburgh, North Sea, DENMARK, Visby, Riga, PRINCIPALITY OF MOSCOW, Armagh, Carlisle, Newcastle, Baltic Sea, Copenhagen, Smolensk, York, Königsberg, ORDER, ENGLAND, Chester, Lincoln, Lübeck, Danzig, TEUTONIC, WALES, Norwich, FRIESLAND, Hamburg, POMERANIA, Warsaw, L I T H U A N I A, Bristol, Bury St Edmunds, London, Winchester, Amsterdam, SAXONY, BRANDENBURG, Bremen, Brunswick, Magdeburg, POLAND, Bruges, Antwerp, Ghent, HOLLAND, R. Rhine, R. Elbe, R. Oder, Cracow, Kiev, R. Dnieper, Rosebeke 1382, Ypres, FLANDERS, Aachen, Cologne, SILESIA, UKRAINE, Agincourt, Crécy, Liège, HOLY, Prague, Amiens, Trier, Mainz, Frankfurt, BOHEMIA, MORAVIA, Rouen, Mello 1358, Rheims, FRANCONIA, ROMAN, R. Dniester, Paris, Meaux 1358, Chartres, LORRAINE, Regensburg, Passau, Tabor, BRITTANY, R. Loire, Orléans, Troyes, Strasbourg, BAVARIA, Vienna, MOLDAVIA, SWABIA, Augsburg, AUSTRIA, Buda, Pest, Poitiers, BURGUNDY, Basle, Munich, Constance, Salzburg, FRANCE, Lausanne, SWISS CONFED., EMPIRE, CARINTHIA, H U N G A R Y, Geneva, Lyons, Bordeaux, R. Dordogne, SAVOY, Milan, Trieste, R. Danube, Bucharest, ENGLISH GASCONY, AQUITAINE, R. Rhône, DAUPHINÉ, Turin, Venice, REPUBLIC OF VENICE, WALLACHIA, Cahors, Genoa, Ravenna, Belgrade, Black Sea, NAVARRE, Toulouse, Montpellier, Avignon, PROVENCE, Narbonne, Marseilles, Pisa, Florence, Ancona, BOSNIA, BULGARIA, Saragossa, CATALONIA, Siena, PAPAL, Adriatic Sea, SERBIAN PRINCES, Ragusa, Adrianople, ARAGON, Barcelona, Corsica, STATES, Rome, KINGDOM, Sardinia, OF, Constantinople, Valencia, Balearic Islands, Naples, NAPLES, Amalfi, PRINCIPALITY OF ALBANIA, Salonica, OTTOMAN TURKS, Mediterranean, Palermo, Messina, DUCHY OF Athens, ACHAEA, ATHENS, KINGDOM OF SICILY, Sea, Rhodes, Crete

57

Medieval trade routes
c.1000-1500

Trading connexions had been remarkably widespread during late antiquity, and they had brought with them important cultural interchanges (page 24). The barbarian invasions, beginning c.300 AD and lasting some 200 years, had disastrous results. The Silk Route from Rome to China was cut, and even within the Roman empire communications broke down. There was a short-lived recrudescence in Carolingian times, involving trade in the North Sea, centred on Dorestad and Quentovic; but it was only after c.1000, with the restoration of relatively stable conditions, that trade picked up. In particular, the Italian cities, already in contact with the Near East (page 36), established connexions with north-west Europe, where the fairs of Champagne were becoming clearing-houses for trade between Italy and the rising industrial centres of Flanders (map 1).

The consolidation of the German empire under the Saxon and Salian dynasties gave impetus to trade from west to east, along a line running from the Low Countries via Cologne to Magdeburg, and along the Main valley to Bamberg and Prague. German control of the Alpine passes, particularly after the opening of the Septimer and St. Gotthard passes during the Hohenstaufen period, stimulated trade with Italy, which contributed to the growing wealth of the south German cities, among them Augsburg, which later became a major commercial and financial centre after the rise of the Fugger merchant family in the fifteenth century. In the north the most important city was Lübeck (founded 1158), the key point controlling trade between the North Sea and the Baltic and the seat of the Hanseatic League, an association of German merchants which took shape in 1259 and was formally constituted in 1358. With its far-flung network of associated cities, and with branches in London, Bruges and Bergen, the Hansa dominated the trade of northern Europe in the fourteenth and fifteenth centuries. It also had connexions with Venice and Genoa, the cities which dominated Mediterranean and Levantine commerce (map 2).

Levantine trade fell into two broad categories: the spice trade, in which Venice predominated, and the silk trade, largely in the hands of Genoa and its merchant colonies in Constantinople and at Kaffa, Tana and Trebizond. The latter profited greatly from the restoration of order and settled government in central Asia by the Mongols (page 46), which allowed a resumption of overland trade, and for a time there was extensive east-west traffic, exemplified by the famous journeys of Marco Polo between 1271 and 1295 (map 3). But the roads opened by the rise of the Mongol empire in the thirteenth century were closed by its decline in the mid-fourteenth century. The important spice trade from Ormuz to the Black Sea was also badly affected; but the trade via the Red Sea and Alexandria to Venice continued without interruption until the Ottoman conquest of Egypt in 1517 (page 48).

Spices were indispensable, easy to handle and highly profitable, and they were the staple of intercontinental trade in this period. Both Europe and China were dependent for supplies on the spice-producing regions of Asia, particularly the Moluccas and the Malay archipelago, and the resultant transactions, largely in the hands of Arab and Indian middlemen, created a complicated network of sea routes, hinging on Malacca, which stretched from the Red Sea and the Persian Gulf to the South China Sea (map 3). In the early fifteenth century, between 1405 and 1433, the Chinese sent seven expeditions through the Strait of Malacca to the Indian Ocean and beyond; but this enterprise ceased abruptly after 1440. Meanwhile, Portugal was probing down the west coast of Africa (page 64) in search of gold; but later, when Genoa, which had lost its eastern markets after the fall of Constantinople in 1453, provided financial backing for the Portuguese ventures, the main objective became the search for an alternative route to the east, to cut out Genoa's rival, Venice. When the Portuguese reached India in 1498, and Columbus, despatched by Portugal's rival, Spain, reached America, a new era had begun. The thousand-year-old pattern, centred on the Mediterranean, gave way to an Atlantic economy (page 82), and the whole economic and political balance in Europe shifted dramatically.

1 Trade routes in Western Europe, c.1000 - 1150
— trade routes   areas of forest   ▲ fairs

3 Eurasian trade routes, c.1000 - 1500

— principal Eurasian routes   — principal Hanseatic routes
— principal Eurasian sea routes   — trans-Saharan trade routes
▨ area of Muslim domination in the mid-15th century   --- Marco Polo's routes (1271-95)
····· Chinese Admiral Cheng-ho's routes (1405-33)

major commodities:
● camphor   ◀ silks
▣ cottons   ◪ silver
↩ drugs   slaves
⊖ dyestuffs   soap
◪ gold   ▯ spices
◗ ivory   ⦀ sugar
◆ linen   wine
⊞ metalware   ◣ woollens
⊟ pepper
◕ perfumes
porcelain
◇ precious stones

2 Hanseatic trade

- ▣ site of important fair
- ◉ site of lesser fair
- ━━ Hanseatic trade routes

The Hanseatic League:
- ● Wendish and Pomeranian circle
- ◆ Saxony, Thuringia, Brandenburg circle
- ▼ Prussia, Livonia, Sweden circle
- ■ Rhine, Westphalia, Netherlands circle

- ●◆▼■ chief city
- ●◆▼■ associated city
- ◖ kontore
- ◑ subsidiary kontore
- ○ other important city

note: places that are important fairs as well as Hanseatic cities have red symbols

to Trondheim • Bergen
Christiania (Oslo)
Tønsberg
North Sea
Stockholm
Reval
Dorpat
Novgorod
Edinburgh
Visby
Baltic Sea
Pskov
Newcastle
Riga
Polotsk
York Hull
Vitebsk
Boston Yarmouth
Skanör
Kolberg
Danzig
Königsberg
Kovno
Smolensk
King's Lynn
Lübeck
Stralsund
Stargard
Elbing
Stourbridge Ipswich
Groningen Bremen Hamburg
Wismar Rostock
Stettin
Gnesen Thorn
Mogilev
London
Deventer Kampen Lüneburg
Magdeburg
Berlin
Posen
Breslau
Bruges Damme
Osnabrück Brunswick
Frankfurt
Lublin
Turnhout
Dortmund Soest Goslar
Leipzig
Antwerp Cologne
Erfurt
Prague
Cracow
Lemberg
Lille
Friedberg
Bamberg
Kiev
St. Denis Paris
Frankfurt am Main
Nuremberg
Rouen
Strassburg
Nördlingen
Augsburg
Linz
Guibray
Besançon (1535)
Zurzach
Chalon-sur-Saône
St Gotthard Pass
Septimer Pass
Lyons Geneva
Bozen
Bordeaux
Chambéry
Milan
Beaucaire
Piacenza
Aigues-Mortes
Nice
Genoa
Venice
Marseilles
Villalón
Medina de Rioseco
Guimarães
Barcelona
Medina del Campo
Atlantic Ocean
Mediterranean Sea
Corsica

JAPAN
Kara Khoto
Kara Khoto
Peking
Pacific Ocean
Aral Sea
R. Jaxartes
Urgench
Tashkent
Sian
Nanking
Hangchow
Bukhara
Samarkand
Kashgar
TURKESTAN
Chengtu
CHINA
Foochow
Merv
Nishapur
PERSIA
Balkh
TIBET
Amoy
FORMOSA
Yazd
Herat
Yunnan
Canton
Zaranj
Kabul
Kandahar
Khyber Pass
Delhi
R. Indus
R. Ganges
BENGAL
HAINAN
Ormuz
Chittagong
Pagan
Muscat
Surat
INDIA
South China Sea
Vijaya
Arabian Sea
Mang-vu
MOLUCCAS
Calicut
Tani
BORNEO
Banda Sea
Cochin
Quilon
CEYLON
BANDA IS.
Colombo
Baddegama
Galle
Malacca
SUMATRA
TIMOR
Palembang
Indian Ocean
JAVA
Majapahit
Dhofar
Siraf
Persian Gulf

59

African states and empires, c.900-1800

By the end of the first millennium AD great changes had taken place in Africa. The rise of a culture based on iron-working (page 10) led to a large-scale displacement of Khoisan-speaking Bushmen and Hottentots by settled Bantu-speaking agriculturalists (map 3) and to the appearance of extensive states and empires based on trade. In the south, Zimbabwe, with its monumental stone buildings, exported gold and copper to the Orient via the port of Sofala, and the impressive Kongo state on the west coast had an important trade in ivory. Further north, the Arab conquest of the Maghreb and the rise of the Almoravid and Almohad empires (page 40) marked a watershed. The Arabs, great traders, developed and extended the trans-Saharan caravan routes, and there is no doubt that trade was an important factor in the development of the great empires which arose in the sub-Saharan savanna. The early history of Ghana (some 500 miles north-west of the modern state with the same name) precedes the Islamic era; but its successors, Mali and Songhay, owed much of their wealth and civilisation, described in glowing terms by Arab travellers, to the Islamic impact. So also did the Kanem-Borno empire around Lake Chad and, after the fifteenth century, the city states of Hausaland (map 1). Arab merchant colonies also spread far down the east coast from Mogadishu to Kilwa. The staples of trade in all cases were gold, ivory and slaves. According to a conservative estimate, the trans-Saharan slave trade before the coming of the Europeans amounted to almost 5 million.

The arrival of the Portuguese on the African coast and the building in 1448 of a first European fort and warehouse at Arguin, followed (1482) by a second at Elmina on the Gold Coast, had at first little impact on Africa. The immediate objective was to share directly in the gold trade, hitherto dominated by Muslim middlemen, and the slave trade was a secondary by-product. But with the development of sugar plantations in Brazil (page 68) and later in the West Indies, the slave trade became a major source of profit, particularly after Dutch and British traders ousted the Portuguese. Along the length of the Gold and Slave Coasts, from Axim to the Niger Delta, fortified trading stations (or 'factories') were set up as bases for this trade (map 2, inset), and the Portuguese continued to export slaves further south in Angola. Of some 15 million Africans shipped aboard between 1450 and 1870, some 90 per cent went to South America and the Caribbean, most of them between 1700 and 1800. The effects on Africa of this appalling trade in human beings are not easy to quantify, though the effects on the victims themselves need no description. Furthermore, the loss of population was not evenly divided and some areas suffered disproportionately. Others profited from the trade. After the invasion and destruction of the great Songhay empire by Morocco in 1591, the forest states of Asante, Dahomey and Benin, having direct access to the Atlantic and to European trade, increased in importance and political power (map 2). The Europeans remained largely ignorant of the African interior, and their influence was limited. In the far south the Dutch were established in the Cape Colony; but, in a continental perspective, its extent was still minimal. In the north-east Islam was spreading; but the Christian kingdom of Ethiopia, despite a serious setback in the 1520s, still held its own. By 1800, with the exception of the Ottomans in the north (and even their power was more nominal than real), Africa remained independent of foreign control. Nevertheless there is little sign that it was ready to meet the European challenge that developed in the nineteenth century (page 102). It was a world unto itself, but in no position to compete with the technological dynamism of the West.

GOLD COAST, 1700

1 Africa, 900-1500

- state nucleus and sphere of influence
- → spread of Islam
- Islamised North and East Africa
- ■ Muslim colony
- major gold producing region
- Ghana 8th-12th century
- Mali 12th-15th century
- Songhay c.1500

gold		cattle
M musk		C copper
slaves		salt
bananas		millet
rice		ivory

3 African languages

c.3000-2000 BC (right):

- Niger-Kordofanian
- Nilo-Saharan
- Afro-Asiatic
- Khoisan
- unoccupied

c.AD 1000 (above):

- Niger-Kordofanian (including Bantu)
- Nilo-Saharan
- Afro-Asiatic
- Khoisan
- Malayo-Polynesian

SPAIN
○ Granada

OTTOMAN EMPIRE

2 Africa, 1500-1800

→ movement of peoples
→ spread of Islam
▨ area of Islamic influence by 1800
→ trade routes
➤ slave trade routes

➤ Spanish offensives against Algiers and Tunis in the 16th century
➤ Moroccan military expeditions
╌╌ Saladian extension of Moroccan territory c.1591
→ Portuguese voyages to Africa and India
━ areas of Ottoman control

coastal settlements:
○ Dutch
○ French
○ Portuguese
◐ Danish
● Ottoman
● British
◑ Spanish
◐ Brandenburger

Tangier
Fez
Atlas Mts.
MOROCCO
Morocco ruled by Sharifian dynasties 1553-1912
Marrakesh
Sijilmassa

Maghreb
Algiers
ALGIERS
Corsair cities under Ottoman suzerainty 1516
Tunis
Jerba
Tripoli

Mediterranean Sea

Alexandria
Cairo
Ottoman conquest 1517
R. Nile
Red Sea

Wargla
Ghadames
Murzuk

Tuat
Ain Salah
Taghaza
Ghat
Tamanrasset

Sahara Desert

Arab trans-Saharan slave trade route

Suakin

SONGHAY
Tadmekka
AIR
Agades
Bilma

Central Sudan

Massawa

FUNJ 16th C
Sennar

SEGU 18th C
Timbuktu
Gao
Jenne

Sudan

Katsina
Lake Chad
KANEM
WADAI
DARFUR

White Nile

ETHIOPIA 16th C
Zeila
ADAL
Berbera

HAUSA STATES
Kano
Zaria
BORNO

MOSSI STATES 15th C

BORGU STATES
NUPE
Ife
R. Benue
KWARARAFA

SHOA

NILOTES

SOMALI

ASANTE 18th C
DAHOMEY 18th C
Badagri
OYO 17th C
BENIN
Lagos
Accra
Whydah
Slave Coast
IBO
Brass
OLD CALABAR
NIGER DELTA STATES 18th C
Fernando Po

see inset above

West Africa · arrival of Portuguese 15thC and 16thC. Dutch, English and French 17thC.

Principe
São Tomé

TIKAR BAMUM BAMILEKE
BANDA
NZAKARA
AZANDE
NGBANDI
BABWA
MANGBETU
PARANILOTES
NILOTES
GALLA

Mogadishu
Brava

PYGMY
TEKE
MONGO
R. Congo

BUNYORO
BUGANDA
ANKOLE
KARAGWE
Lake Victoria
RWANDA
BURUNDI
KIKUYU
Lamu
▲ Mt Kilimanjaro
Malindi
Mombasa
Pemba
Zanzibar

Vasco da Gama to India April 1498 - Dec. 1498
Arab slave trade

LUANGO
KUBA
TETELA
LULUA
KETE
LUBA 15th C – 16th C
Lake Tanganyika

KONGO
Ambriz
CHOKWE
LUNDA 16th – 17th C
Luanda
MBUNDU
LUENA-LOVALE
BEMBA
SANGA
BISA
Lake Nyasa
Kilwa Kisiwani

Benguela
OVIMBUNDU
LOZI
SAAN
BEMBA
LAMBA
LENJE
TONGA
MARAVI
Comoro Is.
Mozambique

OVAMBO
MWENEMUTAPA 16th C
R. Zambezi
Tete
Sena
Quelimane
Sofala

ROZWI
Great Zimbabwe
KARANGA

settlements of mainland African slaves

HOVA MERINA

TSWANA
HERERO
SOTHO
NGUNI
Delagoa Bay
KHOISAN
R. Orange
SOTHO

Fort-Dauphin

MADAGASCAR

Indian Ocean

Cape established by Dutch East India Company in 1652. Gradual spread of white settlers inland. Occupied by Britain 1798.

CAPE
KHOISAN
NGUNI
Cape Town
Cape of Good Hope

Portuguese slave trade

America on the eve of European conquest

Two great and wealthy civilisations confronted the Spaniards when they arrived in America at the beginning of the sixteenth century: the Aztec empire in Mexico and the Inca empire in Peru. The former had a population of 10–12 millions, the latter 6 millions or possibly considerably more. A few other centres of civilisation existed, such as the Chibcha state in modern Colombia; but the remainder of the continent was sparsely inhabited (perhaps 1 million north of the Rio Grande and 1 million in the rest of South America) and divided among more than a thousand small tribal societies, with distinct, often unrelated languages (map 1). Few regions, particularly in the north, had reached the stage of settled agriculture (map 4).

The Aztec and Inca empires were different in character, and there is no evidence of any contact between them. The Aztecs, like the Toltecs who controlled much of Mexico in the eleventh and twelfth centuries, were raw warriors from the north who entered Mexico during the thirteenth century and settled on islands in Lake Texcoco, where c.1325 they founded the town of Tenochtitlán, which was to become their capital. The Inca empire was created by one of the numerous tribes of Quechua stock inhabiting the central Andes, which established itself in the Cuzco valley in the twelfth century. The expansion of both came late and only reached its full extent on the eve of the Spanish conquest. In the case of the Aztecs (map 2) the first step was to ally with the neighbouring tribes in Texcoco and Tlacopán against their overlords in Azcapotzalco, and then to turn against their allies. This aggressive policy began c.1427 under Itzcoatl and was continued by Montezuma I. It reached its peak under Montezuma II (1502–20), when the Aztecs, in control of the greater part of Mexico, were beginning to enter Maya territory in Yucatán. Inca expansion began under the eighth emperor, Viracocha, and his son Pachacuti (1438–63), whose son Topa subdued the coastal civilisation of Chimú (1470), and then, after his accession as emperor (1471), pushed south into Chile and northern Argentina (map 3). Huayna Capac (1493–1525) advanced north into modern Ecuador, where he founded a second capital at Quito. By now the Inca empire was some 200 miles wide and 2500 miles long, held together by an impressive system of highways and post-stations, with relays of runners who conveyed imperial orders to all parts of the empire.

The Incas created a genuine imperial system, with an hereditary dynasty, a Quechua aristocracy and a highly trained bureaucracy. All land was state-owned, and there was a complex system of irrigation. The ordinary Indian spent nine months of the year working for the state, but in return was protected from famine by large state-owned food repositories and provided for in sickness and old age. The Aztec empire, on the other hand, rather like that of the Mongols in Europe (page 46), was essentially a harsh military dominion over vassal peoples, who were left to rule themselves on condition that they paid heavy tribute to Tenochtitlán in food, textiles, pottery and other goods, but increasingly in human beings for sacrifice to the Aztec gods. The number of sacrificial victims rose from 10,000 a year to 50,000 a year at the time of the Spanish conquest. This was certainly one reason why the Totonacs and Tlaxcalans welcomed the Spanish invaders of Mexico (page 68), and resentment against Inca oppression probably played a similar role in Peru. Neither empire was as stable as it seemed. Nevertheless their collapse at the hands of small bands of adventurers (Cortés had only 600 men, a few small cannon, 13 muskets and 16 horses when he invaded Mexico in 1519, and Pizarro had only 180 men, 27 horses and 2 cannon when he attacked the Inca empire in 1531) is not easily explained.

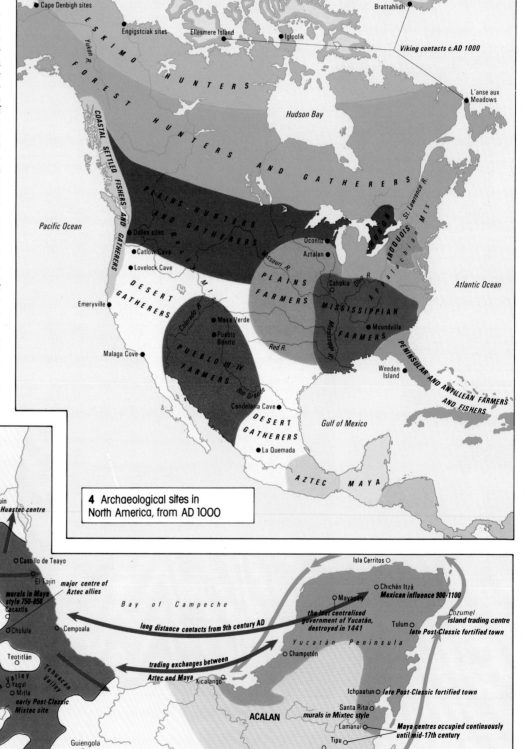

4 Archaeological sites in North America, from AD 1000

2 The Aztec Empire in Mexico

- Maya cultural area
- Postclassic Maya kingdoms
- area of Aztec domination 1519
- → spread of Toltec influence from 9th century AD
- → Postclassic trading routes

1 The American peoples, c.1500

culture areas:

North America
- Arctic
- Sub-Arctic
- Northwest coast
- Plateau
- Great Basin
- California
- Southwest
- Great Plains
- Northeast
- Southeast

Mesoamerica
- Mesoamerica

South America
- Circum-Caribbean
- Savanna-Orinoco
- Andean
- Tropical forest
- Atlantic
- Southern

3 The Inca Empire in Peru

growth of the Inca Empire:
- under Pachacuti 1438-63
- growth under Pachacuti and Topa Inca 1463-71
- growth under Topa Inca 1471-93
- growth under Huayna Capac 1493-1525
- imperial roads

63

European voyages of discovery
1487-1780

The European voyages of discovery opened a new era in world history. They began early in the fifteenth century when Portuguese navigators advanced southward, round the coast of Africa, in search of gold, slaves and spices, until in 1487 Dias and de Covilhã, brought them into the Indian Ocean (map 1). Thenceforth voyages of exploration multiplied, particularly after the resurgence of Islam made the old route to the east via Alexandria and the Red Sea precarious.

While the Portuguese explored the eastern route to Asia, the Spaniards sailed west. Once in the Indian Ocean the former quickly reached their goal: Malabar (1498), Malacca (1511), and the Moluccas (1512). The Spanish search for a western route to the Spice Islands was less successful. Its unintended but momentous result was Columbus' discovery of the New World in 1492 (map 2), followed by the Spanish conquest of America (page 68). But it was not until after 1524, when Verrazzano traced the coastline of North America as far north as Nova Scotia, that the existence of a new continent was generally accepted, and meanwhile the search for a western route to Asia continued, leading to extensive exploration of the Caribbean (map 3). Finally, in 1521, Magellan rounded South America, entered the Pacific, and reached the Philippines, but the route was too long and hazardous for commercial purposes. In 1557 the Portuguese occupied Macao, and after 1571 Spanish galleons traded between Manila and Acapulco in Mexico; but otherwise the exploration of the Pacific was delayed until the eighteenth century (map 4). This was the work of British, Dutch and Russians seeking a navigable passage via the Arctic between the Atlantic and the Pacific, and hoping also to locate a hypothetical southern continent. Both proved illusory; but the result was the charting of New Zealand and the eastern coast of Australia, both in a few years opened to European colonisation (page 112).

Meanwhile England and France, unwilling to recognise the monopoly claimed by Spain and Portugal in the Treaty of Tordesillas (1494), had embarked on a series of voyages intended to reach Asia by a northern route (map 2). All these proved abortive and were abandoned after 1632, but they resulted in the opening of North America to European settlement. The English, French and Dutch were also unwilling to abandon the profitable trade with South and South-East Asia to the Portuguese and Spaniards, and the later years of the sixteenth and first half of the seventeenth centuries saw a determined and ultimately successful effort to breach their privileged position (page 66). After 1500 direct sea contact was established between continents and regions which hitherto had gone their own way in isolation. It was necessarily a slow process, and for long the European footholds in Asia and Africa remained tenuous and precarious. But by the time of the death of the last great explorer, James Cook, in 1779, the worldwide network of relationships had been formed which characterises the modern era and differentiates it from all preceding times.

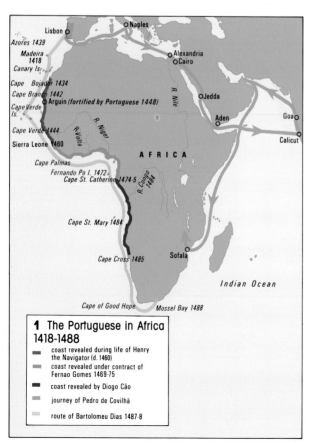

1 The Portuguese in Africa 1418-1488

- coast revealed during life of Henry the Navigator (d. 1460)
- coast revealed under contract of Fernao Gomes 1469-75
- coast revealed by Diogo Cão
- journey of Pedro de Covilhã
- route of Bartolomeu Dias 1487-8

Voyages intended for S. Asia by S.E. Route:
1/Dias 1487/88 (outward) discovered open water S. of Cape Agulhas; entered Indian Ocean; reached Great Fish River.
2/Vasco da Gama 1497–99 (outward) discovered best use of Atlantic winds on way to Cape of Good Hope; reached India, navigated by local pilot.
3/Cabral 1500 (outward) the second Portuguese voyage to India, sighted coast of Brazil at Monte Pascoal, probably accidental

2 Voyages of discovery, 1480-1630

- voyages intended for Southern Asia by South East route
- voyages intended for China and Southern Asia by West or South West route
- voyages intended for Asia by North West and North East routes
- approximate prevailing winds (shown for the first quarter of the year)
- alternating monsoons

Voyages in the Caribbean:
29/Bastidas & La Cosa 1501–02 explored coast from Gulf of Maracaibo to Gulf of Urabá.
30/Pinzón & Solís 1508 sent from Spain to find strait to Asia, coasted E. coast of Yucatán.
31/Ponce de León 1512–13 sailed from Puerto Rico, explored coast of Florida from N. of Cape Canaveral to (possibly) Pensacola. May have sighted Yucatán on return. First explorer to note force of Gulf Stream.
32/Hernández de Córdoba 1516 sailed from Cuba, explored N. and W. coasts of Yucatán. First report of Mayan cities.
33/Grijalva 1517 followed S. and W. coasts of Gulf of Mexico as far as Pánuco River.
34/Pineda 1519 explored N. and W. coasts of Gulf of Mexico from Florida to Pánuco River. Finally ended hope of strait to Pacific in that region.

Voyages in the Pacific:
35/Roggeveen 1721–22 discovered Easter Island and some of the Samoan group. Circumnavigation.
36/Bering 1728 sailed from Kamchatka, discovered strait separating N.E. Asia from N.W. America.
37/Wallis 1766–68 discovered Society Islands (Tahiti), encouraged hope of habitable southern continent. Circumnavigation.
38/Cook 1768–71 charted coasts of New Zealand, explored E. coast of Australia, confirmed existence of Torres Strait. Circumnavigation.
39/Cook 1772–75 made circuit of southern oceans in high latitude, charted New Hebrides, ended hope of habitable southern continent. Circumnavigation.
40/Cook & Clerke 1776–80 discovered Sandwich Islands (Hawaii), explored coast of N. America from Vancouver to Unimak Pass, sailed through Bering Strait to edge of pack ice, ended hope of passage through Arctic to Atlantic.

4/First Portuguese voyage to Malacca, 1509.
5/Abreu 1512–13 visited Moluccas.
6/First Portuguese visits to Canton River, 1514.

Voyages intended for China and S. Asia by W. or S.W. Route:
7/Columbus 1492–93 (outward and homeward) discovered islands in Bahama group, explored N. coasts of Cuba and Hispaniola; interpreted discoveries as part of Asia; found best return route.
8/Columbus 1493–94 (outward) explored S. coast of Cuba; reported it as peninsula of mainland China.
9/Columbus 1498 (outward) discovered Trinidad and coast of Venezuela; recognised coast as mainland, surmised it to be

terrestrial paradise.
10/Columbus 1502–04 explored coast of Honduras. Nicaragua and the Isthmus. Believed Honduras to be Indo-China.
11/Ojeda & Vespucci 1499–1500 (outward) reached Guiana coast, failed to round Cape São Roque, coasted W. to Cape de la Vela. First report of Amazon.
12/Coelho & Vespucci 1501 (outward) coasted S. from Cape São Agostinho to (possibly) 35°S.
13/Solis 1515 entered Plate River estuary and investigated N. bank.
14/Magellan & Cano 1519–22. Discovered Strait of Magellan, crossed Pacific. Reached Moluccas via Philippines. Revealed Pacific as separate ocean of immense size. First circumnavigation.
15/Saavedra 1527 discovered route from coast of Mexico across Pacific to Moluccas.

16/Urdaneta 1565 found feasible return route Philippines to Mexico in 42°N. using W. winds.
17/Schouten & Le Maire 1616 discovered route into Pacific via Le Maire strait and Cape Horn.

Voyages intended for Asia by Northern Route:
18/Cabot 1497 (outward) rediscovered Newfoundland, first sighted by Norsemen in 11th century; took it for N.E. extremity of Asia.
19/Corte-Real 1500 rediscovered Greenland.
20/Verrazzano 1524 traced E. coast of N. America from (probably) 34°N. to 47°N.; revealed continental character of N. America.
21/Cartier 1534 and 1535 explored Strait of Belle Isle and St. Lawrence as far as Montreal.

22/Willoughby & Chancellor 1553 rounded North Cape and reached Archangel.
23/Frobisher 1574 reached Frobisher Bay in Baffin Island, which he took for a 'strait'.
24/Davis 1587 explored W. coast of Greenland to the edge of the ice in 72°N.
25/Barents 1596–97 discovered Bear Island and Spitsbergen and wintered in Novaya Zemlya.
26/Hudson 1610 sailed through Hudson Strait to the S. extremity

of Hudson Bay, which he and others took to be the Pacific.
27/Button 1612 explored W. coast of Hudson Bay, concluded Bay land-locked on the W.
28/Baffin & Bylot 1616 explored whole coastline of Baffin Bay and decided that no navigable N.W. passage existed in that area.

4 Voyages in the Pacific, 1720-1780

3 Voyages in the Caribbean, 1493-1519

→ voyages intended for China and Southern Asia by West or South West route

→ voyages exploring the Caribbean

European expansion overseas, 1493-1713

The Portuguese were the first to exploit the European voyages of discovery. Theirs was essentially a trading empire, and by the middle of the sixteenth century they had more than fifty forts and factories reaching from Sofala on the Zambezi to Nagasaki in Japan (map 1). In 1557 they occupied Macao on the Chinese mainland. The Spaniards, on the other hand, set out on a deliberate policy of conquest and settlement, first in Hispaniola and, a decade or so later, in Mexico and Peru. The result was the foundation of the great Spanish colonial empire (page 68). But the Iberian preponderance did not go unchallenged. Particularly after the foundation of the English and Dutch East India Companies, in 1600 and 1602 respectively, Portuguese trade came under attack (map 2). With the acquisition of Batavia (1619) as an eastern headquarters and of the Cape of Good Hope (1652) as a station on the route to the east, Dutch commercial pre-eminence in Asian waters was assured.

While there was no direct attack on Spain's mainland empire the islands of the Caribbean, coveted as a prime source of sugar for the European market, became an object of intense rivalry and competition, in which all the leading powers engaged (map 4). Furthermore, whatever Spanish pretensions may have been, it was unable to make its presence felt much north of the Rio Grande. There was a slow advance in the west into California; but on the east coast Spanish power was limited to a tenuous foothold in Florida. Here the states of northern Europe, led by England and France, took the lead. France, in particular, advancing down the St. Lawrence estuary, penetrated deep into the interior, exploring the whole Mississippi valley (1682) and establishing fortified posts all the way to the Gulf of Mexico (map 3). The English, on the other hand, established a series of settlements along the eastern coast, beginning with Virginia in 1607. The clash of commercial and colonial interests which ensued ushered in the first age of imperial rivalry and conflict (page 86). Its prelude was the Anglo-Dutch wars of 1652–73 (page 80) which resulted in the British seizure (1664) of the Dutch settlement of New Amsterdam, subsequently renamed New York. It marked the decline of the Netherlands and the rise of England and France to the paramount position in the overseas world.

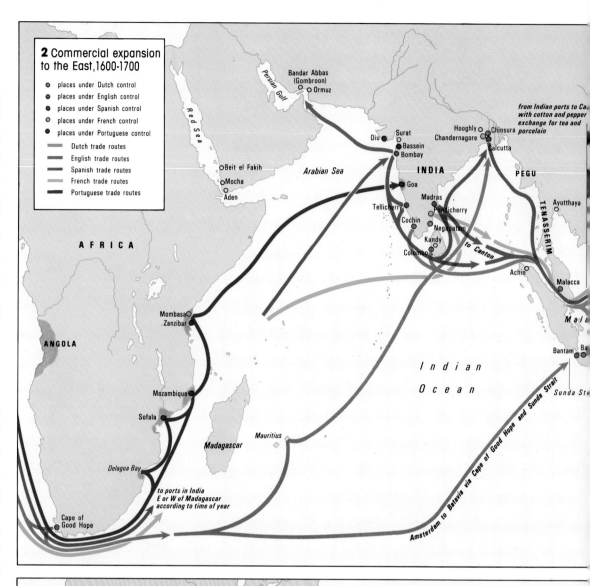

2 Commercial expansion to the East, 1600-1700

- places under Dutch control
- places under English control
- places under Spanish control
- places under French control
- places under Portuguese control
- Dutch trade routes
- English trade routes
- Spanish trade routes
- French trade routes
- Portuguese trade routes

4 The West Indies

- Spanish settlements
- French settlements
- English settlements
- Dutch settlements

CHINA

JAPAN
Nagasaki
Amoy
Canton
Macao
Zeelandia

Pacific Ocean

Manila
Philippines

to Acapulco

from Acapulco

Macassar
Spice Islands
Timor

NEW HOLLAND
(unknown in 1713 except for rough outline of West Coast)

RUPERT'S LAND

NEWFOUNDLAND

Fort Albany (Hudson's Bay Company's trading post) 1679
Rupert House (Hudson's Bay Company's trading post) 1668

ILE ROYALE
ILE ST. JEAN
NOVA SCOTIA

Fort Tadoussac (1600)
St. Lawrence R.

Quebec (1608) *capital of New France*
Trois Rivières (1634)
Richelieu R.

L. Superior

Sault Ste. Marie (1639)

NEW FRANCE
NEW ENGLAND
MAINE
Penobscot 1628

L. Huron

Fort Frontenac (1673)
L. Michigan
Fort Niagara (1679)
L. Ontario
L. Erie

NEW YORK
N.H.
MASS.
CONN.

Portsmouth 1653
Boston 1630
Plymouth 1620
Providence 1636
New Haven 1640

Albany 1664
Hudson R.

Fort Pontchartrain (1701)

PENNSYLVANIA

New York (New Amsterdam 1624-1664)

Fort St. Joseph (1680)
Fort St. Louis (1682)
Fort Crèvecoeur (1680)

Philadelphia 1682
Chester 1682

NEW JERSEY
DELAWARE
Annapolis 1708

Ohio R.

Missouri R.

Cahokia (1698)
Kaskaskia (1703)

VIRGINIA
MARYLAND

Atlantic Ocean

Tennessee R.

NORTH CAROLINA

Fort Prudhomme (1682)

SOUTH CAROLINA

Mississippi R.

LOUISIANA

Pensacola (1696) *founded to counter French claims*
Fort Maurepas (1699)

Gulf of Mexico

3 European settlement in North America

English settlements
French settlements
Spanish settlements

BRITISH TERRITORIES
Carolina Settled from 1663; separated into two colonies 1713.
Connecticut Settled 1635–38; separately incorporated 1662.
Delaware Settled by Swedes from 1638; separate proprietary colony 1704.
Maine Settled from 1622; effectively part of Massachusetts Bay from 1651, formally annexed 1691.
Maryland Settled as proprietary colony from 1632.
Massachusetts Bay Settled 1629 by Massachusetts Bay Co.
Newfoundland Claimed for England by John Cabot 1497; British sovereignty recognised 1713.
New Hampshire Part of Maine 1622; separate province from 1698.
New York Settled as New Netherland from 1624. Seized by English 1664.
Nova Scotia Settled by French (as Acadia) 1604; ceded to English 1713.
New Jersey Part of New Netherland; English proprietary colony 1664.
Pennsylvania Settled as proprietary colony from 1681.
Rhode Island Settled by dissident groups from Massachusetts Bay from 1636; separately incorporated from 1644.
Rupert's Land Fur trading area claimed by Hudson Bay Co. from 1670; claim recognised by France 1713.
Virginia Settled by Virginia Company from 1607; crown colony from 1624.

FRENCH TERRITORIES
New France Settled from c.1608.
Louisiana After exploration of Mississippi by La Salle (1682), France claimed whole Mississippi drainage. Fortified trading posts established at strategic points from Great Lakes to Gulf of Mexico.

SPAIN
Seville
Balearic Is.
MOROCCO

SYRIA
Alexandria
Cairo
EGYPT
R. Nile
Red Sea
KUWAIT
BAHRAIN
Ormuz

SINKIANG

Sea of Japan
JAPAN
Nagasaki

CHINA
R. Yangtze
Canton
Macao
Taiwan
Hainan

Ryukyu Islands
Bonin Islands

R. Indus
R. Ganges
Hooghly
Diu

AFRICA

Arabian Sea

Goa
Calicut
Cochin
Ceylon
Colombo

Laccadive Islands
Andaman Islands
Nicobar Islands

Malay Archipelago
Malacca
Sumatra

Luzon
Manila
Cebu
Philippines

Mariana Islands
Guam
Caroline Islands

Bab el Mandeb
Aden

Maldives

Indian Ocean

Borneo
Brunei

Ternate
Tidore
Moluccas
Celebes
Amboina
Banda Is.

R. Benue
Guato
Elmina
Gulf of Guinea
São Tomé
R. Congo

Malindi
Mombasa
Pemba
Zanzibar
Kilwa

Chagos Arch.

Seychelles

Java
Christmas Island
Timor

Luanda to Bahia with slaves
Luanda
ANGOLA
R. Zambezi
Mozambique
Sofala

Comoro Is.
Agalega Islands

Madagascar
Réunion

St. Helena
...stan da Cunha
...d sugar

Manila galleons with silk
Manila galleons with silver

Lisbon to Goa (alternative route, second half of year)

1 Spanish and Portuguese trade and settlement by c.1600

principal Spanish trade routes
principal Portuguese trade routes
areas under effective Spanish control
areas under effective Portuguese control
important towns in the 16th century
Spanish towns
seat of *Audiencia* (Spanish administrative division)
Portuguese towns

Colonial America
1519-1783

The conquest of Mexico by Hernán Cortés in 1519–20 (map 1), and of Peru by Francisco Pizarro in 1531–33 (map 2), laid the foundations of the Spanish colonial empire in America. With the help of rebellious tribes, oppressed by their Aztec and Inca conquerors (page 62), both were amazingly successful. By 1535, when vice-regal government was set up in Mexico and Lima was founded as the capital of Peru, the first dramatic phase of conquest was over. By 1550 all the chief centres of settled population were in Spanish hands, though the task of pushing forward frontiers into unexplored territory continued until the end of the colonial period (map 3). New viceroyalties were set up in New Granada (1739) and Rio de la Plata (1776), and new military governments in Texas (1718) and California (1767). But none of the later, sparsely inhabited conquests compared with Mexico and Peru in wealth and importance. Potosí in Upper

Peru and Zacatecas in Mexico became the biggest sources of silver in the world, and by 1560 silver was the chief export from the American colonies to Spain.

Elsewhere on the American mainland colonisation was slower to take effect. The Portuguese, on the eastern coast of South America, were only goaded into action by fear of the French. But in 1549 they founded Bahía as an administrative capital, and sugar plantations and mills, worked by slaves from Africa, were introduced. Between 1575 and 1600 coastal Brazil became the foremost sugar-producing territory in the western world, and attracted many land-hungry immigrants from Portugal and the Azores. But the vast Brazilian interior remained largely unexplored and in the hands of native Indian tribes (map 4). The same was true of the whole of North America at this date, beyond the frontier of New Spain. With its harsh climate and poor soil, the eastern seaboard of North America was uninviting territory, and for the first century after its discovery the great Newfoundland fisheries were its main attraction. There was also a fur trade with the natives, and by 1535 French explorers

had penetrated far up the St. Lawrence river in the quest of skins and furs. When, after 1670, the English also built up a fur-trading empire, based on Hudson Bay (map 5), the result was a rivalry which erupted in the colonial wars of the eighteenth century (page 86). Nevertheless, fish and furs were the original staple of North America, and settlement, strongly opposed by fishing interests, only began in the seventeenth century, with the foundation of Acadia, or Nova Scotia, by the French in 1604, of Virginia (1607) and Massachusetts Bay (1629) by the English, and of New Netherland, later New York, by the Dutch in 1623. Even so, progress was slow. As late as the end of the seventeenth century, the total population of the twelve English colonies was a mere 250,000.

The pattern of settlement was also different in the north. The English colonists wanted land for farms and plantations, expelling or exterminating the native population. The history of the British colonies in the eighteenth century is punctuated by savage Indian wars. In Virginia, and later in the Carolinas, where tobacco was introduced as a cash-

crop from Guiana, the plantations were worked by Negro slaves, numbering well over 100,000 by the time of the American War of Independence. The Spaniards, on the other hand, relied on Indian labour, both in ranching and mining, and readily intermarried; hence the extensive *mestizo* population, particularly in Mexico and Peru. At the same time, all the colonies were firmly administered in the interests of the mother country. This inevitably provoked resentment on the part of the colonial élites, and lay behind the demand for independence which erupted in the north in 1775 (page 92) and in Latin America in 1808 (page 96).

4 | Population and settlement

| United States

— frontier of European settlement

--- international boundary

···· provincial boundary

-··- 1763 Proclamation Line

| Indian territory

Negro slavery prominent

1 The Spanish invasion of Mexico 1519-20

← route of Cortés' army 1519

defensive wall of Tlaxcala (approximate position)

Gulf of Mexico

Tenochtitlán · Texcoco · Xocotla · Ixtacmaxtitlán · *Cofre de Perote* · Jalapa · Cempoala · Vera Cruz · Tlaxcala · *Ixtaccihuatl* · Puebla · *Orizaba* · Amecameca · *Popocatepétl* · Cholula

2 The Spanish invasion of Peru 1531-33

route of Francisco Pizarro's army to Cajamarca and Cuzco

route of Hernando Pizarro to Pachácamac and Jauja

✗ battles

5 Trading posts and forts

French fort

British fort

→ major fur routes (to Europe)

Gulf of Guayaquil · Puná Island · Tumbes · Paita · San Miguel · R. Chancay · Cajamarca · Huamachuco · R. Santa · Huaylas · Cordillera Negra · Cordillera Blanca · *Huascarán* · Huaráz · R. Fortaleza · Bombón · *Pacific Ocean* · R. Urubamba · R. Rimac · Jauja · Huancayo · R. Apurímac · Lima-Callao · R. Mantaro · Pachácamac · Huamanga (Ayacucho) · Ollantaytambo · Vilcashuamán · Vilcaconga · Cuzco

(North America map 5)

Bering Strait · *Alaska* · Mackenzie R. · *Pacific Ocean* · Hudson Bay · Fort York 1684 · Fort Bourbon 1742 · RUPERT'S LAND *controlled by Hudson's Bay Company from 1670* · Cumberland House 1774 *(the English break away from shores of Hudson Bay)* · CANADA · Fort Albany 1679 · Fort Charles 1792 (Lake of the Woods) · Fort La Reine (Portage la Prairie) 1738 · Fort Pierre (Rainy Lake) · Fort Kaministikwia 1679 · Fort Frontenac 1673 · Fort d'Huillier 1700 · Fort Niagara 1679 · Missouri R. · St. Lawrence R. · Fort St Louis 1682 · Ohio R. · *Atlantic Ocean* · Fort Orléans 1718 (Missouri) · Fort Massac 1758 · Mississippi R. · Fort Prudhomme 1682 (Memphis)

RUPERT L · NEW SPAIN

3 The development of colonial America

French territory
Spanish territory
Portuguese territory
Dutch territory
Russian territory
British by 1763
ceded by France to Britain 1763
ceded by France to Spain 1763
United States 1783
- - - international boundary
· · · · · provincial boundary
→ major exports
colonisation routes:
Spanish
Portuguese
British
Russian
French

Arctic Ocean
unexplored
Greenland
RUPERT'S LAND
(Hudson's Bay Company)
Hudson Bay
disputed by Russia and Spain
furs
NEWFOUNDLAND
ceded to Britain 1763
QUEBEC
St. Lawrence R.
NOVA SCOTIA
Quebec
Montreal
whale products, fish
UNITED STATES OF AMERICA 1783
Boston
New York
Philadelphia
naval stores, furs, fish, grain
San Francisco
LOUISIANA
Ohio R.
THE THIRTEEN COLONIES
Jamestown
North
Los Angeles (1780)
INTERIOR PROVINCES
Mississippi R.
tobacco, grain
Rio Grande
WEST FLORIDA
New Orleans
EAST FLORIDA (Br. 1763-83)
skins
NEW
BAHAMA ISLANDS (Br. 1783)
sugar, tobacco
Atlantic
SPAIN
Zacatecas
Gulf of Mexico
CUBA
WEST INDIES
silver
Mexico
SANTO DOMINGO
JAMAICA (Br. 1655)
SAINT-DOMINGUE
GUADELOUPE (Fr.)
MARTINIQUE (Fr.)
silver
Belize (Br. 1683)
Caribbean Sea
CENTRAL AMERICA
cochineal, gold
gold
CURAÇAO (Dutch 1634)
Caracas
tobacco, cocoa beans, hides
VENEZUELA
R. Orinoco
Paramaribo
Cayenne
Panama
GUIANA
Santa Fé de Bogotá
NEW GRANADA
drugs, rare plants
Pacific
Quito
gold, naval stores
R. Amazon
Ocean
BRAZIL
QUEBEC
Treaty of Tordesillas 1494, 1506
dyewoods, sugar, tobacco, cotton
slave trade from Africa
Venezuela
PERU
silver, drugs
Lima
Cuzco
R. São Francisco
Bahía
NEW GRANADA
UPPER PERU
gold, diamonds
Potosí
PERU
copper, grain
R. Paraguay
R. Paraná
Rio de Janeiro
BRAZIL
beef
RIO DE LA PLATA
CHILE
RIO DE LA PLATA 1776
hides, silver
CHILE
frontier
Indian
Buenos Aires
South

Spanish American population in 1800 (total 16.9 millions)
Whites 3.3
Indians 7.5
Negros 0.8
Mestizos 5.3

Atlantic Ocean
FALKLAND IS.

Population of the United States and Canada, 1820 (total 11.6 millions)
Whites 9.0
Mulattos 0.1
Negroes 1.9
Indians 0.6

69

South-East Asia, 1511-1826

When European traders and adventurers broke through into the Indian Ocean at the close of the fifteenth century (page 64), the great prize, drawing them forward, was the spices of South-East Asia. Here was untold wealth to be tapped. But here also, at one of the world's main crossroads, where cultural influences from China and India intermingled, they found themselves in a region of great complexity, divided in religion between Buddhism, Hinduism and Islam, and politically fragmented and unstable (map 1). On the mainland, rival peoples and dynasties competed for hegemony. In the Malayan archipelago the empires of Srivijaya and Majapahit (page 50) had disappeared, leaving behind scores of petty states, with little cohesion. This was the situation when Albuquerque conquered the great international emporium of Malacca for the king of Portugal in 1511.

The Portuguese presence changed little at first. Albuquerque and his successors were there to dominate the spice trade through a chain of fortified trading-stations, linked by naval power. Provided this was accepted, they had no wish to interfere with the native potentates. Far more important, after the arrival on the scene of the Dutch and English (page 66), was the challenge to their trading monopoly by their European rivals. For most of the seventeenth century this rivalry was the dominant factor (map 3). The Dutch, in particular, began a systematic conquest of the Portuguese settlements, capturing Malacca in 1641, and then turned against the British. But in doing so, they were inevitably drawn into local politics. After establishing a base at Batavia in 1619, they interfered in succession disputes among the neighbouring sultans, to ensure their own position, and in this way gradually extended control over Java, expelling the British from Bantam in 1682 (map 4). Already earlier they had driven them out of the Spice Islands by the 'massacre of Amboina' (1623) and the seizure of Macassar (1667), in this way forcing the English East India Company to turn instead to the China trade. With this in view the British acquired Penang on the west coast of Malaya in 1786, the first step in a process which was ultimately to make them masters of the Malay peninsula.

But this was still exceptional. European activities encroached on the outlying islands, but had little impact on the mainland monarchies, which had no direct interest in European trade and were mainly concerned with extending their power at the expense of their neighbours. This is a complicated story, because all the main centres were also under pressure from the hill peoples of the interior, always waiting to assert their independence; but the main lines of development are indicated on map 2. They include the advance of Annam at the expense of Cambodia, the rise of a new Burmese empire under Alaungpaya (1735–60), after a Mon rebellion in 1740, and successful Siamese resistance to Burmese encroachment, in spite of Burmese conquest in 1767. These events occurred for the most part without European involvement, but during the struggle for empire between England and France in the eighteenth century (page 86) some states were implicated. Already under Louis XIV France had intervened in Siam against the Dutch. During the Anglo-French war in India after 1746 it supported the Mon rebellion in Burma, and in reply the English East India Company seized the island of Negrais at the mouth of the Bassein river. Later, when the Burmese, foiled in their attempt to conquer Siam, switched their efforts to the north, the British, fearing for the security of Bengal, again intervened. The result was the first Anglo-Burmese war (1824–26) and the British annexation of Assam, Arakan and Tenasserim.

In Malaya there was similar encroachment on the independent rulers when the British, after acquiring Penang in 1786, established Singapore in 1819 as a free trade port after its acquisition by Raffles. This led to a conflict of interests with Holland which was only settled by the Anglo-Dutch treaty of 1824 when the British withdrew from Sumatra in return for Dutch withdrawal from Malacca (map 5). The future Dutch and British colonial empires in South-East Asia were taking shape. But their control was still loose and indirect. Only after the Industrial Revolution in Europe, and the expanding demand for raw materials and markets, were the lives and fortunes of the peoples of the region seriously affected.

1 South-East Asia in 1500

distribution of major religions:

- Theravada Buddhism
- Mahayana Buddhism mixed with Confucianism and Taoism
- Hindu-Buddhism
- Islamic states
- places sending tribute to China between 1370 and 1440

3 European rivalries 1511-1682

- English expeditions
- Dutch expeditions
- Spanish expeditions
- Portuguese expeditions

4 Dutch expansion in Java

1619 – date of Dutch control

Dutch expansion

Java Sea

Bantam
Batavia **1619**
1684-1809
BANTAM
PREANGER DISTRICTS 1677
CHERIBON 1679-1813
Cheribon
Japara
Pekalongan
Semarang
Demak
Rembang
Tuban
Gresik
Surabaya
Sampang
MADURA I. 1705-1743
N.E. COASTAL DISTRICTS **1743**
MANCHANAGARA
SURA KARTA 1830
Madiun
Kediri
JOGJAKARTA
Pasuruan
Malang
BALAM BANGAN 1777

Indian Ocean

5 The Malay states in 1826

Malay states tributary to Siam in 1826

British possessions

SIAM
PERLIS
KEDAH
PENANG
PERAK
KELANTAN
TRENGGANU
Straits of Malacca
SELANGOR
NEGRI SEMBILAN
PAHANG
South China Sea
MALACCA
JOHORE
SUMATRA
SINGAPORE

2 Trade and politics

⊙ principal trading centre

Vietnamese border in 1500

expansion to 1611

further acquisitions from Cambodia in early 18th century

Vietnamese expansion in 19th century

Kingdom of Luang Prabang 1707

area which broke away under Vientiane in 1707

major Burmese conquests

Siamese conquests

trade routes:

routes developed by Dutch and English East India Companies

routes developed by Arab and Gujerati traders

route developed by the Dutch in the 17th century

routes used by English shipping after 1786

route used by the 'Manila Galleon'

→ local trade routes

European possessions in 1826:

British

Dutch

Spanish

Portuguese

New monarchy in Europe, 1453-1547

In Europe revival after the setbacks of the fourteenth century (page 56) began around 1450. The whole continent was affected. In the east Ivan III (1462–1505) profited from the decline of the Mongol khanates (page 46) to inaugurate a rapid expansion of the territory of Muscovy (page 84) and to attack the independence of Tver, Novgorod and the landowning aristocracy. In the west endemic civil war in Spain was ended after the union of Castile and Aragon in 1479. The ending of the Hundred Years' War between England and France (1453) and the expulsion of the English from French territory saw a rapid extension of the area controlled by the French monarchy (map 2), while in England Edward IV (1461–83) began a restoration of royal power which was carried further by the new Tudor dynasty after 1485. Through the Council in the North with its seat at York, and the Council in the March of Wales, with its seat at Ludlow, the turbulent outlying regions were brought under control, while Wales itself and the palatinates of Chester and Durham were integrated into the parliamentary and judicial systems from 1536 (map 4). But an attempt to integrate Ireland by Poynings' Law (1494) had little effect, and although Henry VIII was proclaimed King of Ireland (1541), English power was effectively limited to the Pale around Dublin. Scotland also resisted successfully.

Not all attempts at state-building were a success. The efforts of the dukes of Burgundy to erect an independent state in the rich lands between France and the Empire collapsed when the ambitious Charles the Bold was killed at Nancy in 1477 (map 3). The empire of Matthias

Corvinus of Hungary (1458–90) also proved ephemeral. Italy remained divided, in spite of a marked strengthening of government under rulers such as Lorenzo de' Medici (1469–92) at Florence and Ludovico Sforza (1460–99) at Milan (map 5), and after the French invasion of 1494 internal divisions left Italy a prey to foreign intervention. The main legatee in all instances was the house of Habsburg, which succeeded to the Spanish possessions in 1516 and emerged, under Charles V (1519–56) as the preponderant power in western Europe (map 1). But the diversified Habsburg empire lacked cohesion, and when the Ottoman advance, halted on the middle Danube since 1456, was resumed after 1520 (page 48), and at the same time the emperor was involved in the religious wars in Germany (page 74), the strain was too great. In 1556 Charles V abdicated and the empire was divided between the Austrian and Spanish Habsburgs. Only ten years later the Dutch revolt began.

The Dutch revolt, although the most formidable uprising (page 76), was not exceptional. In England, from Henry VII to Elizabeth I, the Tudors were faced by repeated rebellions, and elsewhere, even in Russia, resistance to centralisation became a powerful force after 1550. The rise of the new monarchies was less a new beginning than the culmination of the long struggle of aristocracy and monarchy. Their financial and administrative machinery was not enough to raise a modern system of government in place of the feudal order, and the decisive change from the old to the new was not made until after another century of strife and turmoil.

2 The reunification of France, 1440-1589

- frontier of France 1493
- Royal Domain c.1475
- lands annexed from Burgundy 1477
- lands of René of Anjou, annexed 1481
- lands of the Duke of Brittany, annexed 1491
- lands brought to the crown by Louis XII, 1498
- lands brought to the crown by Francis I, 1515
- lands of the Duke of Bourbon, annexed 1527
- lands brought to the crown by Henry IV, 1589
- other fiefs annexed with date
- fiefs still independent at end of 16th century
- lands recognising English suzerainty 1429

1 The new monarchies

- Habsburg territory
- Ottoman territory
- Muscovy and territories
- Venetian territories
- Empire of Casimir IV, 1447-92
- Empire of Matthias Corvinus, 1485-90
- **1483** date of conquest

3 The Low Countries, 1467-1548

Charles the Bold's possessions, 1477

Burgundian possessions lost after the death of Charles the Bold, 1477

Emperor Charles V's Burgundian possessions, 1548

1 FRIESLAND	14 CAMBRAI
2 GRONINGEN	15 NAMUR
3 OVERIJSSEL	16 LUXEMBOURG
4 GELDERLAND	17 PONTHIEU
5 UTRECHT	18 AMIENS
6 HOLLAND	19 VERMANDOIS
7 ZEELAND	20 BAR
8 BRABANT	21 LORRAINE
9 LIMBURG	22 BURGUNDY
10 FLANDERS	23 FRANCHE-COMTÉ
11 BOULONNAIS	24 ALSACE
12 ARTOIS	25 TOURNAI
13 HAINAUT	

M. METZ
T. TOUL

4 Extension of Tudor power in Britain

The Pale 1537

The Pale 1596

Principality of Wales before 1536

new Welsh counties after 1536

Council of the Marches of Wales 1525-1642

Council of the North 1537-1641

Council of the West 1539-40

X English attempts to subdue Scots

rebellions against Henry VII, 1485-1509

rebellions against Henry VIII, 1509-47

rebellions against Edward VI and Mary 1547-58

rebellions against Elizabeth I, 1558-1603

5 Renaissance Italy, 1454

boundary of Holy Roman Empire

The Reformation in Europe, 1517-1648

The closing years of the fifteenth century saw a great revival of popular religion in Europe, but the established church, which never fully recovered from the effects of the schism of 1378–1417 (page 56), was ill equipped to satisfy its needs. Except in Bohemia and Moravia, where the Hussites comprised over half the population, and in England, where small groups of Lollards survived, heresy was virtually dead by 1500; but the materialism of the Renaissance popes and the self-seeking of the higher clergy discredited the hierarchy in the eyes of many laymen. Some, like Erasmus of Rotterdam (1466–1536) and Sir Thomas More (1478–1535), still pinned their hopes on spiritual renewal; but elsewhere, particularly in Germany and German-speaking Switzerland, financial and other abuses fired revolt. In 1517 Martin Luther (1483–1546) posted his 95 theses on the church door at Wittenberg. In 1520, under the impulse of Huldreich Zwingli (1484–1531), Zurich renounced allegiance to Rome. Their denunciations of the clergy and the supremacy of the pope and their demand for a return to the standards of early Christianity exercised a vast appeal. By 1560 (map 1) seven out of ten of the Emperor's subjects were Protestants, and the reformed faith prevailed in Scandinavia, Baltic Europe and England. Further impetus came from the teaching of John Calvin (1509–64). In France over one hundred Calvinist churches existed by 1559 and perhaps 700 by 1562, and Calvinism also made rapid progress in Poland, Hungary and Scotland, where it became the official religion in 1560. In addition, a number of more radical sects sprang up, Anabaptists, Mennonites and others (map 2), which rejected theology, ritual and clerical order in favour of Biblical simplicity and often combined evangelism with social protest. They even proclaimed an Anabaptist republic at Münster in 1534, but it was brutally suppressed the next year.

However, the Reformation was soon entangled in politics. Princes and kings, including Henry VIII of England, saw an opportunity to despoil the church of its wealth. Some German princes espoused Protestantism out of fear of imperial power. Luther himself, dependent on princely support, turned against the more radical sectaries and condemned the peasants' revolt of 1525. Foreign policy

also played a part. The Valois kings of France, though combating the protestant Huguenots at home, supported the German Protestant princes against the Habsburg emperor. Although the French Huguenots won toleration by the Edict of Nantes (1598), their numbers were severely reduced during the religious wars between 1562 and 1598 (map 3), and elsewhere in Europe the second half of the sixteenth century saw a great Catholic revival, led by the Jesuit Order, founded in 1534 by St. Ignatius Loyola (1491–1556), and inspired by the reforms of the Council of Trent between 1545 and 1563. Using the Jesuits as their spearhead, Catholic rulers went over to the offensive. Protestants were expelled

from Bavaria (1579) and Styria (1600), and in Poland the number of Protestant churches decreased from 560 in 1572 to 240 in 1650.

The decisive phase of the struggle between Protestants and Catholics, the Thirty Years' War, took place in the Holy Roman Empire (map 4). It began in 1618–21 when the emperor Ferdinand II defeated the Bohemian Protestants at the battle of the White Mountain (1620) and won back Bohemia and Moravia for Catholicism. When he turned against the Protestant princes of Germany, Denmark, England and the Dutch intervened on the Protestant side, but the imperial forces were initially successful and in 1629 an Edict of Restitution was promulgated

which reclaimed large areas of church lands held by Protestant princes. Only the intervention of Gustavus Adolphus of Sweden saved the Protestant cause from collapse. But the Swedish victories at Breitenfeld (1631) and Lützen (1632) brought in Spain on the imperial side, while France allied with Sweden and declared war on Spain (1635). The war was now a struggle in which it seemed that neither side could hope for outright victory, until in 1648 the Peace of Westphalia brought a compromise solution. Lutherans and Calvinists retained the lands they held in 1624, and the wars of religion were over. But Germany, the scene of battle, suffered a lasting setback.

Western Europe, 1558-1648

The second half of the sixteenth and the first half of the seventeenth centuries were a time of turbulence throughout Europe. In Russia the 'time of troubles' after the death of Ivan the Terrible (1584) lasted until 1613. Northern Europe was embroiled in almost continuous war from 1561 to 1658, as Sweden, independent since the time of Gustavus Vasa (1523–60), struggled with Denmark, Russia, Poland and Brandenburg for control of the Baltic and its important trade. The rise of the Swedish empire (map 3), leading to Gustavus Adolphus' intervention in the Thirty Years' War (page 74) and the Swedish acquisition of western Pomerania, Wismar and the bishoprics of Bremen and Verden at the Peace of Westphalia, vitally affected the balance of power in Europe and was one of the most significant developments of the period. In western Europe developments were more confused. The new monarchies of the preceding period (page 72) had over-reached themselves, and from around 1530 reaction set in, particularly when rising prices, recession and widespread unemployment reinforced existing discontents. The Elizabethan Poor Law and other legislation of 1563 was no remedy; indeed, the reign of Elizabeth I (1558–1603), was less auspicious than often painted, and Elizabeth, whose relations with parliament deteriorated sharply at the end of her reign, left her Stuart successors on the English throne a legacy of unsolved problems with which they failed to cope.

From around 1530, sometimes earlier, the history of France and England was punctuated by revolts. As in Germany (page 74), they reflected a combination of religious, social and political grievances. In England the northern risings of 1536 and 1569 (page 72) were Catholic protests against the suppression of the old faith, but they also embodied the resistance of the northern gentry to centralisation and control from London. On the other wing the unrest of radical dissenters combined dissatisfaction with Henry VIII's and Elizabeth's conservative church settlements with resistance to the enclosure of common lands for the benefit of grasping landlords. A similar mixture of motives permeated the frequent uprisings, 500 in all, in France (map 2). These were largely revolts of the common people, driven to extremes by economic hardship; but in the end the most influential factor, visible in France in the revolt of the judges and nobility which drove the king from Paris in 1649, was resistance to autocracy, centralisation and taxation. The Dutch revolt, which began in the North Netherlands in 1572 and ended in 1648 (map 1),

was inspired by fear that the central government, controlled from Spain, intended to override the traditional liberties of the Netherlands. Similar motives underlay the Catalan and Portuguese revolts against Castile (1640).

In the British Isles, united from 1603 under a single monarch, the efforts of Charles I (1625–49) to change the traditional religious and political structure resulted in rebellions in Scotland (1638) and Ireland (1641). The king's innovations were no more popular with many of England's political leaders, called to Parliament to vote the taxes required to restore royal control in the other two kingdoms: their refusal provoked a civil war in England (1642). In a complex sequence of political and military moves (map 4), a small Parliamentary faction not only contrived the defeat and execution of the king (1649), creating an English Republic under the Lord Protector Oliver Cromwell, but went on to establish London's direct control over the entire British Isles (1649–51). Even though the Monarchy was restored in 1660, power was now shared between the crown and Parliament (in constant existence from 1689).

In continental Europe the sequel was different. In France the failure of the Fronde broke the power of the aristocracy and cleared the way for the absolutism of Louis XIV (page 80). Only in Germany was the disarray caused by a century of religious and political conflict enduring. Here the devastation of the Thirty Years' War resulted in a decline of population from some 21 millions in 1618 to around 13 millions in 1648 (map 5), and though some regions were spared, the setback was undeniable. The outcome was a major shift in the European balance. The Habsburgs, who had dominated the previous period, were in retreat, and the future in the West was in the hands of a resurgent France and its rivals, the maritime powers.

The English Civil War (below)

1/Edinburgh 1638: National Covenant signed.

2/Newcastle 1640: Scottish Covenanters invade England and force Charles I to buy them off.

3/Kilkenny 1641: centre of rebellion by Irish Catholics (to 1649).

4/Antrim 1641: massacre of Catholics by Protestants.

5/Westminster 1642: English Parliament raises army against Charles I.

6/Edgehill 1642: first battle of English Civil War, indecisive.

7/Westminster 1643: alliance of English Parliament and Scottish Covenanters against Charles I (to 1648).

8/Nantwich 1644: Parliamentary army defeats Irish Catholic invasion in support of Charles I.

9/Marston Moor 1644: Scots and Parliamentary army defeat Charles I and occupy N. England.

10/Lostwithiel 1644: Parliamentary army loses control of SW England to King.

11/Tippermuir 1644: Montrose and Scottish royalists defeat Covenanters.

12/Philiphaugh 1645: Montrose defeated by Covenanters and forced to flee.

13/Naseby 1645: Parliamentary army defeats Charles I and wins control of all England.

14/Burford 1647: Oliver Cromwell suppresses mutiny of Parliamentary troops (the 'Levellers').

15/Preston 1648: Cromwell defeats Covenanters' invasion of England in support of Charles I.

16/Whitehall 1649: Parliament tries and executes Charles I.

17/Drogheda and Wexford 1649: Cromwell overruns Ireland and ends rebellion there; occupied to 1660.

18/Dunbar 1650: Cromwell defeats Covenanters and occupies Scotland (to 1660).

19/Scone 1651: Charles II crowned king of Scotland by Covenanters.

20/Worcester 1651: Cromwell defeats invasion of Covenanters in support of Charles II who is forced to flee abroad (to 1660).

21/Whitehall 1658: death of Oliver Cromwell (Head of State since 1654).

22/Westminster 1660: coronation of Charles II as king of England.

1 The Dutch revolt, 1572-1648

- boundary of Netherlands 1548
- rebel areas in 1572 (December)
- furthest extent of Dutch revolt (July 1577)
- rebel areas December 1588
- rebel areas December 1606
- Dutch conquests 1621-48
- the Dutch Republic 1648

4 The English Civil War, 1642-45

- area controlled by Parliament August 1642
- Parliamentary gains 1643
- Parliamentary losses 1643
- Parliamentary gains 1644
- area controlled by the King 1644
- area controlled by the King December 1645
- Parliamentary and pro-Parliamentary forces
- Royalist and pro-Royalist forces

Germany and its neighbours
1648-1806

The Peace of Westphalia (1648), besides bringing to a close the wars of religion (page 74), was a milestone in German history. The failure of the emperor to impose his will on the Protestant princes confirmed the political fragmentation which had gathered pace since the fourteenth century (page 54). After 1648 Germany was a patchwork of some 300 small, petty states and free cities (map 1). In addition, the independence of Holland and Switzerland was formally recognised. Theoretically the rights of the princes were limited by the rights of the Holy Roman Empire, but in practice every prince was emperor in his own lands, with full sovereign powers including the laws to make foreign alliances. Political disruption was also compounded by a sharp economic setback, due partly to the devastation and depopulation resulting from the Thirty Years' War, but also to a long-term shift in the European economy. The great south German banking houses of Welser and Fugger went bankrupt in 1614 and 1627 respectively. The Hanseatic League, in disarray since the closing years of the sixteenth century, was dissolved in 1669. Everywhere the towns were in decline, particularly in Austria, Prussia and

Bavaria, but even worse was the plight of the peasantry. In Bohemia and Moravia their legal rights were abolished; in the north and north-east they were ejected from their holdings to permit the consolidation of Junker estates, and reduced to serfdom (page 82). Impoverishment and stagnation were the result. A modest economic recovery occurred after 1750; but with its resources dissipated on ostentatious building and the upkeep of princely households Germany was an economic and social backwater. It was also a pawn in great power politics. Divided among themselves and fearful of Habsburg ambitions, the princes were clients of foreign powers, including Britain and Sweden, but particularly of France, which used its position to make inroads on German territories in the west (page 80), annexing the Franche-Comté of Burgundy (1678), Strasbourg (1681), most of Alsace (1697) and Bar and Lorraine (1766).

After 1648, apart from Austria, only Saxony, Bavaria and Brandenburg could claim even the status of second-rate powers. Saxony, with the mineral resources of the Erzgebirge and its varied industries, was the most advanced, while Bavaria was falling behind; but Brandenburg-Prussia was beginning, under the Great Elector (1640–88) the long climb which made it by 1786 the second German power and the rival of Austria. The rise of Prussia (map 2) is a story of tenacity, unscrupulous diplomacy, but above all of single-

2 The rise of Prussia

- Brandenburg in 1648
- Prussian acquisitions 1648-1707
- acquisitions 1715, 1720
- acquisitions 1742, 1744, 1772
- ✗ battles between Austria and Prussia

3 The growth of the Habsburg Empire

- hereditary Habsburg lands 1525
- acquisitions 1526-1648
- acquisitions 1648-99
- acquisitions 1699-1772
- acquisitions 1772-1805
- boundary of the Holy Roman Empire 1789
- military frontier

minded devotion to building a strong military and administrative apparatus to weld together the scattered territories stretching from the Vistula to the Rhine. The Hohenzollern domains lacked internal and external cohesion. Prussia itself was until 1657 a Polish fief; and it was only in 1772, after the first partition of Poland (map 4) that Frederick the Great (1740–86) succeeded in creating a continuous Prussian territory from Memel to Magdeburg. More impressive, and a cardinal fact in eighteenth-century history, was the recovery of Austria after its setbacks in the Thirty Years' War and the creation of a vast new Austrian empire (map 3). This was largely the work of the great field marshal, Prince Eugene of Savoy (1663–1736). As late as 1683 Vienna itself was besieged by Turkish armies. Eugene turned the tide and by 1699 they had been thrown back and the whole of Hungary brought under Habsburg rule. Austria was now a major power in eastern Europe, while in the west the peace settle-

ment of 1714 brought it the Spanish Netherlands and the Spanish inheritance in Italy. But it was a giant with feet of clay, with weak finances and an inadequate army. Serbia and Belgrade, acquired in 1718, were lost again in 1739, Lombardy and southern Italy in 1734–5. When, on the death of Charles VI (1711–40) and the accession of Maria Theresa (1740–80), Frederick II of Prussia seized Silesia, Austria's inherent weaknesses were exposed. Although the struggle went on until 1763, it proved impossible to dislodge the Prussians. Later both Prussia and Austria took advantage of the disarray of Poland to enlarge their territories in the east. But in the three partitions (map 4) they had to share the spoils with Russia, and their mutual suspicions and rivalry left the west exposed to France. When the French revolutionary armies marched into Germany in 1793 the old order was doomed, and in 1806 the Holy Roman Empire passed unmourned from the map of Europe.

abbreviations:

A.   Archbishopric
B.   Bishopric
C.   County
D.   Duchy
E.   Electorate
L.   Landgraviate
M.   Margraviate
P.   Principality

B. of E.   Bishopric of Eichstätt
B. of H.   Bishopric of Halberstadt
B. of HILDES.   Bishopric of Hildesheim
B. of L.   Bishopric of Lübeck
B. of MIN.   Bishopric of Minden
C. of B.   County of Bentheim
C. of ER.   County of Erbach
C. of HNL.   County of Hohenlohe
C. of RAV.   County of Ravensberg
C. of SCH.   County of Schwarzburg
C. of S.   County of Solms
C. of WAL.   County of Waldeck
C. of L.   County of Limburg
D. of C.   Duchy of Cleves
HOZLN.   Hohenzollern
L. of HESSE-DARM. Landgraviate of Hesse-Darmstadt
P. of Lau.   Principality of Lauenburg
P. of PFALZ-SULZB. Principality of Pfalz-Sulzbach
P. of ZBN.   Principality of Zweibrücken

1 Germany in 1648

Austrian Habsburg

Spanish Habsburg

Wettin (Albertine)

Wettin (Ernestina)

Hohenzollern:

Franconian line

Brandenburg line

Wittelsbach:

Bavarian line

Palatinate line

Oldenburg lands

ecclesiastical lands

imperial cities

Holy Roman Empire 1648

Swedish from 1648

France and Europe
1648 – 1715

Under Louis XIV who succeeded to the throne in 1643, France became the leading country of Europe. His long minority, during Cardinal Mazarin's rule, saw the last major revolts of the aristocracy in defence of its prescriptive rights. When in 1661 Louis became effective ruler, the ground had been prepared for a new regime of centralisation and absolutism. This was the work of Mazarin, who had broken the aristocratic revolts and who turned the *intendants* into permanent representatives of the royal will in the provinces; of Louvois, who reformed the army; and particularly of Colbert's programme of financial reform. At the same time Vauban encircled France with a chain of defensive fortresses (map 1). All this was accompanied by great public works,

including the Languedoc canal, connecting the Atlantic and the Mediterranean, the palace of Versailles, and much building in Paris which became the centre of the cosmopolitan civilisation of Europe.

But Louis XIV's wars, inspired by an almost neurotic fear of the revival of the empire of Charles V and the encirclement of France by Habsburg power, seriously damaged this solid achievement. Beginning with his attack on the Spanish Netherlands in 1667, they imposed a growing burden of taxation and gradually united Europe against him (map 4). England and Holland, maritime and colonial rivals since 1652 (map 3), settled their differences by the Treaty of Breda (1667) and in alliance with Sweden compelled Louis to make peace at Aix-la-Chapelle in 1668. Thereupon Louis detached England from the anti-French alliance by the Secret Treaty of Dover (1670), won over Sweden, and turned against Holland in 1672; but he was halted by an alliance between Austria, Spain and Brandenburg (which

defeated his Swedish allies at Fehrbellin in 1675), and at the Peace of Nimwegen (1678) Holland emerged unscathed.

These inconclusive results convinced Louis that there was little hope of major territorial acquisitions by direct conquest, and after 1679 he turned to a policy of indirect aggression, nibbling away at German territory in the east, particularly in Alsace (map 2), the object being to absorb the remainder of the Burgundian territories which had been partitioned between France and Austria after the death of Charles the Bold in 1477 (page 72). Strasbourg was annexed in 1681, the Palatinate burnt and ravaged in 1689. But these provocative and often brutal actions united German opinion against him, and the revocation of the Edict of Nantes (1685) and the persecution of the French Huguenots incensed the Protestant powers. The result was the formation of the Grand Alliance (1689), led by William of Orange, who had succeeded to the English throne after the revolution

1 France under Louis XIV

frontiers and administration:

〜〜〜 frontier of France 1713-14

〜〜〜 administrative units of Louis XIV's reign, the *généralités* (generalities)

⊚ seat of intendants, Louis XIV's royal commissioners

⊕ *parlement* (law courts)

defence:

■ fortifications (the so-called *barrière* or *frontière de fer*)

◩ fortifications built by Vauban but ceded during reign of Louis XIV

➜ fortification gap, possible invasion route *(porte)*

⚓ galley port

⊞ naval port

economic:

⚓ commercial harbours

major manufactures:

▢ brandy
◭ cloth
▢ glass
⊞ iron
◒ madder dye
◹ paper
⚱ pottery
⚒ printing
▤ salt
◉ silk
◿ soap
▨ tapestry and carpets
▼ wine

80

of 1688 and the deposition of James II. Louis' attempts to foment rebellion in Ireland failed after the defeat of the French navy at La Hogue (1692), but fighting continued inconclusively on the continent until 1697, when the Peace of Ryswick registered Louis' first serious setback.

A new phase opened with the death without heirs of Charles II of Spain in 1700. This event had long been anticipated, but plans to divide the Spanish dominions in such a way as to maintain the balance of power were thwarted not only by the rivalry of France and Austria, but also by the maritime powers (England and Holland), which feared French ascendancy in overseas trade if it acquired the Spanish overseas empire. The result was the long War of the Spanish Succession (map 5), ended, in spite of the victories of Prince Eugene of Savoy and the Duke of Marlborough, by the compromise Peace of Utrecht in 1713. The French candidate retained the Spanish throne as Philip V, and France kept most of its gains on its eastern frontier (map 2). But the ruinous expense of Louis' wars left France in a desperate situation, with a legacy of financial disorder and internal discontent from which his successors never fully recovered.

4 The wars of Louis XIV 1667-1697
- → main lines of French advance
- main theatres of operation
- ■ towns occupied by France
- ✕ French victory
- ✕ Allied victory
- ✕ English victory

Triple Alliance 1668

Coalition of 1673

The Grand Alliance 1689

2 The north-east frontier, 1648-1714
- French frontier 1713/14
- French gains to 1659
- gains to 1679
- gains to 1679 later lost
- gains by Treaty of Ryswick 1697

3 The Anglo-Dutch wars, 1652-1673

First Anglo-Dutch War:
1 Kentish Knock, 1652
2 Dungeness, 1652
3 Three Days' Battle, 1653
4 Gabbard Shoal, 1653
5 Scheveningen, 1653

Second Anglo-Dutch War:
6 Lowestoft, 1665

7 Four Days' Battle, 1666
8 St James's Day Fight, 1666
9 'Holmes's Bonfire' (Terschelling), 1666
10 Chatham Raid, 1667

Third Anglo-Dutch War:
11 Sole Bay, 1672
12 Schooneveld I, May 1673
13 Schooneveld II, June 1673   14 Texel, 1673

✕ English victory
✕ Dutch victory

5 The War of the Spanish Succession 1702-1713
- to Spanish House of Bourbon
- to Great Britain
- to Austria
- to Savoy
- to France
- to Prussia
- ✕ Allied victory
- ✕ Bourbon victory
- ✕ indecisive

The European economy
c.1500-1815

Recovery from the economic setbacks of the fourteenth century (page 56) began around 1450, and Europe's population expanded rapidly, though the fast growth of the sixteenth century was interrupted by war, rebellion, famine and plague in the seventeenth century and not resumed until the middle of the eighteenth century. Overall it increased from an estimated 69 million in 1500 to 188 million in 1800, but the increase was uneven and most marked in Britain and the Netherlands, by 1700 the greatest textile producers of Europe, the most active traders, with the largest merchant fleets and rapidly growing shipbuilding and metalware industries. The result was a shift in the economic axis. In 1500 industry was concentrated in the narrow corridor running north-south from Antwerp and Bruges through Ulm and Augsburg to Milan and Florence. By 1700 the axis ran west-east from England and Holland through the metal and woollen districts of the lower Rhine to the industrial concentrations of Saxony, Bohemia and Silesia, and thence to Russia, now beginning to build up an industrial base (map 4). The great expansion of overseas trade, particularly after 1700, also favoured the maritime powers (map 5). A consequence was the decline of the great trading cities of northern Italy, dominant two centuries earlier. In 1500 only four cities – Paris, Milan, Naples and Venice – had more than 100,000 inhabitants. By 1700 this number had trebled, and the majority of the rising urban centres lay west of the Rhine. London and Paris had already passed the half-million mark.

Significant as these developments were, agriculture was still Europe's most important industry. As late as 1815 three-quarters of its population were employed on the land, though here again there were sharp regional differences. In most of Europe farmers were subsistence peasants, whose smallholdings of 2–10 hectares produced only about 20 per cent more than their immediate needs. But in the west the need to feed growing urban populations led, first in Holland and then in Britain, to an agricultural revolution. The Dutch poured capital into land reclamation, recovering some 180,000 hectares between 1540 and 1715 (map 3), and developed intensive cultivation, eliminating the need to leave land fallow by means of a rotation of crops, which was later taken over in England. The growing population was also sustained by the introduction of new, more productive crops, mainly from America, including maize, which gave a far higher yield than the old regional cereals of southern Europe, and the potato, introduced in c.1565, which spread slowly until it became a key field crop after 1700 (map 2). Urban demand also stimulated specialisation (Holland was exporting 90 per cent of its cheese by 1700), and generated a massive demand in western Europe for wheat and rye from Pomerania, Prussia, Poland and Russia, greatly to the profit of Holland which virtually monopolised the Baltic carrying trade in the sixteenth and seventeenth centuries.

The profitable grain-export trade of eastern Europe adversely affected the position of the peasant population which had enjoyed relative freedom before 1500 but now was reduced to a state of abject serfdom on large commercial estates. Only on the frontiers (e.g. in Hungary and on the Volga) where they performed military service, did the peasants retain freedom. Otherwise emancipation (postponed in Russia until 1861) only came slowly after the French Revolution, and the same was true in western Germany where, following the savage repression of the great peasant revolt of 1525, feudal relationships persisted (map 1). A few rulers, notably the emperor Joseph II (1780–90), realised that improvement of productivity depended on breaking the old feudal relationships; but they were frustrated by landed interests. The position in north-west Europe was very different. Serfdom had disappeared in the Low Countries by 1300. In France and England feudal services had been replaced, even before 1500, by money rents; and although, when prices rose after 1700, French lords sought to recoup themselves by reviving ancient dues (only abolished in 1793), peasant ownership was protected by the courts. Rising prices led, in England, to enclosure of the common fields, a precondition for agricultural improvement. Rich peasants benefited, but poor peasants, driven off the land, flocked to the towns, where they provided the labour force for the new industries.

1 The emancipation of the peasantry

- free settlement
- freed early during transition from labour services to payment of money rents
- in process of achieving freedom in 1789
- completely freed during French Revolutionary period (1789-1815)
- personally free 1799-1815 after surrendering land in exchange
- emancipation starting 1807 (smaller holdings excluded)
- emancipation beginning 1815
- peasants remaining unfree 1815
- great German peasant revolt 1525

4 Trade and industry in the 18th century

population per sq. km.:
- under 20
- 20 to 40
- 40 or more

town population:
- ⊙ 500,000+
- ⊕ 200,000+
- ○ 100,000+
- ○ 30,000+
- ○ less than 30,000
- ● financial centres
- metallurgical industries
- textile industries
- ◣ wool
- + linen
- ▶ cotton
- ◀ silk

3 Land reclamation in the Netherlands
— the Dutch Republic in 1648
- before 1600
- 1600-1800

North Sea
FRIESLAND
HOLLAND
Zuider Zee
ZEELAND

2 The introduction of the potato

FINLAND 1735
SWEDEN 1726
○ Edinburgh
from Chile 1580
○ Dublin
1599
London
1621 1708
BELGIUM 1566
Frankfurt 1580 ○ Breslau 1708
○ Paris
Vienna 1580
Budapest ○ HUNGARY 1654
Lyons ○ Milan ○
from Peru 1565
1600 1625 ○ Venice
○ Madrid
Rome 1566

5 The main trading flows c. 1775
- → exports to Britain
- → exports to United Provinces
- → exports to Spain
- → exports to Portugal
- → exports to France

Glasgow ○ Liverpool ○
Bristol ○ Amsterdam ○
London ○
Nantes ○
La Rochelle ○
Bordeaux ○
Lisbon ○
Cadiz ○

£5.6 million
£5.2 million
£4.9 million
£1.8 million
all Asiatic trade · value unknown
£1.4 million
£2.4 million
£2.2 million

St Petersburg
Vilna
Moscow
Sofia
Adrianople
Constantinople
Salonica

NORWAY *SWEDEN* *FINLAND*
○ Stockholm
St Petersburg ○
Baltic Sea
○ Riga
PRUSSIA ○ Königsberg
Danzig ○
POLAND ○ Moscow
Warsaw ○
R U S S I A
○ Kiev
○ Lemberg
Saratov ○
AUSTRIA-HUNGARY
Vienna ○ Budapest ○
Odessa ○
The Military Frontier
OTTOMAN EMPIRE
○ Bucharest
R. Volga
○ Sofia
Black Sea
○ Salonica
○ Constantinople
○ Athens
Mediterranean Sea

65°
60°
55°
50°
40°

The expansion of Russia, 1462-1905

The rise of modern Russia dates from the reign of Ivan III (1462–1505). During the preceding century the principality of Moscow had expanded at the expense of its immediate neighbours; but it was still a tributary of the Mongols (page 46), and in the west it was hemmed in by the great Polish-Lithuanian state, which extended deep into the Ukraine (page 56). Ivan III threw off the Mongol overlordship (1480), and in the west his conquest of the ancient republic of Novgorod (1478) opened the way to Livonia and the White Sea. Under his son Vassily (1505–33) and his grandson Ivan IV (1533–84) the advance continued. The subjection of the Khanate of Kazan (1552) opened the way across the Urals into Siberia; the conquest of the Khanate of Astrakhan (1556) gave Moscow control of the Volga to the Caspian Sea. But in the west Lithuania and Poland, joined after 1560 by Sweden, fought back vigorously, and during the 'time of troubles' following the death of Ivan IV made substantial gains at Russian expense (map 1). This, on the other hand, was the time of the great Russian thrust across Siberia, which, beginning in 1582, reached the Sea of Okhotsk by 1639 (map 2).

Siberia, where the population in 1720 was only about 400,000, still counted for little. The axis of Russian expansion was in the west, its thrust symbolised by Peter the Great's foundation of the new capital, St. Petersburg (1703). His long Swedish wars, concluded by the Peace of Nystad (1721), brought him Estonia, Livonia and part of Karelia. Russia now had free access to the Baltic. Under Catherine II (1762–96) it won control of the northern shore of the Black Sea, where Odessa (founded 1794) became a main outlet for Russian exports. But the question of secure access from the Black Sea to the Mediterranean remained unsolved. It was to be a central concern of Russian policy in the nineteenth century, and when it was thwarted by the other European powers in 1856 and again in 1878 Russia turned from

Europe to Asia, securing control of the Caucasus (1857–64) and then of the Khanates of Tashkent (1865), Samarkand (1868), Bukhara (1868), Khiva (1873) and Kokand (1876), while in the Far East it conquered the Amur and Ussuri regions at the expense of China (map 3). But defeat in the Crimean War (1854–56) convinced Russia of its backwardness, and in 1861, as a first step to modernisation, the serfs were liberated. Some went to Siberia, far more to the towns, where they provided a working force for industrialisation which began in the 1870s and was especially rapid 1893–1904 and 1909–13, when it exceeded the American growth rate. A metallurgical industry was developed in the Ukraine (map 4) producing mainly rails for the expanding railways. But the achievement was unstable. Russian ambitions in the Far East excited British and Japanese fears, and the result was the Anglo-Japanese alliance (1902) and the Russo-Japanese war of 1904–5 (page 126), which halted Russian expansion until 1945. At home the consequences were even more ominous. An urban proletariat had been formed which became the mainstay of the revolution of 1905 and more fatefully still in 1917.

4 The industrialisation of the Ukraine, 1861-1913

1861-1890	1890-1913	
raw materials:		
●	●	coal
▲	▲	iron
industry:		
■	■	metals
◆	◆	machinery
❙	❙	chemicals
✛	✛	textiles
◗	◗	food (mainly sugar refining)
M	M	miscellaneous
— — —	— — — —	railways

3 Russia in Asia, 1815-1900

▨ The Russian Empire in 1815	▨ acquisitions 1877-1900
▨ acquisitions 1816-56	▨ vassal khanates
▨ acquisitions 1856-76	—— railway

2 Russian expansion in Siberia, 1581-1800

- Russian territory in 1581
- territory added 1581-98
- territory added 1598-1618
- territory added 1618-89
- territory added in 1650s; returned to China 1689
- territory added 1689-1725
- territory added 1725-62
- territory added 1762-1800

YAKUTS native peoples
○ Bratsk 1630 forts and trading posts (with date of foundation)

1 Muscovy and the Russian Empire, 1462-1815

boundary of Russian territories in 1462

boundary of Lithuania in 1462

the expansion of Muscovy :

Moscow territory at end of 13th century

1478 date of acquisition by Muscovy

acquisitions to 1462

acquisitions under Ivan III, 1462-1505

acquisitions during 16th century (1505-86)

acquisitions during 17th century

acquisitions during 18th century

acquisitions 1801-15

territory ceded to Sweden 1617 and Poland 1618

recovered from Poland 1634

recovered from Poland 1667

area affected by Pugachev uprising 1773-4

route of Pugachev rebels

Orel 1564 date of foundation of new town

The struggle for empire
1713-1805

The Treaty of Utrecht (1713), which ended the War of Spanish Succession (page 80), sought to establish stability in Europe and overseas on the basis of a balance of power. But owing to commercial disputes and colonial rivalries, particularly in America, peace remained precarious. In 1739 war broke out between England and Spain; in 1740 Frederick II of Prussia, supported by France, seized Silesia (page 78); and when France, supporting Spain, declared war on England in 1744, the European and overseas wars were fused into a single global conflict. It also quickly turned into a duel between England and France, particularly when, after the inconclusive Treaty of Aix-la-Chapelle (1748), fighting again broke out in North America in 1754. Here the French, with their strategically situated forts, were initially successful. But the whole situation changed when William Pitt the Elder, later Earl of Chatham, became British prime minister in 1756. By allying with and subsidising Prussia, struggling to retain Silesia against an overwhelming French-Austrian-Russian coalition, Pitt compelled France to concentrate on the continental war. Naval victories at Quiberon Bay and Lagos in 1759 assured British control of the Atlantic and prevented reinforcements reaching Canada (map 1). The result was the loss of the French and, when Spain entered the war on the French side in 1761, of the

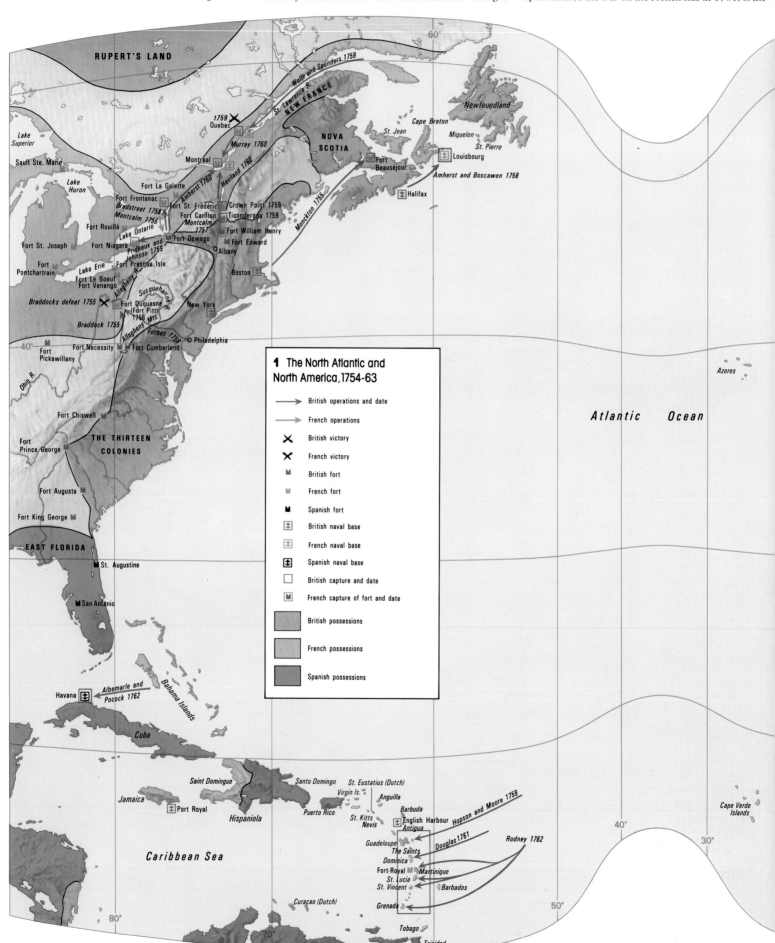

1 The North Atlantic and North America, 1754-63

→ British operations and date
→ French operations
✕ British victory
✕ French victory
▣ British fort
▣ French fort
▣ Spanish fort
⊞ British naval base
⊞ French naval base
⊞ Spanish naval base
☐ British capture and date
▣ French capture of fort and date

British possessions
French possessions
Spanish possessions

Spanish colonial empires in North America. At the Peace of Paris (1763) the French and Spanish possessions in the West Indies were restored, but England retained the North American mainland east of the Mississippi, including Florida which was ceded by Spain.

The British triumph was nevertheless short-lived. When the thirteen colonies rebelled in 1776 (page 92), France, which had rebuilt its navy, supported the rebels and by naval action compelled Great Britain to recognise American independence in the Treaty of Versailles (1783). In India, on the other hand, Britain built an empire which lasted until 1947. Here again, sea-power was decisive, enabling the English East India Company to checkmate the ambitions of the able French governor, Joseph Dupleix, to expand French influence in south India (map 2). By 1763 France was eliminated as a rival in India. An important determinant of the pace of British expansion was the decline of the Mughal Empire (page 48) after the death of Aurangzeb in 1707. Some states, the Marathas and the Sikh Punjab for example, asserted their independence, while former Mughal provinces, such as Oudh, Bengal and Hyderabad, achieved virtual autonomy. The British both feared, and profited from these developments. By the end of the governor-generalship of Richard Wellesley (1797–1805) British supremacy was an acknowledged fact. Revolutionary France attempted a comeback, and Napoleon planned an invasion of India (page 90). But once again sea-power was decisive, and in 1815 Great Britain occupied an unrivalled position in the colonial world.

3 The growth of British power in India to 1805

territory ceded to Britain by 1805

2 The Franco-British conflict in India

territory under British control by 1783

territory under British control by 1815

Indian states in subsidiary alliance with Britain by 1815

- gained by British 1815 → French attacks with date
- gained by British from French 1815 → British attacks with date
- gained by British from Dutch 1815 ✕ British victory
- French towns and territory ✕ French victory
- Portuguese towns ✕ Afghan victory over Marathas

The age of revolution
1773-1810

1755, 1793 Corsica Local clans led by Paoli rebelled against Genoese rule and established independent democratic government. France bought island from Genoa in 1768, crushed revolt. Second attempt by Paoli to secure independence from (revolutionary) France, 1793, resulted in brief British occupation; rise of Bonaparte, himself a Corsican, put an end to separatist movement.

1768 Geneva Middle-class citizens of small city-state rebelled against domination by few patrician families; with French support the latter stayed in control.

1773 South-East Russia Serfs, Cossacks and Asiatic tribes rebelled in Volga and Ural region under leadership of Pugachev, a Don Cossack. Russian army put down revolt in 1774.

1775 America Resistance by Britain's Thirteen Colonies to her financial policies resulted in open warfare and Declaration of Independence, 1776.

1784 Dutch Netherlands Three-cornered struggle for power between Stadtholder, patrician families who controlled Estates General, and middle class Patriot party which aimed to democratise government. In 1787 Prussian troops defeated Patriot army and restored Stadtholder with greater powers.

1787 Austrian Netherlands (Belgium) Revolt against centralising policy of Emperor Joseph II, leading to proclamation of the Republic of the United Belgian Provinces (1790). Fights broke out between aristocratic and middle-class rebels; Austrian Emperor reconquered area, 1790.

1789 France (See main text). Risings by peasantry and Parisians overthrew feudal social and political order; Louis XVI's opposition and attempted flight led to abolition of monarchy (1792). King and Queen were guillotined as traitors (1793). Threat of invasion led to Jacobin 'reign of terror', ended by fall and execution of Robespierre (1794). Following weak and corrupt rule of Directory (1795–99) power passed to Napoleon Bonaparte.

1789 Liège Middle-class citizens supported by workers and peasants expelled prince-bishop and abolished feudalism. Bishop restored by Austrian troops, 1790.

1790 Hungary Magyar nobles rejected edicts of Austrian emperor and demanded greater independence for Hungary within Habsburg Empire; later, frightened by peasant disturbances, accepted compromise with the monarchy.

1791 Poland King, supported by lesser nobles, adopted new constitution designed to strengthen Poland against Russian encroachment. Catherine II of Russia, at invitation of greater nobles, invaded, destroyed constitution and divided large areas of Polish territory between Russia and Prussia. Attempt by Kościuszko and lesser nobles to strengthen surviving Polish state (1794) crushed by Russia and Prussia; Poland partitioned and ceased to exist as a separate state.

1791 Haiti Slave rising in western (French) part of island (Saint Domingue) resulted in rise of black leader; Toussaint l'Ouverture; by 1801 had conquered rest of island from Spaniards and secured virtual independence. Island then seized by the French, rising suppressed, and independence not fully secured until 1825.

1793 Sardinia In return for expelling French revolutionary invaders, islanders demanded autonomy within combined kingdom of Piedmont-Sardinia. King reasserted his authority when French threat subsided in 1796.

1798 Ireland Rebellion of United Irishmen seeking independence from England, put down by British army. Suicide of Wolfe Tone.

1804 Serbia Peasant rising against local garrison developed into demand for autonomy within Ottoman Empire. Under Karageorge Serbs fought fiercely for three years before revolt crushed by Turks.

1808 Spain After Napoleon placed his own brother, Joseph, on throne, a peasant rebellion gave assistance to British expeditionary force under Wellington. Middle-class intellectuals proclaimed constitution, but it did not survive restoration of Bourbon king in 1814.

1809 Tyrol After Austria renewed war against Napoleon, the peasants of Tyrol, whose territory had been taken from Austria by Napoleon in 1805 and given to Bavaria, rebelled under Hofer against new rulers. Revolt was crushed by Bavarian and French troops.

1810 Spanish America (See page 96).

1 Revolts and revolutions in Europe and America

— boundaries at 1789   ▉ areas affected by revolution

The second half of the eighteenth century was a time of revolutionary ferment throughout the western hemisphere, from the Volga, where a great peasant insurrection under Pugachev in 1773 took Kazan and threatened Moscow, to Haiti, where the black population rose in rebellion in 1791 under Toussaint l'Ouverture and won control of the island by 1801. The character of the many rebellions of the period (map 1) was varied, but all derived, directly or indirectly, from the Enlightenment, with its assertion of the rights of man, its rationalism and rejection of traditional authority. Paradoxically, it was enlightened rulers, such as Catherine II of Russia (1762–96) and Joseph II of Austria (1780–90), searching for more modern and efficient foundations for government, who gave practical expression to the new ideas, thus provoking the opposition of vested interests, aristocratic and provincial. Provinces like the Austrian Netherlands (1787) and Hungary (1790) rose in rebellion against the centralising policies and reforming edicts of progressive rulers; colonial peoples resisted dictation by the home government and demanded autonomy or

at least no taxation without consent, as in North America in 1775 (page 92) and in South America after 1808 (page 96). The demand for independence was the commonest motive for revolt, and lay behind the risings in Ireland (1798), Corsica (1755, 1793), Sardinia (1793), Spain (1808), Serbia (1804), and the Tyrol (1809). Sometimes they were underpinned by social unrest; but this was exceptional. Serfdom was abolished in Savoy (1771), Austria (1781), Baden (1783) and Denmark (1788), and peasants had more to hope for from reforming monarchs than from nobles who were their oppressors. Hence their failure to support the gentry in the Polish revolts of 1791 and 1794. Revolts against patrician oligarchies occurred in Geneva (1768) and the Netherlands (1784–87); but usually it was only when concerted aristocratic opposition to the monarchy opened the flood-gates that the peasants and the labouring class took a hand. This was what happened in France after 1787.

The immediate cause of the French revolution was the financial crisis arising from the American war (page 86). By

1786 the government was faced with bankruptcy, and after a vain attempt to persuade an Assembly of Notables to tax the privileged classes, Louis XVI was forced by a rebellious aristocracy to summon the Estates-General which had not met since 1614. When the Estates-General turned itself into a National Assembly on June 17, 1789, the revolution had begun, but it was still a middle-class revolution, and the constitution drawn up in 1791 showed their distrust of the masses by limiting the right to vote. But they counted without the workers, exasperated by a serious economic crisis and by fear of counter-revolution. In Paris, a popular rising stormed the Bastille (July 14, 1789); in the provinces peasants burned châteaux and murdered landlords. Matters now proceeded apace (map 2), particularly when Austria and Prussia threatened invasion. This sealed the fate of constitutional monarchy. In 1792 a republic was proclaimed; in 1793 Louis XVI was executed and a Committee of Public Safety set up, first under Danton and then under Robespierre, which instituted a reign of terror against enemies at home, while Carnot mobilised an army

of 770,000 men against enemies abroad.

By 1795 the French armies were victorious and the revolution had spent itself. Spain and Prussia made peace; French troops held Belgium and the left bank of the Rhine, while William V of Holland was deposed and his country turned into a Batavian republic, closely bound to France, forerunner of other similar republics from Naples to Switzerland (map 3). French influence was spreading far and wide, a victory not simply for French arms but for the ideas and achievements of the revolution, equality before the law, the abolition of feudalism, and the 'rights of man' as defined in the famous declaration of October 2, 1789. When French troops entered the Rhineland in 1792 they were welcomed as liberators and 'brothers' by the educated middle classes. Except among the conservative peasantry, who fought the revolution in France itself from 1793 to 1802, the principles of the French revolution had immense appeal; and though their appeal was later dimmed, they lighted a torch which was never extinguished, even during the reaction which set in after 1815.

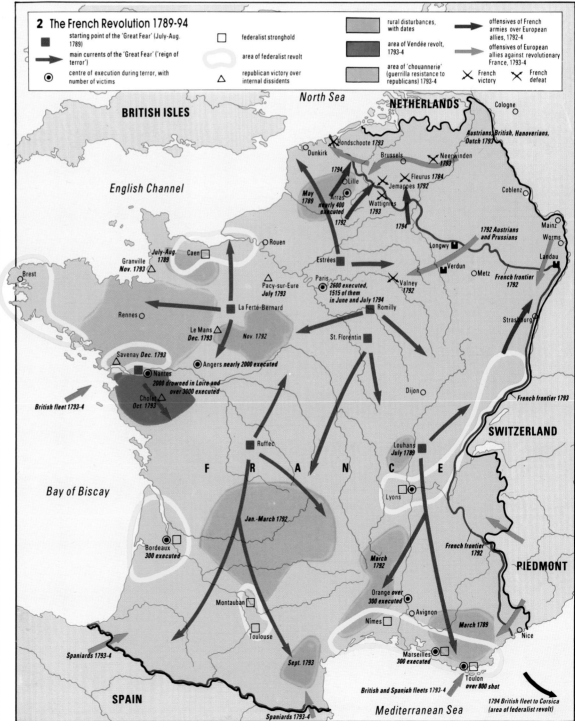

Napoleonic Europe

In 1799 the 31-year-old general Napoleon Bonaparte seized power in France and was to rule until 1814, first as First Consul and then, after 1804, as emperor. His reign was a watershed in the history not only of France but of the whole of Europe. Napoleon had won his reputation by his spectacular victories over Sardinia and Austria in the Italian campaign of 1796; but after 1799, particularly during the Consulate, he proved as brilliant a statesman and administrator as a general. In 1799 Frenchmen, particularly the urban and rural middle classes, wanted peace and security. Napoleon gave them both. The wars were ended by the treaties of Lunéville (1801) and Amiens (1802); for the first time in ten years there was general peace in Europe. At home he gave the citizens who had supported the 'Thermidorian reaction' of 1794 the stability which the Directory (1795–99) had

failed to provide. But he was no reactionary. He made it his task to mould the essential achievements of the revolution into permanent institutions. In 1800 the 83 *départements* into which France had been divided in 1789 were reorganised under prefects responsible to the First Consul. The new civil code of 1804 confirmed the property rights created by the revolution and won him the lasting support of the peasant proprietors who were the backbone of the country. At the same time a career open to talents was provided for men of ability rising through the system of state schools and universities established in 1802.

These achievements outlived Napoleon himself, but peace proved elusive. A durable settlement might have been reached with the continental powers, Prussia and Austria; but the issues between France and England were too deep-seated for compromise, and in 1803 Great Britain declared war on France.

Thereafter war continued almost without interruption until 1815. In essence it was a continuation of the Anglo-French conflict of the eighteenth century (page 86), complicated by the traditional British fear, ever since the French occupation of the Austrian Netherlands in 1792, of a hostile great power on the Scheldt. From that time Great Britain was the moving spirit behind the anti-French coalitions which it kept going, as in the Seven Years' War, by subsidies. France, on the other hand, had not abandoned the hope of recovering the overseas empire lost in 1763. Napoleon's expedition to Egypt (1798–99) was intended to open the back door to India, and there were other plans for recuperating France's position in the Caribbean and on the American mainland. They were foiled by British control of the sea. Nelson's destruction of the French fleet at Aboukir sealed the fate of the Egyptian expedition (map 2), and elsewhere the French navy was no

match for the British, which thwarted French attempts to intervene in Ireland (1797–98) and a projected invasion of England in 1804 (map 3). After Nelson's victory at Trafalgar (1805), British control of the seas was assured, and Napoleon had no alternative except to turn against Britain's continental allies, hoping in this way to seal off Europe and bring Britain to heel by economic pressure.

Napoleon's campaigns against Austria, Prussia and Russia in 1806 and 1807 were brilliantly successful, and 1810 saw him at the peak of his power, directly controlling the whole of western Europe from Catalonia to Lübeck as well as Italy west of the Apennines, with satellite kingdoms and duchies in Spain, the remainder of Italy and Westphalia (map 1). But so long as Britain held out, Napoleon's position was insecure. Control of the sea enabled the British to land an expeditionary force under the future Duke of Wellington in Spain (1808). His attempt to close the continent to British trade led to his breach with Russia. The invasion of Russia (1812) was an act of desperation, a gamble which failed, and after the retreat from Moscow and the battle of Leipzig (1813) Napoleon's fate was sealed. In the reaction which followed much, but not all, of his system perished. In Germany, in particular, the Napoleonic settlements of 1797–98 and 1803 reduced the 234 territories of the old empire to 40 (map 4), and after 1815 there was no going back. Equally important were the institutional changes introduced on the French model. A society based on wealth and merit rather than prescription and privilege was introduced in the Netherlands, the Rhinelands and north-east Italy, and even countries like Prussia reformed to meet the French challenge. The political geography of Europe was rationalised and the modern national state was born, fragile at first but destined to command the future.

4 Napoleonic Germany 1806
— Confederation of the Rhine 1806
1 Württemberg
2 Baden
3 Würzburg
4 Thuringian states
5 Electorate of Hesse
6 Swedish Pomerania
7 Oldenburg
8 Hesse
9 Berg

1 The empire of Napoleon

French territories ruled directly from Paris c.1810

states ruled by members of Napoleon's family c.1810

other dependent states c.1810

British or British occupied territory

✗ French victory   ✗ French defeat

battles of the Italian campaign

battles of the War of the Second Coalition

battles of the War of the Third Coalition

battles in the Austrian War of 1809

battles in the Peninsular War

battles of the Russian campaign

battles of the War of Liberation from French Rule

battles in the defence of France

battles in the War of the 100 Days

The United States
1783-1865

The disputes and difficulties leading to the American War of Independence and the foundation of the United States began almost immediately after the English victory over France and the acquisition of Canada at the Peace of Paris in 1763 (page 86). When the British government reorganised its vastly expanded North American possessions, establishing a huge Indian reserve west of the Alleghenies (1763) and extending the boundaries of Quebec to the Mississippi and Ohio rivers (1774), its measures were bitterly resented by the colonists in New England, Virginia and Pennsylvania as a check to westward expansion. This resentment, combined with resistance to English tax demands and trade controls, was one of the factors behind the revolt of the American colonies. The War of Independence (map 1) began at Lexington and Concord in Massachusetts in April 1775 and was ended, after the British surrender at Yorktown (October 1781), by the Treaty of Versailles (1783), which extended the frontiers of the newly independent United States to the Great Lakes in the north and the Mississippi in the west.

Once independence was achieved, expansion proceeded rapidly. In 1783 the new republic comprised some 800,000 square miles of territory. The purchase of Louisiana from France (1803) more than doubled its extent. Thereafter expansion in the south and west was largely by conquest at the expense of Mexico (map 2), though the Oregon question, finally settled in 1846, looked for a moment as though it might bring war with Great Britain. In the north settlers moved into the 'back country' in increasing numbers after 1800, but it was the arrival of a new wave of European immigrants, predominantly German and Irish, which populated the Midwest. By 1850 the frontier of settlement had reached the 100th meridian, the dividing line between sparse and adequate rainfall.

This vast territorial expansion, which raised the population from approximately 3,000,000 in 1783 to 31,000,000 on the eve of the Civil War, had important political consequences. By 1860 the original 13 states had increased to 34. The result was a deterioration in the relative position of the Southern states with their plantation economy and black slave population, as a result of which the plantation aristocracy saw itself being swamped by the industrialising North and the growing Midwest. This, rather than the simple issue of slavery, was the underlying cause of the American Civil War, but the issues were in fact inseparable because, with over 90 per cent of the black population living in the South (map 3), the moral question was also a regional question. Abraham Lincoln, elected President in 1860 by a northern vote, was right when he said that the nation could not permanently remain 'half-slave and half-free.'

The North fought at first to preserve the Union; but, significantly, it was over the question of whether slavery should be permitted in Kansas and Nebraska that the conflict came to a head. Soon after Lincoln's election South Carolina seceded from the Union and was quickly joined by ten other states (map 4) which came together as the Confederate States of America with their capital at Richmond, Virginia. The course of the war, which opened with an attack on Fort Sumter in April 1861, can be followed on map 5. Northern strategy was to deny the South vital resources by a naval blockade, to gain control of key river routes and forts in the west and to capture the Confederate capital of Richmond. In spite of the preponderance of the North in manpower and resources, the South held out for four years, a fact which heightened the bitterness and resentment during the subsequent period of Reconstruction. The outcome has been called 'the Second American Revolution'; by crippling the Southern ruling class and liberating its labour force, it determined that the thrusting, urban, industrialised North, with its creed of competitive capitalism, would stamp its pattern – for good or ill – on the entire post-bellum United States.

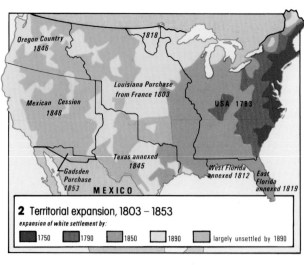

2 Territorial expansion, 1803 – 1853

expansion of white settlement by:

1750   1790   1850   1890   largely unsettled by 1890

1 The American War of Independence, 1775 – 1783

the Thirteen Colonies

Indian Reserve 1763

Quebec 1763-74

Quebec under Quebec Act 1774

other British possessions

Spanish territory

American War of Independence 1775-83:

✕ U.S. victory

✕ British victory

1763 Proclamation Line

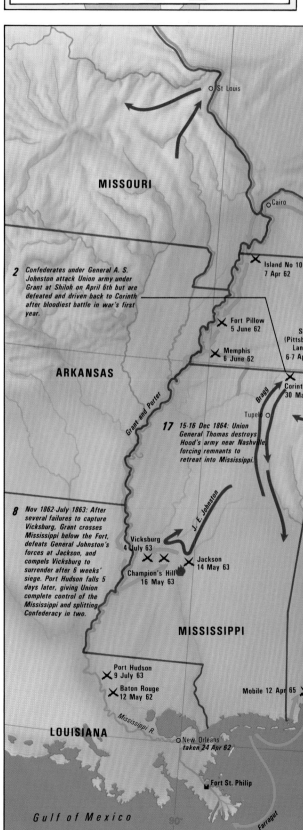

2 Confederates under General A. S. Johnston attack Union army under Grant at Shiloh on April 6th but are defeated and driven back to Corinth after bloodiest battle in war's first year.

17 15-16 Dec 1864: Union General Thomas destroys Hood's army near Nashville forcing remnants to retreat into Mississippi.

8 Nov 1862-July 1863: After several failures to capture Vicksburg, Grant crosses Mississippi below the Fort, defeats General Johnston's forces at Jackson, and compels Vicksburg to surrender after 6 weeks' siege. Port Hudson falls 5 days later, giving Union complete control of the Mississippi and splitting Confederacy in two.

→ Union campaigns   **1-20** chronology of campaigns

→ Confederate campaigns   ✕ major battle, with date

4 Union and Confederate states

- Union states
- Confederate states
- slave states that stayed in the Union

WASHINGTON TERR.

OREGON

territories not yet states

MINNESOTA

WISCONSIN

MICHIGAN

MAINE

VT NH

NEVADA

CALIFORNIA

UTAH TERR.

NEBRASKA TERR.

IOWA

ILLINOIS

INDIANA

OHIO

PENN

NEW YORK

MASS
RI
CONN

NJ
MD DEL

W.VA

NEW MEXICO TERR.

KANSAS

MISSOURI

KENTUCKY

VIRGINIA

NORTH CAROLINA

INDIAN TERR.

ARKANSAS

TENNESSEE

ALABAMA

GEORGIA

SOUTH CAROLINA

TEXAS

LOUISIANA

MISS

FLORIDA

1 Feb-June 1862: Union forces under Generals Grant, Pope and Buell aided by river gunboats seize key points on the Mississippi, Tennessee and Cumberland rivers.

6 Aug-Sept 1862: Lee invades Maryland but is stopped by McClellan at Antietam and retreats to Virginia.

WEST VIRGINIA

5 Mar-June 1862: Confederate General Jackson's brilliant campaigns in Shenandoah Valley keep Union troops from reinforcing McClellan near Richmond.

10 June-July 1863: Lee invades Pennsylvania, suffers defeat by Meade at Gettysburg 1-3 July, retreats into Virginia.

PENNSYLVANIA

○ Pittsburgh   ○ Harrisburg   Philadelphia ○ —40°

○ Gettysburg 1-3 July 63

NEW JERSEY

Antietam 17 Sept 62

Winchester 13-14 June 63   ○ Baltimore

Kernstown 23 Mar 62   MARYLAND

Washington   DELAWARE

Strasburg   1st and 2nd Bull Run (Manassas) 21 July 61 and 29-30 Aug 62

Cedar Mountain 9 Aug 62   Fredericksburg 13 Dec 62

Wilderness 5-6 May 64   Chancellorsville 1-4 May 63

Spotsylvania 8-12 May 64   VIRGINIA

Louisville ○   Frankfort ○

Buell

Bragg   E. K. Smith

KENTUCKY

Perryville 8 Oct 62

14 May 1864-April 1865: In the longest campaign of the war, Grant invades Virginia, fights several indecisive battles with heavy casualties, forces Lee into defensive lines around Richmond and Petersburg.

9 Dec. 1862-May 1863: Union armies under Burnside and Hooker invade Virginia but are repulsed by Lee and Jackson at Fredericksburg and Chancellorsville.

Lynchburg ○   Grant   Richmond burned 3 Apr 65

Appomattox   ○ Petersburg

Bowling Green ○   Cumberland R.

7 Oct 1862: Attempt by Confederate Generals Bragg and Smith to gain control of Kentucky defeated at Perryville, ensuring Union domination of border states.

4 Mar-July 1862: Gen. McClellan's peninsular campaign fails to capture Richmond; Union forces retreat after bloody 7 Days' Battles.

Sheridan   Merrimac and Monitor 9 Mar 62   Fort Monroe

Norfolk 9 May 62

✕ Fort Donelson 16 Feb 62

Fort Henry 6 Feb 62

Nashville 15-16 Dec 64

Tennessee R.

20 26 April 1865: Johnston surrenders to Sherman at Bennett's House, ending war.

Franklin 30 Nov 64

11 Jan-Aug 1863: After drawn Battle of Murfreesboro, Union troops under General Rosecrans force Bragg back to Chattanooga.

Knoxville 2 Sept 63

Murfreesboro 31 Dec 62-2 Jan 63

TENNESSEE

Allegheny Mts

Raleigh 11 Apr 65

19 2-9 April 1865: Lee abandons Richmond and Petersburg; Grant and Sheridan pursue him to Appomattox Courthouse, where he surrenders 9 April.

NORTH CAROLINA

J. E. Johnston

Goldsboro 23 Mar 65

Lookout Mt 24 Nov 63

Chattanooga 25 Nov 63

Chickamauga 19-20 Sept 63

Hood

12 Aug-Nov 1863: Confederates under Bragg evacuate Chattanooga, defeat Rosecrans's advancing forces at Chickamauga, besiege the Unionists in Chattanooga for two months until Federals under Grant break siege and drive Confederates into Georgia.

New Bern ○

Sherman

Fayetteville 12 Mar 65

Sept-Dec 1864: Confederates under Hood invade Tennessee, hoping to cut Sherman's supply lines.

SOUTH CAROLINA

○ Wilmington evacuated 22 Feb 65

Kenesaw Mt 27 June 64

13 May-Sept 1864: Sherman invades Georgia, captures Atlanta after prolonged campaign.

Columbia burned 17 Feb 65

Fort Fisher 15 Jan 65

Atlanta burned 1 Sept 64

Sherman

18 Feb-Mar 1865: Sherman marches northward from Savannah, driving Johnston before him and hoping to catch Lee in a pincers between himself and Grant.

Blockade 1861-5: Union navy blockades 3,500 miles of southern coastline from beginning of war, but not until last 2 years of conflict is blockade effective. By 1865 there are 500 northern ships patrolling southern coast, capturing half the blockade runners trying to get vital supplies to Confederacy.

ALABAMA

○ Macon

Fort Sumter 12-14 Apr 61 bombarded by Confederates

Atlantic Ocean

15 15 Nov-13 Dec 1864: Sherman marches from Atlanta to the sea, destroying Confederate resources.

Savannah evacuated 21 Dec 64

GEORGIA

○ Pensacola

Fort Pickens

FLORIDA

○ Jacksonville

Olustee 20 Feb 64

—30°

April-May 1862: Union ships under Admiral Farragut aided by troops under General Butler capture forts at mouth of the Mississippi, force New Orleans to surrender and gain control of the Mississippi as far north as Port Hudson.

3 Slaves, 1850

- 10% – 30%
- without slaves
- 30% - 50%
- under 10%
- 50% and over

The expansion of the United States
1803-1898

The dominant fact in the history of the United States during the nineteenth century was the opening of the continent. In 1783 the effective frontier of the new Republic was the Allegheny Mountains (page 92). The Louisiana Purchase (1803) opened vast new areas for explorers, led by the famous expedition of Lewis and Clark (1804–8), and for settlers who quickly followed in their wake (map 1). After the Mexican wars (1846–8) and the discovery of gold in California (1848) prospectors, miners, speculators and settlers pushed west across the mountain chains from Salt Lake City and Santa Fe or by the Overland Trail from San Antonio. The great westward movement, bolstered by a confident belief in America's 'manifest destiny', could not, however, proceed without brutal disregard for the native population. The destruction of the North American Indians had begun much earlier in New England in the Pequot war of 1636, and the Delaware Indians were uprooted and driven west before the end of the eighteenth century; but it was in the 1830s, when the land-hunger of the white planters and settlers became insatiable, that the expulsion of whole tribes, Cherokee, Chocktaw, Creek and Chickasaw, and their deportation to the Midwest (and later to Indian reservations) got underway. By 1850 the frontier had reached the 100th meridian, and it was here, in the Midwest and West, that the great battles of the 1860s and 1870s took

place, which reduced the Indian population to scarcely more than 200,000 by the end of the nineteenth century (map 2).

In their place, and usurping their lands, poured in a flood of immigrants, mainly from Europe, which reached its peak in the last decade of the century (diagram 4). In the later phases most of the immigrants (from southern and eastern Europe) remained in the cities on the eastern seaboard, where they swelled the industrial proletariat; but by mid-century Germans and Scandinavians had formed a preponderant element on the farming frontier of Wisconsin, Iowa and Minnesota, and in the last quarter of the century British and Irish settlers, as well as native Americans, played an important part in the development of cattle ranching

and stock raising in Texas, Wyoming and New Mexico. British capital and British land companies also contributed. But the most important area of European investment before 1914 was the financing of American railways, particularly the transcontinental lines. Railroads in operation in 1840 were confined to a few industrial regions in the east. British capital provided the finance to double the mileage between 1866 and 1873 and to carry it west, and this westward shift of transport and population was accompanied by a similar shift of agricultural production (map 3). The effects were dramatic. By 1890, when the rail network was larger than that of the whole of Europe, including the British Isles and Russia, a population moving onto virgin lands, with improved mechanisation, such as the steel plough, new strains of cotton, wheat and maize, and the ubiquitous barbed wire fence, had made the United States the world's leading agricultural producer.

By 1890 the frontier was closed, the prospect of indefinite opportunities within the boundaries of the United States becoming a thing of the past. West of the 100th meridian population was still sparse, and urban and industrial development negligible (page 110); the great upsurge in the colonisation and development of California and the Pacific seaboard was still to come. Nevertheless 1890 marked a turning point, registered in 1898 when the United States, denying its own past refusal to involve itself in other continents, turned from the American continent to the wider world of Asia. In 1898 American history merged into world history, with incalculable consequences for the future.

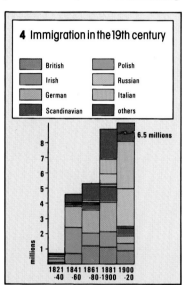

4 Immigration in the 19th century

British	Polish
Irish	Russian
German	Italian
Scandinavian	others

6.5 millions

1821-40, 1841-60, 1861-80, 1881-1900, 1900-20

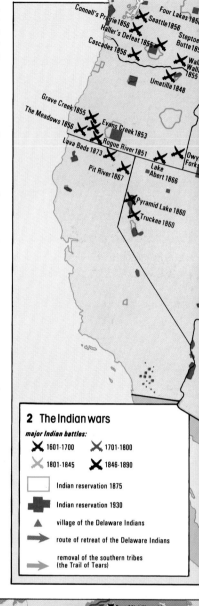

2 The Indian wars

major Indian battles:

✗ 1601-1700   ✗ 1701-1800
✗ 1801-1845   ✗ 1846-1890

▢ Indian reservation 1875

✚ Indian reservation 1930

▲ village of the Delaware Indians

➔ route of retreat of the Delaware Indians

➔ removal of the southern tribes (the Trail of Tears)

1 The opening of the continent

➔ explorers' routes
➔ settlers' routes
▨ cattle trails
○ cow town
➔ fur traders' routes

■ fur station
◣ pass
◣ mining area
⛉ Catholic mission
⛪ Protestant mission

Bear Paw Mountains 1877
Killdeer Mountain 1864
Clearwater 1877
Cedar Creek 1876
Yellowstone 1873
Big Hole 1877
Little Big Horn 1876
Rosebud 1876
Fetterman's Defeat 1868
Slim Buttes 1876
Point of Rocks 1874
Hole-in-the-Wall 1876
Grattan's Defeat 1854
Wounded Knee 1890
Mud Springs 1865
Rush Creek 1865
Ash Hollow 1855
Fort Sedgwick 1865
Milk Creek 1879
Sand Creek 1864
Crooked Creek 1859
Washita 1868
Round Mountain 1861
Chustenahlah 1861
Bird Creek 1861
Fort Gibson
Fort Coffee
Fort Smith
Little Rock
Wichita Village 1858
Fort Towson
Washington
Camden
Monroe
Dove Creek 1863

Big Mound 1863
Stony Lake 1863
Dead Buffalo Lake 1863
Whitestone Hill 1863
Arickara 1823
Acton 1862
Wood Lake 1862
Redwood Ferry 1862
New Ulm 1862
Bad Axe 1832
Stillman's Defeat 1832
Tippecanoe 1811
Springfield
Jonesboro
Batesville
Memphis
Paducah
Nashville
Murfreesboro
Huntsville
Tuscumbia
New Echota
Guntersville
Etowah 1793
Arkansas Post
Montgomery's Point
Talladega 1813
Horseshoe Bend 1814
Fort Mitchell
Montgomery
Vicksburg
Fort Mims 1813
Burnt Corn 1813
Mobile
New Orleans

Bloody Ridge 1763
Detroit 1712, 1763
Fort Dearborn 1812
Haman's Defeat 1790
Fallen Timbers 1794
St Clair's Defeat 1791
Fort Pitt 1763
Fort Ligonier 1763
Bushy Run 1763
Old Chillicothe 1779
Logan's Fort 1777
Bloody Run 1676

CHEROKEE
CHICKASAW
CHOCTAW
CREEK
SEMINOLE

Cherokees 1760
Tomassee 1776
Yamasees 1715
Sharon 1782
Withlacoochee 1835
Swamp 1835
Fort Mellon 1837
Dade Massacre 1835
Lake Okeechobee 1837

Pemaquid 1747
Lovewell's Fight 1725
Sudbury 1676
Bloody Brook 1676
Narragansett Fort 1675
Great Swamp 1637
Pequot Fort 1637
Piscataway Fort 1675
Pamunkey 1624
York River 1676
Tuscararas 1713, 1712

Boston
Albany
Worcester
Plymouth
Hartford
Natick
Providence
New York
Post Road
Great Genesee Road
Philadelphia
Salem
Pennsylvania Road
Baltimore
Washington
Valley Road
Norfolk
Path
Charleston
St Augustine
Atlantic Ocean

3 Railroads and agriculture

railroads in operation in 1840
railroads in operation in 1870
railroads in operation in 1920
leading cotton-growing states in 1840
leading cotton-growing states in 1926
principal wheat and corn (maize) states in 1859
principal wheat and corn (maize) states in 1919

Chicago
New York
Kansas City
San Francisco
New Orleans

Independent Latin America
1808-1910

Napoleon's invasion of Spain and Portugal in 1808 (page 90) enabled their colonies to assert their independence. The revolt began in Argentina in 1810 and Venezuela in 1811, and was later helped by Great Britain and the United States which prevented intervention by the Iberian powers. After the fall of Lima (1821) and Bolívar's victory at Ayacucho (1824) Spain's fate in South America was sealed. In the north, early revolts in Mexico were suppressed, but in 1823 a republic was proclaimed, and a last Spanish attempt at reconquest in 1829 was defeated by Santa Ana. Only Brazil made the transition to nationhood peacefully. Here Portugal agreed to a constitution, and in 1822 the Portuguese king's eldest son became ruler of an independent Brazilian empire, as Pedro I. Only in 1889 when, following the abolition of slavery (1888), disgruntled plantation-owners rose in revolt, was the empire replaced by a federal republic.

Independence essentially was a political movement in the hands of the colonial aristocracy, who wanted a transfer of authority but a minimum of social upheaval. After 1826 the old colonial division between a privileged minority, monopolising land and office, and a barely subsisting mass of peasants, grew sharper. Though the period was rarely without civil strife, the *caudillos*, or military dictators, who dominated the scene during the 50 years following independence, ruled in the interests of the privileged classes, and there was only marginal reform before the Indian, Benito Juárez, took over in Mexico in 1861 (map 1). There were also repeated territorial disputes between the different republics, the fiercest being the War of the Pacific for control of the Atacama Desert nitrate deposits (map 4), to say nothing

of the wars with the United States (page 92) which deprived Mexico of 40 per cent of its territory. Bolívar had plans for an all-encompassing South American Union, but they came to nothing at the Congress of Panama (1826). Instead, such federations as existed (e.g. Great Colombia, 1819-30) quickly fell apart into their constituent elements, usually representing former Spanish administrative units.

For most of the century there was virtually a subsistence economy in most republics. Brazil, with its coffee plantations based on slave labour, was an exception. Elsewhere the *hacendados* treated their estates more or less as self-supporting and self-sufficient, and had little interest in production for the market. Change only came after about 1880 when foreign investment, hitherto modest, increased rapidly (map 3). Even so, it was highly selective, concentrated mainly in Argentina, Brazil, Mexico and Chile. Except in Mexico, where the United States predominated, Britain had the lion's share,

much of it in railways. The stimulus was undoubted, but it also shifted the economy sharply to the export of primary products. Argentina's 'revolution on the pampas' made it a main supplier of grain and meat; Chile was the world's leading producer of nitrates; Brazil exported coffee and rubber, and American food corporations invested heavily in the so-called 'banana republics.' The economic 'take off' also attracted a new wave of European, mainly Italian and Spanish, settlers, notably in Argentina, which greatly altered the population profile (map 2). Urbanisation increased apace, and with it came the beginning of a new urban and industrial proletariat and a middle class growing rich on the export trade. But unbalanced growth also produced new problems. The dictatorship of Porfirio Díaz (1877-1910) brought spectacular economic progress to Mexico, but the mass of the people were left in abject poverty. The result was the Mexican revolution of 1911, the harbinger of a new era in the history of Latin America.

	population	
	1825	1900
Cuba	700,000	1.6 m
Mexico	6.8 m	13.6 m
Guatemala		1.4 m
El Salvador		1.2 m
Honduras		400,000
Nicaragua		400,000
Costa Rica		300,000
Brazil	4.0 m	17.0 m
Colombia	1.3 m	4.1 m
Peru	1.4 m	3.8 m
Venezuela	800,000	2.3 m
Ecuador	550,000	2.0 m
Bolivia	1.1 m	1.7 m
Argentina	630,000	4.7 m
Chile	1.0 m	2.9 m
Uruguay	50,000	800,000
Paraguay	180,000	690,000

2 Population and immigration

UNITED STATES

MEXICO
1828-29

Gulf of Mexico

MEXICO

CENTRAL AMERICA

WEST INDIES

CUBA 1886

slave trade from Africa to Cuba 1822-67 400,000

VENEZUELA 1854

COLOMBIA 1851

ECUADOR 1853

PERU 1854

BRAZIL 1888

PERU AND CHILE

BOLIVIA

CHILE 1823

PARAGUAY

ARGENTINA 1853

URUGUAY

Immigrants to Argentina: country of origin

1857-1924

ITALY

FRANCE

OTHERS

SPAIN

3 Exports and foreign investment

- commodities exported
- major US company
- major UK company

Guggenheim (mining)

tobacco

oil

MEXICO

Standard Oil

sugar

J.P.Morgan (railways)

oil

CUBA

Weetman Pearson (contracting/oil)

oil

United Fruit Company (plantations)

Foreign investment in Mexico (1911) £388 million

USA — UK

GERMANY — FRANCE

HOLLAND

Total British investment in Latin America

ARGENTINA

BRAZIL

CHILE

CUBA

MEXICO

PERU

URUGUAY

OTHER

1913 total £999 million

1890 total £427 million

1880 total £179.5 million

bananas

cacao

ECUADOR

coffee

cacao

tobacco

coffee

VENEZUELA

COLOMBIA

sugar

PERU

copper

guano

silver

tin

BOLIVIA

nitrates

John Thomas North (nitrates)

copper

Antony Gibbs and Sons (finance/trading)

CHILE

wheat

ARGENTINA

cattle

Williamson Balfour (finance/trading)

wool

British railways, public utilities, shipping, land

Liebigs (beef products)

rubber

BRAZIL

cotton

sugar

coffee

British investment in government bonds

PARAGUAY

cattle

URUGUAY

hides

beef

beef

Foreign investment in Latin America (1913) about £2000 million

UK

GERMANY

FRANCE

USA

Foreign investment in Argentina (1913) £650 million

UK

OTHER

USA

GERMANY

FRANCE

1 Political development

- boundary of Mexico 1824
- Mexico 1867
- **1821** date of independent statehood
- Republic of Colombia, 1819-30
- United Provinces of Central America, 1823-38
- later Brazilian acquisitions
- areas affected by Mexican revolution from 1910
- dispute between Ecuador and Peru
- disputed area, Bolivia and Paraguay
- ▽ caudillismo (military dictatorship)
- ○ revolutionary movements
- ◇ constitutionalism
- □ radical reformism
- French territory
- British territory
- Dutch territory
- Spanish territory

CALIFORNIA
UTAH
ceded to USA by Mexico 1848
sold by Texas to USA 1853
UNITED STATES

NEW MEXICO
Texas 1850

San Diego
sold to USA 1850
Rio Grande
TEXAS
independent 1838-45

LOWER CALIFORNIA
SONORA
MEXICO
1821
CHIHUAHUA
COAHUILA
DURANGO
TAMAULIPAS
N
SINALOA
ZACATECAS
S
A
G
Q
H
ME
TT
M
P
O
V
C
TEPIC
JALISCO
COLIMA
MICHOACÁN
GUERRERO
OAXACA
CHIAPAS

Pancho Villa 1914
Santa Ana 1834-55
Madero 1911
Zapata 1910
Morelos 1811-15

Carranza 1913
Ten Years' War 1868-78
Liberal reform 1855-7
War of Reform 1857-60
Benito Juárez 1867-72
Caste war of Yucatán 1848

YUCATÁN
TABASCO
BRITISH HONDURAS
GUATEMALA 1838
HONDURAS 1838
EL SALVADOR 1838
NICARAGUA
COSTA RICA 1838
MOSQUITO COAST 1860 to Nicaragua

BAHAMA IS. (British 1783)

CUBA 1898
US Protectorate

JAMAICA British
REPUBLIC OF HAITI 1804

DOMINICAN REPUBLIC 1844
to Spain 1808-22 to Haiti 1822-44

PUERTO RICO Spanish to USA 1898
VIRGIN IS. (east) British (west) Danish, to USA 1917

ANTIGUA British
GUADELOUPE French
SABA Dutch
MARIE GALANTE French
ST EUSTATIUS Dutch
DOMINICA British
ST CHRISTOPHER British
MARTINIQUE French
NEVIS British
ST LUCIA British
ARUBA Dutch
ST VINCENT British
BARBADOS British
CURAÇAO Dutch
BONAIRE Dutch
GRENADA British
TRINIDAD British

Páez 1830-48
Guzmán Blanco 1870-88

A AGUASCALIENTES
C CAMPECHE
G GUANAJUATO
H HIDALGO
ME MÉXICO
M MORELOS
N NUEVO LEÓN
P PUEBLA
Q QUERÉTARO
S SAN LUIS POTOSÍ
T TLAXCALA
V VERA CRUZ

Cartagena
Maracaibo
Panama
Mompós
Caracas
R.Orinoco
Angostura
VENEZUELA 1830
Georgetown
BRITISH
DUTCH
Cayenne
FRENCH
GUIANA
to Britain 1904

violent constitutionalism

PANAMA 1903
Antioquia
NEW GRANADA 1831
Bogotá
COLOMBIA 1886

Quito
ECUADOR 1803
to Ecuador 1880
Oriente

Guayaquil
García Moreno 1860-75
Iquitos
Tabatinga
to Ecuador 1880

R.Amazon
Manaus
PARÁ
MARANHÃO
CEARÁ
Cabanagem 1835-40
Balaiada 1839
Confederation of Equator 1824
RIO GRANDE DO NORTE
PARAÍBA
PERNAMBUCO
ALAGOAS

RIO NEGRO (later Amazonas)
PIAUÍ

million people
3.0
2.5
2.0
1.5
1.0
0.5

racial profiles 1825:
Whites
Mestizos, Mulattos
Indians
Blacks
1854 date of abolition of slavery
unconquered Indians

Immigrants to Brazil: country of origin
ITALY
OTHERS
SPAIN
PORTUGAL

PERU
to Peru 1902
to Peru 1909
Lima
Callao
Ayacucho
Cuzco
Castilla 1845-62
PERU 1821

BOLIVIA 1825
La Paz
Potosí
MATO GROSSO
Corumbá
GOIÁS
BAHIA
Santa Cruz
Minas Novas
MINAS GERAIS
Diamántina
ESPIRITO SANTO
RIO DE JANEIRO
Rio de Janeiro

EMPIRE OF BRAZIL (kingdom 1815, empire 1822, republic 1889)

slave trade from Africa 1800-55 1.2 million

Puno
L. Titicaca
La Paz
Moquegua
Tacna to Peru 1929
Arica

PERU
BOLIVIA

Chilean gains
Melgarejo 1864-71
GRAN CHACO
Concepción
Ciudad Real
SÃO PAULO
São Paulo
Sabinada 1837
Praieira 1848-9

PARAGUAY 1811
Asunción
SANTA CATERINA
RIO GRANDE DO SUL
Liberal Revolution 1842
Farroupilha Revolution 1835-45

South
Atlantic
Ocean

TARAPACÁ (former Peruvian province)
Iquique
Pozo Almonte
La Central
Atacama Desert

ANTOFAGASTA (former Bolivian province)

Calama

Taltal
Miraflores
CHILE

4 The War of the Pacific, 1879-83
Chilean gains
nitrates

Pacific Ocean

Córdoba
Mendoza
Valparaíso
Santiago
San Luis
Constitución
Rosario
ARGENTINA 1810
San Juan
Montevideo
Rio de la Plata
Buenos Aires

URUGUAY 1828 part of Brazil 1816-28
Battle 1903-15
Rosas 1829-52

aristocratic presidentialism
conservative republic 1862-1910

Valdivia
C H I L E 1818

War of the Desert 1880-81
Patagonia

FALKLAND IS. (ISLAS MALVINAS)
1770-1820 Spanish
1820-33 Argentine
1833 British

The Industrial Revolution in Europe, 1760-1914

The Industrial Revolution, which began in England in the reign of George III (1760–1820), was the catalyst of the modern world. Nevertheless the speed of change should not be exaggerated. Even in continental Europe its impact was limited before 1850 to a few industrial enclaves, and it was not until the last quarter of the nineteenth century – in the case of France, Italy and Russia only after 1890 – that the great surge forward occurred. Outside Europe, with the sole exception of the United States, its impact was delayed for much longer (page 108). Even in Germany 35 per cent of the population was engaged in agriculture in 1895, and most of eastern Europe (Poland, Romania, Bulgaria) and much of southern Europe (Spain, Greece, southern Italy) was virtually untouched by industry. Until 1900, when it began to be challenged by Germany and the United States, the United Kingdom was the workshop of the world, and its industrial strength, which enabled it to dominate world markets, accounts for its pre-eminence in the age of imperialism (page 100).

population of main towns 1801:

London: 959,000
Liverpool: 82,000
Manchester: 77,000
Glasgow: 77,000
Birmingham: 71,000
Bristol: 61,000
Leeds: 53,000
Sheffield: 46,000
Newcastle upon Tyne: 33,000
Hull: 30,000
Nottingham: 29,000
Bradford: 13,000

time taken for fastest mail coach from London to:

Carlisle: 41 hours
Liverpool: 32 hours
Manchester: 28 hours
Great Yarmouth: 21 hours
Birmingham: 16 hours

1 The beginning of the Industrial Revolution: Great Britain, c.1750-1820

population per sq. mile in 1801 (data based on county divisions):

- under 50
- 50 to 100
- 100 to 150
- 150 to 200
- 200 to 260
- 260 to 390
- 390 to 800
- river
- narrow canal
- broad canal

- ○ town connected with water transport system
- □ expanding port
- ○ expanding town
- coalfields
- ▲ iron ore mining
- C copper mining
- lead mining
- tin mining
- salt mining
- slate mining

3 The economic unification of Germany, 1828-88

- Prussian Customs Union 1828
- Deutscher Zollverein (German Customs Union) 1834
- New Zollverein 1867
- additions to 1888

Many factors account for the precedence of Great Britain. It was not only that it was well endowed with coal, iron, and other basic materials; so were many other countries. It was also spared the ravaging effects of warfare on its own soil, unlike most of continental Europe during the revolutionary and Napoleonic wars (pages 88, 90). Unlike France and Germany, where markets and trade were limited by a multiplicity of customs barriers and internal and external frontiers, Great Britain after the union of England and Scotland in 1707 was a single economic unit, where men and goods moved freely. It also enjoyed an advantageous position in Atlantic trade, from which capital flowed into industry. In an age of sailing ships, ports like Liverpool, Glasgow and Bristol had obvious advantages over Hamburg and Bremen. The English social structure was also favourable. In contrast to continental Europe, where most peasants were still tied to the soil (page 82), the early disappearance of serfdom in England meant that the surplus labour released by the enclosure of common land during the eighteenth century could move, without legal obstacles, to the growing industrial centres. Finally, England had a unique network of navigable rivers and canals (map 1), which was of inestimable importance before the railway age for moving both raw materials and finished goods.

In its earliest phase English manufacture had relied on water power; hence the location of the early cotton and woollen mills on the slopes of the Pennines. But essentially the Industrial Revolution, in the century to 1870, was a revolution of coal and iron. Its basis was the application of steam power to machinery, and a series of technical innovations – Watt's rotative engine (1782) and Cartwright's power loom (1792) among others – quickly demonstrated the superiority of steam-power driven machines. In continental Europe, apart from Belgium, where industrialisation proceeded rapidly after 1820, the use of steam power came more slowly. The famous German steel firm of Krupp, later to be a giant of German industry, was founded in 1810 in green fields outside Essen, where a stream provided water power; it had only 7 employees in 1826 and 122 in 1846. Here, and elsewhere, large-scale industry was held back by political fragmentation, lack of capital, and, above all, by poor communications, which severely limited markets. What changed this, above all else, was railway development, beginning in the 1830s. By 1860 the railway networks of Britain, Belgium and Germany were virtually complete, although in Austria-Hungary and Russia large-scale construction was only beginning (map 2). With their demand for rails, sleepers, engines and carriages, railways also provided immense impetus to heavy industry. A second factor was the dismantling of obstructions to trade. In France internal tariffs had been demolished in 1790 as part of the revolutionary reorganisation. In 1818 Prussia followed suit, setting up free trade between its provinces, followed by a Prussian Customs Union (1828) including other smaller

German territories, and finally (1834) the German Customs Union, or *Zollverein*, comprising 17 states and some 26 million people (map 3). Here was a solid basis for the development of German industry.

A new period, sometimes called the Second Industrial Revolution, opened after 1870. The new German Empire, founded in 1871, was in the forefront. Coal and iron were still basic, and here Germany forged ahead, increasing its coal output from 38 million tons in 1871 to 279 million tons in 1913 and its iron output from 1.5 million tons to 15 million tons. But it was in the new branches of industry – steel, electricity and chemicals – that Germany outpaced all other nations. German steel production leapt from 1.5 million tons in 1880 to over 13 million tons in 1910, by which time Krupps was employing 70,000 men. Steel, electricity and chemicals were the index of the new industrial society, and at a time of growing international tension (page 116) Germany's headstart was bound to produce a defensive reaction among its rivals. The intensive industrialisation which occurred in France after 1895 and in northern Italy after 1905 represented a deliberate national effort not to be left behind. The same was true of the great upsurge of Russian industry after 1890, particularly the massive development of the iron and steel industry of the Donets basin (page 84). By now much of heavy industry was keyed to armaments. Industrialisation had changed the face of Europe by 1914; but it had also made it more dangerous and more explosive.

2 The Industrial Revolution in Europe, 1860-1914

- areas of industrial concentration 1870-1914
- centres of textile industry
- centres of chemical industry
- centres of shipbuilding industry
- coalfields
- centres of engineering, armaments and metal industries
- iron ore fields
- lignite fields
- potash fields
- centres of petroleum industry
- European railway network 1870 (largely complete)
- railway development 1870-1914
- canals

European imperialism
1815-1914

Between 1815 and 1914, under the impact of the Industrial Revolution, the character of European imperialism changed. Earlier the motivating force had been the search for the riches of the Orient, and the European stake in Asia and Africa was confined to trading stations and the strategic outposts necessary to protect the trade. In 1815, with the important exception of India, this was still the situation. But in the nineteenth century two new factors came into play. The first was the enforced opening of the world – Turkey and Egypt (1838), Persia (1841), China (1842), even Japan (1858) – to European, particularly British, commerce; in short, the breaking down of barriers to European penetration. The second, setting in around 1880, when a new phase of the Industrial Revolution got under way (page 98), was the search for the raw materials without which industry, in its new form, could not exist. Tin and rubber from Malaya, nickel from Canada, copper from Australia and South America were now the sinews of European industry; and so the scramble for natural resources began, providing a new impetus for colonial expansion. Between 1880 and 1914 Europe added over 8½ million square miles, or one-fifth of the land area of the globe, to its overseas colonial possessions.

Nevertheless no clear line divides the period before and the period after 1880. Criticism of imperialism was certainly strong in the first half of the century. Free traders of the so-called 'Manchester School' argued cogently that empire was unnecessary, even detrimental,

to commerce, and the burgeoning trade with the ex-colonial countries of North and South America seemed to prove their point. Nevertheless imperial expansion was continuous after 1815. Both Great Britain and France – particularly France, which had lost its first empire in 1815 and was determined to constitute a new empire – steadily advanced (map 1). The French conquered Algeria in the 1830s, annexed Tahiti and the Marquesas in the 1840s, expanded their colony in Senegal in the 1850s, and began the conquest of Indo-China in 1859. Great Britain, which had retained the Cape of Good Hope, the maritime provinces of Ceylon and other strategically important footholds (Malta, Mauritius, the Seychelles) in 1815, also continued to expand. Fearing a French challenge, it claimed sovereignty over Australia and New Zealand (page 112). It built up its power in India (page 104), acquired Singapore (1819), Malacca (1824), Hong Kong (1842), Natal (1843), Lower Burma (1852) and Lagos (1861). Many of these acquisitions were defensive reactions against France; most were intended to secure its position in India which, with its army of 150–200,000, made Britain the strongest territorial power in the east. Even so, except for India, imperialism still only touched the outer fringes of Asia and Africa. Even the Russian empire, which by 1886 was to engross much of central Asia (page 84), still only affected the periphery.

After 1880 a fundamental change came about. Its causes were partly economic, but still more important were the rivalries of the European powers, each of which feared that its competitors would steal a march on it. Comparison of maps 1 and 2 points out the difference. Even as late as 1870 colonial penetration was

marginal. By 1914 the European powers had engrossed nine-tenths of Africa and a large part of Asia. Between 1871 and 1914 the French empire grew by nearly 4 million square miles and 47 million people, mainly in north and west Africa and Indo-China, but also in the Pacific islands and Madagascar. But a significant factor was the entry of new claimants, particularly Germany and Italy, challenging the old imperial powers. Germany acquired an empire of 1 million square miles and 14 million colonial subjects in South-West Africa, Togoland, the Cameroons, Tanganyika and the Pacific Islands. Italy obtained Tripoli and Libya, Eritrea and Italian Somaliland, but failed in 1896 to conquer Abyssinia. But the greatest gains of all were made by Great Britain, which secured control over Nigeria, Kenya, Uganda, Northern and Southern Rhodesia, Egypt and the Sudan, as well as areas in the Pacific including Fiji and parts of Borneo and New Guinea. The keystone of the British empire was India, and its acquisitions were made with a view to bolstering British control over access to India and the Indian Ocean via the Suez Canal and East Africa, but also via Singapore and the south Pacific (map 3). So long as it was assured of control of the Indian Ocean, the British imperial position was secure.

In retrospect, the fragility of the European empires so hastily assembled between 1884 and 1914, is obvious. None of the imperial powers had the resources to govern them adequately. European imperialism was more ephemeral than anyone, at the close of the nineteenth century, could have believed; and yet it left an indelible impression on the peoples of Asia and Africa, propelling them willingly or unwillingly into the twentieth century.

3 British control of the Indian Ocean
— British controlled sea routes
▨ British controlled territory

Nineteenth century Africa

Although European exploration began in the eighteenth century (map 1), its impact on Africa was limited until after 1870, except in the far south where Dutch settlers, or Boers, in Cape Colony, who had been brought under British rule in 1806, moved north in the Great Trek (1835) in search of land and freedom, and founded settlements which eventually became the republics of the Orange Free State and Transvaal (map 2). The only other area of European settlement was Algeria, conquered by France between 1830 and 1847 after fierce resistance under Abd al Kadir. Nevertheless this was a period of great change and instability in Africa. In the north-east the dominating fact was the advance of Egypt under Mohammed Ali, who conquered northern Sudan in 1820, founded Khartoum as its capital in 1830, and inaugurated the attempt to build a great Egyptian empire reaching the length of the Nile and east to the Horn of Africa. In the north-west a great Muslim religious revival, beginning around 1804 under Uthman dan Fodio, carried the Fulani south into Hausaland, where they founded the Sultanate of Sokoto. Later, another empire was carved out further west, between the Ivory Coast and the Upper Niger, by a Mandingo Muslim leader, Samory. In the south, the outstanding event was the rise of the Zulus, which resulted in a great political and demographic revolution (the so-called *Mfecane* or 'time of troubles'), as the local tribes were driven west and north into Rhodesia, Malawi and Zambia.

This was the situation when the European 'scramble for Africa' got under way after 1882 (page 100), and the countries named above were leaders of African resistance (map 3). The Zulus, hard pressed between British and Boers after the British annexation of Natal (1845), held out fiercely until the war of 1879–81, when their country was annexed (map 2). Resistance elsewhere was

equally strong. Samory was only defeated by the French in 1898; Sokoto only fell to the British in 1903. In the north the British established a *de facto* protectorate over a bankrupt Egypt after 1882 (turned into a full-scale protectorate in 1914); but they were only able to secure control of the Sudan in 1898 after the slaughter of some 20,000 Sudanese. Nowhere was occupation unchallenged, as the great Herero and Maji-Maji revolts of 1904–6 against German colonialism showed. But the only lasting success was the Ethiopian defeat of Italy at Adowa in 1896. Morocco kept a precarious independence until 1912 before being divided between France and Spain, and Libya and Cyrenaica were occupied by Italy in the same year. By 1914 the European powers were in full control (map 5). Apart from Ethiopia, only Liberia could claim independence.

The position of the Boer republics in the south was different. Transvaal also had been annexed by Great Britain in 1877 and then restored to independence in 1881. But the discovery of diamonds at Kimberley and of gold on the Witwatersrand (1886) sealed their fate. The entry of foreign speculators (*Uitlanders*) sparked Boer hostility, and when an attempt by Cecil Rhodes (Prime Minister of Cape Colony, 1890–96) to stage a take-over failed dismally (Jameson Raid, 1895), the outcome was the Boer War (1899–1902), in which, after initial Boer successes, ruthless British suppression forced the Boers to capitulate (map 4). Nevertheless the Afrikaners secured favourable terms after the Peace of Vereeniging (May 31, 1902), including the use of their own language and the exclusion of blacks from the franchise, and this compromise made possible the formation (1910) of the Union of South Africa as a dominion of the British Commonwealth. It was nevertheless a betrayal of black Africans by Britain which led step by step to the policy of *Apartheid* (1948) and to the radical conflicts which bedevilled South Africa after the rest of the continent had won its independence.

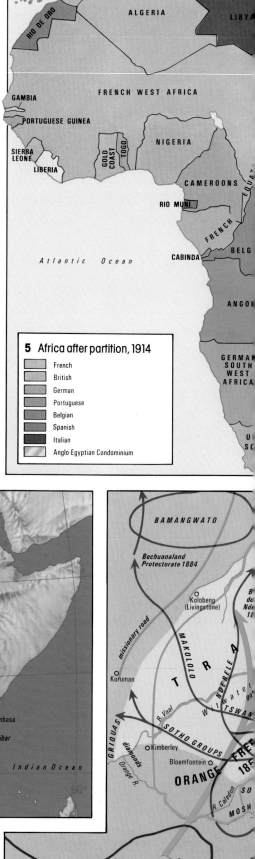

5 Africa after partition, 1914

- French
- British
- German
- Portuguese
- Belgian
- Spanish
- Italian
- Anglo-Egyptian Condominium

1 European exploration in Africa 1769-1887

- Bruce 1769-72
- Mungo Park 1795-97
- Mungo Park 1805-06
- Mollien 1818
- Clapperton 1822-27
- René Caillié 1828
- Livingstone 1841-56
- Barth 1850-56
- du Chaillu 1855-65
- Burton and Speke 1857-59
- Livingstone 1858-64
- Livingstone 1866-73
- Nachtigal 1869-74
- Stanley 1871-72
- Stanley 1874-77
- Brazza 1875-79
- Wissmann 1880-87

EGYPT
(toman dominion er British control 1882)

NGLO-EGYPTIAN **SUDAN**

ERITREA

FRENCH SOMALILAND
BRITISH SOMALILAND

ETHIOPIA

UGANDA

ITALIAN SOMALILAND

BRITISH EAST AFRICA (KENYA)

Indian Ocean

NGO

GERMAN EAST AFRICA

RHODESIA

NYASALAND

NORTHERN RHODESIA

MOZAMBIQUE

SOUTHERN RHODESIA

MADAGASCAR

RICA

SWAZILAND

HU-
LAND

BASUTOLAND

RICA

4 The Boer War and the Union of South Africa, 1899-1910

BECHUANALAND

GERMAN SOUTH-WEST AFRICA
(Protectorate 1884)

R. Limpopo

SOUTH AFRICAN REPUBLIC (TRANSVAAL)

Kamati Poort

Pretoria *Diamond Hill* June 1900
June 1900
Rustenburg
Mafeking besieged Oct.1899-May 1900
Johannesburg *May1900*
Belfast *Aug. 1900*
Barberton
Lourenço Marques
SWAZILAND *(British Protectorate 1907)*

BRITISH BECHUANALAND *annexed 1885: to Cape Colony 1895*
Vereeniging *peace signed May 31, 1902*
Standerton
Vryburg
R. Vaal
ORANGE FREE STATE
Kroonstad
N A T A L *Crown Colony 1856 incorporating Zululand 1897*

GRIQUALAND WEST *to Cape Colony 1880*
Dundee
Kimberley *Dec. 11, 1899*
Paardeberg *Feb. 1900*
Bloemfontein *March 1900*
Ladysmith *besieged Nov. 1899-Feb. 1900*
Magersfontein *Dec. 1899*
Spion Kop *Jan. 1900*
Colenso *Dec. 1899*
Pietermaritzburg
Wepener
Indian Ocean
Durban

Atlantic Ocean
Springfontein
Orange R.
BASUTOLAND *(British Protectorate 1884)*

De Aar
Coleberg
Middelburg
Stormberg *Dec. 10, 1899*

CAPE COLONY
Great Fish R.
Graaff Reinet
East London

Cape Town
Port Elizabeth

→ Boer offensives Oct.1899-Feb. 1900
✕ Boer victories
→ British offensives Feb.1900-May 1902
✕ British victories
— boundary of Union of South Africa 1910

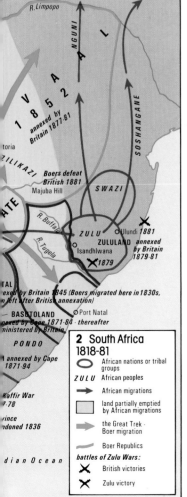

R. Limpopo

NGUNI

V
A
L
1
8
5
2
annexed by Britain 1877-81

SOSHANGANE

ZILIKAZI

Boers defeat British 1881 Majuba Hill

SWAZI

R. Buffalo
ZULU
R. Tugela
ZULULAND *annexed by Britain 1879-81*
Isandhlwana ✕ *1879*
Ulundi *1881*

TAL
exed by Britain 1845 (Boers migrated here in 1830s, n left after British annexation)

BASUTOLAND *oxed by Cape 1871-84 - thereafter ministered by Britain*

Port Natal

PONDO
n annexed by Cape 1871-94

Indian Ocean

Kaffir War
-78
vince ndoned 1836

2 South Africa 1818-81
○ African nations or tribal groups
ZULU African peoples
→ African migrations
▨ land partially emptied by African migrations
→ the Great Trek - Boer migration
⟶ Boer Republics
battles of Zulu Wars:
✕ British victories
✕ Zulu victory

3 European penetration after 1880

Tangier
International Zone 1923
Fez ★
MOROCCO 1912 *French protectorate*
Marrakesh
Agadir
Algiers 1830 *(French occupation)*
Tunis
ALGERIA 1870 ★
TUNIS
TRIPOLITANIA
Tripoli 1911
Benghazi 1912
Alexandria
CYRENAICA ★
Cairo ★
Mediterranean Sea

Canary Islands
SPANISH SAHARA 1912
RIO DE ORO *1885*
In Salah 1901 *(French)*
Atlas Mts
L I B Y A
FEZZAN
EGYPT
ARABIA
Sahara Desert
Red Sea

Taoudenni 1906 *(French occupation)*
Tamanrasset 1902 *(French)*
S   u   d   a   n
Bilma
SUDAN *Sudan – Anglo-Egyptian Condominium established 1899*
Massawa
Aden (British)

St. Louis
R. Senegal
Dakar
SENEGAL
Kayes
FRENCH SUDAN
Timbuktu 1894
Gao
R. Niger
Agadès
NIGER
Zinder 1899
Mahdist State in the Sudan 1881/98
Omdurman ★ Khartoum
Adowa 1896 ★
Italian invasion defeated
ITALIAN SOMALILAND 1889-1892

Empire of Ahadu Sefu (son of al-Hajj Umar)
GAMBIA
Bamako 1883
Ségou ★
Sokoto 1903 *(British)*
Say 1896
Lake Chad
Fort Lamy
RABIH'S DOMAIN ★
Fashoda 1898 (British)
ETHIOPIA
SHOA ★ Addis Ababa
Berbera 1892

FOUTA DJALLON 1887-96
UPPER VOLTA
Ouagadougou 1896
NIGERIA
Kano 1902
Zaria
SOKOTO
Northern Nigeria occupied by Royal Niger Company
Ethiopian expansion under Emperor Menelik

Conakry
FRENCH GUINEA
Samory's Empire
Nikki 1894
ILORIN
NUPE
Lokoja 1885
Gondokoro
SIDAMA KINGDOMS

Freetown
SIERRA LEONE
Monrovia
LIBERIA
Kumasi 1896
TOGO
DAHOMEY
Ibadan
YORUBA
Lagos
CAMEROONS
UGANDA 1893
Lake Victoria
Kampala 1890
BRITISH EAST AFRICA KENYA
Mogadishu ★

IVORY COAST 1891
GOLD COAST 1874
Accra
Fernando Po *(Spanish)*
Douala 1884
Principe *(Portuguese)*
São Tomé *(Portuguese)*
RIO MUNI GABON
FRENCH CONGO
CONGO FREE STATE *King Leopold's Congo Free State (became Belgian Congo in 1908)*
Imperial British East African Company
Nairobi ★
Mombasa

Atlantic Ocean
Cabinda
R. Congo
TIPPU TIB'S DOMAIN ★
Lake Tanganyika
GERMAN EAST AFRICA
Zanzibar (British 1890)
Dar es Salaam 1885 *(German occupation)*

Luanda
ANGOLA
Benguela
Moçamedes
KATANGA ★
NORTHERN RHODESIA
Lake Nyasa
BRITISH CENTRAL AFRICA (Nyasaland) Protectorate 1891
Zomba
Mozambique
Indian Ocean

Swakopmund
GERMAN SOUTH WEST AFRICA
Walvis Bay (British) 1878
Lüderitz
Orange R.
BRITISH BECHUANALAND
SOUTHERN RHODESIA
Salisbury ★
Rhodes' British South Africa Company 'Pioneer Column' 1890
Beira
R. Zambezi
MOZAMBIQUE
Quelimane
MADAGASCAR *Merina Kingdom*
Tamatave
Tananarive

TRANSVAAL
Pretoria
Johannesburg
Delagoa Bay
ORANGE FREE STATE
NATAL
Kimberley
CAPE COLONY
Cape Town
Port Elizabeth
East London
Durban

— French colonies or settlements 1880
→ French penetration
— British colonies or settlements 1880
→ British penetration
— Portuguese colonies or settlements 1880
→ Portuguese penetration
→ German penetration
→ Italian penetration
→ Spanish penetration
→ Belgian penetration
★ anti-colonial resistance

India under British rule, 1805-1947

By 1805 the hegemony of the English East India Company in the Indian sub-continent was an established fact. With the conquest of Sind (1843) and the Sikh kingdom of the Punjab (1849) its dominion became co-terminous with the country's natural frontier in the north-west, while in the north a war with Nepal (1814–16) extended it to the Himalayan foothills (map 1). To the east the British clashed with the Burmese empire and in 1826 and 1852 annexed most of its territories, including Assam. Upper Burma itself was brought under British rule in 1886 (map 2). Within India Dalhousie's Doctrine of Lapse led to the absorption of several small kingdoms in central India, and in 1856 the kingdom of Oudh was annexed following charges of 'misgovernment'. Not surprisingly, this policy provoked disaffection which found a violent outlet in the rebellion of 1857. Beginning as a mutiny of the Company's Indian sepoys, the revolt soon involved princes, landlords and peasants throughout northern India, but the loyalty of the Sikhs and the passivity of southern India enabled the British to crush it after fourteen months of bitter fighting.

The mutiny was a watershed in the history of British India. It discredited the Company and in 1858 the British government assumed direct control, though the autonomy of the Indian princes was respected. The impetus to economic development was immediate. First-class roads were built, totalling 57,000 miles by 1927, but it was the railways which made possible the exploitation of raw materials and the profitable introduction of export crops, such as tea. Between 1869 and 1929 India's foreign trade increased sevenfold. How far this benefited the rural masses is a moot question; but modern industries brought into existence an Indian entrepreneurial class. After 1919, when protective tariffs were introduced, industrial expansion made further progress (map 3).

With the rise of a new middle class, partly through industry but more through the recruitment of educated Indians into the colonial administration, came a reawakened political consciousness. The Indian National Congress (1885) accepted British rule, though in 1905 there were periodic outbreaks of terrorist violence. But it was only after 1919 that Congress, under Gandhi's leadership, fought actively for Home Rule and, after 1929, for independence (map 4). Gandhi's civil disobedience campaigns galvanised the Indian masses; but Congress's claim to represent all Indians, Hindu and Muslim alike, alienated the Muslim minority and led to conflicts which resulted in 1947 in partition (map 5). Faced by mounting unrest and the naval mutiny of 1946, the Labour government in Britain realised that a transfer of power could not be delayed; but in 1946–7 the gradual breakdown of law and order, including communal riots, forced its hand. Plans for partition were hastily drawn up. But the boundary award in Kashmir, Punjab and Bengal resulted in large-scale disturbances in which some 500,000 lost their lives and many millions became refugees, leaving a tense situation which erupted in wars between India and Pakistan (1965, '71) and separatist violence in Kashmir since 1977.

1 India, 1805-57

- territory under British rule in 1805
- boundary of Ranjit Singh of Lahore's territories 1835
- territory under British rule at close of Lord Dalhousie's administration 1856
- main area affected by Indian mutiny 1857
- ○ main centres of rebellion

2 The annexation of Burma, 1826-86

- British India 1826
- area annexed by British 1826
- area annexed by British 1852
- area annexed by British 1886, pacified by 1890-1915
- — boundary of modern Burma

India's Road to Independence (right)
1885 creation of Indian National Congress
1906 Muslim League formed
1915 Gandhi returns to India. Following death of Gokhale (1915) and Tilak (1920) emerges as leader of Congress
1916 Lucknow Pact: Congress and Muslim League agree to co-operate in demand for home rule (*swaraj*)
1917 Montagu Declaration: Britain's goal is 'responsible government for India as an integral part of the British Empire.' But
1919 Government of India Act: some Indian ministers, but central admin. and power in British hands
1919 Amritsar Massacre: troops fire on demonstrators and kill 379 Indians
1920 Khilafat Committee of Hindus and Muslims adopts Gandhi's programme of peaceful non-cooperation (*satyagraha*)
1920 First Civil Disobedience campaign
1922 after violence at Chauri Chaura and Moplah rising in South India
1922–29 Gandhi (in prison 1922–24) withdraws from active politics
1928 Revival of political activity; rise of Jawaharlal Nehru (President of Lahore Congress, 1929). Widening rift between Congress and Muslim League
1929 Lahore Congress demands immediate independence
1930 Gandhi's march to the sea opens Second Civil Disobedience campaign, 90,000 arrests
1930–32 Round Table Conference breaks down over question of separate electorates for Muslims, Sikhs and Untouchables
1935 Government of India Act. Denounced by Nehru as 'satanic', but main provisions accepted by Bombay Congress which agrees to participate in provincial elections
1937 Congress wins 8 out of 11 provinces in elections, but Muslim opinion alienated
1938 Jinnah reorganises Muslim League
1939 resignation of Congress ministries after Viceroy declares war without consulting Indian leaders
1940 Lahore resolution of Muslim League in favour of independent Pakistan
1942 Congress rejects British offer of Dominion Status after war. Gandhi launches 'Quit India' campaign. 'August Revolt' suppressed and Congress leaders imprisoned
1946 Second British Cabinet Mission fails. Communal violence in Calcutta, E. Bengal, Bihar and Punjab; half-million deaths
1947 partition and independence

4 The Indian Nationalist Movement, 1915-47

- British India and Ceylon
- Princely States

China under the Ch'ing Dynasty, 1644-1911

A new era in Chinese history opened in 1644 when the Ming dynasty, beset for a century by Mongol invasions, Japanese raids and civil war, was displaced by a line of foreign, Manchurian, emperors which ruled China until 1911. The Ch'ing, or Manchu, dynasty was resisted in south China for half a century but it quickly established good relations with the dominant Chinese gentry (*shen-chin*) and with its support began a successful policy of territorial expansion which went on until late in the eighteenth century (map 1).

At the same time there was a great economic upsurge (map 2) and a huge increase in population, from 100 million in 1650 to 300 million in 1820 and 420 million in 1850. There was also a considerable export trade in tea, silk and porcelain with the West from Canton and with Russia from Kyakhta. But the financial strain of the wars of expansion and the pressure of the growing population on the land imposed hardships which led to recurrent unrest and revolts, not only among the minority peoples who were harshly exploited by Chinese and Manchus alike, but also in the heart of China itself. Of these the most serious was the White Lotus rebellion between 1795 and 1804. Meanwhile the export surplus was converted after 1825 into a net outflow as a result of the opium trade. Manchu China was still the world's largest and most populous empire. But its growing economic difficulties, coupled with the failure to expand the administration to match the rapid growth of population, and the pressures of the Western powers, seeking to open the China market for their manufactures, resulted in a crisis which came to a head after Chinese attempts to halt the illicit opium trade were decisively defeated by the British in the Opium War of 1839-42.

The Opium War had two major consequences. First, it resulted in the cession of Hong Kong to the British and in the opening of the first five Treaty Ports (their number was thereafter steadily in-creased) in which foreigners enjoyed extra-territorial rights. Secondly, it weakened imperial authority and led to the great Taiping rebellion (1850-64), the most serious but only one of many rebellions which shook Manchu power to its foundations (map 3). The Taiping and Nien rebellions alone left 25 million dead and vast areas, including the wealthy region around Nanking, were devastated. They also convinced the Western powers that Ch'ing China was on the point of collapse and inaugurated a scramble for concessions (map 4).

The response of the Manchu court and bureaucracy was hesitant and half-hearted, more intent on maintaining traditional institutions and Confucian values than on modernisation. Foreign powers had taken advantage of the situation: the British and French occupied Peking in 1856 and forced open more treaty ports, the Russians occupied the Amur region in 1858 and the Maritime Province in 1860 and China was defeated by France in a war over Indo-China in 1884-85. But it was the overwhelming success of Japan in the war of 1894-95 that convinced a section of the Chinese intelligentsia that only a break with the past could save China, and they secured the support of the young emperor Kuang-su. But the reform movement of 1898 was defeated by the dowager empress Tzu-hsi whose reaction was to turn the popular discontent against the foreigners. The result was the Boxer Rising of 1900, an outburst of xenophobia savagely suppressed by the Western powers, who imposed a heavy indemnity and wrung still further concessions from China. By now even the imperial government realised that modernisation was imperative; but, in spite of a number of reforms, its attitude was still essentially conservative. Convinced that the imperial government was the main obstacle to change, revolutionary groups sprang up everywhere after 1901, and when in 1911 a small-scale army mutiny broke out in Wuchang, disaffection spread throughout the whole country (page 122). The imperial government fell, almost without fighting; but China had still to undergo more than forty years of tribulation before it finally made the transition to the modern world.

2 17th century trade

main manufacturing and trading areas, 16th and 17th centuries

major trade routes with principal trade commodities (*grain*)

▲ iron ■ gold
☑ silver C copper
▬ lead ▬ tin
M mercury
⬛ silk textiles
⬛ cotton textiles

☞ paper ● coal
◆ tea ■ salt
⬚ sugar
▼ iron utensils
⬡ ceramics (porcelain)

1 Imperial expansion, 1644-1760

Manchu expansion
Phase 1: China

Manchu homeland

expansion before 1644

expansion 1644-59

1644 date of incorporation

Phase 2: New Territories

1724 date of incorporation

tributary states:

before 1644

after 1644

⊗ seat of main Lamaistic patriarch

★ risings of non-Chinese peoples

sectarian risings of Chinese

■ official centre of foreign commerce

➤ military expeditions

border of China under the Ch'ing dynasty, at its greatest extent c.1760

Map 1 (left panel):

furs, gold, ginseng

Peking

SHANTUNG

Lintsing

Tsining

Sian

Hwaian

raw cotton, grain

Grand Canal/Yün Ho

Nanking

Yangchow

Soochow

Hangchow

HUPEH AND HUNAN

copper

R. Yangtze

C

Changsha

Nanchang

tea, porcelain, silk, cotton

FUKIEN

...EICHOW

KWANGSI

limited Dutch trade

Amoy

Canton

KWANGTUNG

overseas trade with West
tea, silk, fine cottons,
porcelain, lacquer

Map 3 Rebellions and foreign attacks 1840-1901

Legend:
- Taiping control early period 1853-7
- Taiping control late period 1857-63
- routes of Taiping rebels
- other areas of rebellion (named on map)
- British attacks
- French attacks

NORTH-WESTERN MUSLIM RISING 1862-73

JEHOL

FENGTIEN

KAN SU

Lanchow

SHANSI

SHENSI

Peking

Tientsin

CHIHLI Boxer uprising 1900-01

principal area affected by Boxer uprising 1900-1901

mouth of Yellow River after 1855

Nien invasion 1868

SHANTUNG

Taiping northern expedition 1853-54

Grand Canal

Nien rebels 1853-68

main Nien centre

Kaifeng

HONAN

mouth of Yellow River to 1853

Anglo-French campaigns 1858-60

KIANGSU

Yangchow

Chinkiang

Nanking Taiping capital

Shanghai

Sungkiang

SZECHWAN

HUPEH

R. Yangtze

Hankow

ANHWEI

route of Taiping advance to Szechwan 1856-63

Hangchow

Ningpo

CHEKIANG

Taiping advance 1850-53

KIANGSI

YUNNAN

Yunnanfu Yunnan Muslim rebellion 1855-73

KWEICHOW
Kweichow Miao tribal rising 1854-72

HUNAN

Opium War 1839-42

FUKIEN

Foochow

KWANGSI

Amoy

Tamsui

Chinese attacks during Sino-French war 1883-85

Chintien

outbreak of Taiping rebellion 1850

Hakka-Cantonese war 1855-57

Canton

KWANGTUNG

Hong Kong

Hanoi

Sino-French war 1883-85

Map 4 The dismemberment of the Chinese Empire, 1842-1911

RUSSIAN EMPIRE

Russian protectorate 1912

TANNU TUVA

Manchouli

MARITIME PROVINCE

to Russia 1858

Aigun

R. Amur

MONGOLIA

autonomous 1912

Harbin

occupied by Russia 1897-1905 Japanese influence after 1905

Suifen

R. Ussuri

Ili to Russia 1871-81

to Russia 1864

SINKIANG

Yellow River (Huang Ho)

Kalgan

Peking

Tientsin

Taiyuan

Changchun

Mukden

Newchwang

Dairen

Port Arthur

to Russia 1898 to Japan 1905

KOREA

Hunchun

Vladivostok

Antung

Chefoo

Weihaiwei British 1898

Tsinan

Tsingtao German 1898

Japanese 1910

TIBET
autonomous after 1912 under British influence

CHINA

R. Yangtze

Chungking

Ichang

Hankow

Pukow

Chinkiang

Nanking

Wusung

Soochow

Shanghai

NEPAL

BHOTAN

SIKKIM British protectorate 1817

ASSAM British 1826

Yochow

Kiukiang

Wuhu

Hangchow

Ningpo

JAPAN

Ryukyu Is

to Japan 1872

BRITISH INDIA

Changsha

Wenchow

Santuao

FUKIEN

Foochow

Tamsui

Taiwan to Japan 1895

BURMA British 1886

Kunming

Tengyueh

Szemao

Mengtze

Manhao

Lungchow

Nanning

Canton

Macao Portuguese 1557

Kowloon British 1898

Hong Kong British 1842

New Territories British 1898

Amoy

Swatow

FRENCH INDO CHINA 1884

Pakhoi

Kwangchowan French 1898

Haiphong

LAOS French 1893

Kiungchow

Hainan

SIAM

Legend:
boundary of Ch'ing Empire in 1850

colonial possessions:

spheres of influence:

railways:
- Russian
- British
- Japanese
- French
- German
- Chinese

states formerly tributary to China

Treaty ports and towns:
- 1842 Treaty of Nanking
- 1858 Treaty of Tientsin
- 1860 Peking Convention
- 1876 Chefoo Convention
- 1897 Sino-French Trade Convention
- additional ports opened by 1911

The world economy, 1850-1929

After the middle of the nineteenth century the Industrial Revolution, which had radiated from Great Britain to north-west Europe and the eastern seaboard of the United States, spread to the rest of the world. The result, by 1914, was the formation of a single interdependent world economy. But the impact was extremely varied. Though the United States after 1890 was becoming an important subsidiary centre, the focus throughout was on Europe, and most of the development was keyed to the needs of European industry for raw materials and fed by European capital. In 1914 Great Britain was the largest source of foreign investment, with overseas assets totalling nearly £4,000 million, while the United States, like Russia, was still a net borrower (map 3); but in world trade it was losing the predominance it had enjoyed in 1860 to Germany and the United States (diagram 5).

One factor behind these developments was the vast, unprecedented flow of population, mainly from Europe to the New World, but also from China and India to South-East Asia and East Africa (map 2). Between 1850 and 1920 over 40 million Europeans emigrated overseas or to Siberia, carrying with them European institutions and skills which they used to exploit the vast overseas territories. Much foreign investment went into building the infrastructure of railways, ports and shipping and creating the network of communications upon which the functioning of the world economy depended. Outside Europe and the United States there were only 9,100 miles of railroad track in 1870. By 1911 it had increased

to 175,000 miles. Equally important was the expansion of world shipping and the replacement of sailing ships by ocean-going steamships of large capacity. The opening of the Suez Canal (1869) and the Panama Canal (1914) gave a great fillip to world trade (diagram 4). Traffic via Suez rose from 437,000 tons in 1870 to over 20 million tons in 1913, and foreign trade increased threefold in volume during the same period.

Nevertheless the effects of industrialisation were distinctly one-sided. The main shipping routes (map 3) were between the advanced countries and the white dominions, or between them and the producers of raw materials. Even as late as 1929 the world was still a white man's world. A few countries such as India (page 104) and China had begun to develop their own industries; but, with the exception of Japan, they were small enclaves in a vast rural population. In 1914 there were still only 900,000 factory workers in the whole of India, and 69 per cent of cotton operatives in 1919 were in Bombay province. Nowhere outside the United States and Europe was the income produced by manufacturing substantial in 1930 (map 1) and in most cases it accrued to foreign investors. This was true of Malaya, which by 1900 was producing nearly half the world's tin and by 1910 was a major exporter of rubber, and of Katanga, where copper production rose from nothing in 1900 to 305,000 tons (including Northern Rhodesia) in 1930. Here, as elsewhere, the bulk of the population benefited only marginally, and per capita income in most countries seems actually to have declined. This was the situation which led, a generation later, to the conflict of rich nations and poor nations (page 150) and the demand for a New International Economic Order.

2 Population movements 1820-1910

→ emigration from Europe
→ emigration from Japan
→ emigration from China
→ emigration from India

3 Trade and investment

— major sea routes
— international telegraph cables

concentration of investment 1914 (in $ million):

UK German French USA

Top left hemisphere (Asia/migration):

JAPAN
CHINA
ASIA
BURMA SIAM MALAYA
INDIA
CEYLON

A 550 000 Russians 1860-1900
...dessa
...illion ...ssians ...USA
slaves to Arabia

2 million British to Australia and New Zealand
Mauritius
...E NATAL
...LONY

Right hemisphere (Trade and investment map labels):

UNITED STATES 2800 480
CANADA
850 4250 950 200 550
500 400
400 MEXICO 400
Gulf of Mexico
Pacific Ocean
JAPAN
RUSSIA 2400 400
CHINA 200 600
SIAM 200
200 1700 AUSTRALIA 300 NEW ZEALAND
Panama Canal (1914)
COLOMBIA VENEZUELA
Atlantic Ocean
investment in the rest of Europe 3180 535
1050 UNITED KINGDOM 420
GERMAN EMPIRE 750
FRANCE AUSTRIA HUNGARY
650 450
OTTOMAN EMPIRE
ECUADOR
PERU BOLIVIA
DUTCH GUIANA
CHILE 1550
400 200 BRAZIL 700 500
300 700
ARGENTINA URUGUAY 200
Straits of Magellan
ALGERIA 200 EGYPT
LIBYA
Suez Canal (1869)
Indian Ocean
100 FRENCH WEST AFRICA 500
NIGERIA SUDAN
FRENCH EQUATORIAL AFRICA 600 UGANDA BRITISH EAST AFRICA
GERMAN EAST AFRICA 500 (all of Africa)
MOZAMBIQUE
GERMAN SOUTH WEST AFRICA 1550
UNION OF SOUTH AFRICA
Cape of Good Hope
INDIA 1850

Foreign investment in 1914 (in $ million)

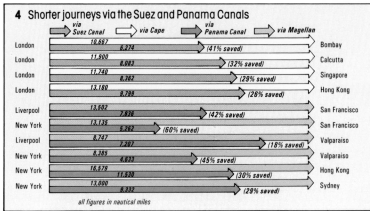

Russia 500
Belgium 900
USA 3510
Holland 4100
Germany 5650
France 9280
United Kingdom 19935

1 Industrialisation outside Europe

% working population engaged in non-agricultural occupations in 1930:

- over 90%
- 81%-90%
- 71%-80%
- 61%-70%
- 51%-60%
- 41%-50%
- 31%-40%
- 21%-30%
- 10%-20%
- unknown

$45M net income produced by manufacturing 1920-30 ($M = millions of US dollars)

$200 gross national product per capita 1930

major industrial regions (excluding Europe)

- ● major coalfield
- ■ iron and steel works
- ⊞ machinery and hardware
- I chemicals
- ◡ woollen industry
- ▶ cotton spinning
- ▣ cotton textile industry

**Map labels:**

ALASKA $1100M
$1330
CANADA
Vancouver
Indianapolis Milwaukee Montreal
...lt Chicago Detroit Pittsburgh Boston
City Denver Cincinnati New York Philadelphia
Memphis Washington Richmond
Knoxville Norfolk
Birmingham Charleston
New Orleans Savannah
USA
Atlantic Ocean $15000M
MEXICO
Gulf of Mexico
Cuba Dominican Republic
Mexico City Haiti
Caribbean Sea
$1380
VENEZUELA BR
$350 COLOMBIA (DUT/FR GUIANA)
Pacific Ocean
ECUADOR
PERU BRAZIL
$115M
$48M $435
$350
BOLIVIA
PARAGUAY Rio de Janeiro Santos
CHILE
URUGUAY $45M
Valparaiso Montevideo Buenos Aires $650
ARGENTINA
$105M
$550 $325M $1000

ALL OTHER LATIN AMERICAN COUNTRIES $350

Iceland

5 Balance of world trade, 1860 and 1913

		Europe	N. America	S. America	Asia	Africa
UNITED KINGDOM	imports 1860	419	252	96	143	80
	exports	358	132	74	139	36
	imports 1913	1,548	848	393	458	220
	exports	917	265	272	620	248
USA	imports 1860	217	—	80	29	—
	exports	249	—	46	11	—
	imports 1913	893	199	381	298	26
	exports	1,479	469	294	140	29
FRANCE	imports 1860	234	47	41	16	34
	exports	293	49	53	3	45
	imports 1913	880	187	183	192	148
	exports	937	89	94	36	181
HOLLAND	imports 1860	92	5	3	32	—
	exports	87	2	1	14	—
	imports 1913	624	190	87	274	14
	exports	1,131	57	9	73	14
GERMANY	imports 1913	1,402	423	290	250	118
	exports	1,828	184	183	130	50
RUSSIA	imports 1913	556	—	—	—	—
	exports	719	—	—	—	—

figures in million dollars US

4 Shorter journeys via the Suez and Panama Canals

via Suez Canal via Cape via Panama Canal via Magellan

From		To
London	10,667 / 6,274 (41% saved)	Bombay
London	11,900 / 8,083 (32% saved)	Calcutta
London	11,740 / 8,362 (29% saved)	Singapore
London	13,180 / 9,799 (26% saved)	Hong Kong
Liverpool	13,502 / 7,836 (42% saved)	San Francisco
New York	13,135 / 5,262 (60% saved)	San Francisco
Liverpool	8,747 / 7,207 (18% saved)	Valparaiso
New York	8,385 / 4,633 (45% saved)	Valparaiso
New York	16,579 / 11,530 (30% saved)	Hong Kong
New York	13,000 / 9,332 (29% saved)	Sydney

all figures in nautical miles

The United States and Canada, 1865-1920

The rise of the modern United States dates effectively from the Civil War, but development was very uneven. For the defeated South the period of Reconstruction (1865–77) was a bitter experience. South Carolina had ranked third in the nation in per capita wealth in 1860; ten years later it was fortieth, and Mississippi, Alabama and Georgia fared no better. Worst of all was the position of the 4 million liberated slaves, who found themselves (as the black leader Frederick Douglass said) without money, property or friends. The great upsurge in population, from 31 million in 1860 to 92 million in 1910, by-passed the South and concentrated wealth and power in the north-east where, with the exploitation of the rich ore reserves of the Mesabi Range in Minnesota and the vast coal reserves of the Appalachians, industry spread rapidly from the original manufacturing belt between Boston and New Jersey to Pitts-

burgh, Detroit and Chicago. Only around 1920 did cheap labour attract the textile industry from New England to the South (map 2).

The Civil War itself had stimulated Northern industry. After 1865 it forged ahead. But the most striking achievement of the immediate post-war period was the opening of the Great Plains, made possible by the railroad boom after 1870. In 1860 some 30,000 miles of railway were in operation, but few lines extended beyond the Great Lakes. By 1870 the mileage had reached 53,000, by 1880 93,000 and by 1890 163,000 miles (page 94). Land grants of more than 132 million acres encouraged railway promoters, and homestead grants of 285 million acres attracted settlers. The number of farms rose from 2 million in 1860 to 6 million in 1910, and grain exports, which the rail network made possible, were an important source of capital for industrial development. The population west of the Mississippi rose from 6 million in 1870 to 26 million in 1910. Nevertheless the bulk of the population was concentrated

in the north-east (map 5), and most of the 25 million immigrants between 1870 and 1914 remained there, providing cheap labour for American industry. Their miserable conditions, and those of the southern blacks, lay behind the unrest which erupted in the 1890s (map 2).

In Canada railway development was even more important than in the United States. Hitherto the 'small and unimportant' eastern colonies (as Lord Durham described them in his famous Report of 1839) had gone their separate ways, more closely linked to the United States, which made no secret of its hope to absorb them, than with each other. After the acquisition of Alaska from Russia (map 4), United States' pressure grew, and to meet it the Canadian Federation was formed in 1867 and completed by the adhesion of Manitoba (1870) and British Columbia (1871). The great transcontinental railways – the Great Western and Canadian Pacific (completed 1885), followed by the Canadian Northern and Grand Trunk Pacific – were the lifeblood of the new Dominion and

changed the axis of Canadian life. Railway development opened Manitoba and Saskatchewan, and made Canada into one of the world's leading wheat producers (map 1). It also led to the discovery of rich mineral deposits, particularly copper and nickel (1883). The other major industry in 1914 was lumber and the manufacture of paper and newsprint. In general, however, industrialisation was only beginning, though the value of Canada's industrial output increased from $190 million in 1890 to over $500 million in 1914.

In the United States, on the other hand, the 1880s and 1890s saw an astounding industrial upsurge. Output of coal and iron increased twenty times between 1870 and 1913, by which date steel production exceeded that of Britain and Germany combined. But the 'Gilded Age' was also a time of gross inequalities, and speculation and over-production caused serious economic setbacks, particularly in 1873 and 1893, which led not only to industrial unrest but also to a search for new markets, particularly in

3 US economic growth

- cotton (raw cotton consumed, in millions of bales)
- corn (millions of bushels harvested)
- wheat (millions of bushels harvested)
- steel (thousands of long tons manufactured)

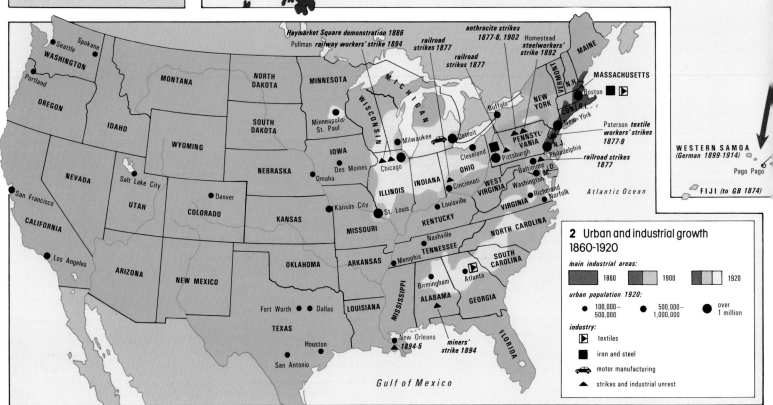

2 Urban and industrial growth 1860-1920

main industrial areas:
1860   1900   1920

urban population 1920:
- 100,000–500,000
- 500,000–1,000,000
- over 1 million

industry:
- textiles
- iron and steel
- motor manufacturing
- strikes and industrial unrest

eastern Asia. Already in 1867 the United States had annexed Midway Island as a Pacific base; in 1887 it secured Pearl Harbor. The other area of advance was the Caribbean and Latin America, where, by the Hay-Pauncefote agreement of 1901, Great Britain gave the United States a free hand. But the turning point came with the Spanish-American war of 1898, which made Cuba into an American protectorate and brought the Philippines – 'a stepping-stone to China' – under American rule (map 4). By 1914, when the Panama Canal was opened, the United States was the world's greatest industrial power. It was also, without fully realising it, involved in world politics. The way was prepared for the United States' entry into the First World War.

5 Population density in 1900

inhabitants per square mile:

	0-2
	2-6
	6-18
	18-45
	45-90
	90 and over

ALASKA (purchased from Russia 1867)

4 American expansion in the Pacific and Caribbean, 1867-1917

→ US influence
→ US possession
→ US protectorate
→ military action by US

HAWAIIAN ISLANDS (annexed by US 1898)

PUERTO RICO (ceded to US by Spain 1898)

VIRGIN ISLANDS

Panama Canal (open 1914, Canal Zone leased to US)

1 The development of Canada, 1867-1920

	land occupied prior to 1851	
	land occupied 1851-1871	
	land occupied 1871-1901	
	land occupied 1901-1921	

population 1871:
□ towns of 25,000 to 100,000 people
■ towns of over 100,000 people

population 1911:
● towns of 25,000 to 100,000 people
● towns of over 100,000 people

ALBERTA 1905 date of accession to Dominion of Canada

railways 1916:
—— Canadian Pacific Railway
---- Canadian Northern (Main Line)
······ National Transcontinental Railway
⬭ main industrial regions

Australia and New Zealand from 1788

Although Australia and New Zealand were discovered by the Dutch explorer Tasman in 1642, colonisation only began after Cook hoisted the British flag at Botany Bay in 1770 (page 64). New South Wales served as a penal colony from 1788 to 1839, Van Diemen's Land (later Tasmania) from 1804 to 1853, and in 1829 the British government, fearing to be forestalled by the French, claimed the whole Australian continent. Fear of France also led to the annexation of New Zealand in 1840. But in both lands geographical obstacles, lack of exportable products, and, in the case of New Zealand, the bitter Maori wars between 1860 and 1871, made the early years of colonisation difficult. New South Wales was hemmed in by the Blue Mountains. Beyond the Great Dividing Range the country soon became arid and inhospitable. Coastal settlements at Perth (1829), Melbourne (1835), and Adelaide (1836) established bridgeheads for exploration in the west (map 5), but as late as 1850 the total white population was only around 350,000, while in New Zealand it was still below 100,000 in 1860. Inducements to settle were few. Neither country was self-supporting, and early trade (chiefly seal products and sandalwood) was insufficient to pay for imports (map 4), and was further hampered by the East India Company's monopoly in the area.

The discovery of gold in New South Wales and Victoria in 1851 and in Otago (South Island) in 1861 initiated a new phase. Even more important was the rapid growth of sheep farming. In 1850 Australia sent 39 million lb. of wool to Great Britain. By 1879 the quantity had increased to 300 million lb. In New Zealand, where wool was largely a South Island product, exports rose from £67,000 in value in 1853 to £2,700,000 twenty years later. The development of the North Island, held back by the Maori wars, came later, after the introduction of refrigeration. Refrigeration made possible the large-scale export of frozen lamb from the South Island, but it also lay behind the growth of dairy farming in the north, which now, stimulated by the exports trade in butter and cheese, drew ahead of the south in population.

Political development kept pace with economic growth. In 1855 New South Wales, Victoria, South Australia and Tasmania became self-governing colonies, followed by Queensland in 1859, and in 1901 joined together to form the Commonwealth of Australia. New Zealand, which had been divided in 1852 into six provinces, each with an elected council, became a united Dominion in 1876, after measures had been taken to safeguard the rights of the Maori population. Both dominions remained heavily dependent on primary exports. For long they enjoyed preferential treatment in the British market; but developments after 1945, particularly the British retreat from Asia, brought important changes. In 1952 both dominions joined for security with the United States in the ANZUS Pact, and when Great Britain entered the European Common Market (1973) and dismantled imperial preference, they were forced to diversify their economies and seek new markets. The process of reorientation is still continuing.

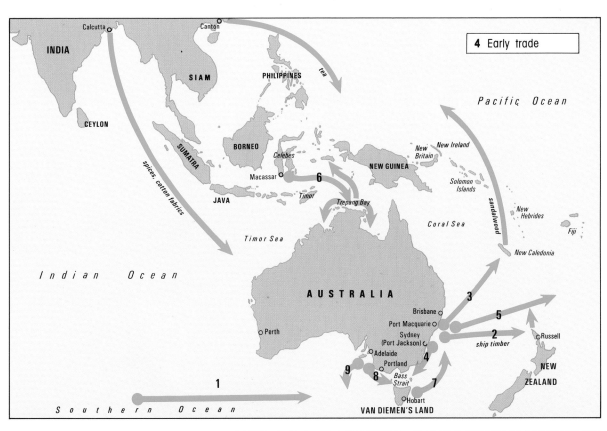

4 Early trade

Early trade (left)
1/Main route from Europe via Cape of Good Hope. First colonisation fleet to New South Wales 1788, mainly convicts and marines. By 1790, with arrival of second fleet, it was clear that the colonies would be reliant upon regular supplies from Europe.
2/Convict transport ships return to U.K. via New Zealand for timber, and Canton for tea or Calcutta for oriental goods.
3/Sydney-based ships to Pacific islands for sandalwood to trade for tea at Canton.
4/Sydney-based ships to Bass Strait islands for seal skins and oil (first major exports to U.K.). Seal fields soon exhausted. Eastern colony ports used as bases for American and British whaling ships, an industry developed by colonists from 1820s.
5/Sydney to Tahiti for pork for provisioning convicts.
6/Macassan fishermen to northern Australian coast to collect trepang (sea cucumbers) to trade with Chinese merchants.
7/Van Diemen's land grain to Sydney.
8/South Australian grain to eastern colonies.
9/South Australian grain to Europe. From 1840s wool and minerals, the basis of late nineteenth century trade with Europe.

1 The settlement and development of Australia

areas occupied by 1850
areas occupied by 1890
more than 2 persons per square mile 1961 (by statistical division)
no significant use c.1960
penal settlements
settlements
railways:
before 1881
1881-1900
1901-1920
after 1920

minerals
gold   T tungsten
iron ore   N nickel
C copper   tin
silver   A alumina/ bauxite
lead   U uranium
Z zinc   M manganese
natural gas   blast furnace
A oil

European nationalism
1815-1914

The flame of nationalism was kindled in Europe by the French revolution. In France itself the revolution forged a sense of national unity, and elsewhere, notably in Spain and Prussia, the humiliation of defeat and French occupation after 1807 produced a short-lived national reaction. For the most part, however, nationalism was confined to a narrow segment of the middle class. It was anathema to the ruling classes, and rarely touched working people. Polish peasants held aloof from the insurrections of 1831, 1846 and 1863; in Ireland only acute agrarian distress after 1877 lined them up behind the nationalists. Down to 1848 liberal and constitutional reform was the main demand, and it was against this, rather than nationalism, that the victorious powers set their faces after the fall of Napoleon at the Congress of Vienna in 1815. Their other main objective was to erect a barrier against a resurgence of revolutionary France. Hence their decision to transfer the Austrian Netherlands (later Belgium) to Holland, to install Prussia in Westphalia and most of the Rhineland, and to hand over the ancient republic of Genoa to Sardinia-Piedmont. As compensation for the loss of the Netherlands, Austria received the Venetian republic and the duchy of Milan, as well as indirect control of Parma, Modena and Tuscany. Sweden, which had to surrender Finland to Russia, was compensated with Norway.

The overriding objective of the great powers after 1815 was to uphold the Vienna settlement and to combat the threat of liberalism and nationalism, but by 1830, when a new wave of liberal and nationalist agitation broke out, the eastern and western powers were drawing apart. By destroying a common front, their divergence of interests enabled Greece (page 116) and Belgium to obtain independence, although in the latter case the territorial settlement, including the disposal of Limburg and Luxembourg was postponed until 1839 (map 5).

In Norway the forced union with Sweden aroused resentment similar to that felt in Belgium towards Holland. There was friction, but little active resistance, and eventually a Norwegian declaration of independence was accepted by Sweden (map 4). The course of events in Poland (1831, 1846) and in Italy, Germany and Hungary in 1848-49 was more eventful. Here nationalist agitation erupted in full-scale war; but the solidarity of the conservative powers and divisions among the nationalists themselves brought all to nothing.

What changed this situation was the rise of a new generation of statesmen. Louis Napoleon, emperor of France since 1852, Cavour, who became prime minister of Sardinia-Piedmont in the same year, and Bismarck, minister-president of Prussia after 1862, all toyed with nationalism, confident of their ability to use it for their own ends. These were not the ends of the liberals who had led the nationalist movements of 1848–49. Cavour's purpose was to ensure that Italian unification was carried out by and in the interests of Sardinia; hence his opposition to the famous Sicilian expedition of the patriot Garibaldi (1807–82) in 1860. Bismarck was determined to ensure that Germany was merged in Prussia, not Prussia in Germany. Both also realised that their objectives could only be achieved by war and diplomacy. Hence Cavour's alliance with France against Austria (1858) and Bismarck's wars of 1864, 1866 and 1870. The result was the unification of Italy (except for Venetia and the Papal State) in 1861 (map 3) and the unification of Germany in 1871 (map 2). Both were retrospectively endorsed by liberal nationalists, but neither satisfied the nationalism they aroused. Italy still laid claim to the Alto Adige, Fiume and Trieste. Bismarck's 'small German' solution, excluding Austria, disappointed those who hankered after a Greater Germany. Indeed, it was after 1870, when the problems of the multi-national Austro-Hungarian state came to the fore, that nationalist claims became loudest. The confusion of peoples and languages in eastern Europe (map 1) defied easy solutions and exacerbated the conflicts which led, step by step, to war in 1914.

5 Belgian independence 1830-39

4 The Scandinavian kingdoms

3 The unification of Italy, 1859-70

- Kingdom of Sardinia in 1815
- territory annexed 1859
- territory annexed May 1860
- territory annexed November 1860
- territory annexed 1866
- territory lost to France 1860
- French from 1768, formerly Genoese
- - - - international frontier 1914

1 Peoples, languages and political divisions in the 19th century

—— national frontiers 1914	Romansch
- - - national frontiers in 1815 where different	Macedonian Slavs

Atlantic Ocean

NORWEGIANS
SWEDES
FINNS
ESTONIANS
GREAT
RUSSIANS
SCOTS
DANES
LATVIANS
LITHUANIANS
WHITE
RUSSIANS
IRISH
WELSH
ENGLISH
DUTCH
FLEMINGS
WALLOONS
POLES
UKRAINIANS
BRETONS
G E R M A N S
CZECHS
SLOVAKS
FRENCH
AUSTRIANS
HUNGARIANS
SLOVENES
ROMANIANS
CROATS
PORTUGUESE
BASQUES
SERBS
BULGARIANS
SPANIARDS
CATALANS
I T A L I A N S
CORSICANS
ALBANIANS
GREEKS
TURKS

DENMARK
Baltic Sea
SCHLESWIG
Tilsit
R. Niemen
North Sea
Schleswig
Kiel
Königsberg
HOLSTEIN
Lübeck
Rostock
EAST PRUSSIA
Hamburg
MECKLENBURG
Danzig
POMERANIA
WEST PRUSSIA
Stettin
OLDENBURG
Bremen
S
HANOVER
R. Elbe
Amsterdam
Hanover
U
R. Warthe
POSEN
The Hague
Münster
BRUNSWICK
Berlin
R. Vistula
NETHERLANDS
WESTPHALIA
Göttingen
ANHALT
BRANDENBURG
Posen
Antwerp
Dortmund
R
Kassel
RUSSIA
Brussels
Düsseldorf
P
Leipzig
Breslau
POLAND
RHENISH
Aachen
Erfurt
Dresden
R. Oder
S I L E S I A
BELGIUM
PRUSSIA
Cologne
WETZLAR
THURINGIA
SAXONY
Koblenz
HESSE
Sedan
NASSAU
Frankfurt
Sadowa
1870
Luxembourg
Darmstadt
1866
Prussians
occupy
Paris 1871
Verdun
Metz
PALATINATE
Prague
BOHEMIA
Nancy
LORRAINE
Karlsruhe
Strassburg
Nuremberg
FRANCE
ALSACE
WÜRTTEMBERG
HOHENZOLLERN
Stuttgart
B A V A R I A
R. Meuse
R. Rhine
BADEN
Ulm
R. Danube
Vienna
Basle
Munich
Constance
SWITZERLAND
AUSTRIA

2 The unification of Germany, 1815-71

Prussia in 1815	acquired by Prussia 1815-66
—— boundary of German Confederation of 1815	
- - - boundary of North German Confederation 1866	
Imperial territory of Alsace-Lorraine 1871	
—— boundary of German Empire 1871	
←- - - Austro-Prussian forces attack Denmark 1864	
←—— Prussian armies in the war with Austria 1866	
←- - German armies in the Franco-Prussian war 1870-71	

The European powers
1878-1914

After the unification of Germany and of Italy (page 114), it seemed for a time as though the major questions which had disturbed the peace of Europe since 1848 had been resolved. Bismarck, the architect of German unification, concentrated his efforts after 1871 upon building a system of alliances which would ensure the future of the new German Reich. The 'wild Junker' had become a conservative, anxious only to preserve what had been won; and his alliances were defensive. But the history of the next forty years is the story of how alliances, originally defensive and stabilising in intent, turned into an aggressive and destabilising system. Furthermore, the unification of Germany and of Italy, far from marking a halting place, opened up a hornet's nest of nationalist revindications. After 1870 the nationalist

movement which had agitated western Europe for forty years, spilled over into the Balkans; and the struggles of the Balkan peoples for independence (map 1) inevitably involved the powers who were their supporters or adversaries, particularly Russia and Austria-Hungary, which, after its exclusion from Germany and Italy after 1866, was essentially an eastward-looking Balkan power.

The evolution of the relations between the great powers between 1879, when Bismarck tried to reconcile his sympathies with a conservative Russia with support for Austria-Hungary, and 1914, when the whole precarious balance fell apart, is indicated diagrammatically on maps 2(a) to 2(f). Until the beginning of the new century the system worked reasonably well. Revolts in the Balkans between 1875 and 1878, culminating in Russian intervention and war with Turkey, thoroughly alarmed the powers; and after the Congress of Berlin (1878) Balkan affairs took a secondary place. Checked in Europe, Russia turned to central Asia and the Far

East, and during the first half of the period the dominant themes were Anglo-Russian rivalry in Asia and Anglo-French rivalry in Africa. What changed this situation was the decision of Germany under William II, particularly after Bülow became chancellor in 1900, to seek 'a place in the sun'. This was not unreasonable; but by now most places in the sun had been occupied, and German policy was seen as a threat by the established imperial powers. The result was the Anglo-French reconciliation (1904) and the Anglo-Russian reconciliation (1907). German 'world policy' also required a navy, resulting in the naval competition which soured Anglo-German relations between 1906 and 1912. After 1907 the Triple Entente with France and Russia became the lynch-pin of British policy, the only firm assurance against the German 'threat'. Germany, on the other hand, saw itself being 'encircled' by a hostile ring constructed by Great Britain.

The result was that the lines between the Triple Alliance and the Triple Entente were drawn tighter. Also

1 The Balkans, 1878-1913

- – – frontier of Ottoman Empire 1800
- —— proposed Bulgaria under Treaty of San Stefano 1878
- ━━ national frontiers after the Balkan wars 1912-13

Germany was driven closer to its only dependable ally, Austria-Hungary. When Austria annexed Bosnia-Herzegovina in 1908, Bülow lent full support, and Austro-Russian antagonism in the Balkans, hitherto suppressed, was rekindled. The climax was postponed until the outbreak of the Balkan wars in 1912. The aggrandisement of Serbia which resulted was viewed by Austria as an intolerable threat. Russia, on the other hand, could not leave Serbia in the lurch without losing credibility. The result was the stupendous build-up of armaments (diagram 3) as the grinding logic of the system came into play. When in 1914 the murder of the Austrian archduke Franz Ferdinand brought matters to a head, the combustible material was piled up which exploded in the First World War.

2 European alliances

- ↓ Austro-German Alliance (the Dual Alliance) 1879-1918
- ♔ Three Emperors' Alliance 1881-87
- ▨ Austro-Serbian Alliance 1881-95
- ▲ Triple Alliance 1882-1915
- ■ Austro-German-Romanian Alliance 1883-1916
- ○ Franco-Russian Alliance 1894-1917
- ✐ Russo-Bulgarian military convention 1902-13

stripes, similar and identical colours indicate an entente or community of interests

2a/The Dual Alliance: October 1879, resulted from the Balkan upheavals of 1875-8. When Russia attacked Turkey and imposed the Treaty of San Stefano, the Austro-Russian understanding of 1873 broke down. Bismarck's purpose in the Dual Alliance was to stabilise the situation. Germany could not afford to let Austria-Hungary succumb to a Russian attack; but the alliance was strictly defensive. It did not imply a common front against Russia, understanding with which was still a basic element in Bismarck's policy, still less a German commitment to underwrite Austrian ambitions in the Balkans. Nevertheless the Dual Alliance marked a turning point: the era of formal alliances had begun.

2b/Bismarck's system at its zenith: 1883. The formation of the Three Emperors' Alliance (1881) appeared to have restored stability in Eastern Europe. But the smouldering Austro-Russian antagonism continued, brought to a head again by the Bulgarian crisis of 1886-7. Alliances with Serbia (1881) and Romania (1883) sought to limit Russian influence in the Balkans. The Triple Alliance of Germany, Austria and Italy (1882) insured Austria against Italian attack in case of war with Russia. After the Three Emperors' Alliance broke down, Bismarck sought security by his Reinsurance Treaty with Russia (1887), while Austria joined in a 'Mediterranean agreement' with Britain, Italy and Spain against France and Russia.

2c/The 'New Course' in Germany: 1891. Even before Bismarck's fall in 1890, it was evident that his complicated system of alliances was running into difficulties. Russo-German relations deteriorated sharply after 1887 as a result of tariff and loan disputes. When the new German chancellor, Caprivi, dropped Bismarck's Reinsurance Treaty, renewed the Triple Alliance, and lined up with the 'Mediterranean entente', Russia replied by a military convention and alliance with France (1894). But the 'new course' was short-lived. After 1895 Germany saw more profit in co-operation with France and Russia in the Far East, while Austria-Hungary and Russia agreed (1897) to put Balkan problems on ice.

2d/The Anglo-French entente: 1904. The decision of William II and Bülow after 1897 to move from a continental, European to a 'world' policy challenged all three established imperial powers and brought about a major realignment. In 1902 France settled its long-standing dispute with Italy; in 1904 it reached a similar settlement with Great Britain. Germany's attempt to exploit Russia's weakness after the Russo-Japanese war and the 1905 revolution to prise apart the Franco-Russian alliance misfired. Franco-British ties were strengthened; Russia and England settled their colonial differences in 1907, and the three powers joined in the Triple Entente to counter and contain Germany.

2e/Europe after the Bosnian crisis: 1909. The Austrian annexation of Bosnia and Herzegovina, a response to the Turkish revolution of 1908, ended the Austro-Russian Balkan entente of 1897 and caused a major crisis in international relations. When Russia protested, Germany gave Austria full support, reversing Bismarck's defensive interpretation of the Dual Alliance, and forced Russia to back down. Henceforward Austria-Hungary and Russia were at loggerheads in the Balkans. Anglo-German relations also were at their nadir, a consequence of growing naval rivalry. The result was to consolidate the Triple Entente, particularly after the second Morocco crisis (1911), when Britain took the lead in opposing Germany.

2f/Europe on the eve of war: 1914. Between 1911 and 1914 the front between the Triple Alliance and the Triple Entente hardened. During the Balkan wars (1912-13), when Serbia, Greece and Bulgaria combined to drive Turkey out of Europe, the two groups still co-operated. But Austria was aghast at the consequent enlargement of Serbia and feared pro-Serb irredentism in its Slav provinces, and Germany was haunted by the spectre of encirclement. When, after the assassination of Franz Ferdinand at Sarajevo on 28 June 1914, Austria decided to punish Serbia and Berlin threw itself unreservedly behind Vienna, the system of alliances almost automatically led to general war.

The First World War
1914-1918

When the assassination of the Austrian heir-presumptive, Archduke Franz Ferdinand, by Bosnian terrorists at Sarajevo on June 28, 1914, sparked off the immediate sequence of events that led to the First World War, the European powers were already divided into heavily armed camps (page 116), and neither was prepared to risk diplomatic defeat. Germany already had its battle plan prepared: the famous Schlieffen Plan, drawn up in 1905, to trap and annihilate the French army by a great encircling movement through Belgium before France's Russian ally had time to mobilise. The expectation everywhere was for a short war, over by Christmas 1914, and only after this expectation proved false did the search for allies begin in earnest. Germany and Austria were joined by the Ottoman Empire and Bulgaria, the Entente powers by Italy, Romania and Greece, and eventually by the United States (map 1).

The German strategy was very nearly successful and brought the German armies within 40 miles of Paris (map 2). It was frustrated by the unexpectedly rapid mobilisation of Russia, which invaded East Prussia and defeated the German 8th Army at Gumbinnen (August 20, 1914). Although the Russians were repulsed at Tannenberg (August 26–29), their offensive drew off German reserves, which helped the French and British armies in the west to halt the German advance in the battle of the Marne (September 5–8), while the Russians simultaneously inflicted a crushing defeat on Austria at Lemberg. The Schlieffen Plan had failed, Germany was forced to despatch troops to the east to prop up the Austrian front, and in the west the war became a war of trenches, artillery, barbed wire and machine guns. Each side launched offensives, with sickening casualties, but without succeeding in advancing more than a few thousand yards. Railways could bring up reinforcements to the front before slow-moving advancing troops could make good any advantage they might have created. The question for both, by the end of 1915, was how to break the stalemate. The answer of the Entente, sponsored by Winston Churchill, was to attack Germany from the rear by campaigns in the Dardanelles and Mesopotamia (page 124), at Salonika, and, after Italy entered the war on May 23, 1915, against Austria on the Isonzo. All were failures. The German answer was to bring Great Britain to its knees by crippling losses at sea. The submarine campaign, initiated on February 1, 1917, was nearly successful, and only defeated when Lloyd George introduced the convoy system in May. But its result was to bring the United States into the war on the Entente side on April 6, 1917.

Even so, the German position was not hopeless. Huge losses in the Brusilov offensive of 1916 and economic chaos at home had broken the Russian fighting spirit, and the Russian revolutions of March and October 1917 (page 120) enabled Germany to transfer troops from the Eastern to the Western Front in the hope of victory before the United States could mobilise. On March 21, 1918,

1 The line-up of the Powers

- Central Powers
- Entente (Allied) Powers
- neutral states
- total mobilised forces
- neutral states that later joined Central Powers, with date
- neutral states that later joined Entente Powers, with date
- killed and died (1914-1918)
- * estimated figures

3 The war in Europe, 1914-18

- major Central Powers offensives
- major Allied offensives
- major battles
- battles costing over 250,000 killed
- naval mutinies
- army mutinies
- food riots
- naval bases
- major naval battles
- German raids on English coast

all battles, offensives, mutinies etc. coloured according to year:

| 1914 | 1916 | 1918 |
| 1915 | 1917 | |

- furthest German advance in the west, 1914
- the trench line, November 1914
- furthest Russian advance in the east, 1914-15
- Russian front, November 1915
- territory held by Central Powers, December 1917 (close in the west to the "Hindenburg line")
- front line at time of Brest-Litovsk armistice between Germany and Russia December 1917
- German penetration of Russia, February 1918
- armistice line in the west, November 1918
- railways

4 Allied shipping losses, 1914-18

figures in tons

- Russia 183,000
- Greece 346,000
- US (while neutral) 56,000
- US (while belligerent) 397,000
- Italy 872,000
- France 900,000
- Great Britain 7,800,000

Hindenburg and Ludendorff launched their great offensive in the west (map 3). Once again it was a near success, but the Allied line held, and on July 18 the French commander Foch launched the counter-offensive which was to be the decisive campaign of the war. On September 29 Ludendorff acknowledged defeat. By now war weariness was rampant. Austria and Bulgaria were near to collapse; the British blockade had brought Germany to the edge of starvation; and the German government, fearful of a Bolshevik revolution, sued for an armistice. On November 11, 1918, fighting ceased. Over 8 million men had perished, as had three empires, the Tsarist, the Austro-Hungarian and the Ottoman. In retrospect the war of 1914–18 was the great European civil war, which destroyed the old European order, squandered Europe's human and material resources, and jeopardised its future. Few people realised in 1918 what had happened; but the age of European predominance was over and a new age of global politics had begun.

2 The German attack in the West, August 1914

German "Schlieffen Plan" to encircle Paris

actual route of German armies

Allied counter offensives

The Russian Revolution
1905-1925

Revolution came to Russia suddenly, but not unexpectedly, in the wake of the unsuccessful Russo-Japanese war of 1904–05 (page 126). Intensive industrialisation since 1890 had created a large, profoundly discontented urban proletariat, and it was they who spearheaded the revolution of 1905, although their revolt sparked off widespread unrest in the countryside (map 1). The Tsar was forced to grant a constitution, including a *duma*, or parliament, but by 1907 the government was back in full control. Nevertheless the 1905 revolution irreparably weakened the old order, and after 1912, following the shooting of strikers in the Lena goldfields in Siberia, a great new wave of social unrest swept the empire. Internally, Russia was in no position in 1914 to meet the challenge of the First World War; and when in the winter of 1916–17 economic dislocation, hunger and sheer incompetence brought the crisis to a head, the government capitulated almost without resistance. This was the February revolution of 1917, which placed power in the hands of liberal Duma politicians. But the Provisional Government's authority was circumscribed by the powerful Petrograd Council (or Soviet) of Soldiers' and Workers' Deputies, and it was also compromised by its commit-

ment to continue the war. When, in April, Lenin returned from exile in Switzerland, promising peace, land and bread, and demanding all power for the Soviets, its days were numbered. An attempt in September by the Commander-in-Chief, General Kornilov, to seize the capital miscarried when his troops rebelled, and on November 7 (October 25 by the old calendar) the Bolsheviks struck, arrested the Provisional Government, and assumed power in the name of the Soviets. This was the October, or Bolshevik, revolution.

The odds were weighted heavily against the new government. The overriding need was peace, and Lenin insisted, against strong opposition, on accepting the onerous terms imposed by Germany in the Treaty of Brest-Litovsk (March 1918). But immediately the Bolsheviks were faced with civil war and foreign intervention, as White Russian armies with British, French, Czech and other support, attacked the new republic (map 2). Lenin pinned his hope on war-weariness and revolution in the west (map 3) and on uprisings among subject peoples in the east (map 4), but to little avail. In Europe, particularly in Germany, revolutionary currents were strong between 1919 and 1923, but they were met by counter-revolutionary forces, including Hitler's National Socialists. However, foreign intervention and the threat of a White Tsarist restoration rallied support for the Reds, and by 1920 the civil war had been won. But the devastation was immense. Industrial production

in 1920 was down to one-seventh of the 1913 level, and shortages provoked a wave of strikes and riots, culminating in the Kronstadt naval mutiny (February 1921). Lenin's answer was the 'New Economic Policy' (NEP), in effect a relaxation of requisitioning and controls. The new policy worked: by the end of 1925 industrial production had regained its pre-war level. Furthermore, the overt hostility of the West relaxed. War with Poland, which had invaded Russia in 1920, was ended by the Treaty of Riga (March 1921), and at the same time a treaty of friendship was signed with Turkey. It was followed by the Rapallo Treaty with Germany (1922) and in 1924 by diplomatic recognition from Britain, France and other European countries.

After Lenin's death in 1924 and a period of disputed succession Lenin's eventual successor, Stalin, ousted Trotsky, with his policy of 'permanent revolution'. Stalin's policy of 'socialism in one country', implying large-scale industrialisation and a re-shaping of inefficient agriculture, placed Russia, at a terrible human cost, in the first rank of industrial and international powers. Inaugurated by the first Five Year Plan of 1928, in many respects it marked a sharp break with the revolution of 1917. But it was also a fulfilment of Lenin's work. Even at the time of Lenin's death Russia was backward and under-developed. By 1939, as Lenin foresaw, Bolshevism had become 'a world force', changing the course of history.

boundary of the Russian Empire, 1914

front between Russia and Central Powers, March 1917

principal towns where Bolsheviks took power, Nov. 1917-Feb. 1918 (dates in new calendar)

boundary of Russian territory occupied by Central Powers following the Treaty of Brest-Litovsk, March 1918

boundary of area controlled by the Bolsheviks, August 1918

eastern boundary of area controlled by the Bolsheviks, April 1919

area controlled by the Bolsheviks, October 1919

boundary of Soviet Territory, March 1921

boundary of areas controlled by anti-Bolshevik forces, May 1920

White Russian armies

non-Russian anti-Bolshevik forces

Barents Sea

NORWAY

SWEDEN

Entente fleet

Murmansk

BRITISH FRENCH CANADIANS ITALIANS SERBS

White Sea

CANADIANS AMERICANS

FINLAND

FINNS

independence of Finland recognised December 1917

Archangel 17 Feb 1918

BRITISH FRENCH

L. Ladoga

L. Onega

Petrozavodsk 17 Jan 1918

Helsinki

Kronstadt

Petrograd (Lenigrad) 7 Nov 1917

Vologda 8 Feb 1918

Vyatka 8 Dec 1917

Perm 14 Nov 1917

Nicholas II and family shot by Bolsheviks July 1918

Revel (Tallinn) 8 Nov 1917

Yudenich

Kornilov's attack on Petrograd September 1917

Novgorod 27 Nov 1917

Kostroma 15 Dec 1917

Yekaterinburg (Sverdlovsk) 8 Nov 1917

British fleet

ESTONIA

Pskov 15 Nov 1917

Yaroslavl 9 Nov 1917

Izhevsk 9 Nov 1917

LETTS

Baltic Sea

Riga

LATVIA

BALTIC GERMANS

Tver (Kalinin) 10 Nov 1917

Ivanovo 7 Nov 1917

Nizhny Novgorod (Gorkiy) 10 Nov 1917

Kazan 8 Nov 1917

Ufa 8 Nov 1917

Kolchak 1918-19

B O L S H E V I K   R U S S I A

LITHUANIA

GERMANY (E. PRUSSIA)

Vitebsk 9 Nov 1917

Moscow 15 Nov 1917

Smolensk 12 Nov 1917

Kaluga 11 Dec 1917

Trans-Siberian Railway

CZECHS

Minsk 7 Nov 1917

Mogilev 1 Dec 1917

Tula 20 Dec 1917

Samara 9 Nov 1917

Warsaw

Brest-Litovsk

Orel 14 Nov 1917

Penza 4 Jan 1918

Orenburg 31 Jan 1918

POLAND

POLES

Gomel 12 Nov 1917

Tambov 13 Feb 1918

Saratov 9 Nov 1917

Zhitomir 22 Jan 1918

Kiev 8 Feb 1918

Denikin 1919

Voronezh 12 Nov 1917

Tsaritsyn (Stalingrad) (Volgograd) 27 Nov 1917

Ural Cossack Army 1918-20

CZECHOSLOVAKIA

HUNGARY

Poltava 19 Jan 1918

Kharkov 24 Dec 1917

Don Cassacks 1917-19

R. Don

ROMANIANS

BESSARABIA

Yekaterinoslva (Dnepropetrovsk) 11 Jan 1918

Novocherkassk 25 Feb 1918

R. Volga

ROMANIA

Kishinev 10 Dec 1917

Nikolayev 27 Jan 1918

Rostov-on-Don 10 Nov 1917

Cossacks

Astrakhan 7 Feb 1918

Odessa 31 Jan 1918

Wrangel 1920

Caspian Sea

Sevastopol 29 Dec 1917

Simferopol 26 Jan 1918

Novorossiysk 14 Dec 1917

BULGARIA

FRENCH

Black   Sea

BRITISH

Entente fleet

BRITISH

Georgians 1919-20

Batum

Mensheviks

Baku 15 Nov 1917

Krasnovodsk

Tiflis (Tbilisi)

BRITISH

Kars

TURKEY

Tabriz

1918-19

BRITISH

PERSIA

The Chinese Revolution
1911-1949

By 1911 the imperial government of China was thoroughly discredited, and it only needed an army mutiny at Wuchang to repudiate its authority (map 1). But the republic proclaimed in 1912, with Sun Yat-sen as its first president, was overwhelmed by its inherited problems, and within weeks Sun was displaced by Yuan Shih-k'ai, the most powerful general of the old regime. After Yuan's death in 1916 the government in Peking lost control and power passed into the hands of provincial warlords, whose armies caused untold damage

and millions of casualties. Compounding this misery were the expansionist policies of Japan, which had secured control of Shantung and Manchuria in 1915 (page 126), as well as the presence of foreign powers, based in the Treaty Ports, who interfered in Chinese politics and exploited the struggling Chinese economy.

In 1919, when the Paris Peace Conference refused to abrogate Japanese and other foreign privileges, this desperate situation exploded in a massive upsurge of Chinese nationalism, which found vent in the 4 May Movement of 1919, a spontaneous uprising of students and urban workers, which was the real starting point of the Chinese revolution. It provided a new constituency for Sun Yat-sen, who had taken refuge at Canton,

and in 1923 Sun reorganised his Nationalist (Kuomintang, KMT) Party, allied with the Chinese Communist Party (CCP, founded in 1921), and prepared to reunite the country. But Sun died in 1925, and it was Chiang Kai-shek, the Moscow-trained general of the KMT army, who led the great Northern Expedition of 1926 which aimed at the elimination of the warlords and the unification of the country (map 2). Helped by peasant and workers' uprisings along its route, it was astonishingly successful, and by April 1927 Chiang established his capital at Nanking. But the uneasy alliance of KMT and CCP could not hold, and in 1927 Chiang turned on his allies, massacring the Communists in Shanghai. Furthermore, the warlords were not entirely eliminated, and

1 The revolution of 1911

● 8 Nov. 1911 revolt, with date of province's independence

2 The Northern Expedition 1926-27

warlord groups:

area controlled by Feng-tien faction (Chang Tso-lin)

area controlled by Kuominchün (Feng Yü-Hsiang)

area controlled by Chihli faction (Sun Ch'uan fang)

area controlled by Chihli faction (Wu P'ei-fu)

T'ang Chi-yao, warlord of Yunnan and Kweichow

Kwangsi clique (group of warlords)

the Northern Expedition:

area controlled by Kuomintang

main Kuomintang forces

minor Kuomintang forces

Yen Hsi-shan (warlord of Shansi, 1912 onwards)

Kuominchün

4 The Chinese Communist movement to 1945

abortive urban insurrections after the break with Kuomintang 1927

position of early Communist army groups

early Soviets (self-governing Communist areas) 1927-35

route of the 'Long March', Oct. 1934–Oct. 1935, of Chinese Communists after Kuomintang assaults on Kiangsi Soviet area

main Communist base area, governed from Yenan 1935-45

area occupied by Japan end 1938

area occupied by Japan after 1944 offensives

'liberated areas' dominated by local Communist groups by 1945

railways in 1937

main industrial centres 1937

other industrial centres 1937

main industrial areas 1937

Chiang's direct rule was limited effectively to the lower Yangtze (map 3). Finally, the Japanese, fearing the potential challenge from a reunited China, decided to reinforce their hold in the north. After 1931, when Japan overran Manchuria, Chiang had to meet simultaneously the Japanese threat from without and the Communist threat at home.

Chiang's purge had virtually eliminated the Communists in the cities, but peasant disaffection, arising from his failure to carry out land reform, provided them with new possibilities in the countryside. It was Mao Tse-tung who realised this, and his base at Chingkang Shan in a remote mountainous area was the main, though not the only, seedbed of the revitalised Communist movement. KMT attacks drove Mao to Kiangsi where the most important Soviet was established and where the Communists ruled an area of several million people developing reform programmes as a peasant-based party rather than an urban, proletarian party on the Russian model. Further KMT attacks forced the Communists to abandon Kiangsi and it was on the famous Long March, to Yenan (map 4), where Mao gathered widespread support by his reform programmes and by spearheading resistance to the Japanese invasion, that his peasant-based wing of the party gained ascendancy. The result was that large areas of China passed under Communist control, while Chiang's government, which had withdrawn under Japanese pressure to the remote fastness of Chungking, was unpopular and out of touch. This was the situation in 1945 after the defeat of Japan, though other factors, particularly the growing Soviet-American involvement, played a part. Negotiations for a political settlement broke down and in 1947 open civil war broke out. The Communists defeated the Nationalists in Manchuria and took Peking in January 1949 (map 5). The great battle around Suchow (November 1948–January 1949) opened the way south. On October 1, 1949, the People's Republic was proclaimed, and the Nationalists fled to Taiwan. But the civil war compounded the devastation of the previous decades and China's new rulers were left with a formidable task of reconstruction.

The Ottoman Empire
1800-1923

The Ottoman Empire gradually disintegrated between the beginning of the nineteenth century and the end of the First World War. Steady European economic and colonial penetration weakened the economy, and the success of the nationalist movements in the latter part of the century caused large areas either to break away or to fall effectively under foreign control.

Austria and Russia had been making inroads into the empire throughout the last decades of the eighteenth century; they were joined by France, whose expedition to Egypt in 1798 eventually resulted in the end of effective control from Constantinople and the creation of a dynasty by the Ottoman viceroy, Mohammed Ali Pasha, which lasted from 1805 to 1952. His son, Ibrahim Pasha, led expeditions to subdue the Wahabi rulers of Nejd, inaugurated a period of Egyptian rule over the

Sudan, and conquered the whole area between what is now Turkey and Egypt between 1831 and 1839.

In the face of this and other challenges, the empire began a series of major reforms, first of its military establishment and then in the fields of law, education and administration. Two major edicts in 1839 and 1856 stressed the subjects' rights to equality and security of life and property. However, especially in the Balkans, the Powers' claims to be able to intervene on behalf of their protégés had the effect of encouraging the nascent nationalist movements; southern Greece, Bulgaria, Montenegro, Romania, and Serbia had all become independent by 1878.

At the same time France was making substantial inroads into North Africa, while Italy invaded Libya in 1911. There were also stirrings of discontent in other Arab provinces, particularly during the long and oppressive reign of Abdul-Hamid II (1876–1909), when ideas of autonomy gradually gained currency, encouraged by the revival of Arabic literature and campaigns to reform

the Arab language. Opposition to Abdul-Hamid's rule culminated in the Young Turk revolution of 1908–09, but the policies pursued by the Young Turks alienated much of the Arab population, and contributed substantially to the Arabs' willingness to seek accommodation with Britain in the course of the war. They were to be disappointed, since the peace settlement put most of the Middle East firmly under British and French control. After Turkey's defeat the caliphate was abolished and a secular republic established.

Similar developments took place in Iran, where the Qajar dynasty (1779–1924) had faced constant Russian and British interference in their internal affairs, culminating in an agreement to divide the country into the spheres of influence of the two powers in 1907. However, the combination of foreign pressures and movements for reform within the country helped to arouse national consciousness and political awareness, and the Constitutional Revolution of 1905–1911 marked a major advance in political self-confidence and maturity.

The Middle East and North Africa 1800–1923 (below)

Afghanistan Independent state under Durrani dynasty to 1842; remained independent despite Russian invasions and wars with Britain 1839–42, 1878–90, 1919.

Albania Ottoman province since 14th century; independent principality 1912; kingdom 1928–39.

Armenia Western part in Ottoman Empire, eastern part in Persia until Russian occupation 1804; independent republic 1918–1920; subsequently absorbed into Turkey and USSR.

Azerbaijan Part of Persia until early 19th century; partly under Russian occupation 1803–28; northern part independent republic 1918–1920; northern part incorporated into USSR after 1920.

Bahrain Independent sheikdom under al-Khalifa family since 1783; under British protection since 1820, formalised in 1892.

Bessarabia Ottoman province; Russian 1812–56; ceded to [Ottoman] Moldavia 1856; Russian 1878; Romanian since 1918.

Bosnia-Herzegovina Ottoman province since 15th century; Austrian administration after 1878; part of Yugoslavia since 1918.

Bukhara Independent khanate; Russian protectorate 1868; part of USSR since 1924.

Bulgaria Ottoman province since 14th century; given autonomy but partitioned 1878; independent kingdom 1908; present (1991) boundaries since 1919.

Daghestan Part of Iran; incorporated into Russia/USSR since 1859.

Dodecanese Ottoman since 16th century; occupied by Italy 1912; to Greece 1947.

Eastern Rumelia Ottoman province since 14th century; part of Bulgaria since 1885.

Georgia Independent kingdom under intermittent Persian control; incorporated into Russia 1801; independent republic 1918–20; part of USSR since 1920.

Greece Ottoman rule since 14th century; independent since 1833; enlarged by additions of Crete and Macedonia in 1913.

Hejaz Under Ottoman suzerainty since early 16th century but generally autonomous under Sharifs of Mecca until 1916; independent 1916–24; absorbed into Saudi Arabia 1925.

Iraq Formed from Ottoman provinces of Basra, Baghdad and Mosul 1920; under Hashemite monarchy 1921–58; British mandate 1920–32.

Kars and Ardahan Ottoman provinces since 16th century; to Russia 1878; in Armenian republic 1918–20; part of Turkey since 1920.

Khiva Independent khanate; Russian occupation 1873.

Kokand Independent khanate; Russian occupation 1876.

Kuwait Ottoman province under hereditary rule of Al Sabah family since c.1756; treaty of protection with Britain 1899–1961.

Lebanon Ottoman conquest 1516–17; Mount Lebanon ruled by independent

dynasties to 1840; given special status within the Ottoman Empire after civil war of 1860; under Ottoman Christian governors 1861–1915; enlarged and made a republic under French mandate 1920–1946.

Macedonia Ottoman province since 14th century; divided between Bulgaria, Greece and Serbia (later Yugoslavia) 1913.

Montenegro Ottoman province since 14th century but generally under autonomous rule; independent 1878; incorporated into Yugoslavia 1918.

Nejd Under Saudi family from 1746; occupied by Egypt for the Ottomans 1818–1822; Saudis regain control 1902; Kingdom of Saudi Arabia incorporating Hasa, Hejaz, Nejd, 1932; Asir added 1934.

Palestine Ottoman province since 16th century; British occupation 1917; assigned to Britain as mandate 1920–1947 with British obligation to facilitate creation of Jewish National Home.

Persia (Iran) Independent kingdom under Qajar Shahs 1779–1924; partition into British and Russian spheres of influence 1907; under Pehlevi dynasty 1924–79.

Qatar Autonomous sheikdom under al-Thani family; British protection 1916–1971.

Romania Formerly Ottoman provinces of Moldavia and Wallachia (since 14th

century); united 1861, independent 1878; enlarged to present (1991) boundaries with the addition of Bessarabia 1918.

Serbia Ottoman province since 14/15th century; autonomous since 1817; separate kingdom 1878; part of Yugoslavia since 1918.

Syria (Name formerly applied to whole area of modern Jordan-Lebanon-Palestine/Israel-Syria.) Ottoman province since 1516; British occupation 1917; Arab kingdom of Damascus 1918–20; French occupation and mandate 1920–1946; sanjak of Alexandretta ceded to Turkey 1939.

Transjordan Part of Ottoman province of Damascus; emirate under British mandate 1923–1946.

Tunisia Ottoman conquest 1574; virtually independent under Husainid dynasty 1705–1881; French conquest 1881; French protectorate 1881–1956.

Turkey Core of Ottoman Empire (early 14th century to 1923); Turkish Republic created 1924.

Yemen Local rulers belonging to Za'idi (Shi'i) sect; nominally part of Ottoman Empire since 1517; Aden occupied by Britain 1839; parts of south in treaty relations with Britain 1886–1954; independent state in north 1918.

3 Agreements between the powers

- zones of control
- zones of influence
- international frontiers 1914
- frontier according to the Treaty of Sèvres 1920

4 The Greco-Turkish War, 1920-22

- area under Greek control 1920
- limit of Greek advance 1921
- direction of Greek offensive 1921
- boundary of Greek control 1921-22
- direction of Turkish offensive 1922

Agreements between the Powers (*above*)

In 1907 parts of Persia became British and Russian spheres of influence (**1**). During the First World War, Britain, France, Italy and Russia made provisional arrangements to divide the Ottoman Empire; in 1915 Russia was given Constantinople, the Straits and the Dardanelles (**2**), France a sphere of influence in Syria and Cilicia (**3**) and Italy in south-west Turkey and the Dodecanese islands (**4**). Under the Sykes-Picot agreement (1916) Palestine was to be internationalised (**5**), Britain was to be given Mesopotamia (**6**), Haifa and Acre on the Mediterranean coast, and the area between (**7**); France gained Aleppo, Damascus, Mosul and their hinterlands (**8**); Russia gained north-west Anatolia, and parts of Kurdistan and Armenia (**9**); subsequently the Italians were promised most of south-west Anatolia (**10**). The British, seeking Arab support, promised Sharif Husain of Mecca a state extending over most of the Arab provinces of the Ottoman Empire. Finally, the Balfour Declaration of 1917 stated that Britain favoured 'the establishment of a national home in Palestine for the Jewish people.' In 1920, the Treaty of Sèvres gave Smyrna (Izmir) and its hinterland to Greece (**11**) and created autonomous states in Armenia and Kurdistan, although the rise of the Turkish Republic meant that the Treaty was never ratified. Most of the present boundaries of the area were agreed at the Lausanne Conference (1923)

1 The disintegration of the Ottoman Empire, 1805-1923

- approximate frontiers in 1800
- Ottoman Empire in 1800
- frontiers after First World War

areas of rule or control:

- British
- French
- Spanish
- Italian
- Russian

Small sheikdoms under British protection 1820s-1971

Independent sheikdom under Al Bu Said family since 1741; British protectorate 1891-1971

Aden port annexed by Britain 1839; treaties of friendship and protection between Britain and local rulers 1886-1954

2 The Middle East in the First World War, 1914-18

- Ottoman Empire in 1914
- under British Empire in 1914
- under Russian Empire in 1914
- Turkish forces
- Russian forces
- French forces
- Allied forces
- Arab forces with Col. T. E. Lawrence
- area of Arab revolt against Ottomans
- Turkish lines at time of surrender, 30 Oct, 1918
- railways

Modern Japan, 1868-1941

The Tokugawa shogunate, established in 1609 (page 50), gave Japan two hundred years of peace and prosperity. But a generation before 1868 it was evident that internal tensions were building up and that the *bakufu* (or Shogun's government) in Edo was losing control. Peasant unrest and discontent among impoverished *samurai*, whose position had been undermined by the growth of a money economy, was compounded by British, Russian, French and American pressure for the opening of Japan to foreign trade. A period of complicated manoeuvring ensued, in which the four western feudal domains (*han*), Satsuma, Choshu, Tosa and Hizen, took the lead (map 1). The outcome was the so-called Meiji restoration, when the emperor, supported by dissident elements, moved from Kyoto to Edo, now re-named Tokyo (or eastern capital), displaced the Shogun, and took direct control of government.

The Meiji restoration of 1868 was in reality a revolution, carried out with the definite aim of modernisation and westernisation. The old feudal structure was replaced in 1871 by a modern system of prefectures. Samurai privileges were abolished (1873), though samurai from Choshu had a leading place in the new conscript army. A western style peerage (1884), cabinet government (1885) and a two-chamber parliament (1889) laid the foundations of political stability; a national education system was instituted (1872) providing teaching for 90 per cent of children by 1900. At the same time economic development was taken in hand (map 2). The first railway was opened in 1872, and by 1906 the main network was completed. Industrialisation proceeded more slowly, beginning effectively only at the end of the 1800s. By 1889 the number of

cotton mills had risen from 3 in 1877 to 83, and by 1913 Japanese production dominated the home market and had a substantial foothold abroad, particularly in China. Nevertheless agriculture remained the main employment until after the First World War. The number employed in agriculture fell from 70 per cent of the population in the 1870s to 57 per cent in 1914, but still provided almost all the foodstuffs for a population which rose from 39 million in 1868 to 56 million in 1918.

International recognition of Japan's new status was nevertheless slow in coming. It had been forced in the 1850s to negotiate unequal treaties with the western powers, and it was not until 1894 that foreign consular jurisdiction was abolished and only in 1911 that Tokyo regained tariff autonomy. These concessions were a tribute to Japan's military successes, seen above all in the war with China (1894–95) and in the Russo-Japanese war (map 4). The first overseas ventures, in the Bonin and Ryukyu islands and in Taiwan, were undertaken primarily to still unrest at home, but in 1894 Japan embarked on a full-scale imperialist policy (map 3). Even so, it was forced by the European powers to return all its conquests except Taiwan; but the Anglo-Japanese treaty of 1902, inspired by mutual fear of Russia, was a turning point. In the war with Russia (1904–05), Japan's forces achieved a series of victories culminating in the fall of Port Arthur (January 1905), the battle of Mukden (February–March), and the destruction of the Russian Baltic fleet in the Tsushima Straits (May). After the war the two combatants rapidly reached agreement over a division of spheres of interest, which allowed Japan to annex Korea in 1910. It had embarked on the creation of a Japanese empire on the Asian mainland, and the war of 1914–18 and the Russian revolution (page 120) enabled it to gain a foot-

hold in Shantung and Manchuria. Although once again western pressure compelled it to withdraw, Japan was recognised at the Peace Conference in 1919 as a major power with a permanent seat on the Council of the League of Nations.

During the 1920s Japanese policy veered between cooperation with the west and an inherent anti-foreign feeling, fed by a sense of discrimination. Until 1932 cooperation prevailed, but the impact of the Great Depression (page 130) swung the balance in the opposite direction, and, beginning with the advance into Manchuria in 1931, Japan set out to carve out an empire in East Asia. After the Japanese attack on the Chinese mainland in 1937, tension grew with the United States. The lines of the Second World War were already being drawn. When Germany defeated France and Holland in 1940, Japan's moment seemed to have arrived, and the advance into South-East Asia began (map 5). In spite of astounding initial successes (page 134), it was a gamble that failed. But paradoxically the failure, and the subsequent American occupation, propelled Japan even more decisively into the modern world than the Meiji restoration, socially authoritarian and backward-looking, had done.

1 Japan in 1868

- provincial borders
- Five highways
- extensions to the Five Highways
- secondary roads
- sea-routes
- ◆ important castle towns

feudal territories:
- major Tokugawa domains
- major anti-Bakufu domains
- → American, Russian, British and other naval visits

2 Industrialisation and economic growth, c. 1880-1922

town population 1918:
- ○ less than 50,000
- ◉ 50,000-100,000
- ⊕ 100,000-500,000
- ⊠ 500,000-1 million
- ■ over 1 million

- railways in 1906
- additions to railways 1906-1918
- main manufacturing areas
- **KYOTO** prefecture

minerals:
- ● coal
- C copper
- ▲ iron
- ■ oil

industry:
- ceramics
- chemicals
- food
- machinery
- manufacturing industry
- ■ metal
- shipbuilding
- + textiles
- wood
- silk

3 The growth of the Japanese empire, 1872-1918

- Japan's possessions at the end of 1875
- territorial acquisitions 1894-1914
- spheres of Japanese influence in 1918

4 The Russo-Japanese War 1904-05

⟵ movements of Japanese forces 1904-05

— railways in 1918

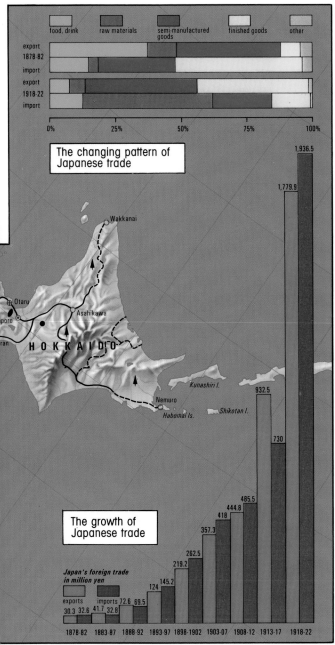

food, drink | raw materials | semi-manufactured goods | finished goods | other

export 1878-82
import

export 1918-22
import

The changing pattern of Japanese trade

The growth of Japanese trade

Japan's foreign trade in million yen

exports imports

1,936.5
1,779.9
932.5
730
485.5
444.8
418
357.3
262.5
219.2
145.2
124
72.6 69.5
41.7 32.8
30.3 32.6

1878-82 1883-87 1888-92 1893-97 1898-1902 1903-07 1908-12 1913-17 1918-22

5 Japanese expansion, 1931-41

- Japan 1928
- expansion to 1933
- expansion to 1941
- ● Chinese capitals
- ✸ Japanese conflict with USSR
- ⟵ Japanese attacks
- ◉ Japanese support for independence movements
- ▪ Allied bases

European political problems, 1919-1939

The First World War shattered the equipoise of 1914. The long-term goal after 1918 was a return to 'normalcy', but it was always an illusion. Not merely had the collapse of the Habsburg Empire, the defeat of Germany, and the Bolshevik Revolution completely altered the balance of power in Europe, but the pre-war economic equilibrium also was destroyed. All the victorious powers were in debt to the United States, and Great Britain, which had largely financed its allies, never fully recovered. These facts weighed heavily at the Paris Peace Conference in 1919, but the dominant fact was probably fear of the spread of revolution from Russia. This accounts for the relatively lenient treatment of Germany, which suffered only minor territorial losses, except for the restoration to the newly independent Poland of the lands seized in the partitions at the end of the eighteenth century. The real problem facing the peacemakers was the tangle of nationalities in Europe. Finland, Estonia, Latvia and Lithuania were detached as independent republics from Russia, which was not represented at the Conference, and Russia also lost Bessarabia to Romania and a large part of White Russia to Poland after the Russo-Polish war of 1920. However, the independent republics of White Russia, Georgia, Armenia and Azerbaijan were brought back into the Soviet Union in 1921 (map 2). The main beneficiary of the peace settlement was Romania, which, in addition to Bessarabia, acquired the Dobruja from Bulgaria and Transylvania from Hungary. But the projected dismemberment of Turkey was thwarted by the national revival under Mustapha Kemal Atatürk (page 124), and in 1923 the new republic was recognised by the Treaty of Lausanne.

The peace treaties left dissatisfied minorities everywhere, and there were widespread movements of refugees, the most extreme case being the wholesale exchange of populations negotiated after the Greco-Turkish war of 1920–22 (map 3). More important politically, they also created a lasting sense of injustice and discrimination. It was inconceivable that either Germany or Russia, once they recovered their strength, would accept a position of inferiority. In addition, there was the irredentism of Hungary, the country which had suffered most from the peace settlement, which was exploited, after 1927, by Mussolini's Fascist Italy, which

hoped in this way to build up for itself a dominant position in the Danubian basin. Thus Europe was divided between revisionists and anti-revisionists, and the only hope for the latter was to support the status quo by a system of military pacts. France, with its alliances with Poland (1921) and Czechoslovakia (1924), underpinning the 'Little Entente' between Czechoslovakia, Yugoslavia and Romania (1921), was the heart and soul of this security system (map 1). It operated effectively until the Great Depression (page 130) and the instability it engendered in France, which undercut France's credibility among its East European clients. When Poland signed a Neutrality Pact with Germany in 1934, it marked the beginning of the collapse of the French security system.

The Locarno treaties (1925), whereby Germany recognised the post-war frontier settlements with France and Belgium, marked the end of the long years of frustration, civil disorder and conflict which had bedevilled Europe since 1918. Germany was welcomed back into the community of nations; so also, after 1925, was Soviet Russia. But the stabilisation of 1925–29 was more apparent than real. With the exception of Czechoslovakia, none of the new states of eastern Europe was economically viable, and the onset of the Depression exposed their weaknesses and left them a prey to German infiltration. Spain also, where the monarchy had been superseded by a republic in 1931, was caught up in its repercussions, which brought a confrontation of left and right and undermined the republican government. The result, in 1936, was civil war (map 4), in which eventually the rebels under General Franco, supported by Italy and Germany, were successful. The failure of France and England to aid the republic discredited them in the eyes of their allies and encouraged Italian and German aggression. Hitler's repudiation of the Locarno treaties, followed by the annexation of Austria (1938) was a clear sign of his intentions; but the destruction of Czechoslovakia, abetted by Poland and Hungary, and the Italian annexation of Albania (1939), further exposed the ambivalence of the western powers (map 5). Whether an alliance with the Soviet Union would have halted the aggressors is a matter of dispute. However, when negotiations between the Soviet Union and the Western powers broke down in 1939, and the Russians, fearing a war of two fronts with Germany and Japan, signed the notorious Nazi-Soviet Non-Aggression Pact, the collapse of the unstable European balance of 1919–39 was inevitable.

1 The European security system, 1921-36

- French alliances
- Little Entente
- Italian alliances
- German alliances
- Soviet alliances
- Balkan pact
- Baltic Entente
- Locarno treaties

The Great Depression
1929-1939

After 1925 it appeared that the disorders of the post-war world had been overcome and a period of relative stability and prosperity had begun. The Great Depression quickly dispelled this illusion. Conventionally its starting point was the financial crash on Wall Street in October 1929; but this was only the manifestation of deeper weaknesses in the world economy. In the United States business was in trouble long before the crash. Worldwide, commodity prices had been falling since 1926, impairing the capacity of exporters such as Australia to buy products from Europe and the United States. The German economy also was faltering by 1928. However, more important than the causes of the depression were its consequences. These were almost instantaneous, although it was only after 1930 that dislocation reached its peak. Its most arresting manifestation was unemployment which reached record heights in 1932. In many industrial countries over a quarter of the labour force was thrown out of work. Industrial production fell to 53 per cent of its 1929 level in Germany and the United States, and world trade sank to 35 per cent of its 1929 value. Attempts to solve the problem only made things worse. As early as 1930 the United States imposed the Hawley-Smoot Tariff, the highest in its history. The United Kingdom responded in 1932 by negotiating the Ottawa Agreements, a series of preferential tariffs for the Commonwealth. Another expedient was competitive devaluation. After England left the Gold Standard in 1931, country after country followed suit and the result was the development of closed currency blocs (map 1), which inhibited international trade still further.

Economic nationalism fostered political nationalism, just as unemployment and the erosion of middle-class living standards fostered political extremism. The fall of the Hamaguchi government in Japan in 1931 marked the end of constitutional democracy and the beginning of Japanese aggression in Manchuria (page 126). In Germany, Brüning's deflationary policies, raising unemployment from under 3 million in 1930 to 6 million two years later, paved the way for Hitler. Hitler's accession to power in January 1933 was followed by Dollfuss's dictatorship in Austria, and eastern Europe, with the exception of Czechoslovakia, quickly followed suit (map 3). France remained precariously democratic until 1940, and in the United Kingdom, where a right-wing 'national' government won a huge majority in 1931, Mosley's fascist movement made little headway. But even here and in the United States, where F. D. Roosevelt was elected president in 1932 with a promise of a 'New Deal', fascist movements exercised considerable pressure (map 2). Only the Soviet Union, isolated from the world economy, was able to sustain economic growth (map 1) – a fact which was to be of cardinal importance after 1941. Roosevelt's New Deal made initial progress, but faltered after 1936 when a new phase of economic down-turn began. By 1939 the United States had not regained the level of industrial output of 1929, and only the Second World War, and the boost it gave to production pulled it out of depression.

The effects of the depression also hit the primary producing countries of Asia, Africa and Latin America. Here, as the crisis radicalised peasants and workers, nationalist and revolutionary movements gained new bases of support. In this respect, as in many others, the Great Depression was the catalyst of the modern world.

1 The world economy, 1929-39

major currency blocs:
- gold bloc
- yen bloc
- German-dominated exchange control area
- dollar area
- sterling area
- areas of shifting or dubious allegiance due to German-American rivalry
- ● areas of loose currency bloc allegiance

production indices:
- 1929 = 100
- 1930
- 1932
- 1934
- 1936
- 1938

3 Social unrest and political movements in Europe

political regimes:
- fascist
- repressive or conservative
- democratic
- 👤 percentage of industrial workers unemployed 1932 *23.2*

major movements of protest and dissatisfaction:
- ◆ strike wave
- ▲ sitdown strike
- ■ riot, demonstration, or single strike
- ● right-wing activity

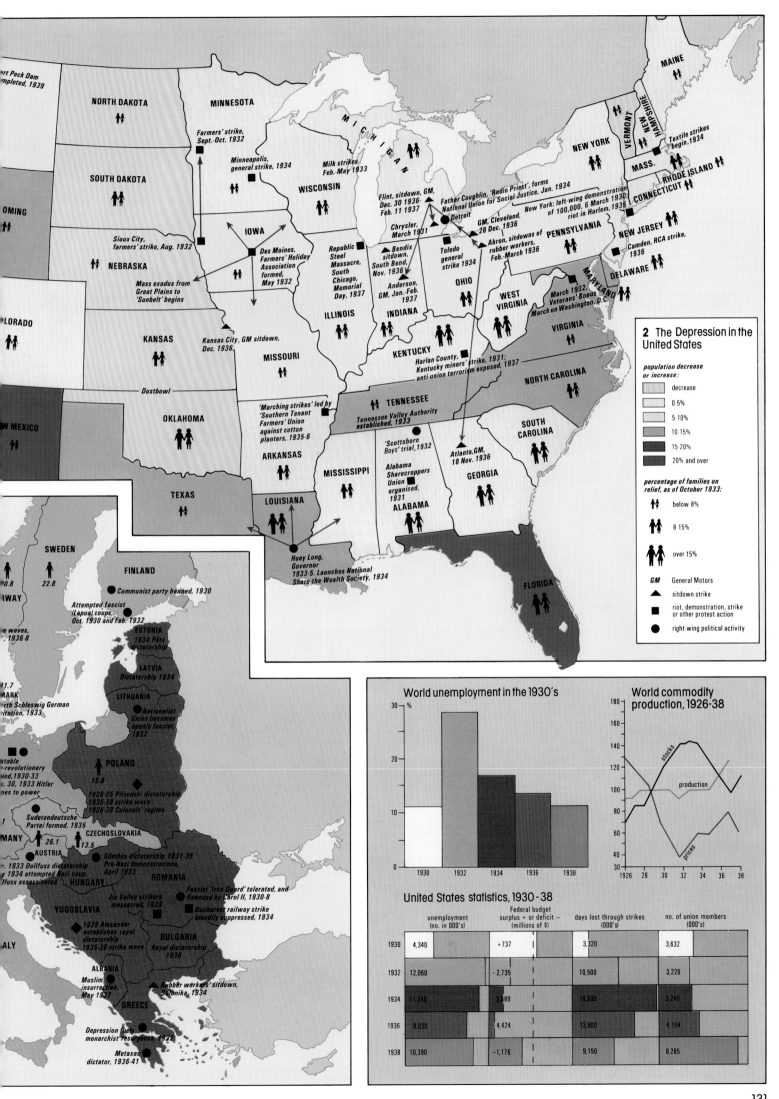

rt Peck Dam
mpleted, 1939

NORTH DAKOTA

MINNESOTA

MICHIGAN

MAINE

NEW HAMPSHIRE

VERMONT

Farmers' strike,
Sept.-Oct. 1932

Minneapolis,
general strike, 1934

Milk strikes
Feb.-May 1933

NEW YORK

Textile strikes
begin, 1934

SOUTH DAKOTA

WISCONSIN

MASS.

RHODE ISLAND

CONNECTICUT

OMING

Flint, sitdown, GM,
Dec. 30 1936-
Feb. 11 1937

Father Coughlin, 'Radio Priest', forms
National Union for Social Justice, Jan. 1934

New York: left-wing demonstration
of 100,000, 6 March 1930;
riot in Harlem, 1935

IOWA

Sioux City,
farmers' strike, Aug. 1932

Chrysler,
March 1931

Detroit

GM, Cleveland,
28 Dec. 1936

PENNSYLVANIA

NEW JERSEY

Camden, RCA strike,
1936

NEBRASKA

Des Moines,
Farmers' Holiday
Association
formed, May 1932

Republic
Steel
Massacre,
South
Chicago,
Memorial
Day, 1937

Bendix
sitdown,
South Bend,
Nov. 1936

Toledo
general
strike 1934

Akron, sitdowns of
rubber workers,
Feb.-March 1936

DELAWARE

MARYLAND

LORADO

Mass exodus from
Great Plains to
'Sunbelt' begins

Anderson,
GM, Jan.-Feb.
1937

OHIO

**WEST
VIRGINIA**

March 1932,
Veterans' Bonus
March on Washington, D.C.

VIRGINIA

KANSAS

Kansas City, GM sitdown,
Dec. 1936

ILLINOIS

INDIANA

KENTUCKY

Harlan County,
Kentucky miners' strike, 1931;
anti-union terrorism exposed, 1937

NORTH CAROLINA

W MEXICO

MISSOURI

Dustbowl

'Marching strikes' led by
'Southern Tenant
Farmers' Union
against cotton
planters, 1935-6

TENNESSEE

Tennessee Valley Authority
established, 1933

**SOUTH
CAROLINA**

OKLAHOMA

'Scottsboro
Boys' trial, 1932

Atlanta, GM,
18 Nov. 1936

ARKANSAS

MISSISSIPPI

Alabama
Sharecroppers
Union
organised,
1931

GEORGIA

TEXAS

LOUISIANA

ALABAMA

Huey Long,
Governor
1933-5. Launches National
Share-the-Wealth Society, 1934

FLORIDA

SWEDEN

FINLAND

Communist party banned, 1930

0.8

22.8

Attempted fascist
(Lapua) coups,
Oct. 1930 and Feb. 1932

ESTONIA
1934 Päts
dictatorship

RWAY

e waves,
1936-8

LATVIA
Dictatorship 1934

LITHUANIA

1.7

ARK

rth Schleswig German
itation, 1933

Nationalist
Union becomes
openly fascist,
1932

stable
-revolutionary
iod, 1930-33
. 30, 1933 Hitler
es to power

POLAND

15.6

1926-35 Pilsudski dictatorship
1935-38 strike wave
1936-38 Colonels' regime

Sudetendeutsche
Partei formed, 1935

CZECHOSLOVAKIA

1

MANY

26.1

13.5

. 1933 Dollfuss dictatorship
y 1934 attempted Nazi coup,
lfuss assassinated

AUSTRIA

Gömbös dictatorship 1931-35
Pro-Nazi demonstrations,
April 1933

HUNGARY

ROMANIA

Fascist 'Iron Guard' tolerated, and
financed by Carol II, 1930-8

Jiu Valley strikers
massacred, 1929

Bucharest railway strike
bloodily suppressed, 1934

YUGOSLAVIA

1929 Alexander
establishes royal
dictatorship
1935-38 strike wave

BULGARIA
Royal dictatorship
1936

ALY

ALBANIA
Muslim
insurrection,
May 1937

Rubber workers' sitdown,
Salonika, 1934

GREECE

Depression fuels
monarchist resurgence, 1932

Metaxas
dictator, 1936-41

World unemployment in the 1930's

World commodity production, 1926-38

stocks

production

prices

United States statistics, 1930-38

	unemployment (no. in 000's)	Federal budget surplus + or deficit − (millions of $)	days lost through strikes (000's)	no. of union members (000's)
1930	4,340	+ 737	3,320	3,632
1932	12,060	− 2,735	10,500	3,226
1934	11,340	− 3,989	19,600	3,249
1936	9,030	− 4,424	13,900	4,164
1938	10,390	− 1,176	9,150	8,265

The War in the West
1939-1945

Hitler's accession to power in 1933 added a new dimension to international politics. He was held back at first by Germany's diplomatic isolation and by the need to put the shattered economy back on its feet. But by 1936 this phase was over. The re-occupation of the Rhineland, the denunciation of the Locarno treaties (page 128), the Rome-Berlin axis, and the anti-Comintern Pact with Japan, demonstrated the new thrust of German policy. Nevertheless Hitler hoped to get his way by threats and bluster rather than by war, and the unopposed annexation of Austria and the dismemberment of Czechoslovakia in 1938 seemed to prove him right. When in the following year he turned against Poland he expected that England and France would once again give way, and believed that the notorious Nazi-Soviet pact of August 23, 1939, would deter the Western powers from intervention. But this time Hitler miscalculated. When German

troops invaded Poland (September 1, 1939), England and France declared war, though they did nothing to aid the Poles.

For the first three years the German armies, with their *Blitzkrieg* strategy, were extraordinarily successful (map 1). After the fall of Poland Hitler halted, hoping that the Western powers would negotiate a compromise peace. Then, in April 1940, he launched his attack in the west, overran Denmark and Norway, and turned against France, which was knocked out of the war before the end of June. But the new Churchill government in London refused to concede defeat, and Hitler launched a major air offensive, intended to prepare the way for invasion. The victory of the Royal Air Force in the Battle of Britain forced him on September 17, 1940, to call off the projected invasion. Instead, Hitler decided to attack Soviet Russia. The directive for 'Operation Barbarossa' was issued in December 1940, the invasion of Russia launched on June 22, 1941. It nearly succeeded. Before the tide turned, German armies were outside Moscow and Leningrad and had overrun southern Russia to the

Black Sea and the Caucasus.

Meanwhile two other events intervened. One was the lack of success of Italy, which had entered the war in 1940, which forced Hitler, in 1941, to divert troops to conquer Yugoslavia and Greece and to reinforce the African front. Secondly the United States, entering the war in 1941 (page 134), supplied Britain and Russia with much needed arms and equipment, and also helped to defeat the German submarine campaign in the Atlantic (map 3). The British victory at El Alamein (October 1942), the subsequent capitulation of the Italian and German armies in Africa (May 1943), the Anglo-American invasion of Sicily and then Italy, and the fall of Mussolini (July 1943), were major Allied successes. But it was the great Russian victory at Stalingrad (January 1943) that was decisive. The Germans' last major offensive in the east at Kursk failed in July 1943. Thereafter they fought a stubborn defensive war (map 2), but after the Anglo-American landings in northern France (June 1944) and the opening of the Second Front, the ring was closed,

and the bases were lost for the 'secret weapons' which Hitler hoped would force the British to capitulate. The Ardennes offensive (December 1944) was a final attempt to break out in the west; but by now the Allies held the initiative. A major Soviet offensive against East Prussia opened in January 1945, and by April Berlin was under assault. On April 30 Hitler committed suicide, and on May 7 his successor, Admiral Doenitz, surrendered unconditionally. The costs were appalling: 15 million military and 35 million civilians had perished, 20 million of whom were Soviet citizens. Some 6 million Jews were exterminated in concentration camps or otherwise. Anglo-American saturation bombing reduced many German cities to rubble, and 25 million Russians were left homeless. Europe was in ruins, and already the differences between the victorious powers, which were to darken the post-war years (page 136), were visible.

1 The German advance, 1939-43

- Axis territory 1 September 1939
- Axis satellites
- Axis occupied
- German advances 1939 41
- Italian advances
- Axis attack on USSR 1941
- Axis advances in USSR 1942
- Allied forces
- cities severely damaged by bombing
- Soviet occupied territory 1939-40
- British Empire
- airborne landings
- Allied withdrawals
- neutral powers

principal German concentration and extermination camps:

1 Auschwitz–Birkenau	7 Flossenbürg	14 Ravensbrück
2 Belzec	8 Gross Rosen	15 Sachsenhausen
3 Bergen-Belsen	9 Majdanek	16 Sobibor
4 Buchenwald	10 Mauthausen	17 Stutthof
5 Chelmno	11 Mittelbau	18 Theresienstadt
6 Dachau	12 Natzweiler	19 Treblinka
	13 Neuengamme	

The War in Asia and the Pacific
1941-1945

Japanese expansionism in the 1930s was the product of a desire to achieve economic self-sufficiency, military security and a self-imposed leadership of eastern Asia (page 126). Japan after September 1931 overran Manchuria and then set about the reduction of its neighbouring provinces by overrunning much of China north of the Yangtze and sponsoring puppet regimes in its area of conquest. By 1941, Japan, with no possibility of militarily or politically ending the Chinese war, found its ambitions widening to include the European colonial empires in South-East Asia. These offered the raw materials and markets that would free Japan from an economic dependence upon an increasingly unfriendly United States. The latter's re-armament programmes were scheduled to near completion by 1944–1945; the prospect of future naval inferiority and the economic blockade imposed upon Japan after its occupation of Indo-China in 1940 prompted Japanese action. The attack upon the US Pacific Fleet at Pearl Harbor in December 1940 was an attempt to forestall American military preparation and thereby buy the time needed to secure and develop South-East Asia.

In challenging the United States Japan sought to fight the world's greatest industrialised power to a stalemate that would result in a negotiated peace which would recognise Japanese hegemony in eastern Asia. Within six months of the start of the Pacific war Japanese forces had conquered American, British and Dutch possessions throughout South-East Asia and had carried the war to the borders of India, to the waters that washed Australia and into the south-west Pacific (map 1). Yet in those months Japan failed to inflict a naval defeat sufficient to impair US military capacity and morale: indeed, in attempting to do so the Imperial Navy suffered a reverse in the Coral Sea in May 1942, the devastation of its front-line carrier force off Midway in June and crippling losses in the protracted Guadalcanal campaign of August 1942-February 1943. Thereafter, without the means to end the war that it had initiated, Japanese strategic mobility was rapidly eroded as the Imperial forces became obliged to fight defensively on widely separated fronts against a number of enemies (map 2). The United States no less slowly grew into a force that was able to sustain four major efforts: a devastatingly successful campaign against Japanese naval and merchant shipping; an 'island-hopping' strategy with amphibious forces that bypassed the major centres of Japanese resistance; an ultimately overwhelming carrier offensive that was to carry the war to the Japanese Home Islands; and a strategic air offensive, based upon the

1 The Japanese advance 1941–42

→ Japanese advance or strike 1941-42

● Japanese base

■ Allied base

✕ battle

Marianas, that was to shatter Japanese urban areas in the last six months of the war (map 3). By August 1945, when the US atomic bomb attacks upon Hiroshima and Nagasaki and the Soviet offensive in Manchuria enforced their surrender, the Japanese had been utterly exhausted and defeated. However, the brief Japanese colonial adventure had unleashed forces of revolutionary nationalism that were to shape events throughout eastern and South-East Asia over the next three decades.

3 The bombardment of Japan, 1945

- area of industrial concentration
- ★ the 'Big Six' fire-raid targets
- ✱ secondary fire-raid target
- ▲ mine-laying target
- → naval bombardment
- ⚓ atomic bomb target

KOREA

Sea of Japan

Hokkaido

Shimonoseki Strait

Nagasaki 9 Aug.

East China Sea

Kyushu

Hiroshima 6 Aug.

Kobe

Osaka

Shikoku

Nagoya

Honshu

Linshoten Strait

Kawasaki

Tokyo

Yokohama

Pacific Ocean

J A P A N

SOVIET UNION

Soviet army attacks (9 Aug 1945)

Sea of Okhotsk

Kamchatka

Komandorski Is.

Bering Sea

60

Khabarovsk

MANCHURIA (MANCHUKUO)

INNER MONGOLIA

Sakhalin

Kurile Is.

Hokkaido

Attu Kiska Amchitka

Aleutian Is.

17 Aug 1945

10 Oct 1943

May-Aug 1943

Japanese perimeter Aug 1945

Japanese perimeter Oct 1944

Japanese perimeter March 1944

ian Forces

se advance into Burma
Oct 1943

ese offensive into NE India
ne 1944

a offensive into Burma
Nov 1944

e offensive in Yunnan
944-March 1945
n taken May 1945

Peking

Tientsin

Dairen

Seoul

Pusan

KOREA

China

East China Sea

JAPAN

40

Nanking

Shanghai

1944 Japanese Ichi-go Offensive

Chinese counter-offensive
April-June 1945

Amoy

Okinawa

Formosa

Hiroshima 6 Aug 1945

Nagasaki 9 Aug 1945

Kyushu

Tokyo

Shikoku

bombing attacks from
15 June 1944

Direct air attack on
Japan from Okinawa
April to Aug 1945

Volcano Is.

Bonin Is.

Iwo Jima
Feb-March 1945

20th Air Force maintains
direct air attack on Japan
from 24 Nov 1944-14 Aug 1945

Fighters cover and
sweep over Japan
from May 1945

Kunming

Laokai

Hanoi

Canton

Hong Kong

Gulf of
Tongking

Hainan

Midway

Hawaiian Is.

Oahu
Pearl Harbor

20

SIAM

angoon

Mandalay

FRENCH INDO-CHINA

Bangkok

Pnom Penh

Saigon

Luzon
landings Jan 1945

Manila

Philippine Is.

Mindoro
Dec 1945

25 Oct 1944
Battle of Leyte Gulf.
Heavy Japanese naval losses

Leyte

Leyte landing 20 Oct 1944
23/29 Oct 1944 Major defeat

Battle of Philippine Sea.
Japanese carrier aviation annihilated
June 1944

Marianas

Saipan June 1944

Tinian

Guam
July 1944

Ulithi
Sept 1944

Palau
Sept 1944

Caroline Is.

Truk

Main fleet base of
central Pacific.
In effect abandoned
by Japanese 1944

Eniwetok
Feb 1944

Pacific Ocean
Area Forces

Kwajalein
Feb 1944

Marshall Is.

Majuro
Jan 1944

Christmas Is.

MALAY STATES

Kuala Lumpur

Singapore

Sumatra

Palembang

Mindanao
May 1945

Zamboanga

Sulu Sea

BRUNEI
June 1945

SARAWAK

Borneo

Balikpapan
July 1945

Tarakan
May 1945

Dutch East Indies

Bandjarmasin

Celebes

Macassar

Java Sea

Morotai
Sept 1944

Halmahera

Sansepur
July 1944

Sorong

Noemfoor
July 1944

Biak
May 1944

Hollandia

Wewak

New Guinea

Makin

Tarawa Nov 1943
Abemama

Gilbert Is.

Pacific Ocean

Manus Feb 1944

Admiralty Is.

Bismarck Arch.

Rabaul

New Ireland

Green Is.

New Britain

Bougainville Nov 1943

Ellice Is.

Eastern Solomons

25/26 Oct 1942 Japanese forces repulsed

Battle of Santa Cruz Aug 1942

Solomon Is.

Russell Is.

Tulagi

Guadalcanal some 50 actions 7 Aug 1942-9 Feb 1943

Batavia

Surabaya

Java

Flores

Amboina

Ceram

Tanimbar Is.

Timor

Sumba

Saidor
Jan 1944

Buna

Port Moresby

Cape York

17/25 Sept 1942
Japanese ground
forces repulsed

Coral Sea

South-west
Pacific Area Forces

Espiritu Santo

New
Hebrides

South Pacific
Area Forces

Fiji Is.

Timor Sea

Darwin

Queensland

AUSTRALIA

New Caledonia

Sydney

Melbourne

---

2 The Allied counter-offensive

- → Allied advance
- ⊹ Allied air attack
- ◻ Allied base
- ● Japanese base
- ◉ Japanese base bypassed or neutralised
- ✳ atomic bomb target
- ✕ battle

90 110 130 150 170 190

Europe after 1945

Europe emerged from the war of 1939–45 devastated and politically divided. Major territorial changes in the east, where Soviet frontiers were advanced approximately to the former Tsarist boundary and Poland was compensated with German territory up to the Oder-Neisse line, were accompanied by a vast movement of displaced persons, including over 12 million Germans (map 1). Germany and Austria were divided into occupation zones and placed under four-power control. But growing Soviet-American conflict after the abortive Potsdam conference (July–August 1945) undermined four-power co-operation, and the consolidation of the Soviet hold in eastern Europe (map 4) accelerated the division of the continent into two armed camps, completed by the establishment of the North Atlantic Treaty Organisation (1949) and the Warsaw Pact Organisation (1955) (map 3). In 1949 the three western zones of Germany became the German Federal Republic, while Moscow established the German Democratic Republic in the east. (map 5).

Economic recovery in the West was stimulated by American aid under the Marshall Plan (1947), and after 1950 western Europe experienced an unprecedented economic boom (diagram 2). Simultaneously, the process of economic integration was initiated which led in 1957 to the creation of the European Economic Community (EEC), though at first Great Britain remained outside, founding a rival organisation, EFTA (European Free Trade Association), and only joining the EEC with Denmark and Ireland in 1973 (map 3). In eastern Europe economic growth was slower but continuous, thanks to Stalinist methods of industrial and agricultural development. Harsh conditions led to widespread strikes and demonstrations in eastern Germany in 1953 (map 5) and to national uprisings in Poland and Hungary in 1956, the latter, like the experiment in national communism in Czechoslovakia in 1968, brutally suppressed by Soviet troops. Nevertheless, after 1957 there was

considerable economic progress. East Germany and Romania forged ahead. Elsewhere, progress was sluggish and uneven, notably in Poland where the formation, in 1979, of an active trade union movement, Solidarity, resulted in the imposition of martial law by 1981.

Steady economic growth helped to stabilise Europe politically. Parliamentary democracy flourished in most of western Europe. In 1954 West Germany was integrated into the western bloc, becoming a member of NATO. Austrian sovereignty was restored a year later. By the 1970s links between eastern and western Europe were much improved. At the European Security Conference in Helsinki in 1975 the post-war settlement of Germany and Poland was formally recognised, and a period of détente inaugurated. In the 1970s democracy finally triumphed in Spain, Portugal and Greece, paving the way for their eventual entry into the Common Market. Economic unity in western Europe produced an unprecedented boom which could not be dented even by the oil crisis of 1973 or rising levels of unemployment in the 1979–81 recession. Though there were arguments

about the level of food subsidy and the establishment of a common exchange rate mechanism, the 1980s saw a closer level of economic co-operation which culminated in plans for complete economic unity to be implemented in stages after 1992. Western prosperity led to increased trade with eastern Europe and contributed to a gradual relaxation of economic controls. In poorer or more backward areas old political tensions remained. In Northern Ireland after 1969, economic stress and longstanding ethnic grievances gave rise to a situation at times close to civil war (map 6). Terrorism surfaced in the Basque areas of Spain, and urban ultra-left terrorist groups committed outrages in West Germany and Italy. Political dissatisfaction in eastern Europe exploded and led, in 1989/90, to the rapid overthrow of Communism in favour of popular multi-party political systems. A year later Germany was re-unified and Soviet influence in eastern Europe declined rapidly with the ending of Comecon and the Warsaw Pact. Eastern Europe faced nationalist and religious conflict and adjustment to economic market forces.

1 Territorial change and population movements, 1945-49

- border of Germany in 1937
- Allied control zones of Germany and Austria
- cities divided into four occupation zones
- annexed by Russia 1940–45
- states which became Communist 1945-48
- Yugoslav gains from Italy in 1945

peoples resettled, evacuated or expelled (with numbers):
- Germans
- Baltic peoples
- Finns driven from area bordering Russia
- Soviet nationals
- Russians forcibly repatriated
- Poles
- Czechs
- peoples settled by International Refugee Organisation

2 Post-war industrial recovery

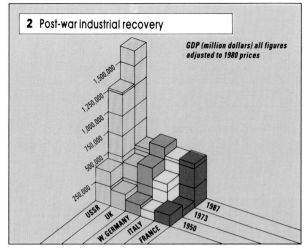

GDP (million dollars) all figures
adjusted to 1980 prices

1,500,000
1,250,000
1,000,000
750,000
500,000
250,000

USSR   UK   W. GERMANY   ITALY   FRANCE

1987   1973   1950

6 Northern Ireland, 1969-90

Roman Catholic majority areas

areas of greatest violence

major incidents

main Irish Republican Army (IRA)
border crossing points

SCOTLAND

North
Channel

1990
human bomb
6 killed

1972 Bloody Sunday
13 killed

Londonderry

Coleraine

1972 Claudy, 9 killed

REPUBLIC

CO. LONDONDERRY

Ballymena

Larne

N O R T H E R N

CO. ANTRIM

1971 McQurk's Bar
15 killed

CO. TYRONE

Lough
Neagh

Belfast

O F

I R E L A N D

Omagh

1972
Bloody Friday
9 killed

1978
La Mon,
12 killed

Dungannon

1987
Remembrance Day
11 killed

Craigavon

Enniskillen

1987
Loughgall,
9 killed

CO. DOWN

CO. FERMANAGH

Armagh

CO. ARMAGH

1976 Kingsmills, 10 killed

IRELAND

Newry

Irish Sea

1988
Ballygawley
8 killed

Crossmaglen

1979 Warrenpoint,
18 killed

4 The Soviet Union and Eastern Europe, 1945-49

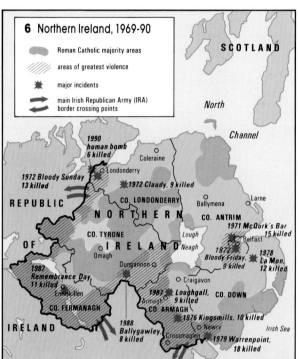

ESTONIA

LATVIA

LITHUANIA

Kaliningrad

EAST
PRUSSIA

U S S R

POLAND
opposition parties
dissolved Nov. 1947

Berlin

EAST
GERMANY
formation of Socialist Unity Party, April 1946
German Democratic Republic established Oct. 1949
Berlin blockade June 1948–May 1949

Prague

NORTHERN
BUKOVINA

Communist coup in Prague
Feb. 1948

CZECHOSLOVAKIA

RUTHENIA

Vienna

Budapest

BESSARABIA

AUSTRIA

HUNGARY
opposition parties dissolved
Nov. 1947

ROMANIA
king abdicated Dec. 1947

Belgrade

Bucharest

YUGOSLAVIA
Tito breaks
with
Moscow,
June 1948

BULGARIA
Dimitrov takes over as
prime minister,
Nov. 1946

ALBANIA

GREECE
civil war 1946
communists suppressed, 1949

Soviet territorial gains
since 1939

Warsaw Pact allies

Polish gains from Germany

air corridors for Western
access to Berlin

Western autobahn to Berlin

ICELAND
EFTA 1970

SWEDEN

FINLAND
associate member
of EFTA 1961

NORWAY

A t l a n t i c

O c e a n

North
Sea

DENMARK

SOVIET UNION

UNITED STATES
AND CANADA

IRISH
REP.
EEC 1973

UK

NETHERLANDS

EAST
GERMANY

POLAND

WEST

BELG.

GERMANY

LUX.

CZECHOSLOVAKIA

GERMANY

FRANCE

AUSTRIA

HUNGARY

ROMANIA

SWITZ.

ITALY

YUGOSLAVIA
limited involvement
in COMECON
from 1964

BULGARIA

PORTUGAL
(joined
EEC 1986)

SPAIN
(joined NATO 1982
joined EEC 1986)

Corsica

Sardinia

ALBANIA

GREECE
(joined EEC 1981)

TURKEY

M e d i t e r r a n e a n   S e a

Sicily

withdrew from
Warsaw Pact, 1968

3 Military and economic blocs, 1980

military partition:

NATO 1949-55

Warsaw Pact Organisation

economic blocs:

original members of EEC

subsequent members of EEC

Benelux Customs Union 1947 (and EEC)

Council for Mutual Economic Assistance (Comecon) 1949

subsequent members of Comecon

members of European Free Trade Association (EFTA) 1960

Denmark and UK leave EFTA Dec. 1972, join EEC Jan. 1973

DENMARK

North Sea

Baltic Sea

SCHLESWIG-
HOLSTEIN

Königsberg
to Russia 1945

Rügen

Danzig

BREMEN AND
BREMERHAVEN
(joint city state)

HAMBURG
(city state)

Kiel

MECKLENBURG

E. PRUSSIA
to Poland 1945

Schwerin

GERMAN

Stettin

to Poland
1945

POMERANIA

Bremen

R. Elbe

R. Oder

NETHERLANDS

LOWER SAXONY

DEMOCRATIC

AND

REPUBLIC

SILESIA

GERMAN

Hanover

BRANDENBURG

Berlin (E. Berlin capital
of Democratic Republic,
W. Berlin separate state of
Federal Republic, 1951)

R. Rhine

NORTH

FEDERAL

SAXONY-
ANHALT

Potsdam

POLAND

Düsseldorf

RHINE-WESTPHALIA

REPUBLIC

Halle

R. Neisse

HESSE

Leipzig

Dresden

Bonn (capital of
Federal Republic,
1949)

Weimar

SAXONY

to Poland 1945

LUX.

THURINGIA

Coblenz
(temporary
capital)

Wiesbaden

Frankfurt am Main

CZECHOSLOVAKIA

RHINELAND
PALATINATE

Mainz

SAARLAND
French occupied;
to Germany 1957

WÜRTTEMBERG
BADEN (1945-52)

BADEN
(1945–52)

BAVARIA

Stuttgart

WÜRTEMBERG
(3 Länder united,
1952)

BADEN
(1945–52)

WÜRTTEMBERG-
HOHENZOLLERN
(1945–52)

Munich

FRANCE

AUSTRIA

SWITZERLAND

5 Post-War Germany to 1990

border of Germany in 1937

border of German Democratic Republic 1949

borders of German post-war administrative regions

administrative capital

centres of the June Uprising 1953

Retreat from empire
after 1947

The European empires of the nineteenth century (page 100) were still intact in 1939, though most German and Ottoman possessions had passed as League of Nations mandates to Britain, France and Japan. Nationalist unrest in the Middle East and Asia exposed the growing fragility of the empires in the 1930s. By the 1950s the demands for independence were irresistible.

None of the European powers surrendered its colonies voluntarily. France fought stubbornly to maintain control in Indo-China, and the Netherlands struggled to contain the nationalists in Java, who had proclaimed an Indonesian republic in 1945. Neither was successful. Vietnamese victory at Dien Bien Phu (1954) forced France to give way (page 148). In Indonesia the nationalists advanced step by step into Kalimantan, Celebes and the Moluccas, until by 1956 they controlled the whole of the former Dutch East Indies except West Irian, which they annexed in 1963 (map 2). The British, also, had no intention of abdicating their imperial position, but continual unrest

forced their hand and in 1947 India and Pakistan became independent (page 104), followed by Burma and Ceylon. Nevertheless Britain still clung to its base at Singapore, fought a long war against Malayan insurgents and resisted Indonesian attempts to annex Sarawak and Brunei. Only after 1967, when Aden was evacuated, did Britain abandon its presence east of Suez, except in Hong Kong, to be retained until 1997, its economic success being of great benefit to China.

Resistance to independence was strongest in colonies with a white settler population, or where there was substantial European investment. This was the situation in the Belgian Congo (Zaire) where, within days of independence, the province of Katanga, with its rich copper and uranium resources, seceded, resulting in prolonged civil war, only halted in 1965 when a government favourable to Western mining interests was set up (map 4). In Algeria, with a white population of one million, the bloodiest war of liberation was fought between 1954 and 1962, first in the countryside and then in the cities (map 3). But conflict was scarcely less bitter in Rhodesia, Kenya and the Portuguese colonies of Angola, Mozambique and Guinea-Bissau.

The British attempted to save the situation in the Rhodesias and Nyasaland by creating a Central African Federation (1953); but when Zambia and Malawi rejected this compromise (1964), Southern Rhodesia declared unilateral independence (1965) in order to ensure white predominance. But the collapse of the Portuguese empire in 1974 forced the Rhodesian government, now surrounded by black states, to cede control to the black majority and Zimbabwe was born in 1980.

By now the formal structures of European imperialism had been dismantled (map 1). In their place came different forms of association, the British Commonwealth and a special relationship between France and its ex-colonies. Britain showed in the Falklands War in 1982 that she was still prepared to fight on behalf of the few islands still directly ruled from London. Only in southern Africa did the white minority try to maintain traditional white rule. But even here the pressure from native nationalist movements compelled change. Namibia won complete independence in 1990, and in South Africa the government gradually abandoned 'apartheid' and accepted the need to co-operate with non-white political forces.

3 The Algerian Civil War 1954-62

☐ French administrative and military territories

⌇ French defensive frontier lines

4 The Congo crisis, 1960-65

☐ area of Katanga secession, 1960-1963

☐ maximum area of rebel advance 1964

● UN troops base

— railways

■ Belgian intervention 1961

centres of 1963-4 rebellion

Belgian paratroop intervention 1964

--- state borders

◆ diamonds

gold

tin

Ⓜ manganese

● coal

Ⓒ copper

Ⓩ zinc

▽ cobalt

⊕ uranium

▲ iron ore

an   *Sea*

Algiers Feb.1959
Tizi Ouzou   Bougie
1954   Collo   Philippeville
   2   *1955*   Bône
GIERS   3   Sétif   Constantine
   Hodna Mts   CONSTANTINE
ulad-Naïl Mts   Batna   1
   1954
   Aures Mts.   *March 1955*
   Oct. 1955   Feriana
at   El Oued   Tozeur
uvement National   Touggourt   TUNISIA
érien (MNA)   *(independent 1956)*
g.1955, "invaded"
FLN Dec.1956
RRITORIES   6
   ▲▲ ○ Ouargla

areas of FLN (Front de Libération Nationale) activity, with date

6 *wilayas*, administrative areas of FLN "shadow government"

oil fields

2 Indonesia and Malaysia, 1945-65

- → → Indonesian confrontation with Malaysia
- → expansion of Indonesian Republic
- areas of unrest
- Republic of Indonesia 1945
- Indonesian states incorporated in Republic, with dates
- Federation of Malaysia 1963

PHILIPPINES
   MINDANAO
Pacific Ocean

South China Sea
SABAH (British North Borneo) claimed by Philippines 1962
BRUNEI
WEST IRIAN (Dutch New Guinea) *annexed by Indonesia 1963*

1964   MALAYA
Medan   Kuala Lumpur
   SARAWAK   *1963-4*
Dutch-Indonesian conflict 1945-9
SUMATRA   Singapore *1959*   *B o r n e o*   *1963-4*   KALIMANTAN 1950   CELEBES (SULAWESI) 1950   MOLUCCAS 1950

1964   Bandjarmasin   REPUBLIC OF SOUTH MOLUCCAS *suppressed by Indonesia 1952*

Palembang
   Makasar
Indian Ocean   Jakarta (Batavia)   MADURA   LESSER SUNDA IS. 1950   PORTUGUESE TIMOR *annexed by Indonesia 1976*
Bandung   J A V A   TIMOR 1950
   Jogjakarta

C H I N A

1 Decolonisation, 1947-90

- ■ territories independent since 1947, with date
- *MPLA* anti-colonial liberation organisations involved in armed struggle

colonies, protectorates and mandates prior to 1947:

British	Spanish	Australian
French	Dutch	South African
Belgian	Italian	New Zealand
Portuguese	U.S.	

☐ dependent states, coloured accordingly

GHANISTAN
PAKISTAN 1947
TIBET *re-absorbed by China 1950; autonomous region 1965*
NEPAL   BHUTAN
SIKKIM *annexed by India 1975*
EAST PAKISTAN 1947 (BANGLADESH 1971)
BURMA 1948
   Anglo-Chinese agreement 1986 for reunification 1997, with Hong Kong able to retain its institutions for 50 years   Hong Kong   Macao

I N D I A   1 9 4 7
   LAOS 1954   NORTH VIETNAM 1954
THAILAND   *insurrection against French rule 1945-54*
   SOCIALIST REPUBLIC OF VIETNAM *unified 1976*
Andaman Is. (Indian)   CAMBODIA 1954   SOUTH VIETNAM 1954   *South China Sea*   PHILIPPINES 1946
Pacific Ocean

SRI LANKA 1948   *called Ceylon until 1972*
BRUNEI 1984   Sabah
MALAYA 1957 *Communist guerrillas 1948-57*
○ MALDIVES 1965   *Sumatra*   MALAYSIA 1963   Sarawak
SINGAPORE 1965   *Borneo*
Celebes
   WEST NEW GUINEA *to Indonesie 1963*   PAPUA NEW GUINEA 1975
Indian Ocean   INDONESIA 1949
Java
   E. TIMOR *FRETILIN (to Indonesia 1976)*

AUSTRALIA

Atlantic Ocean
Bahamas 1973
   CUBA   Turks and Caicos Is.
   British Virgin Is.
   Anguilla
   St. Barthélemy
HAITI   DOMINICAN REP.   Antigua Barbuda 1981
BELIZE 1981 *(formerly British Honduras)*   Puerto Rico *FALN*   St. Christopher Nevis 1983
   Jamaica 1962   American Virgin Is.   Montserrat   Guadeloupe
HONDURAS   St. Martin   Dominica 1978
   Sint-Maarten   Martinique   Barbados 1966
   Aruba   Curaçao   St. Lucia 1979   St. Vincent 1980
NICARAGUA   *Caribbean Sea*   Bonaire   Grenada 1974
   Trinidad and Tobago 1962
PANAMA   COLOMBIA   VENEZUELA

New Ireland New Britain 1975 *(to Papua New Guinea)*   Kiribati 1979 *(formerly Gilbert Is.)*   *Pacific Ocean*
   Nauru 1968   Jarvis I.
   Tuvalu 1978 *(formerly Ellice Is.)*   Marquesas Is.
Solomon Islands 1978   Wallis and Futuna Is.   Western Samoa 1962
AUSTRALIA   Vanuatu 1980 *(formerly New Hebrides)*   American Samoa   Society Is.
   New Caledonia   Fiji 1970   Tonga 1970   Tahiti Is.
   Cook Is.   Gambier Is.
   Kermadec Is.   Pitcairn I.
   Lord Howe I.   Norfolk I.

Asia and Africa after independence

The history of Asia and Africa since independence is one of chronic instability. Three factors stand out: first, the seizure of power by military leaders (Egypt 1952, Pakistan 1958, Ghana 1966, Indonesia 1967), with the aim (rarely successful) of abolishing corruption and stabilising the economy; second, the resurgence of long-standing regional, tribal and religious conflicts (Naga unrest in India, Kurdish revolts in northern Iraq, Turkey and Iran, nationalist uprisings among the Kachins, Mons, Shans and other 'hill peoples' in Thailand and Burma); finally persistent intervention by the great powers, particularly in the Middle East. Sino-Soviet rivalry lay behind the Vietnamese invasion of Cambodia and the Chinese invasion of Vietnam (1979). In Africa the United States and the Soviet Union inter-vened in the Somali-Ethiopian war (1976–78), and France sent troops to Chad, and, with other Western powers, helped to quell the insurrection in Zaire in 1978. The attempted secession of Biafra (map 2), essentially a revolt of the Ibo people in eastern Nigeria against northern domination, was defeated by the federal government, with broad international backing. On the other hand, the secession of Bangladesh from Pakistan (1971) was successful, though only achieved with massive Indian military support.

Two countries alone were exceptions from the general pattern. Japan's progress, after the recovery of independence in 1951, was phenomenal. Maintaining close relations with the United States, successive governments concentrated on industrial development and new technology until in the 1970s Japan emerged as the world's third industrial nation (diagram 4). The case of China is more equivocal. Reconstruction after the Revolution (page 122) proceeded apace; but the 'Great Leap Forward' (1958–60) and the 'Cultural Revolution' (1966–68) brought not only political strife but also severe economic disruption and widespread massacre. After the death of Mao Tsetung (1976) stability returned and there was wide-ranging economic reform, particularly in agriculture; China also became an industrial power. Countries around the Pacific Rim – South Korea, Taiwan, Singapore – made significant economic progress in the 1970s and 1980s based on the cheap production of high-technology goods for the West. Elsewhere poverty remained endemic. In 1985 only 6 out of 47 African countries had an average annual income above $750 a head; only 10 out of 80 states in the whole region had an average annual income above $2,500.

Faced by the threat of internal disruption, governments everywhere looked

1963-74 intermittent intercommunal clashes
1974 Turkish invasion and occupation of northern part of island

1979 Muslim Brotherhood insurgency
1982 army attack on Muslim Brotherhood; many thousands killed

1975-77 civil war, Christians against Muslim leftists and Palestinians
1976 Syrian intervention in south
1978 Israeli intervention in south
1982 Beirut attacked by Israel
Expulsion of PLO from Beirut
1985 formal withdrawal of Israeli troops
1987 Syrian invasion eventually restores some order
1989-90 inter-Christian militia conflicts

1958 King Faisal assassinated; republic proclaimed
1961-75 intermittent fighting in Kurdish areas
1980-88 war with Iran ends with no gains
1988 attacks on Kurdish areas using chemical weapons
1990 invasion and annexation of Kuwait
1991 Defeated by US-led UN forces; suppresses Kurds in north and Shias in south

invaded by Iraq 1990
liberated by US-led UN forces 1991

1960s border conflicts with Morocco
1965 Ben Bella deposed by Col. Boumedienne

1976 Spanish Sahara jointly occupied by Morocco and Mauritania; POLISARIO guerrilla resistance backed by Algeria

1948 state of Israel proclaimed; wars with Egypt (1956), Egypt, Jordan and Syria (1967), Egypt and Syria (1973) (see map 3) 1967 West Bank of Jordan, Sinai and Golan Heights occupied. Sporadic Palestinian Arab resistance, led since 1967 by PLO under Yasser Arafat
1982 withdrawal from Sinai
1986-7 widespread Arab civil disturbances (Intifada)

1990 election of Islamic fundamentalist-dominated chamber of deputies
1991 election results nullified

1973 Aozou strip occupied

1952 King Farouk deposed; replaced by military junta, led by Nasser after 1954
1956 nationalisation of Suez Canal Company and war with Britain, France and Israel
1958-61 union with Syria (United Arab Republic)
1967, 1973 wars with Israel (see map 3)
1970 Sadat becomes president
1979 Egyptian-Israeli peace treaty
1981 Sadat assassinated

1969 border conflict with People's Democratic Republic of Yemen
1990-91 Provided bases for US-led coalition forces in liberation of Kuwait

1969 King Idris deposed; replaced by military junta under Col. Gadhafi
1986 US bomb Tripoli in retaliation for terrorist attacks

1968 civilian government overthrown
1974-85 border conflicts with Burkina

1960 - civil war; FROLINAT guerrillas supported by Libya
1973, 1981 Libyan invasions
1981 Libyan withdrawal
1984- border war with Libya

1963-72 civil war
1969 General Numeiry takes power in military coup, intermittent civil war in South since independence
1984 severe famine
1985 Numeiry overthrown (civil war continues)

1966 Nkrumah deposed
1967-85 series of military coups

1967-70 Nigerian Civil War (see map 2)
1981 civilian rule restored   1984, 85 military coups

1966 military takeover led by Col. Bokassa, crowned emperor 1976
1980 republic restored

1966 Obote expels Kabaka (King) of Buganda
1970 border dispute with Kenya
1971 Obote overthrown by Amin; Asians expelled; large-scale repression
1979 invaded by Tanzania, Amin overthrown; Obote restored (1980), overthrown (Jan 1986)

1970s border disputes with Uganda and Somalia

1960-69 civil war (see p. 138)
1978 invasion of Shaba province by anti-Mobutu dissidents, repelled with French assistance

1962-65 civil war, massacre of Batutsi

1975- Marxist MPLA government in conflict with UNITA guerrillas aided by South Africa

1980- South African intervention in support of MNR guerrillas
1986 President Machel dies in air crash

1980 increasing steps towards once-party state

1972 military takeover

support for black nationalists in Angola, Namibia and Rhodesia
1991 Kaunda defeated in democratic election

1975 invasion of Angola
1976 mounting black urban unrest
1976-81 African homelands (Bantustans) established in Transkei, Bophuthatswana and Ciskei
1984 new constitution: limited representation for Indians and coloureds
1985-87 growing African resistance and civil unrest
1986 commando raids on neighbouring countries

South African presence resisted by SWAPO to 1990
1990 Mandela released, President de Klerk starts to dismantle apartheid

2 Nigeria and the Biafran War 1967-70

Ibo heartland
boundaries of the 12 States
Biafra, declared 30th May, 1967
effectively occupied by Biafra, 9th Aug. 1967
Biafran offensive towards Lagos
Nigerian offensives

NORTH-WESTERN STATE
Kano
KANO
Maiduguri
NORTH-EASTERN STATE
NORTH-CENTRAL STATE
Kaduna
Kainji Lake
DAHOMEY
KWARA
Ilorin
N I G E R I A
Jos
R. Niger
R. Benue
BENUE-PLATEAU
WESTERN STATE
Sept 1967
Ibadan
Ore
Sept 1967
July 1967
July 1967
CAMEROON
LAGOS
Ekitipupa
Sept 1967
EAST CENTRAL STATE
LAGOS (Federal capital)
Benin City
Amichi
SOUTH-EASTERN STATE
MID-WESTERN STATE
BIAFRA
RIVERS STATE
Sept 1967
surrender signed Jan 1970
Calabar
Port Harcourt
rebel advance halted Aug 1967
May 1968
Oct 1967
Bight of Biafra
Enugu

to the great powers for support. Inevitably they were drawn into great-power politics. Iran, where the United States covertly helped the Shah's supporters to oust the nationalist Mossadeq in 1953, was one bastion of American influence in the Middle East until 1979 when Ayatollah Khomeini introduced revolutionary Islamic fundamentalism and a long war with Iraq ensued. The Jewish state of Israel, at war with its Arab neighbours ever since its foundation in 1948 (map 3) received US support. The Soviet Union supported Syria and Egypt until the latter, after the Egyptian-Israeli war of 1973, turned to the United States for financial backing. This diplomatic revolution inaugurated a new phase. At Camp David in 1978 Egypt and Israel came to terms, but the rest of the Middle East remained in a constant state of crisis. From 1980 Iraq and Iran were at war for eight years; Lebanon collapsed in civil war; in 1990 Iraq invaded Kuwait and was driven out by UN forces early the following year.

Democracy made significant gains in the whole area during the 1980s and 1990s (notably in Pakistan, the Philippines, Namibia, South Africa and Zambia) but elsewhere single party or military regimes were still the rule. Prospects for stability and an end to violence and political coercion remained uncertain.

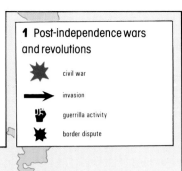

1 Post-independence wars and revolutions

- civil war
- → invasion
- guerrilla activity
- border dispute

nationalist government of Mossadeq ...ved and Shah restored
...79 Islamic revolution; deposition ...ah, Jan. 1979; guerrilla war in ...istan; large scale repression ...ran-Iraq war (1980-88) threatens ...national shipping in the Gulf ... western convoys introduced

... supports Baluchistani ...aratists in Pakistan
...1979 invaded by USSR; ...n killed, Karmal installed as ...ident; continued resistance ...Islamic guerrillas
...1989 USSR withdraws

C H I N A

1950 invasion of Tibet
1953-57 first Five-Year Plan
1958-60 Great Leap Forward; abandonment of Soviet model and beginning of Sino-Soviet dispute
1960- border conflicts with India and USSR
1966-68 Cultural Revolution; mobilisation of Red Guards
1969-75 stabilisation and economic progress
1971 China admitted to United Nations
1972 Nixon's visit to Peking and normalisation of Sino-American relations
1976 death of Mao Tse-tung; political reorientation under Hua Guofeng and Deng Xiaoping, leading to a limited revival of private sector trade and production
1989 Demonstration for democracy by Beijing students crushed

GHANISTAN

PAKISTAN **INDIA**

spasmodic unrest among Nagas, Sikhs and Tamils
1962 Sino-Indian border war
1975-77 state of emergency proclaimed
1980 further emergency measures
1984 Sikh separatist uprising suppressed
Indira Gandhi assassinated

1958 military coup by Ayub Khan
1965 border clashes with India in Rann of Kutch
1965 war with India over Kashmir, 1972 ceasefire lines established
1971 war with India over Bangladesh
1977 military coup by Zia ul-Haq
1988 Democratic elections. Benazir Bhutto prime minister

1965-75 Marxist insurgency by People's Democratic Republic of Yemen defeated with British and Iranian help

...2-69 civil war
...-79 intermittent war with ...le's Democratic Republic of Yemen ...ns united 1990

... war against Eritrean secessionists ... Emperor Haile Selassie overthrown ...my junta
...88 severe famine, aid from West ...Mengistu flees, Eritrean independence agreed

1970 border disputes with Ethiopia and Kenya
...78 occupation of Ogaden and war with Ethiopia

TIBET

BANGLADESH

1971 secession from Pakistan; civil war followed 1975 by murder of Sheikh Mujib and military control

BURMA

continuing guerrilla activity since independence (1948) by Communist and minority groups, united in 1975-76 into Federal National Democratic Front
1958, 1962 military coups
1974 Socialist People's Republic inaugurated
1988 military coup

SRI LANKA

1958, 1961 fighting between Sinhalese and Tamils
1971 government assumes emergency powers after rural guerrilla uprisings; 1984 intercommunal rioting
1986-90 Indian intervention to crush Tamil rebellions

1948 Democratic People's Republic of Korea proclaimed
1950 invasion of South Korea

NORTH KOREA

SOUTH KOREA

1948 republic of Korea proclaimed
1950 Korean War (see p.148)
1961 military coup followed by dictatorship of Park Chung Hee (assassinated 1979); mounting opposition from 1974
1979 martial law (relaxed 1981)

J A P A N

Kurile Islands incorporated in USSR 1945; claimed by Japan
1951 peace treaty with USA and end of occupation
1956 agreement with USSR, ending state of war; cession of territories (including S. Sakhalin) taken from Russia in 1905
1960 widespread demonstrations against security treaty, granting US military bases in Japan and Okinawa
1972 normalisation of relations with China
1974 beginning of incipient trade disputes with US and EEC
1990 formal agreements with USSR (formal end to 1945 war)

occupied by US after 1945, reverted to Japan 1972

OKINAWA

seat of Chinese Nationalist government under Chiang Kai-shek since 1949
1958 territorial dispute with mainland China over Quemoy and Matsu

TAIWAN

1954 French withdrawal followed by civil war and foreign intervention 1956-75 (see p. 148)
1976 North and South Vietnam reunified under Viet-Minh rule
1978 invasion of Cambodia and border clashes with China
1979 Chinese invasion

VIETNAM

LAOS

1953-73 civil war
1975 monarchy abolished; Pathet Lao seizes power

THAILAND

1947 military takeover, guerrilla activity by Communist and minority groups since 1960
1976 border clashes with Cambodia
1978 Cambodian refugee camps in E. Thailand become bases for anti-Vietnamese factions
1987 border clashes with Laos

CAMBODIA

PHILIPPINES

Communist and Muslim insurgency since 1968, erupting into civil war 1972-78
1986 Marcos regime ousted following general election

Mindanao

1970 monarchy abolished
1970-74 civil war; victory of Khmer Rouge who conduct massacre of civilians
1978 Vietnamese invasion overthrows Khmer Rouge
1989 Vietnamese forces withdraw

1969 risings by Chinese minority groups
1975-78 Communist guerrilla activity
1978 renewed racial and religious conflict

M A L A Y S I A

IRIAN JAYA

I N D O N E S I A

1967 Sukarno ousted by military coup; suppression of Communists
1976 resistance to Indonesian rule in E. Timor
1977-79 secessionist rising in Irian Jaya

E. Timor

3 Israel and Palestine, 1947-80

350,000 from Europe ○ Beirut
283,000 from M. East

- Jewish state under UN partition plan for Palestine 1947
- Israel after Arab invasion and War of Independence 1948
- Israel conquests 1967
- Egyptian re-conquests, and Israeli conquests 1973

LEBANON
SYRIA
Tyre
Damascus
Golan Heights
Qunaytirah
Sea of Galilee
Haifa
Samaria
Nablus
West Bank
R. Jordan
Tel-Aviv
Jaffa
Jerusalem
Amman
Jericho
Gaza
Hebron
Dead Sea
Gaza Strip
Judaea
Rafah
Beersheba

ISRAEL

Mediterranean Sea

264,500 from N. Africa

Port Said
El Arish

JORDAN

Ismailia
Giddi Pass
Suez
Mitla Pass

Negev

SAUDI ARABIA

Sinai Peninsula
returned to Egypt 1981

Elat
▲ Abu Rudeis oilfield
Aqaba

E G Y P T

population movements:
→ Jewish immigration 1948-64
→ Arab emigration 1948 (total 726,000)
→ Arab emigration 1967 (total 400,000)

Gulf of Suez
Suez Canal
Gulf of Aqaba
Strait of Tiran
Sharm el Sheikh
Red Sea
Ras Muhammad

4 Japanese industrial production, 1945-80

index of industrial production (1945=100)

2684.1
1736.4
487.8
112.2

1980
1970
1960
1950

cameras †: 16,317,000 (1980); 13,804,000; 10,172,000; 7,290,000; 5,813,000; 1,859,000; 193,000
cars †: 13,500,000; 7,038,100; 3,178,000; 185,100; 1,800
televisions and computers
ships *: 1,807,000; 227,000

growth of industrial production

† units
* metric tons

141

Latin America since 1930

The world depression of 1930 (page 130) was a watershed in the history of Latin America. Heavily dependent on primary exports (map 2), all the republics were hit by the drop in world trade. Chile's exports fell by over 80 per cent between 1929 and 1933; those of Bolivia and Peru by 75 per cent. In Brazil coffee was burnt. Only oil-exporting Venezuela more or less weathered the storm. The result was widespread disillusion with the middle-class liberal or radical parties, themselves apparently helpless. In 1930 and 1931, 11 of the 20 republics south of the Rio Grande experienced revolutionary changes of government. In Mexico, where Cárdenas (1934–40) revived the

land distribution policies of 1911, the shift was to the left, but the swing was mainly to the right, though not back to nineteenth century *caudillismo* (page 96), the social bases of which were being eroded by urbanisation and population movements (map 3). The new dictators were populists, appealing directly to the masses and cooperating with organised labour and the trade unions. They also introduced programmes of industrialisation, following Soviet or, more often, fascist models, to reduce dependence on overseas markets and hasten economic development.

Manufacturing industry was given a further boost by the Second World War, which cut off imported consumer goods and stimulated the industrial sector. But industrialisation made Latin America dependent upon imported capital goods,

raw materials, technology and finance, creating enormous foreign debts. Multinational corporations exploited the cheap labour markets of Latin America without stimulating economic development. Social tensions arose from income concentration, unemployment, lack of opportunities and the presence of foreign interests. Social revolutions were attempted but frustrated in Guatemala, Bolivia and Chile (map 1), and this underlined the obstacles to change when economies are too narrowly based to sustain welfare programmes and when local élites are prepared to collaborate with the United States. Cuba from 1959 attempted to achieve social change, economic growth, and freedom from the United States simultaneously. The revolution led to greater social equality and an improvement in the prospects of rural workers but it also involved a commitment to a repressive government and a dependence on the Soviet Union.

In the face of revolutionary change, many governments closed their ranks. With some support from the upper and middle classes, military governments in the south combined political repression with economic liberalisation. Other than in Chile, in the mid-1980s the world recession drove the military back to their barracks. By the late 1980s, three problems dominated: the debt crisis; the watchful suspicions of the military in the southern cone over the new democracies; and the civil conflicts in Central America, a continuing barrier to economic and political development, though the defeat of the Sandinistas in Nicaragua in 1990 in democratic elections suggested the possibility of returning stability.

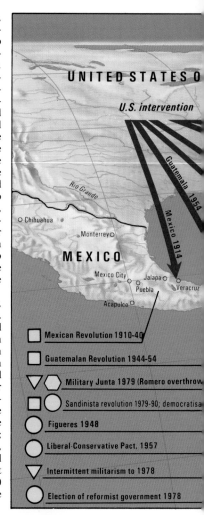

U.S. intervention

☐	Mexican Revolution 1910-40
☐	Guatemalan Revolution 1944-54
▽⬡	Military Junta 1979 (Romero overthrow
☐◯	Sandinista revolution 1979-90; democratisa
◯	Figueres 1948
◯	Liberal-Conservative Pact, 1957
▽	Intermittent militarism to 1978
◯	Election of reformist government 1978

2 Economic development

direct US investment in Latin America:

1952 – millions of $
1943 – millions of $
1929 – millions of $

chief exports of Latin America 1958:

●● represents more than 50% of total exports

● represents more than 25% of total exports

Venezuela: oil production 1940-1975 (million barrels)

1940	1945	1950	1955	1960	1975
186	325	500	700	1041	856

families benefited

600,000
500,000
400,000
300,000
200,000
100,000
0

Mexico: agrarian reform – land distribution:

land area distributed in hectares (1 hectare = 2.471 acres)

10,000,000
5,000,000
0

1916-34 | 1934-40 | 1940-45 | 1945-52 | 1952-58 | 1958-63 | 1963-67

urbanisation in 1970: %age of population living in cities of over 100,000 inhabitants

Argentina, Bolivia, Brazil, Chile, Colombia, Cuba, Ecuador, Guatemala, Honduras, Mexico, Nicaragua, Paraguay, Peru, El Salvador, Uruguay, Venezuela

1 Social and political movements, 1930-90

⬜ **Social revolution** Fundamental change (attempted or achieved) in economic and social structure by nationalist or Marxist movements

⬤ **Reformism** Moderate socio-economic change or modernisation by democratic or other process

☆ **Populism** Revolutionary change by dictatorships appealing to popular forces, especially urban labour

◇ **Christian Democracy** Radical socio-economic change by Christian Democrat parties

▽ **Militarism** Military dictatorship of the right, with or without social or modernising programme

⬡ **Indigenous guerrilla movements** Urban guerrillas from late 1960's following failure of Cuban-inspired rural guerrillas

Atlantic Ocean

Washington

Grenada 1983

Dominican Republic 1916-24, 1965-66

Haiti 1915-34

Cuba 1921-23, 1933, 1961

Panama 1903-18, 1989

Nicaragua 1912-33

Bahama Islands

Miami

Havana

CUBA

Santiago

HAITI

DOMINICAN REPUBLIC

Dominica

Martinique

St. Lucia

St. Vincent

Barbados

Tobago Trinidad

Cuban Revolution 1959 ⬜

Cuban inspired guerrilla movements 1959-68

US invasion 1983

BELIZE

GUATEMALA

Guatemala City

HONDURAS

Managua

NICARAGUA

EL SALVADOR

San José

COSTA RICA

PANAMA

Panama City

San Juan

Caracas

VENEZUELA

Georgetown

Paramaribo

Cayenne

SURINAM

GUYANA

FRENCH GUIANA

Macapá

Cartagena

COLOMBIA

Bogotá

Quito

ECUADOR

Guayaquil

R. Negro

Manaus

R. Amazon

Gurupá

Belém

Fortaleza

PERU

Piura

R. Purus

Recife

Trujillo

Huánuco

B R A Z I L

Callao Lima

Cuzco

Brasília

Salvador (Bahia)

Arequipa

La Paz

BOLIVIA

Sucre

Belo Horizonte

PARAGUAY

São Paulo

Santos

Rio de Janeiro

Asunción

Military dictatorship Stroessner 1954
Rodriguez 1989 ▽

Antofagasta

Florianópolis

Pôrto Alegre

San Miguel de Tucumán

Copiapó

Rio Grande

R. Uruguay

Santa Fé

Córdoba

URUGUAY

Fray Bentos

Rosario

Montevideo

Valparaíso

Mendoza

Buenos Aires

Santiago

C H I L E

ARGENTINA

Concepción

Bahia Blanca

Valdivia

Osorno

Rawson

Patagonia

Comodoro Rivadavia

Santa Cruz

Falkland Islands (Islas Malvinas)
occupied by Argentina 1982;
occupation ended by UK
Task Force June 1982

Tierra del Fuego

Rómulo Betancourt 1945-48, 1959-64
Carlos Andrés Pérez 1974-79 ⬤

Rafael Caldera 1969-7; Luis Herrera Campins 1979; Jaime Lusinchi 1984 ◇

Getulio Vargas 1930-45, 1950-54 ☆
João Goulart 1961-64 ▽
Modernising militarism 1964

Civilian rule 1985; democratisation 1986 ⬤

Batllismo 1903-33 ⬤

Tupamaros ⬡

Military 1973 ▽

Civilian rule 1985; democratisation 1986 ⬤

Montoneros ⬡

Juan Domingo Perón 1943-55, 1973-4 ☆

Military 1976-83 ▽

Democratisation and civilian rule 1983 ⬤

☆ **Radical militarism 1968**
⬤ **Return to civilian rule 1980**

⬜ Bolivian Revolution 1952-64

⬜ Che Guevara (killed 1967)

▽ Military 1980; democratisation 1982

◇ Eduardo Frei 1964-70

⬜ Salvador Allende (Popular Unity) 1970-73

▽ Pinochet 1973- free market economy

3 Population growth and change

middle class, as % of total population (1963):

▫	5%-20%
▫	20%-30%
▫	30%-40%
▫	40%-50%
▫	over 50%
▫	no available information

percentage of population engaged in agriculture (1963) 50%

Rio de Janeiro

Mexico: population increase 1900-80

67.0
48.2
35.0
25.8
19.7
16.6
14.3
15.2
13.6

millions

Mexican Revolution | Post-Revolution

1900 10 20 30 40 50 60 70 80

Brazil: population increase 1920-80

millions

120
100
80
60
40
20
0

1920 1940 1950 1960 1970 1980

143

The United States from 1945

The years from 1940 to 1980 saw economic, demographic, and social changes in the United States that transformed the lives of its people. The agricultural, industrial, and service sectors of the economy reached unprecedented levels of productivity. Fewer farmers provided not only for a population which, by 1980, was overwhelmingly urban, but also a significant proportion of the world's production of major staples such as wheat, corn, and soya beans (diagram 5, A–C). Mechanisation (under 10 per cent of the cotton crop was harvested by machine in 1949, 96 per cent in 1969), greater yields from improved seed and fertilisers, and an intensely market-oriented and government subsidised system of sales and distribution made this possible. The economy at large grew at a comparable pace until the 1970s. The gross national product (in constant 1958 dollars) was $227.2 billion in 1940, $722.5 billion in 1970. The service sector expanded more rapidly than did manufacturing, and cities such as Atlanta and Houston in the South and South west, and Los Angeles, San Francisco, and Denver in the West, became major centres of economic activity (map 4).

This economic growth was accompanied by massive flows of people both within and into the country. With the end of large-scale immigration in the 1920s and the relative im-mobility of the 1930s, it seemed as though the mobility of American life was over. But the armament build-up during the Second World War attracted many people to the old industrial centres of the Northeast and the Midwest, and to new plants elsewhere. Economic expansion after the war sustained these flows. Millions of blacks and whites left the Southern country-side for the East, the Midwest, and the far West; many more agricultural, industrial, and professional families moved to the West, the Sun Belt of the South and Southwest, and to burgeon-ing cities around the nation (map 1). An interstate system of highways totalling about 40,000 miles by 1980 facilitated the long-distance movement of people, and the rise of complex networks of residence and work (map 2). By 1980 only a third of the population lived in non-metropolitan areas.

About 10 million immigrants arrived in the US between 1950 and 1980 (map 1) (plus millions more illegally). Perhaps the most dramatic social change was in the realm of race relations. Between 1940 and 1980 a centuries-old structure of formal, explicit racial discrimination against blacks and Asians all but disappeared. Minorities made major gains in education, income, and social acceptance. But this revolution in race relations was not without strains. The massive black and Hispanic migration to American cities exploded in substantial urban riots during the troubled years of the 1960s (map 3). A further strain was imposed by the war in Vietnam, particularly after President Johnson's decision in 1965 to commit ground troops on a massive scale (page 148). By 1968 opposition to the war had become a further divisive factor in American society.

Vietnam also imposed serious strains on the American economy. After 1967 the United States entered a period of inflation and deficits, abandoning the Gold Standard and depreciating the dollar in 1971. Competition from the EEC and Japan brought US industrial predominance to an end; by 1980 unemployment, particularly among blacks and other minorities, became a serious problem. In the 1980s economic growth revived and American rearmament brought a revival in America's international position. The result was an end to the arms race with the Soviet Union and an end to Cold War conflicts. American intervention in Grenada, Panama and the Middle East produced a growing nationalism at home, and growing confidence that the American conception of 'liberal capitalism' was still a viable one.

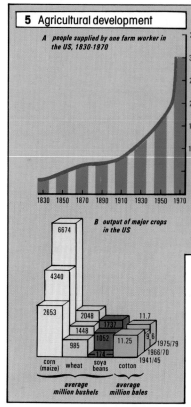

5 Agricultural development

A *people supplied by one farm worker in the US, 1830-1970*

B *output of major crops in the US*

corn (maize) · wheat · soya beans · cotton

average million bushels · *average million bales*

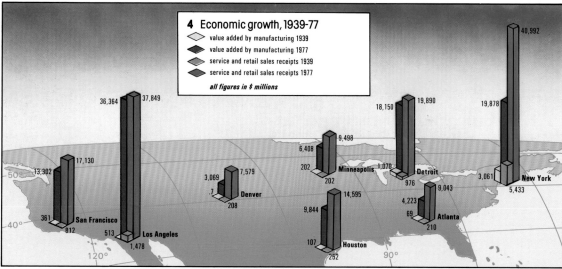

4 Economic growth, 1939-77

- value added by manufacturing 1939
- value added by manufacturing 1977
- service and retail sales receipts 1939
- service and retail sales receipts 1977

all figures in $ millions

2 Growth of metropolitan areas 1940-75 (standard)

- 1940
- 1960
- 1975
- interstate highways 1980

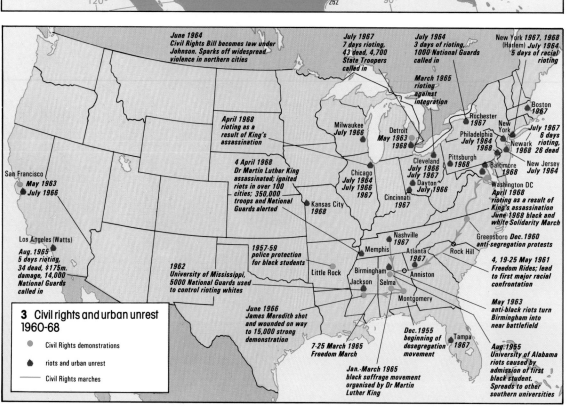

3 Civil rights and urban unrest 1960-68

- ● Civil Rights demonstrations
- ♣ riots and urban unrest
- — Civil Rights marches

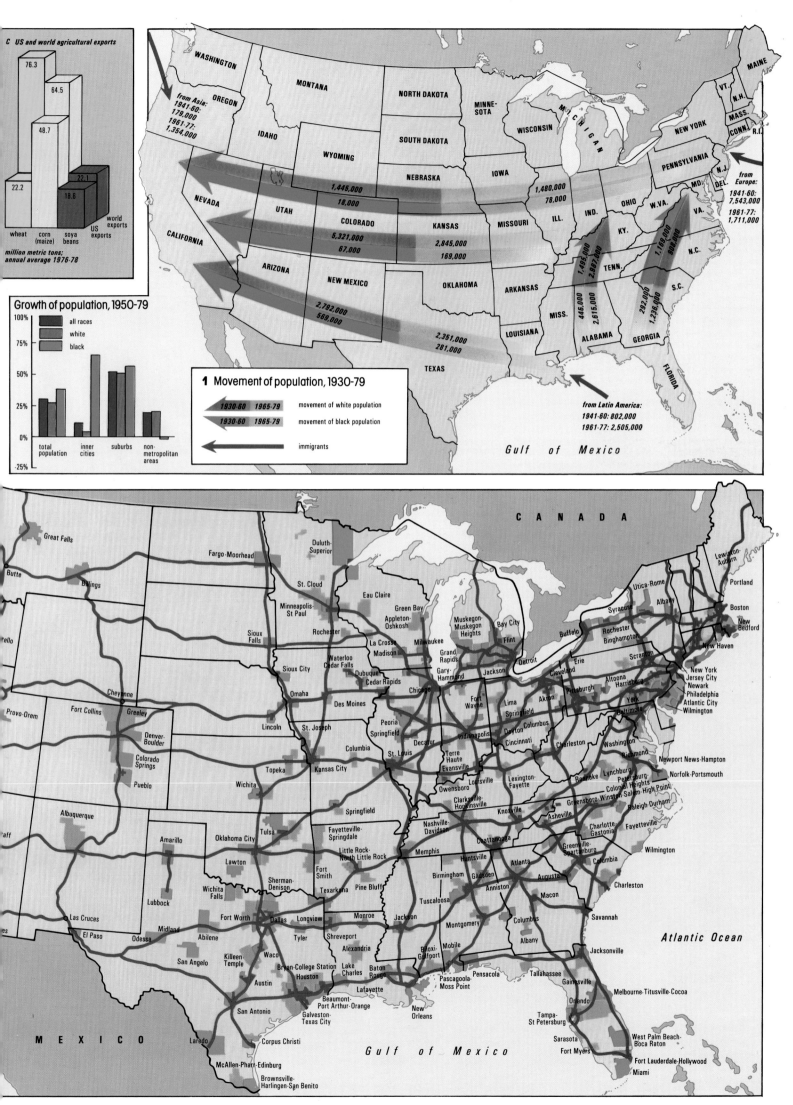

C US and world agricultural exports

| 76.3 | 64.5 | 48.7 | 22.2 | 22.1 | 18.6 |

wheat   corn (maize)   soya beans

world exports
US exports

million metric tons; annual average 1976-78

Growth of population, 1950-79

- all races
- white
- black

100%
75%
50%
25%
0%
-25%

total population   inner cities   suburbs   non-metropolitan areas

WASHINGTON
OREGON
MONTANA
IDAHO
WYOMING
NEVADA
UTAH
CALIFORNIA
ARIZONA
NEW MEXICO
COLORADO
NORTH DAKOTA
SOUTH DAKOTA
NEBRASKA
KANSAS
OKLAHOMA
TEXAS
MINNE-SOTA
IOWA
MISSOURI
ARKANSAS
LOUISIANA
WISCONSIN
MICHIGAN
ILL.
IND.
KY.
TENN.
MISS.
ALABAMA
GEORGIA
FLORIDA
OHIO
W.VA.
VA.
N.C.
S.C.
NEW YORK
PENNSYLVANIA
MAINE
VT.
N.H.
MASS.
CONN.
R.I.
N.J.
DEL.
MD.

from Asia:
1941-60: 179,000
1961-77: 1,354,000

from Europe:
1941-60: 7,543,000
1961-77: 1,711,000

1,445,000
18,000

5,321,000
67,000

2,792,000
569,000

2,351,000
281,000

2,845,000
169,000

1,480,000
78,000

1,495,000
2,887,000

446,000
2,615,000

1,169,000
808,000

292,000
1,236,000

1 Movement of population, 1930-79

1930-60   1965-79   movement of white population
1930-60   1965-79   movement of black population
immigrants

from Latin America:
1941-60: 802,000
1961-77: 2,505,000

Gulf of Mexico

CANADA

Great Falls
Butte
Billings
Fargo-Moorhead
Duluth-Superior
St. Cloud
Minneapolis-St Paul
Eau Claire
Green Bay
Appleton-Oshkosh
Muskegon-Muskegon Heights
Bay City
Lewiston-Auburn
Portland
Utica-Rome
Albany
Boston
New Bedford
Rochester
Binghampton
Syracuse
La Crosse
Madison
Milwaukee
Grand Rapids
Flint
Buffalo
Erie
Scranton
New Haven
Waterloo-Cedar Falls
Dubuque
Cedar Rapids
Gary-Hammond
Jackson
Detroit
Cleveland
Pittsburgh
Altoona
Harrisburg
New York
Jersey City
Newark
Philadelphia
Atlantic City
Wilmington
Sioux Falls
Sioux City
Omaha
Chicago
Fort Wayne
Lima
Akron
York
Baltimore
Cheyenne
Provo-Orem
Fort Collins
Greeley
Denver-Boulder
Colorado Springs
Pueblo
Lincoln
St. Joseph
Des Moines
Peoria
Springfield
St. Louis
Decatur
Terre Haute
Evansville
Indianapolis
Dayton
Springfield
Cincinnati
Columbus
Charleston
Washington
Richmond
Newport News-Hampton
Norfolk-Portsmouth
Topeka
Kansas City
Columbia
Owensboro
Louisville
Lexington-Fayette
Roanoke
Lynchburg
Petersburg
Colonial Heights
Wichita
Clarksville-Hopkinsville
Knoxville
Asheville
Greensboro-Winston-Salem-High Point
Raleigh-Durham
Albuquerque
Springfield
Nashville-Davidson
Chattanooga
Charlotte-Gastonia
Fayetteville
Wilmington
Amarillo
Oklahoma City
Tulsa
Fayetteville-Springdale
Little Rock-North Little Rock
Memphis
Huntsville
Atlanta
Greenville-Spartanburg
Columbia
Charleston
Lawton
Sherman-Denison
Fort Smith
Pine Bluff
Birmingham
Gadsden
Anniston
Augusta
Macon
Wichita Falls
Texarkana
Tuscaloosa
Montgomery
Columbus
Savannah
Lubbock
Las Cruces
Midland
Odessa
El Paso
Fort Worth
Dallas
Longview
Monroe
Jackson
Abilene
Tyler
Shreveport
Alexandria
Mobile
Biloxi-Gulfport
Pensacola
Tallahassee
Gainesville
Albany
Jacksonville
San Angelo
Killeen-Temple
Waco
Bryan-College Station
Austin
Lake Charles
Baton Rouge
Lafayette
Pascagoola-Moss Point
Melbourne-Titusville-Cocoa
Orlando
San Antonio
Beaumont-Port Arthur-Orange
Galveston-Texas City
Houston
New Orleans
Tampa-St Petersburg
Sarasota
Fort Myers
West Palm Beach-Boca Raton
Laredo
Corpus Christi
Fort Lauderdale-Hollywood
Miami
McAllen-Pharr-Edinburg
Brownsville-Harlingen-San Benito

M E X I C O

Gulf of Mexico

Atlantic Ocean

145

The Soviet Union
1926-1991

By the time of Lenin's death in 1924 the new Bolshevik state had survived the perils of civil war and foreign intervention (page 120). The future character of the Soviet Union was decided principally by the policies introduced by Stalin after 1928: the first Five Year Plan and the forced collectivisation of agriculture, both implemented with massive brutality. Collective farming claimed at least 2–3 million victims. Nevertheless, by 1939 a much reduced agricultural population was tilling a larger area than in 1929 and getting a harvest 20 per cent bigger. The surplus population moved into industry. Between 1926 and 1940 the industrial labour force grew by 30 million, and output increased enormously, providing the Soviet Union with the industrial basis to withstand the German onslaught in 1941.

The war against Germany (page 132), in which some 20 million Russians perished, caused immense devastation; 1,700 towns and 70,000 villages were destroyed. But major new industrial centres, such as Magnitogorsk in the southern Urals and Stalinsk (Novokuznetsk) on the Kuzbass coalfield (map 1), were beyond the reach of the German armies, and during the war more than 1,000 important factories were evacuated from western Russia to the Urals and beyond. Nevertheless the setback was undeniable. Industrial production was down by over 30 per cent in 1946 as compared with 1940. What was remarkable was the speed of recovery. By 1953 the pre-war level was passed, but at immense human cost. Massive reparations, particularly from eastern Germany, accounted in part for the recovery, but more important was the large-scale use of forced labour, drafted into the hitherto barren north and north-east. The result was a shift in the centre of economic gravity and the foundation of towns far from the old industrial centres. But the onset of the Cold War (page 148) necessitated a diversion of productive capacity to armaments and, as in the pre-war period, heavy industry was the priority. The improvement of living standards lagged far behind. Agriculture was neglected. In 1953, grain production still hovered around its 1913 level.

Stalin's death in 1953 brought an immediate reaction against his heavy-handed rule, even more marked after Khrushchev's denunciation of Stalinism at the 20th Party Congress in 1956. Under Khrushchev (1955–64) there was genuine relaxation, both abroad, where the reduction of Cold War tension seemed to open new prospects, and at home. At the 21st and 22nd Party Congresses (1959, 1961) Khrushchev held out glowing promises of a future of plenty. In fact, Khrushchev's crash programme to open up the 'virgin lands' of Siberia and Kazakhstan failed to live up to expectations, and in 1963 it was necessary to import grain from Canada. Simultaneously, renewed tension with the United States, culminating in the Cuban missile crisis (page 148), enforced a further shift of productive capacity back to armaments. In addition, Soviet industrial growth slowed significantly. These setbacks sealed Khrushchev's fate. Under Kosygin (1964–80) and Brezhnev (1964–82) there was no abrupt reversal of direction. The Soviet economy continued to expand: between 1960 and 1980 oil production quadrupled; steel output doubled; grain harvests trebled. Nonetheless, increasingly the Soviet Union abandoned its role as the centre of world revolution to face its mounting economic problems.

By Brezhnev's death popular pressure for reform was growing. A cautious start was made under his successors, notably Andropov (1982–84). Under Gorbachev (1985–91) the pace quickened dramatically. Paradoxically, reform tended only to highlight the country's economic weaknesses and, by allowing greater freedoms, to encourage nationalist disturbances. The subsequent eclipse of the Communist Party, accompanied by what had now become a massive economic crisis and the imminent break-up of the union, prompted a conservative backlash in August 1991. Quickly put down, the attempted coup sparked the final disintegration of the Soviet Union as republic after republic, taking their cues principally from Russia itself and the now-independent Baltic republics, declared independence and allegiance to democracy. By Christmas 1991 Gorbachev was forced to resign. Lenin's revolution was over.

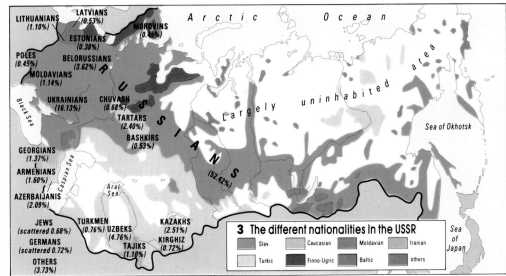

3 The different nationalities in the USSR

Slav	Caucasian
Moldavian	Iranian
Turkic	Finno-Ugric
Baltic	others

2 The constituent republics

- – – – USSR boundary
- ——— RSFSR boundary (Russian Federation)
- other Soviet Republics
- principal groups with autonomous status
- territory acquired since 1939

SSR — Soviet Socialist Republic
ASSR — Autonomous Soviet Socialist Republic
AR — Autonomous Region
AD — Autonomous District

1 Industrial expansion
1926–80

- ● coal mining
- ◐ lignite mining
- ⊺ petroleum extraction
- ⊹ natural gas extraction
- ⊖ oil shale mining
- ▲ iron ore mining
- ⊗ electricity generation
- ■ integrated iron and
  steel industry
- ⊠ steel making
- ◆ non-ferrous metal industry
- ⊞ metal working and
  machine building industry
- ı chemical industry

periods of industrial expansion:

- ■ 1926-1940
- ■ 1941-1945
- ■ 1946-1980

147

The Cold War from 1947

With the elimination of Germany, Japan and Italy and the weakening of Great Britain and France in the Second World War, the USA and the USSR emerged as the two 'super-powers'. The Cold War was the expression of their political and ideological confrontation. Conflict was already visible before the end of the war. In view of the US monopoly of the atom-bomb and the potential threat it implied for the USSR, Stalin decided, after the failure of the Potsdam Conference (July–Aug. 1945), to consolidate Soviet control in eastern Europe (page 136). In reply, the USA built up the defence of western Europe, with the formation of the North Atlantic Treaty Organisation (NATO) in 1949.

Starting as a conflict over central Europe and divided Germany, the Cold War soon developed into a global confrontation. For the United States the Korean War (1950) was evidence of a world-wide Communist conspiracy, although, in fact, the Chinese only intervened when the American advance to the Yalu river seemed to threaten their security (map 2); but American policy hereafter was to 'contain' the Communist powers by a series of encircling alliances. NATO was followed by SEATO (South-East Asia Treaty Organisation, 1954) and the Baghdad Pact (1955), converted into CENTO (Central Treaty Organisation) in 1959. By this time the USA had over 1400 foreign bases, including 275 bases for nuclear bombers, in 31 countries around the Soviet perimeter (map 1). Meanwhile the USSR had acquired nuclear weapons (A-bomb 1949, H-bomb 1953), and when it launched the first space satellite (Sputnik) in 1957, a new dimension was added. Although the intercontinental ballistic missile (ICBM) did not make the American bases obsolete, it meant that, in the event of nuclear war, each of the two super-powers could attack the other's cities directly. The resulting 'nuclear stalemate' enforced a gradual reappraisal.

There were other contributory factors. The monolithic blocs were showing signs of strain, evidenced on the Soviet side by Polish and Hungarian uprisings (1956) and growing signs of a Sino-Soviet rift. In western Europe, France under General de Gaulle rejected American political leadership after 1958. Furthermore, the Baghdad Pact, far from increasing security in the Middle East, divided it into hostile camps, opening it, after America declined to finance the Aswan high dam and after the Suez War (1956), to Soviet influence (map 4). For the USA the

Cuban revolution (1959) posed more immediate problems. When, after an unsuccessful attempt by US-supported dissidents to unseat Fidel Castro, the USSR sent nuclear missiles to Cuba, war seemed imminent, until Khrushchev agreed (Oct. 26, 1962) to their removal (map 5). But in Indo-China, where the US had refused in 1954 to endorse the settlement of the long anti-colonial war against France (page 138) and had set up a counter-revolutionary regime in Saigon, the situation remained tense. In the end the US was forced to intervene directly, and by 1968 some 543,000 American ground troops, as well as substantial naval and air forces, were committed. But this failed to defeat the guerrilla tactics of the Vietnamese National Liberation Front (map 3), and in 1973, with the US economy under severe pressure, President Nixon called a halt. In 1972 Nixon signed the first SALT treaty limiting nuclear armaments, but after the Soviet invasion of Afghanistan (1979) a new arms race began, culminating in the controversial US 'Star Wars' programme. A new era of super-power co-operation began under Reagan and Gorbachev, which led to agreement to reduce nuclear arsenals. Soviet withdrawal from Afghanistan and from eastern Europe, and joint agreement on a re-unification of Germany in 1990 brought the 'classical' Cold War to an end.

2 The Korean War, 1950-53

3 The war in Vietnam, 1957-73

- controlled by the NLF
- controlled by the Saigon government
- contested areas

4 The Middle East during the Cold War, 1955-68

- members of Baghdad Pact
- countries opposed to Baghdad Pact
- major pipelines of the Iraq Petroleum Company and Aramco
- major oil fields
- areas occupied by Israel after the 1967 war

decline of British influence:
(1) evacuation of Canal Zone 1954
(2) dismissal of General Glubb 1956
(3) Iraqi revolution, assassination of Nuri es-Said 1958
(4) withdrawal from Aden 1967

Pacific
Ocean

Wake   Kwajalein

Guam

Iwo Jima

JAPAN

US 7th fleet

Okinawa   PHILIPPINES

SOUTH KOREA

KOREA 1950-3   Formosa   Quemoy, Matsu
1954-5 1958

SOUTH VIETNAM
1946-54, 1957-73
INDO-CHINA

LAOS

THAILAND

ALASKA

Baffin Island

GREENLAND

Iceland

SOVIET

UNION

CHINA

MONGOLIA

EAST
PAKISTAN

Indian

Ocean

INDIA

PAKISTAN

DA

Azores

Ocean

HOLLAND
BELGIUM   NORWAY

DENMARK

IRELAND   UNITED
KINGDOM   P

WEST   EG   C
GERMANY   H   ROMANIA
YUGOSLAVIA   BULGARIA
1948-53
ALBANIA
ITALY   GREECE
1945-9
FRANCE

PORTUGAL   SPAIN

MOROCCO

LIBYA

TURKEY
1945-7

ISRAEL

US 6th fleet

IRAN
1945-6, 1951-3

IRAQ
1958

LEBANON
1958

SAUDI ARABIA

1 The Soviet and American blocs, 1949-59

USA and allies

USSR and allies

Soviet ICBM bases (7000 mile range)

other Soviet missile sites

principal Soviet military airfields

US ICBM bases (5500 mile range)

US heavy bomber bases (capable of reaching USSR with
airborne refuelling)

US nuclear and other major bases (Oct. 1962)

strategic US fleets

points of conflict in the Cold War

uprisings in the Communist world

abbreviations:

C	**CZECHOSLOVAKIA**		H	**HUNGARY**
★	1948		★	1956
●	1968		●	1956
EG	**EAST GERMANY**		P	**POLAND**
★	Berlin 1948-9, 1958-62		★	1956
●	Berlin 1953		●	1956

5 The Cuban crisis, 1962

American blockade zone

Soviet mobile missile
and jet bomber bases

US Air Force base

US Naval base

FLORIDA
*USAF and US Army
build-up*

Homestead A F
Miami

Key West

Guanajay

San Cristóbal
Havana   Sagua la Grande
Remedios
Candelaria   Santa Clara
Bay of Pigs
landing April 1961

CUBA   Santiago de Cuba

Guantánamo Bay   HAITI

JAMAICA

Task Force Screen (TF 136)

Air patrol

Bahama
Islands

DOMINICAN
REPUBLIC

Air patrol

149

The world in 1990

From the Second World War global history has been dominated by massive population growth (chart 2), great increases in wealth and income, and exceptionally rapid technological changes. By the 1980s the management of change and growth had become the key priority of governments everywhere.

The growth of the world economy continued at a slower rate in the 1980s and its fruits remained very unevenly distributed. In 1981 2.2 billion people lived in the low-income developing world with an average income of $275 a year. The 700 million living in the developed industrial world had an average annual income of $11,000 (map 1). The bulk of the world's population in the 1980s was composed of poor peasants in the less-developed world. In the United States only 2 per cent worked in agriculture; in China the figure was 69 per cent, in the rest of Asia and Africa between 75 and 93 per cent. In the poor agricultural regions medical and educational provision was much lower (chart 3).

High levels of debt contracted by the less-developed world led to regular default and unstable financial markets. Modern electronic technology produced rising levels of unemployment. Inflation was fuelled everywhere by rising state expenditure. The most successful economies, Japan and West Germany, came to replace Britain and the United States as the major states in the world economy. The USA became a net debtor state and its industrial leadership was challenged by the great industrial potential of the EEC and the states of the so-called Pacific Rim, Japan, South Korea, Taiwan, Singapore. By 1987 the EEC provided 20 per cent of world trade, the USA only 16 per cent.

The other major consequence of economic growth was environmental damage. The scramble to find new areas to farm, and to satisfy the demand for goods, produced high levels of industrial pollution, and the threat of 'global warming' through damage to the ozone layer in the atmosphere. During the 1980s this became a major issue, and agreement was reached between major industrial states to try to limit pollution and control the use of resources. It was recognised that without international action the long-term ecological damage would be difficult to repair. No other issue is as important for the world of the 1990s.

The 1980s also witnessed the retreat of dictatorship and the decline of communist state economies. In the Philippines, Pakistan, and throughout eastern Europe democracy replaced authoritarian rule. Throughout the communist world it was realised that centralised controlled economies could not solve the dilemmas of economic growth and provide their populations with what they wanted. In China and the Soviet Union far-reaching economic reform introduced a measure of private initiative and reduced state regulation. The result was growing demand in both states for greater political freedom. In China this led in 1990 to a return to more repressive policies; in the Soviet Union it led to widespread unrest and violence and a serious crisis of state. The retreat of communism (map 4) made liberal capitalism look more attractive and the western world took the initiative in the late 1980s in promoting greater co-operation in economic affairs, in arms reductions, in ecological initiatives. In 1991 the United Nations, led by

the USA and Britain, intervened militarily in the conflict between Iraq and Kuwait. It was the first time the world had united almost as one to reverse aggression. Yet for all this the world of the 1990s still has issues of poverty, famine and war to confront. For all the evidence of greater co-operation there is the prospect of rapid and unstable political change. The management of change is still a difficult and unpredictable endeavour.

1 ALBANIA	16 JORDAN
2 AUSTRIA	17 KUWAIT
3 BAHRAIN	18 LEBANON
4 BANGLADESH	19 LUXEMBOURG
5 BENIN	20 MALAWI
6 BHUTAN	21 NEPAL
7 BURUNDI	22 QATAR
8 CAMBODIA	23 RWANDA
9 CZECHOSLOVAKIA	24 SIERRA LEONE
10 DJIBOUTI	25 SWITZERLAND
11 EQUATORIAL GUINEA	26 SYRIA
12 THE GAMBIA	27 TOGO
13 GUINEA BISSAU	28 UNITED ARAB EMIRATES
14 HUNGARY	29 YUGOSLAVIA
15 ISRAEL	30 ZIMBABWE

1 Rich nations and poor nations, 1989

countries with a per capita GNP of under US $300
$ 300-$ 750
$ 751-$ 2,500
$ 2,501-$ 6,000
$ 6,001-$ 9,000
$ 9,001-$ 20,000
$ 20,001-$ 30,000

total overseas development aid to individual countries in 1985 (million $US):
⬤ over $600
◗ 300-600
◖ 150-300
○ under 150

international debt:
US $15-30 bn
US $30-50bn
over US $50 bn

■ metropolitan areas of over 7 million inhabitants
▲ OPEC member nations
✳ data not available
✱ 1985 figures

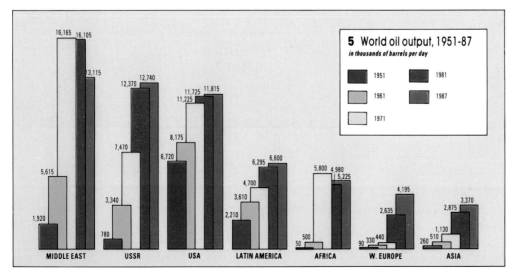

5 World oil output, 1951-87
in thousands of barrels per day

1951   1981
1961   1987
1971

	MIDDLE EAST	USSR	USA	LATIN AMERICA	AFRICA	W. EUROPE	ASIA

4 Collapse of Communist power in Europe, 1989-91
✳ anti-Communist demonstrations
• multi-party elections

1945-47 Guerrilla war, 1956, 1970, 1979-80, 1981-89 under martial law
✳ 1953
1961 Berlin Wall built
1989 Berlin Wall breached March 1990
Germany reunified 1990
June 1989
✳ 1968 Prague Spring ended by Soviet intervention; June 1990 June 1989

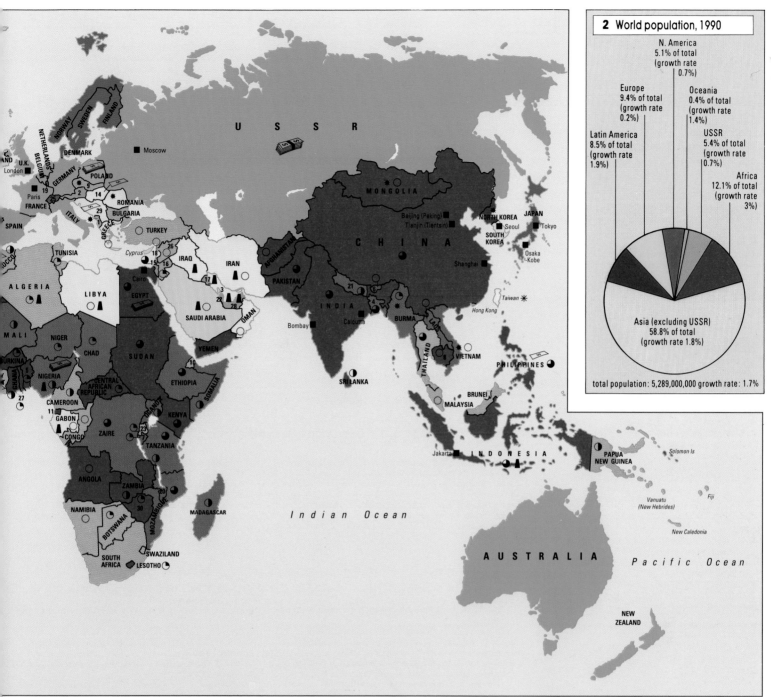

2 World population, 1990

N. America
5.1% of total
(growth rate
0.7%)

Europe
9.4% of total
(growth rate
0.2%)

Oceania
0.4% of total
(growth rate
1.4%)

Latin America
8.5% of total
(growth rate
1.9%)

USSR
5.4% of total
(growth rate
0.7%)

Africa
12.1% of total
(growth rate
3%)

Asia (excluding USSR)
58.8% of total
(growth rate 1.8%)

total population: 5,289,000,000 growth rate: 1.7%

East Germany 1989 (Aug.-Sept.) Mass refugee escape to West Germany via Hungary and Czechoslovakia; (Oct.-Nov.) Mass demonstrations throughout country; (9 Nov.) Berlin Wall breached, formally opened Dec.-Jan. 1990 leading to reunification.
Poland 1980 Formation of independent trade union, *Solidarity*; 1981-89 martial law; 1989 (Sept.) *Solidarity*-led government; 1990 (Jan.) Communist Party dissolved.
Czechoslovakia 1989 (Nov.) Mass demonstrations spread from Prague; collapse of Communist rule.
Hungary 1989 (Oct.) End of Communist rule.
Yugoslavia 1988 Mass demonstrations against falling living standards and corruption; 1989 Slovenia and Croatia legalise opposition parties; 1991 Croatian and Slovenian independence, civil war.
Romania 1989 (Dec.) Armed uprisings in Bucharest and Timişoara; President Nicolae Ceauşescu executed.
Bulgaria 1989 (Nov.) Dictator Todo Zhivkov removed from office by Party opponents.
Ukraine 1989 (July) Coal-miners strike for improved conditions and end to Party monopoly; (Sept.) First National Congress of *Rukh* (Ukrainian Nationalist Party); 1991 Referendum vote for independence; 1991 independence declared; Kravchuk elected president.
Belorussia 1989 (June) Popular Front founded; 1991 independence declared.
Moldavia 1989 (May) Popular Front founded; 1990 (Feb.) Popular Front wins election; 1991 independence declared.
Lithuania 1988 *Sajudis* (independent movement) formed; 1989 (May) Lithuanian Supreme Soviet declares sovereignty 1990; (Feb.) *Sajudis* wins election; independence recognised 1991 by USA, USSR, UN.
Latvia 1988 National Independence Movement formed; 1989 mass anti-Communist demonstrations; 1991 independence recognised by USA, USSR, UN.
Estonia 1988 National Independence Party formed; 1990 (Mar.) Congress of Estonia formed; 1991 independence recognised by USA, USSR, UN.

3 The gap between nations

life expectancy at birth

infant mortality (deaths per 1000 live births)

literacy % of population

Acknowledgements

ACKNOWLEDGEMENTS AND BIBLIOGRAPHY
We have pleasure in acknowledging the following:
Map 5, page 76, is based, with kind permission, on map 2, page 107 in *Grosser Atlas Zur Weltgeschichte*, Westermann
Map 5, page 111, is based, with the kind permission of George Philip & Son Ltd, on page 215 of *The New Cambridge Modern History Atlas* H.C. Darby, H. Fullard (eds.)

Among the large number of works consulted by contributors, the following contain valuable maps and other data that have been particularly useful:

I. History Atlases

Atlas zur Geschichte 2 vols. Leipzig 1976
Bazilevsky, K.V., Golubtsov, A., Zinoviev, M.A. *Atlas Istorii SSR*, Moscow 1952
Beckingham, C.F. *Atlas of the Arab World and the Middle East*, London 1960
Bertin, J. (et al) *Atlas of Food Crops*, Paris 1971
Bjørklund, O., Holmboe, H., Røhr, A. *Historical Atlas of the World*, Edinburgh 1970
Cappon, L. (et al) *Atlas of Early American History*, Chicago 1976
Darby, H. C., Fullard, H. (eds.) *The New Cambridge Modern History* vol. XIV: Atlas, Cambridge 1970
Davies, C.C. *An Historical Atlas of the Indian Peninsula*, London 1959
Engel, J. (ed.) *Grosser Historischer Weltatlas* 3 vols. Munich 1953–81
Fage, J.D. *An Atlas of African History*, London 1958
Gilbert, M. *Russian History Atlas*, London 1972
Gilbert, M. *Recent History Atlas 1860–1960*, London 1966
Gilbert, M. *First World War Atlas*, London 1970
Gilbert, M. *Jewish History Atlas*, London 1969
Hazard, H.W. *Atlas of Islamic History*, Princeton 1952
Herrmann, A. *Historical and Commercial Atlas of China*, Havard 1935
Herrmann, A. *An Historical Atlas of China*, Edinburgh 1966
Jedin, H., Latourette, K.S., Martin, J. *Atlas zur Kirchengeschichte*, Freiburg 1970
Joppen, C., Garrett, H.L.O. *Historical Atlas of India*, London 1938
Kinder, H., Hilgermann, W. *DTV Atlas zur Weltgeschichte* 2 vols. Stuttgart 1964
Matsui and Mori *Ajiarekishi chizu*, Tokyo 1965
May, H.G. (ed.) *Oxford Bible Atlas*, Oxford 1974
Nelson's Atlas of the Early Christian World, London 1959
Nelson's Atlas of World History, London 1965
Nihon rekishi jiten Atlas vol., Tokyo 1959
Palmer, R.R. (ed.) *Atlas of World History*, Chicago 1965
Paullin, C.O. *Atlas of the Historical Geography of the United States*, Washington 1932
Ragi al Faruqi, I. *Historical Atlas of the Religions of the World*, New York 1974
Roolvink, R. *Historical Atlas of the Muslim Peoples*, London 1957
Schwartzberg, J.E. (ed.) *A Historical Atlas of South Asia* Chicago 1978
Shepherd, W.R. *Historical Atlas*, New York 1964
Toynbee, A.J., Myers, E.D. *A Study of History, Historical Atlas and Gazetteer*, Oxford 1959
Treharne, R.F., Fullard, H. (eds.) *Muir's Historical Atlas*, London 1966
Van der Heyden, A.M., Scullard, H.H. *Atlas of the Classical World*, London 1959
Wesley, E.B. *Our United States .... its History in Maps*, Chicago 1977
Westermann *Grosser Atlas zur Weltgeschichte*, Brunswick 1978
Whitehouse, D. & R. *Archaeological Atlas of the World*, London 1975
Wilgus, A.C. *Latin America in Maps*, New York 1943

II. General Works

Ahzweiler, H. *L'Asie Mineure et les Invasions Arabes*, Revue Historique 1962
Ajayi, J.F.A., Crowder, M. *History of West Africa* vols. 1 & 2 London 1974
Allchin, B. & R. *The Birth of Indian Civilisation*, London 1968
Australia, Commonwealth of, Department of National Development, *Atlas of Australian Resources*
Barraclough, G. *Medieval Germany*, Oxford 1938
Basham, A.L. *The Wonder that was India*, London 1967
Beresford, M. *New Towns of the Middle Ages*, London 1967

Berney, M. (ed.) *Australia*, Sydney 1965
Bloch, M. *Les Caractères Originaux de l'Histoire Rurale Française*, Oslo 1931
Boisselier, J. *La Statuaire du Champa*, Paris 1963
Bury, J.B., Cook, S.A., Adcock, F.E. (eds.) *The Cambridge Ancient History*, Cambridge 1923–
Bury, J.B., Gwatkin, H.M., Whitney, J.P. (eds.) *The Cambridge Medieval History*, Cambridge 1911
Chang, K.C. *The Archaeology of Ancient China*, New Haven & London 1968
Cheng Te-k'un *Archaeology in China*, Cambridge 1959
Churchill, Winston S. *The Second World War*, London 1948–53
Coedès, G. *Les Etats Hindouisés de l'Indochine et d'Indonésie*, Paris 1964
Cook, M.A. (ed.) *A History of the Ottoman Empire to 1730*, Cambridge 1974
Cresswell, K.A.C. *A Short Account of Early Muslim Architecture*, Oxford 1958
Crowder, M. *West Africa under Colonial Rule*, London 1968
Cumberland, K.B. *Aotearoa Maori: New Zealand about 1780*, Geographical Review no. 39
Curtin, P. de A. *The Atlantic Slave Trade*, Wisconsin 1969
Dalton, B.J. *War and Politics in New Zealand 1855–1870*, Sydney 1967
Darby, H.C. (ed.) *An Historical Geography of England before AD 1800*, Cambridge 1936 & 1960
Despois, J., Raynal, R. *Géographie de l'Afrique du Nord*, Paris 1967
Dyos, H.J., Aldcroft, D.H. *British Transport*, Leicester 1969
East, W.G. *The Geography behind History*, London 1965
East, W.G. *An Historical Geography of Europe*, London 1966
Edwardes, M. *A History of India*, London 1961
Evans, B.L. *Agricultural and Pastoral Statistics of New Zealand 1861–1954*, Wellington 1956
Ferguson, J. *The Heritage of Hellenism*, London 1973
Fisher, C.A. *South-East Asia*, London 1964
Fletcher, A. *Tudor Rebellions*, London 1968
Fowler, K. *The Age of Plantagenet and Valois*, New York 1967
Fourquin, G. *Histoire Economique de l'Occident Médiéval*, Paris 1969
Ganshof, F.L. *Etude sur le Développement des Villes entre Loire et Rhin au Moyen Age*, Paris–Brussels 1943
Geelan, P.J.M., Twitchett, D.C. (eds.) *The Times Atlas of China*, London 1974
Gernet, J. *Le Monde Chinois*, Paris 1969
Grousset, R. *The Empire of the Steppes: A History of Central Asia*, New Brunswick N.J. 1970
Guillermaz, J. *Histoire du Parti Communiste Chinois*, Paris 1968
Hall, D.G.E. *A History of South-East Asia*, London 1968
Harlan, J.R. *The Plants and Animals that Nourish Man*, Scientific American 1976
Harlan, J.R., Zohary, D. *The Distribution of Wild Wheats and Barleys*, Science 1966
Hatton, R.M. *Europe in the age of Louis XIV*, London 1969
Henderson, W.O. *Britain and Industrial Europe 1750–1870*, Liverpool 1954
Hopkins, A.G. *Economic History of West Africa*, London 1973
Inalcik, H. *The Ottoman Empire: The Classical Age 1300–1600*, London 1973
Jeans, D.N. *An Historical Geography of New South Wales to 1901*, Sydney 1972
Kennedy, J. *A History of Malaya 1400–1959*, London 1962
Kjölstad, T., Rystad, G. *5000 år: Epoker och utvecklingslinjer*, Lund 1973
Konigsberger, H., Mosse, G.L. *Europe in the sixteenth century*, London 1968
Langer, W.L. *An Encyclopedia of World History*, London 1972

La Roncière (et al) *L'Europe au Moyen Age*, Paris 1969
Lattimore, O. *Inner Asian Frontiers of China*, New York 1951
Lyashchenko, P.I. *History of the National Economy of Russia to the 1917 Revolution*, New York 1949
Majumdar, R.C. *The Vedic Age*, Bombay 1951
Majumdar, R.C. *History and Culture of the Indian People, Age of Imperial Unity*, Bombay 1954
Macmillan's Atlas of South-East Asia, London 1964
McBurney, C.B.M. *Proceedings of the British Academy LXI* 1975
McIntyre, W.D., Gardner, W.J. *Speeches and Documents on New Zealand History*, Oxford 1970
McNeill, W.H. *A World History*, New York 1971
Meinig, D.W. *On the Margins of the Good Earth*, New York 1962, London 1963
Mellaart, J. *The Neolithic of the Near East*, London 1975
Ministry of Works *A Survey of New Zealand Population*, Wellington 1960
Miquel, A. *L'Islam et sa Civilisation*, Paris 1968
Morrell, W.P., Hall, D.O.W. *A History of New Zealand Life*, Christchurch 1957
Moss, H. St. L.B. *The Birth of the Middle Ages*, Oxford 1935
Mulvaney, D.J. *The Prehistory of Australia*, London 1975
Mussett, L *Les Invasions: Les Vagues Germaniques*, Paris 1965
Musset, L. *Les Invasions: Le Second Assaut contre l'Europe Chrétienne*, Paris 1971
The National Atlas of the United States of America, Washington DC 1970
Neatby, H. *Quebec, The Revolutionary Age 1760–1791*, London 1966
New Zealand Official Yearbook, Wellington 1893–
Ogot, B.A. (ed.) *Zamani, A Survey of East African History*, London 1974–1976
Oliver, R., Fagan, B. *Africa in the Iron Age c. 500 BC–AD 1400*, Cambridge 1975
Oliver, R., Atmore, A. *Africa since 1800*, Cambridge 1972
Ostrogorsky, G. *History of the Byzantine State*, Oxford 1956
Parker, W.H. *An Historical Geography of Russia*, London 1968
Piggott, S. *Prehistoric India to 1000 BC*, London 1962
Pitcher, D.E. *An Historical Geography of the Ottoman Empire*, Leiden 1973
Sanders, W.T., Marino, J. *New World Prehistory: Archaeology of the American Indian*, Englewood Cliffs, N.J. 1970
Saum, L.O. *The Fur Trader and the Indian*, London 1965
Seltzer, L.E. (ed.) *The Columbia Lippincott Gazetteer of the World*, New York 1952
Simkin, C.F. *The Traditional Trade of Asia*, Oxford 1968
Smith, C.T. *An Historical Geography of Western Europe before 1800*, London & New York 1960
Smith, W.S. *The Art and Architecture of Ancient Egypt*, London 1965
Snow, D. *The American Indians: their Archaeology and Prehistory*, London 1976
Stavrianos, L.S. *The World to 1500*, Englewood Cliffs, N.J. 1975
Stein, Sir Aurel *Travels in Central Asia*, London 1935
Stratos, A.N. *Byzantium in the seventh century*, Athens 1965
Tarn, W.W. *Alexander the Great*, Cambridge 1948
Tate, D.J.M. *The Making of South-East Asia*, Kuala Lumpur 1971
Thapar, R. *A History of India*, London 1967
The Times Atlas of the World, Comprehensive Edition, London 1980
Toynbee, A.J. (ed.) *Cities of Destiny*, London 1967
Toynbee, A.J. *Mankind and Mother Earth*, Oxford 1976
U.S. Strategic Bombing Survey, Summary Report (Pacific War), Washington 1946
Van Alstyne, R.W. *The Rising American Empire*, Oxford 1960
Van Heekeren, H.R. *The Stone Age of Indonesia*, The Hague 1957
Wadham, S., Wilson, R.K., Wood, J. *Land Utilization in Australia*, Melbourne 1964
Watters, R.F. *Land and Society in New Zealand*, Wellington 1965
Wheatley, P. *The Golden Khersonese*, Kuala Lumpur 1961
Wheeler, M. *Early India and Pakistan to Ashoka*, London 1968
Willey, G. *An Introduction to American Archaeology* vols. 1 & 2 Englewood Cliffs, N.J. 1970
Williams, M. *The Making of the South Australian Landscape*, London 1974
Wilson, M., Thompson, L. *Oxford History of South Africa* vols. 1 & 2 Oxford 1969, 1971

INDEX

1 HISTORICAL PLACE NAMES

Geographical names vary with time and with language, and there is some difficulty in treating them consistently in an historical atlas, especially for individual maps within whose time span the same place has been known by different names. We have aimed at the simplest possible approach to the names on the maps, using the index to weld together the variations.

On the maps forms of names will be found in the following hierarchy of preference:

a English conventional names or spellings, in the widest sense, for all principal places and features, e.g., Moscow, Vienna, Munich, Danube (including those that today might be considered obsolete when these are appropriate to the context, e.g., Leghorn)

b Names that are contemporary in terms of the maps concerned. There are here three broad categories:

i names in the ancient world, where the forms used are classical, e.g., Latin or latinized Greek, but extending also to Persian, Sanskrit, etc.

ii names in the post-medieval modern world, which are given in the form (though not necessarily the spelling) current at the time of the map (e.g., St. Petersburg before 1914, not Leningrad).

iii modern names where the spelling generally follows that of *The Times Atlas of the World*, though in the interests of simplicity there has been a general omission of diacritics in spellings derived by transliteration from non-roman scripts, e.g., Sana rather than Şana'ā'.

2 THE INDEX

The index does not include every name shown on the maps. In general only those names are indexed which are of places, features, regions or countries where 'something happens', i.e., which carry a date or symbol or colour explained in the key, or which are mentioned in the text.

Where a place is referred to by two or more different names in the course of the atlas, there will be a corresponding number of main entries in the index. The variant names in each case are given in brackets at the beginning of the entry, their different forms and origins being distinguished by such words as *now, later, formerly* and others included in the list of abbreviations (*right*).

'Istanbul (*form.* Constantinople, *anc.* Byzantium)' means that the page references to that city on maps dealing with periods when it was known as Istanbul follow that entry, but the page references pertaining to it when it had other names will be found under those other names.

Places are located generally by reference to the country in which they lie (exceptionally by reference to island groups or sea areas), this being narrowed down where necessary by location as E(ast), N(orth), C(entral), etc. The reference will normally be to the modern state in which the place now falls unless (a) there is a conventional or historical name which conveniently avoids the inevitably anachronistic ring of some modern names, e.g., Anatolia rather than Turkey, Mesopotamia rather than Iraq, or (b) the modern state is little known or not delineated on the map concerned, e.g., many places on the Africa plates can only be located as W., E., Africa, etc.

Reference is generally to page number/map numbers (e.g., 118/1) unless the subject is dealt with over the plate as a whole, when the reference occurs as 118-19 (i.e., pages 118 and 119). All entries with two or more references have been given sub-headings where possible, e.g., Civil War 129/4. Battles are indicated by the symbol ✕. References to names of persons, treaties, etc., occurring in the text are followed by the abbreviation T. e.g. 'Alexander the Great 22T'.

Though page references are generally kept in numerical order, since this corresponds for the most part with chronological order, they have been rearranged occasionally where the chronological sequence would be obviously wrong, or in the interests of grouping appropriate references under a single sub-heading.

All variant names and spellings are cross-referenced in the form 'Bourgogne (Burgundy)', except those which would immediately precede or follow the main entries to which they refer. The bracketed form has been chosen so that such entries may also serve as quick visual indications of equivalence. Thus Bourgogne (Burgundy) means not only 'see under Burgundy' but also that Burgundy is another name for Bourgogne.

3 ABBREVIATIONS

a/c	also called
AD	Autonomous District
Alb.	Albanian
anc.	ancient
AR	Autonomous Region
Ar.	Arabic
a/s	also spelled
ASSR	Autonomous Soviet Socialist Republic
Bibl.	Biblical
Bulg.	Bulgarian
C	Century (when preceded by 17. 18 etc.)
C	Central
Cat.	Catalan
Chin.	Chinese
Cz.	Czech
Dan.	Danish
Dut.	Dutch
E	East(ern)
Eng.	English
Est.	Estonian
f/c	formerly called
Finn.	Finnish
form.	former(ly)
Fr.	French
f/s	formerly spelled
Ger.	German
Gr.	Greek
Heb.	Hebrew
Hung.	Hungarian
Indon.	Indonesian
Ir.	Irish
Is.	Island
It.	Italian
Jap.	Japanese
Kor.	Korean
Lat.	Latin
Latv.	Latvian
Lith.	Lithuanian
Mal.	Malay
med.	medieval
mod.	modern
Mong.	Mongolian
N	North(ern)
n/c	now called
Nor.	Norwegian
n/s	now spelled
NT	New Testament
obs.	obsolete
OT	Old Testament
Pers.	Persian
Pol.	Polish
Port.	Portuguese
Rom.	Romanian
Russ.	Russian
S	South(ern)
s/c	sometimes called
Som.	Somali
Sp.	Spanish
S. Cr.	Serbo-Croat
SSR	Soviet Socialist Republic
Sw.	Swedish
T	text
Turk.	Turkish
Ukr.	Ukrainian
US(A)	United States (of America)
var.	variant
W	West(ern)
Wel.	Welsh
WW1	The First World War
WW2	The Second World War

Al Quds (Jerusalem)

Al Raydaniyya N Egypt ✕ 49/1

Alsace (*anc.* Alsatia *Ger.* Elsass) in German Empire 55/3; acquired by Habsburgs 78/3; acquired by French 80-81; customs union 98/3; WW1 119/2

Alsace-Lorraine *Ger.* Elsass-Lothringen) region of E France annexed by German Empire 115/2; ceded to France 128/2

Alsatia (Alsace)

Altaich S Germany monastery 34/4

Altamira N Spain Palaeolithic art 5/3

Altan Khan Mongol Chieftain 46T

Altendorf N Germany megalithic tomb 15/3

Altmark region of E Germany 53/3

Alto Adige (South Tyrol)

Altona N Germany customs union 98/3

Altun Ha E Mexico Mayan site 12/2

Altxerri N Spain Palaeolithic art 5/3

Alwa early Christian kingdom of the Sudan 60/1

Alwar district of N India communal riots 104/4

Amalfi S Italy Byzantine port 36/2

Amara Upper Egypt fortress 21/1

Amara NW India pre-Harappan site 9/5

Amarapura C Burma Neolithic site 8/3; early trade centre 71/2

Amaravati E India early trading centre 25/1

Amasia (*mod.* Amasya) E Anatolia archbishopric 27/2; Roman Empire 31/3

Amastris (*earlier* Sesamus) N Anatolia Byzantine Empire 42/2

Amasya (*anc.* Amasia) C Turkey Ottoman town 49/1

Amathus Cyprus ancient Greek colony 19/4

Ambianum (Amiens)

Amboina C Indonesia massacre of English 70/3; trade centre 71/2

Ambriz Angola Portuguese settlement 61/2

Amchitka Aleutian Is. Alaska retaken from Japanese 135/2

Amecameca Mexico on Cortés' route 68/1

America, Central (*a/c* Mesoamerica) early peoples 12-13; agricultural origins 6/4; early civilisations 13/1; Aztec Empire 62/2; Indian tribes 63/1; early voyages of discovery 65/3; colonial expansion 66/1, 68/1

America, North Colonisation 5/2; agricultural origins 6/4; early cultures 12-13, 62/1; Indian tribes 63/1; early voyages of discovery 64/2; colonial expansion 67/3, 69/3; European colonial rivalry 86/1; immigration from Europe 108/2; industrialisation 144/4. See also Canada, United States

America, South Colonisation 5/2; early peoples 12-13; agricultural origins 6/4; early civilisations 13/1; Indian tribes 13/5; Inca Empire 63/3; early voyages of discovery 64/2; colonial expansion 66/1, 68/2, 69/3; industrialisation 96/2; independence 97/1; immigration from Europe 108/2; economic development 96/3; modern politics 97/1; population 97/2

American Samoa S Pacific 139/1 (inset)

Amida (*mod.* Diyarbakir) E Anatolia 31/3; archbishopric and monastery 27/2

Amiens (*anc.* Samarobriva *later* Ambianum) N France 17C revolt 77/2; provincial capital 80/1; WW1 118/3

Amisea N Anatolia Byzantine Empire 43/2

Amisus (*mod.* Samsun) N Anatolia Ionian colony 19/4; early archbishopric 27/2; Byzantine Empire 42/2

Amiternum C Italy 30/1

Amman (*Bibl.* Rabbath Ammon *anc.* Philadelphia) Jordan Levantine city 21/1; 125/2

Ammon ancient country of Palestine 21/2

Ammon, Sanctuary of Egypt Alexander's route 22/3

Amnisos Crete Mycenaean settlement 19/1

Amol N Persia Alexander's route 23/3

Amöneburg W Germany monastery 38/3

Amorium C Anatolia Byzantine Empire 42/2, 43/3

Amoy S China early trade 106/2; treaty port 107/4; Anglo-French attacks 107/3; Japanese influence 107/4; occupied by Japanese 127/5

Amphipolis N Greece ✕ 23/2; Roman Empire 24/2; early church 27/2

Amir NW India Harappan site 9/5

Amritsar N India political disturbances under British rule 104/4

Amselfeld (Kosovo)

Amsterdam Netherlands trading port 83/5; 18C financial centre 82/4

Amud Palestine site of early man 3/3

Amur River Russia/China border 84/2

Anabaptists 74/2, 75/1, T

Anadyrsk E Siberia founded 84/2

Anagnia (*mod.* Anagni) C Italy early town 30/1

Anantapur S India ceded to Britain 87/3

Anatolia early settlement 7/2; early agriculture 7/4; Mycenaean trade 18/2; Hittite cities 21/1; Muslim conquest 42/4; Ottoman conquest 49/1; Black Death 57/1; Italian and Russian spheres of influence 125/3. See also Asia Minor

Anatolic Theme Anatolia district of Byzantine Empire 42/2

Anazarbus SW Anatolia early archbishopric 27/2; Byzantine Empire 42/2

Ancona N Italy Roman Empire 24/2, 30/1, 3; medieval city 56/3

Ancrum Moor Scotland ✕ 73/4

Ancyra (*mod.* Ankara *obs. Eng.* Angora) W Anatolia Alexander's route 22/3; Roman Empire 24/2; 31/3; early archbishopric 27/2; Byzantine Empire 43/1, 3

Åndalsnes C Norway WW2 132/1

Andalusia (*Sp.* Andalucia) region of S Spain reconquest by Castile 37/4

Andaman Islands Indian territory of Bay of Bengal 101/2, 139/1

Andegavum (*earlier.* Juliomagus *mod.* Angers) W France early bishopric 26/2

Andernach (*anc.* Antunnacum) W Germany Palaeolithic art 5/3 ✕ 55/3

Andover S England Industrial Revolution 98/1

Andredescester S England ✕ 33/3

Andredesweald S England 33/3

Anegray E France early monastery 38/3

Anga region of NE India 29/4

Angarsk S Siberia industry 147/1

Angers (*anc.* Juliomagus *med.* Andegavum) W France 17C revolt 77/2; centre of French Revolution 89/2

Angevin Empire France 52T, 52/2

Anghelu Ruju N Sardinia burial site 14/2

Angkor Cambodia Buddhist site 27/1, 51/2

Angkor Borei S Cambodia Hindu-Buddhist remains 51/2

Angles tribe of NW Europe, migrations 32/1, 2; 33/3; 34/1

Angles-sur-l'Anglin SW France Palaeolithic art 5/3

Anglo-Dutch Wars 81/3

Anglo-Egyptian Sudan Ottoman territory under British control 101/2; condominium 102/5

Angola SW Africa Portuguese discovery 64/1; early Portuguese trade 67/1; source of slaves 67/1; Portuguese colonisation 100/2, 102/5, 103/3; independence 138/1; political development 140/1

Angora (*anc.* Ancyra *mod.* Ankara) W Anatolia ✕ 47/4

Angoulême (*anc.* Iculisma) C France region annexed to France 72/2; provincial capital 80/1

Anguilla island of West Indies settled by English 66/4; independence 139/1 (inset)

Anhalt C Germany principality and duchy 79/1, 114/1; Reformation 75/1

Anhui (Anhwei)

Anhwei (*a/s* Anhui) province of E China Manchu expansion 106/1

Ani Persia Byzantine Empire 43/1

Aniane S France monastery 34/4

Aniba Upper Egypt fortress 21/1

Anjira NW India pre-Harappan site 9/5

Anjou region of NW France annexed by France 52/2; province of France 80/1

Ankara (*anc.* Ancyra *obs. Eng.* Angora) W Turkey ✕ 49/1; revolt against Ottoman rule 48/1; Ottoman Empire 124/1

Ankole Uganda kingdom 61/2

Annaba (Bône, Hippo Regius)

Annam N Indo-China under T'ang control 50/1; under Mongol control 47/1; expansion and early trade 71/2

Annapolis (*until* 1694 Anne Arundel Town *earlier* Providence) NE USA 67/3

Ansbach S Germany Reformation 75/1, 74/4; margraviate 79/1

Anshan Manchuria Russo-Japanese War 127/4; industry 123/4

Ansi N China trade 25/1

Anta dos Gorgions S Portugal megalithic tomb 14/3

Antakya (Antioch)

Antalya (Attalia)

Antibes (Antipolis)

Antietam (*a/c* Sharpsburg) NE USA ✕ 92/5

Antigonid Kingdom Mediterranean 22/4

Antigua island of West Indies settlement by British 66/4; colony 97/1; independence 139/1 (inset)

Anting NW China Han commanderie 29/3

Antioch (*Lat.* Antiochia *mod.* Antakya) NW Syria Mediterranean trade 25/1, 37/2, 58/3; spread of Christianity 27/2; Roman Empire 25/2, 31/3; archbishopric 38/2, 39/1; Byzantine rule 43/1, 3; principality 40/3

Antiochia (Antioch, Antakya)

Antipolis (*mod.* Antibes) SE France Ionian colony 19/4

Antium (*mod.* Anzio) C Italy Roman colony 30/1

Antofagasta region of N Chile dispute with Peru and Bolivia 97/4

Antonine Plague 25/3

Antrim N Ireland massacre of Catholics 76/4

Antung (*now* Dandong) Manchuria treaty port 107/4; Russo-Japanese war 127/4

Antunnacum (Andernach)

Antwerp (*Fr.* Anvers *Dut.* Antwerpen) Belgium Hansa city 59/2; trade 59/2; 18C financial centre 82/4; town of Spanish Netherlands 76/1; industrial development 98/2; WW1 118/3; WW2 132/2

Anuradhapura Ceylon Buddhist site 27/1

Anvers (Antwerp)

Anxur (Terracina)

An-yang N China early urban settlement 8/4

Anyer Lor W Java site 8/3

Anzio (*anc.* Antium) C Italy WW2 133/2

Aomori N Japan town and prefecture 126/2

Aornos (*mod.* Tash-Kurghan) Afghanistan Alexander's route 23/3

Apache Indian tribe of SW USA 63/1

Apache Pass SW USA on trail west 94/1

Apamea Syria Roman Empire 25/2, 31/3; early archbishopric 27/2

Aphrodisias SW France Ionian colony 19/4

Apollonia NE Greece Dorian colony 19/4; early church 27/2

Apollonia NW Greece Dorian colony 19/4; Roman Empire 24/2

Apollonia (*mod.* Sozopol) Bulgaria Ionian colony 19/4

Apollonia Libya Greek colony 19/4; Roma Empire 24/2; Byzantine Empire 43/1

Apollinopolis (Edfu)

Appenzell Switzerland Reformation 75/1

Appian Way (Via Appia)

Appomattox SE USA Confederates surrender 93/5

Apulia region of SE Italy unification with Naples 56/3

Apulum (*mod.* Alba Iulia) Romania Roman Empire 24/2, 31/3

Aqaba (Aelana)

Aqsu (Aksu)

Aquileia (*med.* Aglar) N Italy Latin colony 30/1; Roman Empire 24/2; early archbishopric 26/2, 35/4; Byzantine Empire 43/1, 3

Aquincum (*mod.* Budapest) Hungary Chinese finds 24/1; Roman Empire 24/2, 31/3

Aquisgranum (Aachen)

Aquitaine (*anc.* Aquitania *mod.* Guyenne) region of SW France English possession 52/2; Black Death 57/1

Aquitania (*mod.* Aquitaine *later* Guyenne) Roman province of Gaul 30/3; Visigothic territory conquered by Franks 34/1, 35/2

Arabaya Arabia satrapy of Achaemenid Empire 21/5

Arabia early trade 59/3; spread of Judaism 26/1; early Christian activity 39/1; centre of Islam 41/1

Arabian Gulf (Persian Gulf)

Arabia Petraea Roman province of N Arabia 31/3

Arabissos E Anatolia Byzantine Empire 43/1

Arabs territorial losses to Byzantine Empire 43/1; independence from Ottomans 124-125; emigration from Israel 141/3

Arachosia (*a/c* Harauvatish) Afghanistan ancient province of Persian and Alexander's Empires 29/4

Aradus (*Bibl.* Arvad *later* Arward *Fr.* Rouad) Syria Phoenician city 19/4; Alexander's route 22/3

Arago S France site of early man 3/3

Aragon (*sp.* Aragón) region of E Spain at time of Reconquista 37/4; Muslim minorities 75/1; rural uprisings 57/1; acquired by Habsburgs 72/1

Arakan diistrict of SW Burma Islamic states 51/2, 70/1; British control 71/2; annexed by British 104/2

Aralsk C Asia 147/1

Aram ancient country of Middle East 21/2

Arapaho C USA Plains Indian tribe 63/1

Araucanian S America Andean Indian tribe 63/1

Arausio (*mod.* Orange) S France 26/2

Arawak S America Indian tribe 63/1

Arbailu (*a/c* Arbela *mod.* Arbil) Mesopotamia 17/3, 21/1

Arbela (*a/c* Arbailu *mod.* Arbil) Mesopotamia Alexander's route 22/3; early archbishopric 27/2, 39/1

Arcadia country of Ancient Greece 18/3

Arcadiopolis Bulgaria Byzantine Empire 43/1

Archangel (*Russ.* Arkhangelsk) N Russia founded 85/1; Allied occupation 121/2; industry 147/1

Arcole N Italy ✕ 91/1

Arcot S India ceded to British 87/3; ✕ 7/2

Arcy-sur-Cure C France site of early man 3/3

Ardabil Azerbaijan early trade 59/3

Ardales S Portugal Palaeolithic art 5/3

Ardea N Italy ancient town 30/1

Ardennes *forest* Belgium/France WW1 119/3; WW2 ✕ 132/2

Ardmore Ireland early bishopric 26/2

Arelate (*mod.* Arles) S France Roman Empire 24/2, 30/3; archbishopric 26/2

Arene Candide NW Italy site 15/1

Arequipa Peru early Spanish city 66/1

Arezzo (*anc.* Arretium) C Italy medieval city 56/3

Argel (Algiers)

Argentina independence from Spain 97/1; exports and foreign investment 96/2; population 96/2; industrialisation and economy 142/2, 3; 150/1; political developments 143/1

Argentoratum (*mod.* Strasbourg) E France Mithraic site 26/1

Arginusae islands of the Aegean ✕ 23/2

Argissa Greece site 15/1

Argolis country of Ancient Greece 18/3

Argos S Greece 22/1

Arguin island off NW Africa Portuguese settlement 60/2, 64/1; French port 60/2

Århus (*a/s* Aarhus) C Denmark archbishopric 52/3

Aria (*a/c* Haraiva) ancient region of Afghanistan 23/3

Arica Peru trading post 66/1

Arickara E USA ✕ 95/2

Ariha (Jericho)

Ariminium (*mod.* Rimini) N Italy Latin colony 30/1; archbishopric 26/2

Arizona state of USA Depression 130/2; population 145/1

Arjunayanas tribe of N India 29/5

Arkansas state of C USA Depression 131/2; population 145/1

Arkhanes Crete Mycenaean settlement and palace 19/1

Arkhangelsk (Archangel)

Arles (anc. Arelate or Arelas) S France early archbishopric 34/4; medieval trade 55/3

Arlit SE Algeria early site 11/1

Armagh N Ireland archbishopric 26/2; monastery 38/3

Armagnac region of SW France under English rule 52/2; annexed to France 72/2

Armenia (anc. Urartu) country of Caucasus spread of Christianity 26/1; Alexander's Empire 22/3; Roman province 31/3; Muslim conquest 41/1; Ottoman Empire 124/1; independence after WW1 125/3, 129/2; SSR 146/2

Armenia, Lesser region of Asia Minor 40/3

Armeniac Theme Anatolia division of Byzantine Empire 42/2

Armenians emigration from Turkey 129/3

Arpachiyah N Mesopotamia early farming village 7/4

Arpi C Italy early town 30/1

Arpino (Arpinum)

Arpinum (mod. Arpino) C Italy early town 30/1

Arrapkha Mesopotamia trading town 17/4

Arras (anc. Nemetocenna) N France fort 80/1; French Revolution 89/2; WW1 118/3

Arretium (mod. Arezzo) C Italy Etruscan city 19/4, 30/1; Roman Empire 24/2

Arsinoe Libya ancient town 31/3

Artacoana Afghanistan Alexander's route 23/3

Artajona NE Spain megalithic tomb 14/3

Artaphernes Persian general 23/1

Artashat Caucasus patriarchate 27/2

Artaxata Armenia Roman Empire 31/3

Artemision (Cape Artemisium)

Artois region of NE France Burgundian possession 72/2; province of France 80/1

Aruba island of Dutch West Indies 97/1, 139/1 (inset)

Arvad (Arwad)

Arwad (anc. Aradus Bibl. Arvad Fr. Rouad) Syria Assyrian Empire 20/3; Crusader states 40/3

Asahikawa N Japan 126/2

Asante W Africa early state 61/2

Ascalon (mod. Ashqelon) S Palestine Philistine city 19/4; Venetian naval victory 37/2

Ascension Island S Atlantic British colony 100-101

Ascoli Piceno (Asculum)

Ascoli Satriano (Ausculum)

Asculum (a/c Asculum Picenum mod. Ascoli Piceno) N Italy 30/1

Ashdod (Lat. Azotus) Palestine Philistine city 19/4, Levantine city 21/1

Ash Hollow C USA ✕95/2

Ashkenazi N European Jews 39/4

Ashkhabad (from 1919✕27 Poltoratsk) SW Central Asia industry 147/1

Ashqelon (Ascalon)

Ash Sham (Damascus)

Ash Shariqah (Sharjah)

Ashtaroth ancient Israel 21/4

Ashur (mod. Sharqat) Mesopotamia early urban centre 16/1, 17/4; Assyrian Empire 20/3; Mitannian city 21/1

Asia early man 3/3, 4/1, 5/2, 6/7; agricultural origins 7/2, 5; early trade routes 59/3; tribal movements 32/3; expansion of Christianity 39/1; Chinese expansion 28/2; Mongol expansion 46/7; early voyages of discovery 65/2, 67/1; Russian expansion 84/2, 3; industrialisation 108/1; colonial empires 100/101; anti-colonial resistance 139/1

Asia (Byzantine name Asiana) Roman province of Anatolia 31/3, 4

Asiago N Italy WW1 119/3

Asia Minor spread of civilisation 16/1; conversion to Christianity 27/1; Ottoman control 49/1. See also Anatolia

Asiana (Asia)

Asir SW Arabia Ottoman Empire 125/1

Asoka's Empire India 28T; 29/4

Aspendus SW Anatolia Dorian colony 19/4

Aspern/Essling Austria ✕91/1

Assam state of NE India Mongol control 47/1; British control 71/2, 104-5

Assus W Anatolia Aeolian colony 19/4

Assyria Empire 20/3; Roman province 31/3

Astacus (mod. Izmit) NW Anatolia Dorian colony 19/4

Astarac SW France independent fief 72/2

Asti N Italy Lombard League 55/3

Astorga (Asturica Augusta)

Astoria NW USA fur station 94/1

Astrakhan S Russia occupied by Mongols 47/4; Tartar khanate 85/1; Bolshevik seizure 121/2; WW2 133/2

Asturias region of N Spain kingdom 34/4; part of Castile 37/4

Asturica Augusta (mod. Astorga) N Spain Roman Empire 31/3; bishopric 26/2

Asunción Paraguay early Spanish settlement 66/1; 97/1

Aswan (Syene)

Asyut (anc. Lycopolis) S Egypt trade 58/3

Atacama (Sp. Atacameño) S America Andean Indian tribe 63/1

Atacama Desert Chile/Peru War of the Pacific 97/4

Atacameño S America early cultural centre 13/4

Atapuerca N Spain site of early man 3/3

Atchana (Alalakh)

Athenae (Eng. Athens mod. Gr. Athinai) Greece Roman Empire 24/2, 31/3

Athenopolis SE France Ionian colony 19/4

Athens (Lat. Athenae mod. Gr. Athinai) Greece Mycenaean palace 19/1; Greek parent state 19/4; Persian wars 20/5, 22/1; war with Sparta 23/2; Chinese finds 24/1; bishopric 27/2; invaded by Huns 32/1; Byzantine Empire 43/1, 3; WW2 133/2

Athinai (Athens)

Athura Mesopotamia satrapy of Achaemenid Empire 21/5

Atjeh (n/s Aceh) N Sumatra Islamic state 70/1

Atlanta SE USA ✕93/5; industry 110/2; strike 130/2

Atlantic Ocean U-Boat warfare WW2 133/3

Atranji Khera N India site 9/1

Atropatene (Azerbaijan)

Attalia (mod. Antalya) S Anatolia early church 27/2; Byzantine Empire 43/1, 3

Attica ancient state of SE Greece 18/3, 22/1, 23/2

Attigny NE France Frankish royal residence 34/4

Attila ruler of the Huns 32/2

Attirampakkan and Gudiyam Cave S India Stone Age site 9/1

Attu Island Aleutians, W Alaska Japanese attack 134/1

Atwetwebooso W Africa Iron Age site 11/1

Auckland N Island, New Zealand province and second capital 112/2

Audenarde (Dut. Oudenaarde) Belgium fort 80/1

Augila (n/s Awjilah) Libya early trade 60/1

Augsburg (anc. Augusta Vindelicorum) S Germany town of Swabia 55/1; medieval trade centre 59/2

Augusta W Australia early settlement 113/1

Augusta Argentorate (mod. Strasbourg) E France Roman Empire 24/2

Augusta Rauricorum (mod. Augst) W Germany Roman Empire 24/2, 30/3

Augusta Taurinorum (mod. Turin) N Italy early bishopric 26/2

Augusta Treverorum (mod. Trier Eng. Treves) W Germany Mithraic site 26/1; Roman Empire 24/2, 30/3; archbishopric 26/2

Augusta Vindelicorum (mod. Augsburg) S Germany Roman Empire 24/2, 30/3

Augustodunum (mod. Autun) C France Roman Empire 24/2, 30/3; early bishopric 26/2

Augustów NE Poland WW1 119/3

Augustus Roman Emperor 30T

Auliye-Ata (Dzhambul)

Aulon (later Avlona mod. Vlorë) Albania Dorian colony 19/4

Aurangzeb Mughal emperor 87T

Auranitis region of Judaea 26/3

Auschwitz-Birkenau (Pol. Oświęcim) concentration camp 132/1

Ausculum (a/c Ausculum Apulum mod. Ascoli Satriano) C Italy early town 30/1

Austerlitz (mod. Slavkov) Czechoslovakia ✕91/1

Australia (originally called New Holland) early man 3/3; before the Europeans 10/2; early voyages of discovery and exploration 112/5; early trade 113/4; settlement and development 113/1; emergence of Commonwealth 101/1, 2; economy and industrialisation 108/1; WW2 134-135

Austrasia the eastern Frankish Empire, 34/4

Austria (Ger. Österreich) German settlement 55/3; Black Death 57/1; acquired by Habsburgs 56/2, 78/3, 78-9T; War of the Spanish Succession 81/5; attacked by Ottomans 48/2; archduchy 79/1; opposition to Napoleon 91/1; inter-war alliances 128/1; socio-political change 130/3; annexed by Germany 129/5; Allied occupation zones 136/1; EFTA 137/3

Austro-Hungarian Empire agriculture and peasant emancipation 83/1; Military Frontier with Ottoman Empire 78/3; industrial revolution 99/2; ethnic composition 115/1; European alliances 117/2; overseas trade 109/3; WW1 118-9; dismantled 128/2

Autun (Augustodunum)

Auvergne region of C France English possession 52/5; annexed to France 72/2; French province 80/1

Auvernier E Switzerland early settlement 14/2

Auximum E Italy Roman colony 30/1

Ava C Burma political centre 70/1, 71/2

Avanti region of C India 29/4

Avaricum (Bourges)

Avaris (a/c Tanis) Lower Egypt Hyksos capital 21/1

Avars (Chin. Juan-juan) ancient people of Asia and Europe 31/4, 5; 34/1; 35/4

Avdeyevo E Russia Palaeolithic art 5/3

Avenio (Avignon)

Avesnes N France megalithic flint mine 15/3; fort 80/1

Avignon (anc. Avenio) S France Great Schism 57/1; Papal enclave 80/1; annexed by France 88/3

Ávila C Spain expulsion of Jews 38/4

Avlona (Gr. Aulon mod. Vlorë It. Valona) Albania Byzantine Empire 43/1, 3; Ottoman conquest 48/1

Avranches NW France 17C revolt 77/2

Awdaghost W Africa trans-Saharan trade 61/2

Awjilah (Augila)

Axel S Netherlands town of Dutch Republic 77/1

Axim Ghana early Dutch settlement 61/1 (inset)

Axum ancient kingdom of NE Africa 11/1, 25/1, 60/1

Aydhab Sudan early trade 58/3

Aydin W Anatolia emirate 49/1

Ayia Irini SW Aegean Mycenaean settlement 19/1

Ayia Triada (a/s Hagia Triada) Crete Mycenaean village and palace 19/1

Aylesbury S England Industrial Revolution 98/1

Aymará Andean Indian tribe of S America 63/1

Ayodhya (earlier Saketa) NC India town of Kosala 29/4

Ayutthaya (a/s Ayuthia properly Phra Nakhon Si Ayutthaya) S Thailand early political centre 70/1; early trade 71/2

Ayyubids Muslim dynasty, Egypt 60/1

Azak (mod. Azov) S Russia Ottoman conquest 49/1

Azerbaijan (anc. Atropatene) country of the Caucasus Muslim conquest 41/1; Ottoman conquest 48/2; acquired by Russia 85/1, 124/1; independence after WW1 129/2; SSR 146/2

Azincourt (Agincourt)

Azores (Port. Açores) islands of N Atlantic Portuguese discovery 64/1; trade 66/1; Portuguese colony 100/2

Azotus (mod. Ashdod) Palestine bishopric 27/2; in Judaea 26/3

Azov (Turk. Azak) S Russia Ottoman town 49/1

Aztec Empire Mexico 62/2; conquest by Spain 68/1

Baalbek (Heliopolis)

Bab el Mandeb S Arabia land bridge 5/2

Babirush Mesopotamia satrapy of Achaemenid Empire 21/5

Babylon Mesopotamia early urban settlement 16/1; Sumerian city 17/4; Alexander's route 22/3

Babylonia ancient country of Mesopotamia Kingdom 20/4; under Alexander 22/3

Baçain (Bassein)

Bactra (a/c Zariaspa mod. Balkh) Afghanistan silk route 25/1; Alexander's route 23/3

Bactria (a/c Bactriana Pers. Bakhtrish) ancient country of Afghanistan 22T, 23/3

Badajoz SW Spain ✕90/1

Bad Axe N USA ✕95/2

Badegoule SW France Palaeolithic art 5/3

Baden S Germany margraviate 79/1; Confederation of the Rhine 91/4; state 115/2; German customs union 98/3

Badr W Arabia ✕41/1

Badra (Der)

Bad-tibira Mesopotamia Sumerian site 16/2

Baecula SW Spain ✕30/2

Baetica S Spain Roman province 30/3

Baffin, William explorer 65/1

Baffin Island N Canada discovery 64/2

Baghdad Mesopotamia early archbishopric 39/1; Mongol conquest 46/1, 47/4; early trade 58/3; under Ottoman rule 49/1; WW1 125/3

Baghdad Pact 148/4, T

Bagneux NW France megalithic tomb 14/3

Bagram (Begram)

Bagrationovsk (Eylau)

Bahadarabad NW India site 9/1

Bahamas islands of N Caribbean discovery 64/2; British colony 66/4, 69/3, 86/1, 97/1, 100/2; independence 139/1 (inset)

Bahawalpur native state of NW India under British rule 104/1; joins Pakistan at Partition 105/5

Bahçesaray (Bakhchesaray)

Bahia E Brazil Portuguese control 66/1; province 97/1

Bahrain (f/s Bahrein Ar. Al Bahrayn) island of Persian Gulf Ottoman siege 48/2; independent sheikhdom 125/1; independence 138/1

Baile Átha Cliath (Dublin)

Bailén S Spain ✕90/1

Baiovarii tribe of S Germany 32/2

Bairat (a/c Bhabra) N India site 9/1

Bakhchesaray (Turk. Bahçesaray) Crimea Ottoman Empire 49/1

Bakhtrish (a/c Bactria) Afghanistan Achaemenid province 21/5

Baku Azerbaijan Muslim trade 59/3; conquered by Ottomans 48/2; Congress of Peoples of the East 120/4; British occupation 121/2; industry 147/1

Balagansk SC Siberia founded 84/2

Bala-Kot NW India Harappan site 9/5

Balambangan district of Java Dutch control 71/4

Bâle (Basle)

Balearic Islands W Mediterranean Byzantine Empire 42/1; attacked by Saracens 36/2; conquest by Pisa 37/4; reconquered by Aragon 37/4; to Spain 81/5

Balikpapan E Borneo recaptured from Japanese 135/2

Balkan (anc. Bactra a/c Zariaspa) Afghanistan early bishopric 39/1; Muslim conquest 41/1; early trade 59/3

Balkhash C Asia 147/1

Ballarat SE Australia goldfield 113/1

Ballinamuck N Ireland ✕90/3

Ballynagilly Ireland site 15/1

Baltic Viking trade 37/1

Baltic Entente 128/1

Baltic States (Estonia, Latvia, Lithuania)

Baltimore E USA industry 110/2

Baluchistan region of NW India tribal agency 105/3; joins Pakistan after Partition 105/5

Countries 73/3; annexed to France 72/2; province of France 80/1

Burkina (Faso) see Upper Volta

Burma spread of Buddhism 70/1; Mongol invasion 47/1; early state 51/2, 71/2; tributary state of Chinese Empire 106/1; annexed by Britain 104/2; under British rule 101/2, 105/3; Indian National Army 105/4; Japanese support for independence movements 127/5; Japanese occupation 134/1; retaken by Allies 135/2; independence 139/1; political development 141/1

Burnley N England Industrial Revolution 98/1

Burnt Corn SE USA ✕ 95/2

Bursa (*anc.* Prusa *later* Brusa) W Anatolia Byzantine Empire 42/4; centre of Ottoman state 49/1

Burundi (*form.* Urundi) country of C Africa native state 61/2; independence 138/1; political development 140/1. See also Ruanda-Urundi

Burwell E England Industrial Revolution 98/1

Bury N England Industrial Revolution 98/1

Buryat-Mongol ASSR E USSR 146/2

Buryats Mongolian tribe 47/1

Bury St. Edmunds E England Industrial Revolution 98/1

Bushy Run NE USA ✕ 95/2

Bussa W Africa reached by Mungo Park 102/1

Buto Egypt early urban centre 16/1

Button, Sir Thomas explorer 64/1

Buxar NE India site 9/1; ✕ 87/2 (inset)

Buxentum (*Gr.* Pyxous, *a/s* Pyxus) S Italy Roman colony 30/1

Byblos (*mod.* Jubail) Syria early trade 17/4; Mycenaean trade 18/2; Phoenician city 19/4; Levantine city 21/1; Alexander's route 22/3

Byelorussia (Belorussia)

Bylany Czechoslovakia site 15/1

Bylot, Robert explorer 64/1

Byzantine Empire (*a/c* East Roman Empire) 30T; 36/2, 37/1, 40/2, 41/1, 42-43; conflict with Seljuks 41/2

Byzantium (*Eng.* Constantinople *mod.* Istanbul) E Thrace Dorian colony 19/4; Peloponnesian War 23/2; Roman Empire 24/1, 2; Achaemenid Empire 20/5

Cabeço da Arruda C Portugal megalithic tomb 14/1

Cabinda coastal district of SW Africa occupied by Portuguese 103/3

Cabral, Opero Portuguese explorer 64/2

Cacaxtla C Mexico early site 12/4

Cáceres W Spain Civil War 129/4

Cachar district of E India annexed by British 104/2, 105/3

Cacheu W Africa Portuguese settlement 60/2

Caddo S USA Indian tribe 63/1

Cádiz (*anc.* Gades) SW Spain reconquered from Muslims 37/4; trading port 82/4; naval base 87/2; Civil War 129/4

Caen N France 80/1; French Revolution 89/2; WW2 132/1, 2

Caere (*mod.* Cerveteri) C Italy Etruscan city 19/4

Caerleon (Isca)

Caernarvon (*Wel.* Caernarfon *anc.* Segontium) N Wales castle 53/7

Caesaraugusta (*mod.* Zaragoza *Eng.* Saragossa) N Spain Roman Empire 24/2, 30/3; early archbishopric 26/2

Caesarea C Israel Roman Empire 25/2, 31/3; early archbishopric 27/2; town of Judaea 26/3

Caesarea (*mod.* Cherchell) N Algeria Roman Empire 30/3

Caesarea (*a/c* Caesarea Cappadociae, *mod.* Kayseri) C Anatolia early archbishopric 27/2; Roman Empire 31/3; Byzantine Empire 43/1

Caesarodunum (Tours)

Caesaromagus (Chelmsford)

Cagliari (Carales)

Cahokia C USA early site 12/3; French post 67/3; fur station 94/1

Caiguá forest Indian tribe of S Brazil 63/1

Cairns E Australia early settlement 113/1

Cairo (*Fr.* Le Caire *Ar.* Al Qahirah and Al Fustat – Old Cairo) Egypt Muslim conquest 41/1; early trade 58/3, 61/2; captured by Ottomans 49/1; Ottoman Empire 48/2

Cajamarca C Andes site 12/4, 5

Cajamarqilla C Andes site 12/5

Cajon Pass SW USA 94/1

Calabria region of S Italy part of Kingdom of Naples 56/3

Calagurris (*mod.* Calahorra) N Spain Roman Empire 30/3

Calais N France 100 Years War 56/5; WW1 118/3; WW2 132/2

Calcutta E India trade 67/2; British settlement 66/2; industry 105/3; naval mutiny 105/4

Çaldiran (*a/s* Chaldiran) E Turkey ✕ 49/1

Caldy Island S Wales monastery 38/3

Caledonia (Scotland)

Cales C Italy Latin colony 30/1

Calgary W Canada growth 111/1

Calico Hills W USA early site 5/2

Calicut (*a/c* Kozhikode) SW India trade 59/3, 67/1; industry 105/3

California state of SW USA ceded by Mexico 97/1; Depression 130/2; population 145/1

Callao Peru trade 66/1

Callatis Bulgaria Ionian colony 19/4

Calleva (*mod.* Silchester) S England Roman Empire 30/3

Callipolis (*mod.* Gallipoli) S Italy Greek colony 19/4

Calne SW England Industrial Revolution 98/1

Calusa Indian tribe of SE USA 63/1

Camarina Sicily Dorian colony 19/4, 23/2

Cambaluc Mongolia early bishopric 39/1

Cambodia (*known formally as* Democratic Kampuchea *earlier* Khmer Republic) early sites 8/3; temple kingdoms 51/2; invaded by Siam and Vietnam 71/2; French protectorate 101/2; independence 139/1; Vietnamese war 148/3; political development 141/1

Cambous S France early settlement 14/2

Cambrai N France Burgundian possession 73/3; WW1 118/3 (inset)

Cambria (*mod.* Wales) expansion of Christianity 38/3

Cambridge E England castle 36/3; Industrial Revolution 98/1

Camden SE USA ✕ 92/1

Cameroon (*f/s* Cameroons, Cameroun *Ger.* Kamerun) country of W Africa German colony 100/1, 102-103, independence 138/1; economy 151/1

Campa forest Indian tribe of S America 63/1

Campania region of C Italy Roman Empire 30/1

Camp David Agreement 140T

Campeche province of S Mexico 97/1

Camulodunum (*mod* Colchester) S England Roman Empire 24/2, 30/3

Cana (*a/s* Cane) S Arabia early port 24/1

Canada early trade 68/5; Confederation 101/1; development 110-111; NATO 149/1; economy 109/1, 150/1

Canadian Pacific Railway 111/1

Çanakkale (*f/s* Chanak) W Turkey Greco-Turkish War 125/4

Çanakkale Boğazi (Dardanelles]

Canal de Briare N France 80/1

Canal Royal S France 80/1

Canary Islands Portuguese exploration 64/1; on early trade routes 66/1; Spanish sovereignty 87/1, 138/1

Canaveral, Cape (*for a short time called* Cape Kennedy) SE USA 65/3

Canberra SE Australia capital territory 113/1

Candamo N Spain Palaeolithic art 5/3

Çandar (*a/c* Kastamonu) early emirate of N Anatolia 49/1

Candelaria W Cuba Soviet missile site 149/5

Candida Casa S Scotland monastery 38/3

Çankırı (Gangra)

Cannae S Italy ✕ 31/2

Canterbury (*anc.* Durovernum *ecclesiastical Lat.* Cantuaria) S England monastery 38/3; Industrial Revolution 98/1

Canterbury S Island, New Zealand 112/2

Cantigny NE France WW1 118/3 (inset)

Canton S China trade 25/1, 59/3; treaty port 107/4; captured by Japanese 127/5

Canton River S China first European visit 65/2

Cantuaria (*mod.* Canterbury) archbishopric 26/1

Canusium (*mod.* Canosa di Puglia) S Italy Roman Empire 30/1

Canute the Great 38/2, 53/4

Caparcotna Palestine Roman Empire 25/2

Cap Blanc SW France Palaeolithic art 5/3

Cape Artemisium (*mod. Gr.* Artemision) E Greece ✕ 22/1

Cape Bojador NW Africa ✕ 60/2

Cape Breton Island E Canada French possession 86/1

Cape Coast Castle (*a/c* Cape Coast) Ghana early British settlement 60/2 (inset)

Cape Colony S Africa early settlement 60T; captured by British from Dutch 87/2; British colony 102-103 (inset)

Cape Finisterre NW Spain ✕ 90/3

Capeletti N Algeria cattle domestication 11/1

Cape of Good Hope S Africa first European voyage 65/2; Dutch settlement 61/2

Cape Province S Africa established by Dutch East India Co. 61/2

Cape St. Vincent S Portugal ✕ 90/3

Cape Town South Africa Dutch settlement 61/2

Cape Verde Islands W Africa Portuguese exploration 60/2; Portuguese sovereignty 100/2; independence 138/1

Capitanata region of C Italy part of Kingdom of Naples 56/3

Caporetto N Italy WW1 ✕ 119/3

Cappadocia (*Pers.* Katpatuka) county of E Anatolia Alexander's Empire 22/3; independent state 22/4; Roman province 31/3; Byzantine province 42/2, 43/1

Capsa (*mod.* Gafsa) Tunisia Roman Empire 30/3

Capua S Italy Mithraic site 26/1; Roman Empire 24/2, 31/3

Caracas Venezuela colonised 69/3

Carajá forest Indian tribe of C Brazil 63/1

Carales (*mod.* Cagliari) Sardinia Roman Empire 30/3; archbishopric 26/2

Carapito N Portugal megalithic tomb 14/3

Carchemish (*Turk.* Karkamiş) E Anatolia 20/2, 21/1

Cardiff S Wales Industrial Revolution 98/1

Caria (*Pers.* Karka) country of W Asia Minor Persian province 23/1

Carib Indian tribe of Caribbean 63/1

Caribbean early voyages of discovery 65/3; European settlement 66/1; colonial expansion 69/3; US involvement 111/4, 142/1

Carinthia (*Ger.* Kärnten) province of S Austria Frankish duchy 54/1; medieval German Empire 55/3; acquired by Habsburgs 56/2, 78/3; Habsburgs duchy 79/1

Carlisle N England rebellion against Henry VIII 73/4; Industrial Revolution 98/1

Carmana (Kirman)

Carmania county of E Persia 23/3, 29/4

Carnatic (*a/c* Karnataka) coastal region of SE India 87/2

Carniola (*Ger.* Krain) region of Austria/Yugoslavia medieval Germany 55/3; acquired by Habsburgs 56/2, 78/3; Habsburg duchy 79/1

Carnuntum ancient town of Austria Mithraic site 26/1; Roman Empire 24/2, 31/3

Carolina N America British settlement 67/3

Caroline Islands C Pacific German sovereignty 101/2; captured by US from Japanese 135/2

Carolingian Empire (Frankish Kingdom)

Carpathos (*It.* Scarpanto) island of E Mediterranean colonisation 19/1

Carpi N Italy ✕ 81/5

Carreg Cennen S Wales castle 53/7

Carrier sub-arctic Indian tribe of NW Canada 63/1

Carson City W USA mining site 94/1

Cartagena (*anc.* Carthago Nova) SE Spain naval base 87/1, Civil War 129/4

Carteia S Spain Roman Empire 30/3

Carthage (*Lat.* Carthago) Tunisia Stone Age site 11/1; Phoenician colony 19/4; Roman Empire 24/2, 30/2, 3; early archbishopric 27/2; Byzantine reconquest 32/1; Muslim conquest 40/1

Carthago Nova (*mod.* Cartagena) SE Spain Roman Empire 24/2, 30/2, 3, 32/3; archbishopric 26/2

Cartier, Jacques French explorer 64/2

Cascades NW USA ✕ 95/2

Cashel Ireland bishopric 26/2

Casimir I king of Poland 72/1

Caspian Gates N Persia Alexander's route 23/3

Cassano N Italy ✕ 81/5

Cassel N France ✕ 81/4

Cassino C Italy WW2 133/2

Castellón de la Plana E Spain Civil War 129/4

Castiglione N Italy ✕ 91/1

Castile region of Spain at time of Reconquista 36/2; acquired by Habsburgs 72/1

Castillo N Spain Palaeolithic art 5/3

Castillo de Teayo Mexico Aztec town 62/2

Castle Cavern S Africa Iron Age site 11/1

Castoria N Greece Byzantine Empire 43/3

Castra Regina (*mod.* Regensburg *form. Eng.* Ratisbon) C Germany Roman fort 24/2

Castulo (*mod.* Cazlona) S Spain Roman Empire 30/3

Catalans people of NE Spain 115/1

Catalonia (*Sp.* Cataluña *Cat.* Catalunya) region of NE Spain reconquest by Aragon 37/4; under French rule 90/1; autonomous 128/2

Catana (*mod.* Catania) Sicily ally of Athens 23/2; Roman Empire 31/3; medieval German Empire 55/3

Catanzaro S Italy WW1 119/3

Catawba Indian tribe of SE USA 63/1

Cattaro (*mod.* Kotor) E Adriatic WW1 119/3

Caucasus early urban settlement 16/1; Muslim expansion 41/1

Cawahib forest Indian tribe of W Brazil 63/1

Cawnpore (*n/s* Kanpur) N India Indian Mutiny 104/1; civil unrest 104/4

Cayapó forest Indian tribe of C Brazil 63/1

Cayenne French Guiana colonisation 69/3

Çayönü E Anatolia early farming site 7/4

Cazlona (Castulo)

Ceará NE Brazil Confederation of the Equator 97/1

Cebu island of C Philippines Spanish control 67/1

Cedar Creek C USA ✕ 95/2

Cedar Mountain SE USA ✕ 93/5

Cefalù (*anc.* Cephaloedium) Sicily medieval German Empire 55/3

Celebes (*Indon.* Sulawesi) island of East Indies Muslim expansion 40/5; occupied by Japanese 134/1; state of Indonesia 139/2

Celenderis S Anatolia Ionian colony 19/4

Celts tribe of W Europe, France 19/4; expansion 15/5

Cempoala Mexico Aztec town 62/2; on Cortés' route 68/1

Cenomani early people of N Italy 30/1

CENTO treaty organisation 148T

Central African Federation (Northern Rhodesia, Southern Rhodesia, Nyasaland)

Central African Republic (*form.* Central African Empire *form.* Ubangi-Shari) independence 138/1; political development 140/1

Central Asian Gasfield USSR 147/1

Central India Agency Indian states under British control 104/1, 105/3

Central Provinces (*now* Madhya Pradesh) state of central India 105/3

Ceos (*mod.* Kea) island of the Aegean colonisation 19/1

Cephaloedium (Cefalù)

Cephalonia (*mod.* Kefallinia) island of the Ionian Byzantine Empire 43/3; Venetian territory 48/1

Cerdagne (*Sp.* Cerdaña) region of France and Spain Habsburg territory 80/1

Cerdicesford S England ✕ 33/2

Ceredigion district of Wales 53/7

Cerebon (Cheribon)

Goa district of W India early trade 66/2, 67/1; Portuguese settlement 48/2, 87/3, 105/3
Godavari district of E India ceded to Britain 87/3, 104/4
Goias province of Brazil 97/1
Gokomere S Africa early site 11/1
Golan Heights Syria occupied by Israel 141/3
Gold Coast (now Ghana) early European settlement 103/3 (inset); British colony 100/2, 103/3
Golden Bull 54/T
Golden Horde Khanate of C Asia 47/3, 4
Goldsboro SE USA✕93/5
Gombroon (Bandar Abbas)
Gomel WC Russia WW1 119/3; industry 147/1
Go Mun N Vietnam Neolithic site 8/3
Gondeshapur Persia early archbishopric 27/2
Gönnersdorf W Germany Palaeolithic art 5/3
Go Oc Eo Indo-China trade 25/1
Good Hope, Cape of S Africa Portuguese discovery 64/1
Goole N England Industrial Revolution 98/1
Gophna Israel city of Judaea 26/3
Gordium C Anatolia early city 16/1; Alexander's route 22/3; Achaemenid Empire 21/5
Gorée W Africa French settlement 61/2
Gorgan (Gurgan)
Gorkiy (until 1932 Nizhniy Novgorod) C Russia industry 147/1
Gorlice SE Poland✕119/3
Gornja Tuzla N Yugoslavia early settlement 14/2
Gorno-Altai AR C Asia 146/2
Gorno-Badakhshan AR C Asia 146/2
Gorodets SW Russia town of Pereyaslavl 45/2
Gortyna Crete Roman Empire 24/2; archbishopric 27/2
Goslar C Germany Hanseatic city 59/2
Gothenburg (Sw. Göteborg) W Sweden 77/3
Goths invasions 32/1
Gotland island of Baltic occupied by Teutonic Knights 54/4; transferred to Sweden 77/3
Gottorp NW Germany Reformation 74/4
Gough's Cave S England site of early man 3/3; Palaeolithic art 5/3
Gournia Crete palace site 19/1
Gouy N France Palaeolithic art 5/3
Goyet Belgium Palaeolithic art 5/3
Grado N Italy bishopric 26/2
Graeco-Bactrian Kingdom Afghanistan 22/4
Graig Llwyd N Wales megalithic axe factory 14/3
Gran (Hung. Esztergom) Hungary bishopric 38/2; Ottoman conquest 48/2
Granada city and region of Spain Muslim kingdom 37/4; acquired by Habsburgs 72/1; 18C urban development 82/4; Muslim minority 74/1; Civil War 129/4
Grand Pressigny W France megalithic flint mine 14/3
Grandson Switzerland✕73/3
Granicus W Anatolia✕20/5, 22/3
Grantham C England Industrial Revolution 98/1
Granville NW France French Revolution 89/2
Grattan's Defeat C USA✕95/2
Grave Creek W USA✕95/2
Gravesend SE England Industrial Revolution 98/1
Great Britain agriculture and peasant emancipation 82/1; trade and industry 82/4; colonisation of North America 86/1; opposition to Napoleon 90-91; colonial empire 100-101; growth in armaments 117/3; 19C European alliances 117/2; WW1 118-9; WW2 132-3. See also England
Great Driffield NE England Industrial Revolution 98/1
Great Genesee Road NE USA 94/1
Great Khan, Empire of the E Asia 47/3
Great Langdale NW England megalithic axe factory 14/3
Great Leap Forward China 140T
Great St. Bernard pass Switzerland/Italy 58/1
Great Swamp NE USA✕95/2
Great Trading Path E USA settlers' route 94/1
Great Yarmouth (a/c Yarmouth) E England Industrial Revolution 98/1
Great Zimbabwe early city of SE Africa 61/2
Greco-Turkish War 125/4
Greece (anc. Gr. Hellas mod. Gr. Ellas) Ancient Greece 18-19, 20-21; Levantine ports 21/1; arrival of Christianity 26-7; invaded by Visigoths 32/1; Black Death 57/1; independent kingdom 116/1; WW1 118/9; conflict with Bulgaria and Turkey 124/1; inter-war alliances 128/1; socio-political change 131/3, 137/4, 5; WW2 133/2; Cold War 149/1
Greeks migration after WW1 129/3
Greenland rediscovered 64/2; US bases 149/1
Grenada island of W Indies British colony 97/1; self-government 139/1 (inset); US invasion 143/1
Grenoble SE France parlement 80/1
Grijalva, Juan de Spanish explorer 64/3
Grimaldi N Italy site of early man 3/3
Grimes Graves E England megalithic flint mine 14/3
Grimsby N England Industrial Revolution 98/1
Griqualand West S Africa 103/4
Griquas tribe of S Africa 102/2
Grønhøj C Denmark megalithic tomb 15/3
Groningen N Netherlands Hanseatic town 59/2; Burgundian possession 73/3
Gross Rosen (now Pol. Rogoźnica) SE Germany concentration camp 132/1
Grotte des Fées SE France burial site 14/2

Groznyy Caucasus industry 147/1
Gruta de Furninha C Portugal farming site 15/1
Gua Cha Malaya early site 8/3
Guadalajara C Spain Civil War 129/4
Guadalajara C Mexico capital of New Spain 66/1
Guadalcanal island of Solomons, S Pacific✕135/2
Guadeloupe island of W Indies French settlement 66/4, 69/3; attacked by British 87/1; French territory 97/1, 139/1 (inset)
Guahibo Indian tribe of S America 63/1
Gua Kechil Malaya early site 8/3
Gua Kepah W Malaya Iron Age site 8/3
Guam island of W Pacific occupied by US 110/1; occupied by Japanese 134/1; recaptured by US 135/2; US base 149/1 (inset)
Guanajay W Cuba Soviet missile site 149/5
Guanajuato province of C Mexico 97/1
Guantánamo Bay E Cuba US naval base 149/5
Guaraní forest Indian tribe of Paraguay 63/1
Guatemala country and city of C America founded 66/1; independence 97/1; US involvement 149/1
Guató Indian tribe of C Brazil 63/1
Guayaquil port of Ecuador 97/1
Guaymí Indian tribe of C America 63/1
Guernica N Spain Civil War 129/4
Guerrero province of S Mexico 97/1
Guiana region of S America discovered 65/3; colonised by Dutch and French 69/3. See also Surinam, French Guiana, Guyana
Guibray NW France medieval fair 59/2
Guildford S England✕73/4
Guinea (form. French Guinea) independence 138/1
Guinea-Bissau (form. Portuguese Guinea) W Africa independence 138/1
Gujerat (n/s Gujarat) region of W India under British rule 87/3, 104/1; Partition 105/5
Gulbarga S India political disturbance 104/4
Gumbinnen E Prussia✕WW1 119/3
Gumma prefecture of C Japan 126/2
Güns (Hung. Köszeg) Hungary Ottoman siege 48/2
Guntur district of S India civil unrest 104/4
Günük (Xanthus)
Gupta Empire India 29/5; destroyed by White Huns 33/1
Gurgan (a/c Gorgan anc. Hyrcania) city and region of N Persia Muslim conquest 41/1
Gurgaon district of N India communal riots 104/4
Guryev Russ. C Asia founded 85/1; industry 147/1
Gusev (Gumbinnen)
Gustavus Adolphus King of Sweden 74/1
Guyana (form. British Guiana) S America 142-3, 150/1
Guyenne (a/c Aquitaine anc. Aquitania) region of SW France English possession 52/2; French Royal domain 72/2; province of France 80/1
Gwadar (f/s Gwador) Pakistan Alexander's route 23/3; ceded by Muscat 105/5
Gwalior former state of C India 104/1
Gwynedd early Welsh principality 33/3, 35/3, 53/7
Gwynllwg early district of S Wales 33/3

Gyulafehérvár (Alba Iulia)

Habsburg Lands 56/2, 57/1
Hacilar N Turkey site 7/4
Hadar Ethiopia site of early man 5/3
Hadhramaut region of S Arabia Muslim expansion 41/1
Hadrumetum (mod. Sousse) Tunisia Phoenician city 19/4; Roman Empire 30/3
Haervej Denmark Land route of Jutland 53/3
Haestingas people of S England 33/3
Hafrsfjord S Norway✕53/5
Hafsids Muslim dynasty of Tunisia 40/2
Haga S Sweden megalithic tomb 15/3
Hagi W Japan 126/1
Hagia Triada (Ayia Triadha)
Hagmatana (a/c Ecbatana) Persia 21/5
Haida coast Indian tribe of NW Canada 63/1
Hailar Manchuria on railway 122/4
Hainan island S China early soviet 122/4
Hainaut (Dut. Henegouwen) district of Belgium under medieval German Empire 55/3; Burgundian possession 73/3
Haiphong N Vietnam early trade 71/2; railway 107/4; Vietnamese war 148/3
Haiti Toussaint l'Ouverture's revolt 88/1; independence 97/1; US intervention 142/1, 2; political development 143/1. See also Hispaniola
Hakka-Cantonese War S China 107/3
Hakodate city of N Japan 126/1
Halab (Aleppo)
Hala Sultan Tekke E Cyprus Levantine port 21/1
Halberstadt N Germany bishopric 79/1
Halicarnassus (mod. Bodrum) W Anatolia Byzantine Empire 43/1
Halidon Hill SE Scotland✕56/4
Halifax N England Industrial Revolution 98/1
Halifax E Canada British naval base 86/1; growth 111/1
Halin N Burma Hindu-Buddhist remains 51/2
Halland province of SW Sweden under Danish rule 53/3; regained from Denmark 77/3
Halle C Germany WW1 119/3

Haller's Defeat NW USA✕95/2
Halwan Mesopotamia early archbishopric 39/1
Halys River C Anatolia✕20/5
Hama (anc. Hamath) W Syria occupied by French 125/3
Hamadan (anc. Ecbatana) W Persia Mongol conquest 47/4; Ottoman control 48/2
Haman's Defeat NE USA✕95/2
Hamath (mod. Hama) Syria Mitannian city 21/1
Hamburg N Germany bishopric 38/2; Hanseatic city 59/2; 18C financial centre 82/4; industrial development 99/3; German customs union 98/3; WW1 119/2; Communist uprising 120/3; WW2 132-3; post-war 137/5
Hami (Kumul)
Hamid early Ottoman principality of SW Anatolia 49/1
Hamilton C Canada growth 111/1
Hammurabi, Empire of 17/4
Han NW China Western Chou domain 9/6; warring state 28/1; expansion 106/1; Empire 107/4
Han sub-Arctic Indian tribe of Alaska 63/1
Hanau W Germany✕90/1
Hanchung C China Han commanderie 29/3
Hangchow C China early agriculture 7/2; provincial capital 51/4; early trade 59/3, 107/2; captured by Kuomintang 123/3; industry 108/1, 123/4
Hang Gon S Vietnam Iron Age Site 8/3
Hankow C China industry 109/1; treaty town 107/4
Hannibal Carthaginian general 30/2
Hannover (Hanover)
Hanoi (form. Thang Long) N Vietnam trade centre 71/2; Japanese occupation 127/5; 1945-75 war 148/3
Hanover (Ger. Hannover) former state of N Germany industrial development 98/3, 99/2; unification with Germany 115/2; WW1 119/2; WW2 133/2
Hanseatic League N Europe 59/2
Haraiva (a/c Aria) region of C Afghanistan satrapy of Achaemenid Empire 21/5
Harappa N India early urban settlement 9/5, 16/1
Harauvatish (a/c Arachosia) region of C Afghanistan satrapy of Achaemenid Empire 21/5
Harbin Manchuria railway 127/4; Russian occupation 107/4; Russo-Japanese war 127/4; industry 123/4
Hare sub-arctic Indian tribe of NW Canada 63/1
Harfleur N France 56/5
Harlech N Wales castle 53/7
Harmozia (later Ormuz or Hormuz) S Persia Alexander's Empire 23/3
Harold Bluetooth King of Denmark 52T
Hartlepool NE England WW1 119/3
Harwich E England Industrial Revolution 98/1; WW1 119/3
Harz mountains of N Germany prehistoric metal-working 14/2
Hasdrubal Carthaginian general 30/2
Hassuna N Mesopotamia early farming village 7/4
Hastings S England Norman castle 36/3
Hatra (mod. Al Hadhr) Mesopotamia Roman Empire 31/3
Hattin Palestine✕40/3
Hattushash (mod. Boğazköy) C Anatolia early urban settlement 16/1; Hittite Empire 20/2
Hausa States (a/c Hausaland) Nigeria 60-61
Havana (Sp. La Habana) Cuba imperial trade 66/1; Spanish base captured by British 86/1
Haveite N Germany megalithic tomb 15/3
Hawaii state of USA military base 149/1 (inset)
Hawaiian Islands (f/c Sandwich Islands) C Pacific early Polynesian settlement 10/2; annexed by US 100/2, 110/4; war in the Pacific 135/2
Hawkes Bay province of N Island, New Zealand 112/2
Hay W England Industrial Revolution 98/1
Hay-Pauncefote Agreement 111/1
Hazor N Palestine Levantine city 21/1
Hebrides (form. Nor. Sudreyar) Scandinavian settlement 37/1; acquired by Scotland 72/1
Hebron (Ar. Al Khalil) Palestine city of Judaea 26/3; West Bank 141/1
Hecatompylos (a/c Qumis) on Silk Road 25/1; ancient city of Persia 25/1; Alexander's route 23/3
Heijo (Pyongyang)
Hejaz (Ar. Hijaz) region of W Arabia centre of Islam 41/1; under Abbasid sovereignty 41/2; Ottoman sovereignty 124-5
Helenopolis W Anatolia Byzantine Empire 43/1
Heliopolis (mod. Baalbek) Syria Roman Empire 31/3
Heliopolis (Bibl. On) Lower Egypt 17/3; Alexander's route 22/3; conquered by Arabs 41/1
Hellespont (Dardanelles)
Hellespontine Phrygia country of NW Anatolia 22/3
Helmantica (Salamantica)
Helsinki (Sw. Helsingfors) S Finland Swedish port 77/3; WW2 133/2
Helvetia (Swiss Confederation)
Helvetic Republic (mod. Switzerland) state under French protection 89/3
Hembury SW England site 15/1
Hemeroskopeion Spain Ionian colony 18/4
Hemudu (Ho-mu-tu)
Henegouwen (Hainaut)
Hengyang SE China industry 123/4
Henry I King of Saxony 54T
Henry II King of England 52/1
Henry IV German king 54T

Malaca (*mod.* Málaga) S Spain Roman Empire 24/2, 30/3

Malacca (*Mal.* Melaka) district of S Malaya early sultanate 51/2; early trade 59/3, 67/1; captured by Portuguese 70/3; European discovery 65/2; captured by Dutch 66/2, 70/3; under Portuguese rule 71/2; British possession 71/5, 101/1

Málaga (*anc.* Malaca) S Spain 18C urban development 83/4✕81/5; Civil War 129/4

Malaga Cove W USA site 62/4

Malagasy Republic (Madagascar)

Malao (*mod.* Berbera) N Somalia early port 25/1

Malapati S Africa Iron Age site 11/1

Malatya (*anc.* Melitene) E Turkey Hittite city 21/1; revolt against Ottoman rule 48/2

Malavas people of NW India 29/5

Malawi (*form.* Nyasaland) country of C Africa independence 138/1; political development 140/1; economy 150/1

Malaya Iron and Bronze Age sites 8/3; early trade 25/1; spread of Islam 40/5, 70/1; British control 101/2; occupied by Japanese 134/1. See also Malaysia

Malaysia (state formed by amalgamation of Malaya, Sarawak and Sabah) independence 139/1; economy 150/1; confrontation with Indonesia 139/2

Malay States SE Asia British protectorate 71/5. See also Malaya, Malaysia

Malbork (Marienburg)

Maldives islands of N Indian Ocean conversion to Islam 41/4; acquired by British 87/2; protectorate 101/1; independence 139/1

Mali (*form.* French Sudan) country of West Africa independence 138/1; political development 140/1; economy 150/1

Mali Empire early state of W Africa 60/1

Malinalco Mexico Aztec temple 62/2

Malindi Kenya Muslim colony 60/1; early Portuguese trade 61/2

Mallia Crete palace site 19/1

Mallorca (Majorca)

Mallus W Anatolia Ionian colony 19/4

Malmédy E Belgium ceded by Germany 128/2

Maloyaroslavets W Russia✕91/1

Malplaquet N France✕81/5

Malta island of C Mediterranean Norman conquest 36/2; British colony 101/2; WW2 133/1; independence 138/1

Mal'ta E Siberia site of early man 3/3; Palaeolithic art 5/3

Malujowice (Mollwitz)

Maluku (Moluccas)

Malvasia (*a/c* Monemvasia) S Greece Venetian territory 48/1

Malvinas, Islas (Falkland Islands)

Mameluke Empire Egypt/Palestine Mongol invasion 46/1

Mamelukes (*a/s* Mamluk) 40/2

Manassas (*a/c* Bull Run) E USA✕93/5

Manchanagara district of Java Dutch control 71/4

Manchester N England industrial development 98/1

Manchouli N China treaty town 107/4

Manchukuo (name given to Manchuria as Japanese puppet state)

Manchuria (*called 1932-45* Manchukuo) region of NE China Manchu homeland 106/1; occupied by Russia 107/4; Russo-Japanese war 127/4; Russian and Japanese spheres of influence 127/3; warlord control 122/2; Japanese puppet state 123/3, 4; 127/5, 134/1; reoccupied by Russia 135/2

Manchus people of NE China, under the Ming 51/4; homeland expansion 106/1

Manda E Africa early trade 11/1

Mandalay C Burma trade 71/2; occupied by British 104/2; terminus of Burma Road 127/5; occupied by Japanese 134/1; retaken 134/2

Mandan plains Indian tribe of C Canada 63/1

Mangalore S India industry 105/3

Mang-vu Siam early trade 59/3

Manhao SW China treaty town 107/4

Manila C Philippines early trade 67/1; Spanish settlement 66/2; captured by Japanese 134/1

Manipur state of E India 71/2, 104/2, 105/5

Manisa W Anatolia Ottoman Empire 49/1

Manitoba province of C Canada economic development 111/1; joins Confederation 101/1

Mannheim W Germany industrial development 99/2 WW2 133/2

Mantinea C Greece✕23/2

Mantua (*It.* Mantova) N Italy Lombard League 55/3; Signorial domination 56/3; 73/5

Manuel I Byzantine Emperor 42T

Manuel's Fort N USA fur station 94/1

Manunggul Cave W Philippines Iron Age site 8/3

Manus Island W Pacific Allied base 135/2

Manzikert E Anatolia✕42/4, 43/1

Mao-Mao Kenyan guerrilla movement 138/1

Maoris New Zealand tribe 112/2, 3

Mao Tse-tung 122T

Ma-pa E China site of early man 3/3

Mapungubwe early state of SE Africa 60/1

Maracanda (*mod.* Samarkand) Alexander's route 23/3; Achaemenid Empire 21/5; early trade 25/1

Maranga C Andes early site 12/4

Maranhão province of Brazil 97/1

Mărăşeşti Romania WW1 119/3

Marash (*Turk.* Maraş) N Anatolia Byzantine Empire 43/3

Maratha Confederacy N India in alliance with British 87/2; 87/3

Marathon C Greece✕20/5, 22/1

Maravi early state of E Africa 61/2

Marche region of C France 52/2; annexed by France 72/2

Marches (*It.* Le Marche) province of Italy unification 114/3

Marches, of Wales 73/4

Marcianopolis Bulgaria early archbishopric 27/2; Byzantine Empire 43/1

Marcomanni early tribe of C Europe 30/3, 31/4

Marco Polo route 59/3

Mardi early tribe of N Persia 22/3

Marengo N Italy✕90/1

Mari Mesopotamia early urban settlement 16/1, 17/4

Mari people of C Russia 44/3, 45/2, 85/1; ASSR 146/2

Marianas (*form.* Ladrones) islands of W Pacific German colony 101/2; US occupation 135/2

Marie Galante island of W Indies French settlement 66/4 (inset)

Marienburg (*Pol.* Malbork) N Poland seat of Teutonic Order 54/4

Marienwerder (*Pol.* Kwidzyn) N Poland founded by Teutonic Knights 54/4; 1920 plebiscite 128/2

Maritime Provinces (*Russ.* Primorskiy Kray) Russ. Far East acquired from China 107/4

Mariupol (*now* Zhdanov) S Russia industry 85/4

Marj Dabik SE Anatolia✕49/1

Mark W Germany Reformation 74/4

Market Harborough C England Industrial Revolution 98/1

Marksville USA Hopewell site 12/3

Marlborough province of S Island, New Zealand 112/2

Marne *river* NE France WW1 119/2; ✕118/3 (inset)

Maroc (Morocco)

Marqab Syria 40/3

Marquesas Islands S Pacific Polynesian dispersal centre 11/2; French colony 139/1 (inset)

Marrakesh (*Fr.* Marrakech) Morocco early trade 58/3, 61/2

Marruecos (Morocco)

Marsala (Lilybaeum)

Marseilles (*Fr.* Marseille *anc.* Massilia) S France Mediterranean trade 58/3; galley port 80/1; centre of French Revolution 89/2

Marshall Islands C Pacific German colony 101/2; occupied by US 135/2

Marshall Plan 136T

Marston Moor N England ✕76/4

Martinique island of W Indies French settlement 66/4, 69/3; attacked by British 86/1; French territory 97/1, 100/2, 139/1 (inset)

Martyropolis E Anatolia early bishopric 27/2

Mary (Merv)

Maryland state of E USA colony 67/3, 92/1; Civil War 93/5; Depression 131/2; population 111/5, 145/1

Masada Judaea Roman siege 26/3

Masai tribe of E Africa 60/1

Masal Hüyük N Anatolia Hittite city 21/1

Masampo S Korea Russo-Japanese war 127/4

Mashdad (Meshed)

Masovia (*a/s* Mazovia *Pol.* Mazowsze) region of Poland 53/1, 54/4

Masqat (Muscat)

Massachusett Indian tribe of NE USA 63/1

Massachusetts state of NE USA British colony 92/1; Depression 131/2; population 111/5, 145/1

Massachusetts Bay NE USA British colony 67/3

Massagetae tribe of C Asia 23/3

Massawa N Ethiopia Ottoman settlement 48/2, 61/2; Italian attack 103/3

Massilia (*mod.* Marseille *Eng.* Marseilles) S France Roman Empire 24/2, 30/2, 3; bishopric 26/2

Masulipatam S India early trade 25/1

Maszycka S Poland Palaeolithic art 5/3

Mataco Indian tribe of S America 63/1

Matadi W Belgian Congo 138/4

Mataram Sultanate of Java Dutch control 71/2

Mathura C India early trading centre 25/1

Mato Grosso province of Brazil 97/1

Matsu *island* SE China Nationalist outpost 149/1

Matsue W Japan 126/2

Matsuyama W Japan 126/2

Matthias Corvinus king of Hungary 72/1, T

Maubeuge NE France WW1 119/2

Mauer Germany site of early man 3

Mauern S Germany Palaeolithic art 5/3

Mauretania region of NW Africa conversion to Christianity 26/1

Maurice (Mauritius)

Mauritania country of NW Africa independence from France 138/1; political development 140/1; economy 150/1

Mauritius (*Fr.* Maurice) *island* Indian Ocean early trade 66/2; British colony 101/1, 2

Mauthausen Austria concentration camp 132/1

Maya people and civilisation of C America 12/2, 13/1, 62/2

Mayapán Mayan city of E Mexico destroyed 62/2

Maysville Road C USA settlers' route 94/1

Mazaca (*mod.* Kayseri) C Anatolia Achaemenid Empire 21/5

Mazouco N Portugal Palaeolithic art 5/3

Mazovia (Masovia)

Mazowsze (Masovia)

Mbandaka (Coquilhatville)

Meadowcroft E USA early site 5/2

Meadows, The W USA ✕94/2

Meath early kingdom of C Ireland 53/6

Meaux N France unrest 57/1; St Bartholomew Massacre 74/3

Mecca (*Ar.* Al Makkah) W Arabia birth of Islam 41/1; early trade 58/3; Ottoman Empire 48/2; Sharifs of Mecca 46/1; WW1 125/2

Mecklenburg N Germany duchy 79/1; Reformation 74/4, 75/1; unification of Germany 98/3, 115/2

Medes ancient people of NW Persia 20T

Media (*a/c* Mada) ancient country of NW Persia 20/4; in Alexander's Empire 22/3

Media Atropatene Hellenised kingdom of NW Persia 22/4

Medina (*Ar.* Al Madinah) W Arabia centre of Islam 41/1; early trade 58/3; Ottoman Empire 48/2; WW1 125/2

Medina del Campo N Spain medieval fair 59/2

Medina de Rioseco N Spain medieval fair 59/2

Medinet Habu C Eygpt New Kingdom temple 21/1

Mediolanum (*mod.* Milano *Eng.* Milan) N Italy Roman Empire 24/2, 30/3; bishopric 26/2

Mediterranean Sea Greek colonisation 18/4; Phoenicians 18/4; Mycenaean trade 18/2; Roman routes 24/2; Saracen invasions 37/1; Norman and Venetian expansion and Byzantine reconquest 36/2; early trade routes 24/2, 58/3; WW2 132-3

Meersen, Partition of 35/6

Meerut N India Indian Mutiny 104/1; riots 104/4

Megara C Greece Greek parent state 19/4

Megara-Hyblaea Sicily Greek colony 19/4

Megiddo Palestine Egyptian fortress 21/1; ✕WW1 125/2

Mehdia (Mahdia)

Mehemmed I Ottoman ruler 48T, 49/1

Mehemmed II Ottoman ruler 48T, 49/1

Mehi N India Harappan site 9/5

Meidum (Maidum)

Meiji Restoration Japan 126T

Meinarti island of Upper Nile Egyptian fortress 21/1

Meissen district of E Germany 52/1, 55/1, 3

Melaka (Malacca)

Melanesia region of W Pacific early settlement 10/2

Melbourne SE Australia founded 113/1

Melilla (*anc.* Rusaddir) N Morocco Mediterranean trade 58/3; acquired by Habsburgs 72/1

Melitene (*mod.* Malatya) E Anatolia spread of Mithraism 26/1; Roman Empire 25/2, 31/3; early archbishopric 27/2; Byzantine Empire 42/2

Melka Kunturé S Ethiopia site of early man 3/3

Mello N France civil unrest 57/1

Melolo S East Indies Iron Age site 8/3

Melville Island N Australia 113/1

Memel (*Lith.* Klaipeda) NW Russia founded by Teutonic Knights 54/4; WW1 119/3

Memel Territory (*Ger.* Memelgebiet *or* Memelland) region of SW Lithuania annexed by Germany 129/5

Memphis Lower Egypt Iron Age site 11/1; city of Ancient Egypt 17/3, 21/1; Alexander's route 22/3; Achaemenid Empire 20/5; Roman Empire 25/2, 31/3; Byzantine Empire 43/1

Memphis SE USA ✕92/5; civil unrest 144/3

Mende N Greece early bishopric 19/4

Menes king of Egypt 16T

Mengtze (*Fr.* Mong-tseu) SW China treaty port 107/4

Meniet S Algeria early site 11/1

Mennonites sect 74/2

Menominee Indian tribe of C USA 63/1

Menorca (Minorca)

Menteşe early emirate of SW Anatolia 49/1

Mercia early kingdom of C England 35/3, 38/3

Meremere N Island, New Zealand ✕112/3

Mérida (*anc.* Emerita Augusta) SW Spain Civil War 129/4

Mérida SE Mexico early Spanish city 66/1

Merimbe Egypt early agricultural site 11/1

Merina early state in Madagascar 103/3

Merkits Mongolian tribe 47/1

Meroë Sudan Iron Age site 11/1; city of Alwa 60/1

Merovingian kingdom 35/2

Merse (of Berwick) SE Scotland acquired by Edward III 56/4

Mersin E Anatolia early site 17/4

Merthyr Tydfil S Wales Industrial Revolution 98/1

Merv (*since 1937* Mary *anc.* Alexandria) Russ. C Asia early trade 25/1, 59/3; spread of Christianity 26/1; early archbishopric 39/1; Muslim conquest 41/1; Safavid Empire 49/3

Mesas de Asta S Spain early settlement 14/2

Mesaverde SW USA site 62/4

Mesembria Bulgaria Greek colony 19/4

Mesen (Messines)

Meshchera E Slav tribe of C Russia 85/1

Meshed (*Pers.* Mashhad) Alexander's Empire 23/3

Mesoamerica classic period 12/2, 13/1

Mesopotamia (*mod.* Iraq) early agriculture 6/2, 7/4; early empires 16-17; spread of Mithraism 26/1; Alexander's Empire 23/2; Roman Empire 31/3; Muslim conquest 41/1; WW1 125/2; British control 125/3

Nagasaki W Japan early European trade 67/1, 66/2; industry 126/2; bombed by US 135/2, 3
Nagidus S Anatolia Greek colony 19/4
Nagorno-Karabakh AR Caucasus 146/2
Nagoya C Japan 126/2, 135/3
Nagpur C India 104/4, 105/3
Nahuatl Indian tribe of C Mexico 63/1
Naimans Mongolian tribe 47/1
Nairobi Kenya occupied by British 103/3
Naissus (*mod.* Niš) S Yugoslavia Roman Empire 24/2; bishopric 27/2
Najd (Nejd)
Najran SW Arabia early bishopric 39/1
Nakhichevan ASSR Caucasus 146/2
Nakhodka Russ. Far East industry 147/1
Nakhon Pathom S Thailand Hindu-Buddhist remains 51/2
Nakhon Ratchasima C Thailand Vietnam war 148/3
Nambicuara forest Indian Tribe of W Brazil 63/1
Namibia (*form.* South West Africa, *earlier* German South West Africa) German colony 101/2, 103/3; independence from South Africa 138/1, 140/1; economy 150/1
Namsos C Norway WW2 132/1
Namur Belgium Burgundian possession 73/3; town of Spanish Netherlands 77/1; WW1 119/2
Nanchang S China Ming provincial capital 51/4; under warlord control 122/2; anti-Nationalist insurrection 123/4; occupied by Japanese 127/5
Nanchao (*mod.* Yunnan) SW China independent kingdom 50-51
Nan Chihli E China Ming province 51/4
Nancy E France✕73/3; WW1 119/2
Nanhai S China Han Commanderie 29/3
Nanking N China Ming provincial capital 51/4; treaty port 107/4; Nationalist capital 122/2; occupied by Japan 127/5
Nanning S China treaty port 107/4
Nantes NW France Scandinavian settlement 37/1; 17C revolt 77/1; trading port 83/5; centre of French Revolution 89/2; industrial development 98/2
Nantwich C England✕76/4
Nanyueh SW China independent kingdom 28/2
Napata Egypt Iron Age site 11/1; fortress 21/1
Napier N Island, New Zealand founded 112/2
Naples (*anc.* Neapolis *It.* Napoli) Mediterranean trade 58/3, 82/4; industrial development 99/2; WW2 133/2
Naples, Kingdom of Black Death 57/1; to Aragon 72/1; acquired by Habsburgs 72/1; to Austria 81/5; satellite of France 91/1; unification of Italy 114/3
Napoleon Emperor of France 90-91
Napoli (Naples)
Naqada Upper Egypt 17/3
Nara C Japan Buddhist site 27/1; prefecture 126/2
Narbo (*mod.* Narbonne) S France Roman Empire 24/2
Narbonensis (*a/c* Gallia Narbonensis) Roman province of S France 30/3
Narbonne (*anc.* Narbo) S France Muslim conquest 40/1; medieval trade 58/1
Nariokotome E Africa site of early man 3/3
Naroch *Lake* W Russia WW1✕119/3
Narosura E Africa early site 11/1
Narraganset Indian tribe of NE USA 63/1
Narragansett Fort NE USA✕95/2
Narva Estonia, W Russia 1905 Revolution 120/1; WW2 133/2
Narvik N Norway WW2 132/1
Narym W Siberia founded 84/2
Naseby C England✕76/4
Nashville SE USA✕93/5
Nashville Road C USA settlers' route 94/1
Nassau principality of C Germany 79/1; Reformation 75/1; unification with Germany 115/2
Natal province of S Africa annexed by Britain 103/2; British colony 103/4
Natchez S USA Indian tribe 63/1
Natchez Trace S USA settlers' route 94/1
Natchitoches S USA fur station 94/1
Natick NE USA Protestant mission 94/1
National Road C USA settlers' route 94/1
Nations, Battle of the (Leipzig) E Germany✕90/1
NATO 137/3, 148T
Naucratis Egypt Iron Age site 11/1; Greek colony 19/4
Nauru *island* W Pacific territory 139/1 (inset)
Nautaca (*mod.* Karshi) C Asia on Alexander's route 23/3
Navajo Indian tribe of SW USA 63/1
Navarino (Pylos)
Navarre (*Sp.* Navarra) region of N Spain/SW France kingdom 37/1; acquired by Habsburgs 72/1; acquired by France 80/1
Navas de Tolosa S Spain✕40/2
Navpaktos (Lepanto)
Naworth Castle N England✕73/4
Naxos Sicily in Mycenaean world 18/2; Greek colony 19/4
Nazca Andean Indian tribe of S America 63/1
Nazlet Khatir E Egypt site of early man 3/3
Ndeni (Santa Cruz)
N'Djamena (Fort Lamy)
Neanderthal Germany site of early man 3/3
Neapolis (*mod.* Napoli *Eng.* Naples) S Italy Greek colony 19/4, 23/2; Roman Empire 31/3; early bishopric 26/2
Near East (Middle East)
Neath S Wales Industrial Revolution 98/1

Nebraska state of C USA Depression 130/2; population 111/5, 145/1
Neerwinden Belgium✕89/2
Nefertara N Greece Mithraic site 26/1
Negapatam (*n/s* Nagappattinam) S India Dutch settlement 66/2;✕87/2 (inset); industry 104/3
Negri Sembilan state off Malaya 71/5
Negroponte (Euboea)
Nehavend (*anc.* Laodicea in Media) W Persia✕41/1
Nejd (*Ar.* Najd) region of C Arabia 124/1, 125/2
Nellore district of SE India ceded to Britain 87/3
Nelson county and town of S Island, New Zealand founded 112/2
Nelson Bay S Africa Stone age site 11/1
Nemausus (*mod.* Nîmes) S France Roman Empire 30/3 early bishopric 26/2
Nemetocenna (Arras)
Nemours region of N France 72/2
Nenets AR N Siberia 146/2
Neocaesarea N Anatolia early archbishopric 27/2; Byzantine Empire 43/1
Nepal tributary state of Chinese Empire 106/1; 107/4; economy 150/1
Nepala (*mod.* Nepal) tributary state of the Guptas 29/4, 5
Nepete N Italy Latin colony 30/1
Nerchinsk SE Siberia founded 84/2
Nerchinsk, Treaty of 106/1
Nerja S Spain Palaeolithic art 5/3
Nestorian churches 39/1
Nesvizh (*Pol.* Nieświez) W Russia town of Turov-Pinsk 45/2
Netherlands (*a/c* Holland *form.* Dutch Republic United Provinces) Burgundian possession 73/3; acquired by Habsburgs 72/1; agriculture and land reclamation 8/3; trade and industry 82/4; independence in north 114/5; industrial revolution 98/2; colonial power 100/2; socio-political development 130/3; EEC and NATO 137/3; economy 150/1. See also Belgium, Flanders, Holland
Netherlands, Austrian (*mod.* Belgium) revolt against Emperor 88/1; occupied by French 88/3
Netherlands East Indies (*now* Indonesia) occupied by Japanese 135/1. See also East Indies, Borneo, Java, Moluccas, Sumatra
Netherlands, Spanish (*later* Holland *or* United Provinces; *and* Belgium) Reformation 75/1; part of German Empire 79/1; Dutch revolt 76/1; territory lost to and gained from France 81/2, 4
Netherlands, United 79/1
Neuchâtel Switzerland Reformation 75/1
Neuengamme N Germany concentration camp 132/1
Neuenheim W Germany Mithraic site 26/1
Neustria the Frankish lands of N France 34/4
Neuve-Chapelle NE France WW1 118/3 (inset)
Nevada state of W USA Depression 130/2; population 111/5, 145/1
Nevers C France independent fief 72/2
Neville's Cross N England✕56/4
Nevis *island* W Indies English settlement 66/4; British colony 97/1; self-government with St. Christopher 139/1 (inset)
New Amsterdam (*earlier* Fort Amsterdam *now* New York city) colonised by Dutch 67/3
New Britain *island* Papua New Guinea early Melanesian settlement 10/2; retaken from Japanese 135/2; to New Guinea 139/1 (inset)
New Brunswick province of E Canada joins Confederation 101/1; 111/1
New Caledonia *islands* S Pacific early Melanesian settlement 10/2; French colony 101/2, 139/1, US base 135/4
Newcastle SE Australia penal settlement 113/1
Newcastle-under-Lyme C England Industrial Revolution 98/1
Newcastle-upon-Tyne N England medieval trade 59/2; Civil War 76/4; industrial development 98/1
Newchwang Manchuria treaty port 107/4; Russo-Japanese war 127/4
New England NE USA British settlement 67/3
Newfoundland province of E Canada rediscovered 64/2; British settlement 67/3, 86/1; British colony 69/3; joins Dominion 111/1
New France French possessions in Canada 67/3, 86/1
New Galicia Spanish colony of C Mexico 66/1
New Granada (*mod.* Colombia) Spanish colony 66/1, 69/3; vice-royalty in rebellion against Spain 88/1, 97/1
New Grange Ireland megalithic tomb 14/3
New Guinea (*now part of* Papua New Guinea) early settlement 10/2; Dutch/German/British control 101/2; attacked by Japanese 134/1; retaken by Allies 135/2. See also West Irian
Newham N England✕73/4
New Hampshire state of NE USA colony 67/3; 92/1; Depression 131/2; population 111/5, 145/1
New Haven NE USA founded 67/3
New Hebrides (*Fr.* Nouvelles Hébrides *now* Vanuatu) *islands* S Pacific early Melanesian settlement 10/2; British/French condominium 101/1; US base 134/1; independence 139/1 (inset)
New Holland (*now* Australia) early voyages 65/4
New Ireland *island* Papua New Guinea early Melanesian

settlement 10/2; occupied by Japanese 135/1
New Jersey state of E USA colony 67/3, 92/1; Depression 131/2; population 111/5, 145/1
New Lanark S Scotland Industrial Revolution 98/1
New Malton N England Industrial Revolution 98/1
New Mexico state of SW USA ceded by Mexico 97/1; Depression 131/2; population 111/5, 145/1
New Netherland (*now* New York State) Dutch colony 67/3
New Orleans S USA French/Spanish occupation 69/3; Civil War 92/5
New Plymouth N Island, New Zealand founded 112/2. See also Taranaki
Newport S Wales Industrial Revolution 98/1
Newport Pagnell S England Industrial Revolution 98/1
New Sarai S Russia Mongol capital 46/1
New South Wales state of SE Australia early exploration 65/4; settlement and development 113/1; statehood 101/1
New Spain (*mod.* Mexico. C America and Caribbean) early voyages of discovery 65/3, 69/3; Spanish vice-royalty 66/1; rebellion against Spain 88/1
New Territories S China acquired by Britain 107/4
Newton C USA cow town 94/1
Newton C USA Industrial Revolution 98/1
Newton le Willows NW England Industrial Revolution 98/1
New Ulm N USA✕95/2
New York (*form.* New Netherland) colony 67/3, 92/1
New York state of E USA Depression 131/2; population 111/5, 145/1; industry 110/2; social unrest 144/3
New York City (1653-64 called New Amsterdam *earlier* Fort Amsterdam) 67/3; British naval base 86/1; industry 110/2; population 110/2; social unrest 144/3
New Zealand early Polynesian settlement 10/2, 3; early voyages 65/4; settlement and development 101/1, 112/2, 3
Neyshabur (*a/s* Nishapur) N Persia 17/4
Nez Perce plateau Indian tribe of W Canada 63/1
Ngandong Java site of early man 3/3
Ngaruawahia N Island, New Zealand 112/3
Ngatapa N Island, New Zealand✕112/3
Ngazargumu W Africa centre of Kanem-Borno 60/1
Nguni (*a/c* Ngoni) tribe of S Africa 61/2, 103/2
Nha Trang S Indo-china Hindu-Buddhist temple 51/2
Niah cave Borneo site of early man 3/3; Bronze Age caves 8/3
Niami W Africa early centre of Mali Empire 60/1
Niaux SW France Palaeolithic art 5/3
Nicaea (*mod.* Iznik) W Anatolia centre of early Christianity 27/2; Roman Empire 24/2, 31/3; Byzantine Empire 43/3
Nicaea NW India Alexander's route 23/3
Nicaragua country of C America early exploration 64/2; independence 97/1; US protectorate 97/1; political development 111/4; Sandanista revolution 142/1
Nicarao Indian tribe of C America 63/1
Nice (*It.* Nizza) S France annexed from Italy 88/3
Nicephorium (*mod.* Rakka) Syria Roman Empire 25/2, 31/3
Nicobar Islands Indian Ocean territory of British India 105/3
Nicomedia *mod.* Izmit) W Anatolia Roman Empire 24/2, 31/3; early archbishopric 26/2; Byzantine Empire 43/1
Nicopolis Lower Egypt 25/2
Nicopolis W Greece archbishopric 26/2; Byzantine Empire 43/3
Nicopolis (*mod.* Nikopol) Bulgaria Byzantine Empire 49/1
Nida W Germany Mithraic site 26/1
Nien rebels N China 107/3
Nieświez (Nesvizh)
Niger country of W Africa French colony 103/3; independence 138/1; economy 150/1
Nigeria country of W Africa British colony 100/2, 102/5, 103/3; independence 138/1; political development 140/1; Biafran war 140/2; economy 150/1
Niigata E Japan 126/1, 2
Nikki Dahomey, W Africa occupied by French 103/3
Nikolayev S Ukraine founded 85/1; 1905 Revolution 120/1
Nikopol (Nicopolis)
Nile (*a/c* Aboukir Bay)✕90/2
Nilotes people of E Africa 60-61
Nîmes (*anc.* Nemausus) S France centre of French Revolution 89/2
Nina C Mesopotamia Sumerian city 16/2
Nindowari N India Harappan site 9/5
Nineveh Mesopotamia early farming village 7/4; 17/4; Assyrian Empire 20/2, 3; Mitannian city 21/1; Alexander's Empire 22/3
Ningsia NW China early bishopric 39/1; Ming frontier defence area 51/4
Ningpo E China treaty port 107/4
Ninus (Nineveh)
Nippur C Mesopotamia Sumerian city 16/2, 17/4, 20/3
Nirou Khani C Crete Mycenaean settlement 19/1
Niš (Naissus, Nish)
Nish (*S. Cr.* Niš *anc.* Naissus) E Yugoslavia Ottoman Empire 49/1; WW1 119/3
Nishapur (*Pers.* Neyshabur) W Persia early bishopric 39/1; Muslim conquest 48/2; Mongol conquest 47/4; Muslim trade 59/3; Safavid conquest 48/2
Nisibis (*mod.* Nusaybin) E Anatolia Alexander's route 22/3; Roman Empire 31/3; early archbishopric 27/2, 39/1

Paderborn N Germany bishopric 79/1
Padua (*It.* Padova *anc.* Patavium) N Italy 56/3; WW1 119/3
Paeckche Korea early state destroyed by T'ang 51/1
Paestum (*earlier* Poseidonia) S Italy Latin colony 25/1
Paez Andean Indian tribe of S America 63/1
Pagan C Burma Buddhist site 27/1; early empire 51/2
Pahang state of Malaya 71/5
Pair-non-Pair SW France Palaeolithic art 5/3
Paita Peru on Pizarro's route 68/2
Paiute Indian tribe of W USA 63/1
Pajajaran Java early kingdom 51/2
Pakhoi S China treaty port 107/4
Pakistan independence 105/5, 139/1; secession of Bangladesh 141/1; boundary dispute with India 141/1; Baghdad Pact and US alliance 149/1; economy 150/1. (For period before 1947 see under India and/or constituent provinces)
Palaiokastro Crete 19/1
Palatinate (*Ger.* Pfalz) historical region of W Germany Wittelsbach territory 72/1; Reformation 75/1; German unification 115/2
Palau (*f/s* Pelew) SW Caroline Islands, W Pacific occupied by US 135/2
Pale, The Ireland 73/4
Palembang SE Sumatra Hindu-Buddhist remains 51/2; trade 59/3
Palenque E Mexico Mayan site 12/2
Palermo (*anc.* Panormus) Sicily medieval German attack 55/3; 18 C urban development 82/4
Palestine (*Lat.* Palaestina *now* Israel and Jordan) early urban settlement 16/1 Levantine cities and ports 21/1; at time of David 21/2; at time of Alexander 22/3; Roman Empire 24/2; emergence of Judaea 26/2; Byzantine Empire 43/1; Muslim reconquest 40/3; Ottoman province 124/1; WW1 125/2; British control 125/1; WW2 132/1; partition between Israel and Jordan 141/3
Pallavas dynasty of S India 29/5
Palmerston North N Island, New Zealand 112/2
Palmyra (*Bibl.* Tadmor *or* Tamar) Syria Roman Empire 25/2; early bishopric 27/2
Pamphylia ancient country of southern Anatolia 19/4, 31/3, 43/1
Pamunkey NE USA✕95/2
Panaji (Nova Goa)
Panama Isthmus discovered 65/3; Canal Zone 111/4; independence 97/1; political development 142-3; US base 149/1; economy 150/1; US intervention 1989 143/1
Panama Canal opening 100/2; 109/4
Panchala early kingdom of N India 29/4
Pandya country and dynasty of S India 29/4, 5
Pangim (*form.* Nova Goa *now* Panaji) W India 105/3
Panipat N India✕48/2, 87/2
P'an-lung-ch'eng (*a/s* Panlongcheng) S China Shang city 8/4
Panmunjom Korea 1953 armistice 148/2
Pannonia C Europe Avar Kingdom 35/4
Pannonia Inferior Roman province of C Europe 31/3, 4
Pannonia Superior Roman province of C Europe 31/3, 4
Panormus (*mod.* Palermo) Sicily Phoenician city 19/4; Roman Empire 24/2, 30/3
Pan-p'o (*a/s* Banpo) C China early settlement 8/2
Pantelleria *island* C Mediterranean WW2 133/3
Panticapaeum (*mod.* Kerch) Crimea Greek colony 19/4; Roman Empire 24/2, 31/3; early trading centre 25/1
Pao W China Western Chou domain 9/6
Pao-an Soviet N China 122/4
Paochi W China Western Chou site 9/6
Papago Indian tribe of N Mexico 63/1
Papal States C Italy expansion 56/3; Black Death 57/1; at time of Habsburg power 72/1, 73/5; Reformation 75/1; unification of Italy 114/3
Paphlagonia ancient country of N Anatolia 19/4, 23/3, 4, 43/1
Paphlagonian Theme N Anatolia district of Byzantine Empire 42/2
Paphos (*Lat.* Paphus) Cyprus Greek colony 19/4; Roman Empire 25/2; bishopric 27/2
Papua Australian territory 101/2
Papua New Guinea SW Pacific independence 139/1; economy 150/1. See also New Guinea
Pará province of N Brazil 97/1
Paraetacene ancient people of NW Persia 23/3
Paraetonium (*mod.* Mersa Matruh) Egypt Alexander's Empire 23/3
Paraguay independence 97/1; political development 142-3; economy 150/1
Paraíba E Brazil Confederation of the Equator 97/1
Paramaribo Dutch Guinea colonised 69/3
Paranilotes people of Sudan 61/2
Parhae (*Chin.* Pohai) early Korean state 51/1
Parihaka N Island, New Zealand early Maori resistance 112/3
Paris N France early bishopric 26/2; 18C financial centre 82/4; St. Bartholomew Massacre 74/3; Fronde revolt 77/2; *parlement* 80/1; centre of French Revolution 89/2;✕91/1; industrial development 98/2

Parma N Italy Roman colony 30/1; Lombard League 55/3; Signorial domination 56/3; acquired by Habsburgs 78/3; occupied by France 88/3; unification of Italy 114/3
Parpalló E Spain Palaeolithic art 5/3
Parsa (*a/c* Persis) S Persia satrapy of Achaemenid Empire 21/5
Parthenopean Republic S Italy state established by French Revolution 89/3
Parthia ancient country of N Persia 23/3, 4
Parthians ancient people of the Caucasus 31/3
Pasargadae SW Persia Alexander's route 23/3;✕25/5
Passau SE Germany bishopric 35/4, 38/2, 3, 79/1
Passchendaele NW Belgium WW1✕118/3 (inset)
Passi di Corvo S Italy farming site 15/1
Patagonia region of S Argentina 97/1
Pataliputra (*mod.* Patna) NE India trading centre 25/1
Patara SW Anatolia Greek colony 19/4; early bishopric 27/2
Patavium (*mod.* Padova *Eng.* Padua) N Italy Roman Empire 24/2
Pathet Lao Laotian Communist movement 140/1
Patna (Pataliputra)
Patras (*mod. Gr.* Patrai *anc.* Patrae) S Greece Byzantine Empire 43/1
Pattala NW India limit of Alexander's journey 23/3
Pau SW France seat of intendant 80/1
Paul, St. journeys 27/2
Paulis (*now* Isiro) NE Belgian Congo Congo crisis 138/4
Pavia (*anc.* Ticinum) N Italy Lombard League 73/5; medieval trade 58/1; Signorial domination 56/3
Pavlodar S Siberia industry 147/1
Pavlov Czechoslovakia Palaeolithic art 5/3
Pavón Mexico early site 12/3
Pawnee plains Indian tribe of C USA 63/1
Paya Indian tribe of C America 63/1
Pearl Harbor Hawaii bombed by Japanese 134/1
Pechenegs tribe of Ukraine, 43/3, 44/1, 45/2
Pechenga (Petsamo)
Pecherskaya Lavra Ukraine monastery 38/2
Pech-Merle SW France Palaeolithic art 5/3
Pechora tribe of N Russia 85/1
Pecsaete tribe of early England 33/3, 35/3
Pedra Branca S Portugal megalithic tomb 14/3
Pedra Coberta NW Spain megalithic tomb 14/3
Pedra Furada Brazil early site 5/2
Peebles county of C Scotland acquired by Edward III 56/4
Pegu early state of S Burma, Buddhist site 27/1; peripheral Mongol control 47/1; early trade 71/2
Pei Chihli NE China Ming province 51/4
P'ei-li-kang (*a/s* Peiliang) NE China early settlement 8/2
Peipus, Lake (*Russ.* Chudskoye Ozero *Est.* Peipsi Järv) W Russia✕45/2
Peking (*form. Mong.* Khanbalik) N China early trade 59/3; Ming capital 51/4; warlord attacks 22/2; Japanese occupation 127/5; industry 108/1
Pelew (Palau)
Pella Palestine early bishopric 27/2
Pella Macedonia 20/5, 22/3
Peloponnesian War 23/2
Peloponnesus (*Eng.* Peloponnese *a/c* Morea) region of S Greece 18-19
Pelusium N Egypt Alexander's Empire 22/3; Roman Empire 25/2, 31/3
Pelym W Siberia founded 84/2
Pemaquid NE USA✕95/2
Pemba *island* Tanzania Muslim colony 60/1
Pembina N USA fur station 94/1
Pembroke S Wales Scandinavian settlement 37/1; WW1 118/3
Penang state of Malaya British possession 71/5; WW2 134/1
Peninj E Africa site of early man 3/3
Peninsular War 90/1
Pennsylvania state of E USA colony 67/3, 92/1; Civil War 93/5; Depression 131/2; population 111/5, 145/1
Pennsylvania Road NE USA settlers' route 94/1
Penobscot NE USA founded 67/3
Pensacola SE USA Spanish post 67/3; fur station 94/1
Penuel Palestine ancient capital 21/2
Penydarran S Wales Industrial Revolution 98/1
Penza C Russia founded 85/1; 1905 Revolution 120/1; Bolshevik seizure 121/2
Pepin King of Franks 34T
Pequot Fort NE USA✕95/2
Perak state of Malaya 71/5
Perath Mesopotamia early archbishopric 27/2
Perche N France fief 72/2
Pereslavets SW Russia 45/2
Pereyaslavl Ukraine bishopric 38/2; early principality 45/2
Pereyaslavl N Russia town of Vladimir-Suzdal 45/2
Pergamum (*Gr.* Pergamon *Turk.* Bergama) W Anatolia Roman Empire 24/2, 31/3; early bishopric 27/2
Perge S Anatolia early archbishopric 27/2
Périgord region of C France English possession 52/2; annexed to France 72/2
Perinthus SE Europe Greek colony 19/4
Perlis state of Malaya tributary to Siam 71/5
Perm (*1940-57 called* Molotov) C Russia founded 85/1; Bolshevik seizure 121/2; industry 147/1

Permians people of N Russia 38/2, 45/2
Pernambuco (*now* Recife) Brazil early Portuguese territory 66/1; Confederation of the Equator 96/1
Perovsk (Kzyl-Orda)
Perpignan S France fort 80/1
Perryville SE USA✕93/5
Persepolis Persia early trade 25/1; Alexander's Empire 23/3; Achaemenid Empire 21/5; Muslim conquest 41/1
Persia (*now* Iran) war with Greece 22/1; Achaemenid empire 21/5; attacked by White Huns 33/1; expansion of Christianity 39/1; Muslim conquest 41/4; under Abbasid sovereignty 41/2; Mongol conquest 46-7; Safavid Empire 49/1; independent kingdom 125/1; British and Russian spheres of influence 125/3
Persian Gulf (*a/c* Arabian Gulf *or* The Gulf) WW1 125/2; oil 151/4
Persis (*a/c* Fars, Parsa) S Persia Alexander's Empire 23/3
Perth W Australia early settlement 113/1
Peru Spanish colonisation 66/1, 69/2; independence 97/1; war with Chile 97/4; political developments 142-3; economy 150/1
Perusia (*mod.* Perugia) N Italy Roman Empire 30/1, 31/3
Pesaro (Pisaurum)
Peshawar Pakistan industry under British rule 105/3; capital of NW Frontier Agency 105/5
Pesto (Posidonia)
Peterborough E England Industrial Revolution 98/1
Petersfels SW Germany Palaeolithic art 5/3
Petra Jordan Roman Empire 25/2, 31/3; early archbishopric 27/2
Petralona Greece site of early man 3/3
Petřkovice Czechoslovakia Palaeolithic art 5/3
Petrograd (*before 1914* St. Petersburg *since 1924* Leningrad) WW1 119/3; Russian Revolution 121/2
Petropavlovsk (*now* Petropavlovsk-Kamchatskiy) Russ. Far East founded 84/2; industry 147/1
Petsamo (*Russ.* Pechenga) NW Russia Russian conquest from Finland 133/2
Pettau (Poetovio)
Pevkakia E Greece Mycenaean settlement 19/1
Pfalz (Palatinate)
Pfalz-Sulzbach W Germany principality 79/1
Phaistos Crete Mycenaean site 19/1
Phalaborwa SE Africa Iron Age site 11/1; 60/1
Phanagoria S Russia Greek colony 19/4
Phan Rang S Indo-China Hindu-Buddhist temple 51/2
Phaselis W Anatolia Greek colony 19/4
Phasis Caucasus Greek colony 19/4; Roman Empire 33/1
Phazania (*mod.* Fezzan) region of S Libya 31/3
Philadelphia (*mod.* Alaşehir) W Anatolia early church 27/2
Philadelphia (Amman)
Philadelphia E USA founded 67/3; industry 109/1
Philiphaugh S Scotland✕76/4
Philippi N Greece Roman Empire 27/2
Philippines early sites 8/3; spread of Islam 40/5; early trade 67/1; Spanish conquest 71/2; acquired by US 102/2, 110/4; occupied by Japanese 127/5, 134/1; retaken by Americans 135/2; independence 139/1; political development 141/1; US bases 149/1; industry and economy 150/1
Philippine Sea✕135/2
Philippopolis (*mod.* Plovdiv *Turk.* Filibe) Bulgaria Roman Empire 31/3; Byzantine Empire 43/1; Ottoman Empire 48/1
Philistia ancient country of Middle East 20/2
Philomelium (*mod.* Akşehir) C Anatolia Byzantine Empire 43/3
Phnom Laang Cambodia early site 8/3
Phnom Penh Cambodia 70/1, 71/2; Vietnam war 148/3
Phocaea W Anatolia Greek colony 19/4
Phocis ancient territory of C Greece 18/3
Phoenicia at time of Greeks 19/4, 21/2; Roman province 31/3
Phoenicians move into Africa 11/1
Phrygia ancient country of W Anatolia 19/4, 22/3; Byzantine Empire 43/3
Phylakopi S. Aegean early settlement 14/2; Mycenaean palace sites 19/1
Piacenza (*anc.* Placentia) N Italy Lombard League 55/3; Signorial domination 56/3; medieval fair 59/2
Piauí state of NE Brazil 97/1
Picardy (*Fr.* Picardie) region of N France annexed from Burgundy 72/2, 80/1; WW1 118/3 (inset)
Picentes early tribe of N Italy 25/1
Pictavi W France early bishopric 26/2
Picton S Island, New Zealand railway 112/1
Picts early tribe of Scotland 32/1, 38/3
Piedmont (*It.* Piemonte) region of N Italy 88/3, 114/3
Pigs, Bay of Cuba CIA invasion 149/5
Pilos (Navarino, Pylos)
Pilsen (*Cz.* Plzeň) Czechoslovakia industrial development 99/2
Pima Indian tribe of N Mexico 63/1
Pindal N Spain Palaeolithic art 5/3
Pinega N Russia town of Novgorod Empire 45/2
Pinkie Scotland✕73/4
Pinsk W Russia town of Turov-Pinsk 45/2
Piombino N Italy Duchy 73/5; French rule 91/1
Piqillacta C Andes early site 12/5
Pi-Ramesse Lower Egypt Egyptian city 21/1

Saitama prefecture of C Japan 126/2
Saka Haumavarga C Asia satrapy of Achaemenid Empire 21/5
Sakas early people of W India 29/5
Sakata N Japan 126/2
Sakhalin (*Jap.* Karafuto) *island* Russ. Far East north acquired by Russia 84/3; south acquired by Japan 127/3; south reoccupied by Russia 135/2; claimed by Japan 141/1
Saksiny tribe of S Russia 45/2
Sala Morocco Roman Empire 30/1
Saladin Muslim conqueror 40/3
Salahiyeh (Dura-Europos)
Salamanca N Spain ✕ 90/1
Salamantica (*a/c* Helmantica *mod.* Salamanca) N Spain Roman Empire 30/3
Salamis (*later* Constantia) Cyprus Greek colony 19/4; Roman Empire 27/2; archbishopric 27/2
Salamis C Greece ✕ 20/5, 22/1
Salankayas people of SE India 29/5
Saldae (Bougie)
Salé N Morocco site of early man 3/3
Salekhard (Obdorsk)
Salem district of S India ceded to Britain 87/3
Salernum (*mod.* Salerno) S Italy Roman colony 30/1; Byzantine port 36/2
Salinelles SE France megalithic flint mine 15/3
Salisbury S England Industrial Revolution 98/1
Salisbury (*n/c* Harare) S Rhodesia 103/3
Salish House NW USA fur station 94/1
Salonae (*a/s* Salona) Albania Mithraic site 26/1; Roman Empire 24/2, 30/3; early archbishopric 27/2; Byzantine Empire 42/1
Salonika (*a/s* Salonica *a/c* Thessalonica *Gr.* Thessaloniki *Turk.* Selanik) N Greece bishopric 38/2; occupied by Ottomans 49/1; 18C urban development 83/4; WW1 119/3
Saltillo N Mexico early Spanish city 66/1
Salt Lake City W USA early trails 94/1
Salzburg Austria bishopric 34/4; archbishopric 38/2, 3, 79/1
Samara (1935-91 Kuybyshev) C Russia founded 85/1; on railway to east 84/3; Bolshevik seizure 121/2
Samaria region of C Palestine 26/3
Samarkand (*anc.* Maracanda) C Asia on Silk Road 25/1; early archbishopric 39/1; Muslim conquest 41/1; Timur's Empire 47/4; early trade 59/3; Soviet Union 147/1
Samarobriva (Amiens)
Samarra N Mesopotamia early farming site 7/4
Samatata early state of E India 29/4, 5
Sambor Prei Kuk Cambodia Hindu-Buddhist temple 51/2
Sambre *river* NE France WW1 119/3 (inset)
Samoa *islands* S Pacific early settlement 10/2; German colony 101/2; annexed by US 111/4. See also Western Samoa
Samogitia (*Lith.* Žemaitija) region of NW Russia occupied by Teutonic Knights 54/4; by Lithuania 28/2, 56/2
Samory's Empire W Africa 103/3
Samos *island* Aegean Sea Greek parent state 19/4; bishopric 27/2
Samosata E Anatolia Roman Empire 25/2; Byzantine Empire 43/1
Samoyeds people of N Siberia 45/2, 84/2
Sampford Courtenay W England ✕ 73/4
Samrong Sen Cambodia early site 8/3
Sana SW Arabia early bishopric 38/1
San Agostín (*now* St. Augustine) SE USA Spanish fort 66/1
San Antonio S USA early Catholic mission 94/1
San Antonio SE USA Spanish fort 86/1
San Candido (Aguntum)
Sanchi C India Buddhist site 27/1
San Cristóbal NW Cuba Soviet missile base 149/5
Šandalja N Yugoslavia site of early man 3/3
Sand Creek C USA ✕ 95/2
San Diego (*form.* San Diego de Alcalá) SW USA early Catholic mission 94/1
Sandinista revolt Nicaragua 143/1
Sandwich Islands (*now* Hawaii) C Pacific discovered 65/4
San Felipe S USA early Catholic mission 94/1
San Fernando Rey de España W USA early Catholic mission 94/1
San Francisco (*form.* San Francisco de Asis) W USA Spanish settlement 69/3; early Catholic mission 94/1
Sanga C Africa Iron Age site 11/1; tribe 60/1
San Gabriel Arcángel SW USA early Catholic mission 94/1
Sangela NW India Alexander's route 23/3
San Gimignano C Italy Republican commune 56/3
Sangiran Java site of early man 3/3
San José Magote C Mexico Olmec centre 12/2
San Juan del Puerto Rico W Indies Spanish fort 66/1
Sankt Peterburg (St. Petersburg)
San Lorenzo C Mexico Olmec centre 12/2
San Luis Obispo de Tolosa W USA early Catholic mission 94/1
San Luis Potosí state of C Mexico 97/1
Sansapow N New Guinea taken by Allies 135/2
San Sebastián N Spain Civil War 129/4
San Stefano, Treaty of 125/3
Santa Barbara W USA early Catholic mission 94/1
Santa Catarina state of S Brazil 97/1

Santa Cruz W USA early Catholic mission 94/1
Santa Cruz (*n/c* Ndeni) Solomon Islands WW2 ✕ 135/2
Santa Fe SW USA on trail west 94/1
Santa Fé de Bogotá (*n/c* Bogotá) Colombia Spanish capital of New Granada 66/1
Santa Marta Colombia Spanish port 66/1
Santa Maura (Leucas)
Santander N Spain Civil War 129/4
Santa Rita E Mexico Mayan centre 12/2
Santa Severina S Italy Saracen occupation 37/1
Santiago Chile founded 66/1
Santiago de Compostela NW Spain bishopric 38/2
Santiago del Estero Argentina early settlement 66/1
Santimamiñe N Spain Palaeolithic art 5/3
Santo Domingo (*now* Dominican Republic) W Indies Spanish colony 66/1, 4; 69/3
Santorini (Thera)
Santuao E China treaty port 107/4
San Xavier del Bac SW USA early Catholic mission 94/1
São Jorge de Mina (Elmina)
São Paulo S Brazil state 97/1
São Tomé *island* W Africa Portuguese colony 103/3
São Tomé and Príncipe *islands* W Africa united as independent republic 138/1
Saracens invasion of S Europe 37/1
Saragossa (*anc.* Caesaraugusta *mod.* Zaragoza) N Spain bishopric 38/2; ✕ 90/1; captured by French 90/1; Civil War 129/4
Sarai S Russia early trade 58/3. See also New Sarai, Old Sarai
Sarajevo C Yugoslavia captured by Ottomans 49/1; Ottoman administrative centre 49/1; WW1 119/3; WW2 132-3
Sarandib (Ceylon)
Saratoga NE USA ✕ 92/1
Saratov C Russia founded 85/1; Bolshevik seizure 121/2
Sarawak country of N Borneo British protectorate 101/2; occupied by Japanese in WW2 134/1; incorporated into Malaysia 139/2
Sarcee plains Indian tribe of W Canada 63/1
Sardes (Sardis)
Sardica (Serdica)
Sardinia (*It.* Sardegna) *island* W Mediterranean Muslim conquest 40/1; Saracen attacks 37/1; Byzantine Empire 42/1; Pisan conquest 36/2; to Aragon 72/1; rebellion against Piedmont 88/3; Kingdom 114/3
Sardis (*a/s* Sardes) W Anatolia Alexander's route 22/3; Roman Empire 31/3; one of seven churches of Asia 27/2; Byzantine Empire 43/1
Sargon King of Akkad 16T
Sarkel S Russia ✕ 44/1
Sarmatians (*Lat.* Sarmatae) tribe of Caucasus and S Russia 19/4, 31/3
Sarmizegetusa Romania Mithraic site 26/1; Roman Empire 31/3
Sarnath E India Buddhist site 27/1
Sarnowo Poland early site 6/2
Sarre (Saar)
Saruhan early emirate of W Anatolia 49/1
Sasanian Empire Western Asia 29/5
Sasebo W Japan 126/2
Saskatchewan province of C Canada economic growth 111/1
Saskatoon C Canada growth 111/1
Satala NE Anatolia Roman Empire 25/2, 31/3; early archbishopric 27/2
Satara district of W India 104/4, 105/3
Satavahana ancient kingdom of India 29/4
Satricum C Italy Latin colony 30/1
Satsuma old province of W Japan 126/1
Saturnia N Italy Roman colony 30/1
Saudi Arabia Kingdom of Arabia 140/1, 149/1, 151/4
Sauk Indian tribe of C USA 63/1
Sault Ste. Marie C Canada French fort 67/3, 86/1
Saumurois region of W France 52/2
Savannah SE USA evacuated 92/5
Savenay NW France French Revolution 89/2
Savignano N Italy Palaeolithic art 5/3
Savoy (*Fr.* Savoie *It.* Savoia) region of France/Italy medieval state 72/1; Calvinism 75/1; annexed by France 88/3; ceded to France 114/3
Saxon March 34/4
Saxons Germanic tribe of NW Europe 34/4, 32/1
Saxony region of N Germany conversion to Christianity 38/3; Frankish Empire 34/4; medieval German Empire 55/1, 3; Black Death 57/1; Wettin territory 72/1; Reformation 75/1; Electorate and Duchy 79/1; unification of Germany 98/3
Say W Africa occupied by French 102/1, 103/3
Sayda (Sidon)
Saylac (Zeila)
Saylan (Ceylon)
Sayn country of C Germany 79/1
Scandia (*mod.* Scandinavia) region of N Europe 30/3
Scandinavia (*anc.* Scandia) Viking invasions of Europe 37/1. See also Denmark, Sweden, Norway
Scania (*Sw.* Skåne) region of S Sweden acquired from Denmark 77/3
Scapa Flow N Scotland WW1 118/3
Scarborough N England WW1 118/3

Scarpanto (Carpathos)
Schism, Great (Western) 56T, 57/6
Schlesien (Silesia)
Schleswig (*Dan.* Slesvig) S Denmark bishopric 52/3; Reformation 75/1
Schleswig-Holstein region of N Germany unification of Germany 98/3, 115/2
Schlieffen Plan WW1 118T, 119/2
Schooneveld I and II S North Sea Dutch naval victories 81/3
Schouten and Le Maire explorers 64/2
Schwaben (Swabia)
Schwarzburg county of E Germany 79/1
Schwarzerden W Germany Mithraic site 26/1
Schweizerbild Switzerland Palaeolithic art 5/3
Schwerin N Germany WW1 119/3
Schwyz Switzerland original canton 54/5
Scodra (*mod.* Shkodër *It.* Scutari) Albania Roman Empire 31/3
Scone S Scotland Edward I's campaign 53/6; Civil War 76/4
Scotland (*anc.* Caledonia) Scandinavian settlement 37/1; Anglo-Scottish wars 56/4; Black Death 57/1; acquires Shetland, Orkney and Hebrides 72/1; Reformation 75/1; in English Civil War 76/4
Scots 31/1
Scots Celtic tribe of N Ireland 52/2
Scupi (*mod.* Skoplje *Mac.* Skopje *Turk.* Üsküb) early archbishopric 27/2; Byzantine Empire 43/1
Scutari (*mod.* Shkodër *anc.* Scodra) Albania conquered by Ottomans 49/1
Scythia ancient country of C Asia 23/3
Scythians ancient tribe of S Russia 19/4, 22/3
Scythopolis N Palestine city of Decapolis 26/3
SEATO 148T
Seattle NW USA ✕ 94/2
Sebaste Palestine bishopric 27/2; town of Judaea 26/3
Sebastopol (*Russ.* Sevastopol) Crimea, S Russia 1905 Revolution 120/1; WW1 119/3; WW2 132-3
Sebta (Ceuta)
Sech S Ukraine 85/1
Sedan N France ✕ 115/2; WW1 119/3; WW2 132/1
Segesta Sicily ally of Athens 23/2
Segontia (*a/c* Segontium *mod.* Caenarvon) Wales Mithraic site 26/1; Roman Empire 30/3
Ségou (*Eng.* Segu) French Sudan 102/1, 103/3
Segovia C Spain Roman Empire 30/3
Segu (*Fr.* Ségou) early city-state of W Africa 61/2
Seibal E Mexico Mayan centre 12/2
Seila Lower Egypt pyramid 17/3
Seistan (*a/s* Sistan) province of E Parsia Muslim conquest 41/1
Selangor state of Malaya 71/5
Selanik (Salonika)
Seleucia (*a/c* Veh-Ardashir) Mesopotamia early trade 24/1
Seleucia (*a/c* Seleucia Tracheotis) SE Anatolia early archbishopric 27/2; Byzantine Empire 43/1
Seleucia-Ctesiphon Mesopotamia early trading centre 25/1; early patriarchate 27/2, 39/1
Seleucian Theme S Anatolia province of Byzantine Empire 42/2
Seleucid Kingdom Anatolia-Persia 22/4
Selinus (*mod.* Selinunte) Sicily Greek colony 19/4, 23/2
Seljuks Turkish Muslim dynasty of Middle East 41/2, 43/3, 46/3
Selkirk county of C Scotland acquired by Edward III 56/4
Selymbria SE Europe Greek colony 19/4; Byzantine Empire 43/1
Semendre (*mod.* Smederevo) N Serbia conquered by Ottomans 49/1
Semgallen (*obs. Eng.* Semigallia) region of NW Russia occupied by Teutonic Knights 54/4
Seminole Indian tribe of SE USA 95/2
Semipalatinsk S Siberia founded 84/2
Semna Upper Egypt fortress 21/1
Sempach C Switzerland ✕ 54/5
Sena Mozambique Portuguese settlement 61/2
Sendai N Japan 126/2
Senegal W Africa French colony 100/2, 101/2, 103/3; independence 138/1; economy 138/1
Senegambia region of W Africa source of slaves 61/2
Sennar Sudan early town 61/2
Sennones early people of N Italy 30/1
Sens NE France French Revolution 89/2
Seoul (*Jap.* Keijo) S Korea Russo-Japanese war 127/4; Korean war 148/2; population 151/1
Sepphoris town of Judaea 26/3
Septimania ancient region of S France, part of Frankish Empire 34/4
Serbia (*now part of* Yugoslavia) country of SE Europe conversion to Christianity 38/2; Byzantine Empire 43/3; Mongol invasion 46/2; empire under Stephen Dushan 56/2; Black Death 57/1; Ottoman province 49/1; independence 116/1, 124/1; industrial development 98/2; WW1 118-9; forms part of Yugoslavia 129/2; WW2 133/2
Serbs Slav tribe of SE Europe 32/2, 33/5
Serdica (*a/s* Sardica *mod.* Sofia) Bulgaria Mithraic site 26/1; Roman Empire 24/2, 31/3; early archbishopric 27/2; Byzantine Empire 43/1
Serpukhov C Russia town of Muscovy 85/1

Uruk (a/c Erech) Mesopotamia early farming village 7/4; Sumerian city 17/2, 4

Üsküb (S. Cr. Skoplje, Maced. Skopje) Yugoslavia Ottoman Empire 116/1

U.S.S.R. formation 120-1; alliances in 1930's 128/1; fighting against Japan 135/1; WW2 132-3; territorial gains after WW2 137/4; constituent republics 146/2; nationalities 146/3; Communism overthrown 146T; Warsaw Pact Comecon 149/1; development 147/1; Cold War 149/1

Ust-Kutsk C Siberia founded 84/2

Ust-Orda Buryat-Mongol AD E USSR 146/2

Ust-Sysolsk (Syktyvkar)

Ust-Vilyuysk E Siberia founded 84/2

Ust-Vym N Russia bishopric 38/2

Utah state of W USA ceded by Mexico 97/1; Depression 130/3; population 111/5, 145/1

Ute Indian tribe of SW USA 63/1

Utica Tunisia Stone Age site 11/1; Punic city 19/4; Roman Empire 30/2

U Tong S Thailand Hindu-Buddhist remains 51/2

Utrecht (anc. Trajectum) Holland bishopric 38/3; Burgundian possession 73/3; province of Dutch Republic 77/1

Uttar Pradesh (from. United Province) state of N India 105/5

Uttoxeter C England Industrial Revolution 98/1

Uvja (a/c Elam) W Persia province of Achaemenid Empire 21/5

Uxii ancient tribe of W Persia 22/3

Uxmal E Mexico Mayan centre 12/2

Uzbeks people of C Asia 146/3

Uzbek SSR C Asia 146/2

Vagarshapat (since 1945 Echmiadzin) Armenia early archbishopric 27/2

Vaisali W Burma Hindu-Buddhist remains 51/2

Valencia (anc. Valentia) E Spain bishopric 38/2; reconquered by Aragon 37/4; 18C urban development 82/4; Muslim minority 75/1, ✕90/1; Civil War 129/4

Valentia (mod. Valence) S France bishopric 26/1

Valentia (Valencia)

Valladolid N Spain Lutheran minority 75/1; Civil War 129/4

Valley Road NE USA settlers' route 94/1

Valmy NE France ✕89/2

Valois region of NE France 72/2

Valona (anc. Avlona Turk. Avlonya now Alb. Vlorë) S Adriatic Ottoman town 48/2

Vancouver W Canada growth 111/1

Vandals Germanic tribe, invasion of Europe and N Africa 32/1, 2; 34/1

Van Diemen's Land (mod. Tasmania) early trade 113/4

Vanga ancient country of E India 29/4

Varangians Russia Viking raiders 44/1/T

Varna (anc. Odessus 1949-57 Stalin) E Bulgaria burial site 14/2; ✕49/1

Vasiliki E Crete Mycenaean settlement 19/1

Vasio S France bishopric 27/2

Vassily III king of Muscovy 72/1

Vatsa early kingdom of N India 29/4

Vaud Switzerland Reformation 75/1

Veletians Slav tribe of NW Europe 55/1

Velia (Elea)

Velikiye Luki W Russia WW2 133/2

Velitrae C Italy Latin colony 30/1

Velsuna (Volsinii)

Vendée region of W France 80/1; uprising 89/2

Vendôme region of NW France 72/2

Venetia (It. Venezia) region of N Italy exchanged for Austrian Netherlands 78/3, 88/3; unification of Italy 114/3

Venetian Empire (Venice)

Venetian Republic NE Italy 79/1. See also Venice

Venezia (Venetia, Venice)

Venezuela European discovery 65/3; independence 97/1; US influence 111/4; political development 143/1; economy 142/2, 3, 150/1

Venice (It. Venezia anc. Venetia) expansion into Adriatic and Aegean 37/4; Reformation 75/1; republican commune 56/3; early trade 58/3; Black Death 57/1; 18C financial centre 82/4; WW1 119/3

Ventspils (Windau)

Venusia (mod. Venosa) C Italy Latin colony 30/1

Vera Cruz E Mexico modern province 97/1

Vercelli N Italy Lombard League 55/3; Signorial domination 56/3

Verdalpino E Spain farming site 15/1

Verden N Germany bishopric 79/1

Verdun E France annexed to France 72/2; WW1 119/2 (inset)

Verdun, Treaty of 35/5

Vereeniging, Peace of Boer War 102T/4

Verkhne-Angarsk S Siberia founded 84/2

Verkhne-Kolymsk E Siberia founded 84/2

Verkhne-Udinsk (Ulan-Ude)

Verkholensk S Siberia founded 84/2

Verkhoturye W Siberia founded 84/2

Verlaine Belgium Palaeolithic art 5/3

Vermandois region of NE France Royal domain 52/2.

Burgundian possession 73/3

Vermont state of NE USA Depression 131/2; population 111/5, 145/1

Vernyy (since 1921 Alma-Ata) Russ. C Asia industry 147/1

Veroia (Beroea)

Verona N Italy Roman Empire 24/2; Lombard League 55/3; Signorial domination 56/3; 18C financial centre 82/4

Verrazzano Italian navigator 65/2

Versailles N France 80/1

Vértesszöllős Hungary site of early man 3/3

Verulamium (mod. St. Albans) S England Roman Empire 30/3; bishopric 26/2

Vesontio (mod. Besançon) E France Roman Empire 30/3; archbishopric 26/2

Vetulonia C Italy Etruscan city 19/4

Via Appia (Eng. Appian Way) C Italy Roman road from Rome to Brindisi 30/1

Via Flaminia (Eng. Flaminian Way) C Italy Roman road from Rome to Rimini 30/1

Via Valeria C Italy Roman road 30/1

Viborg (Viipuri, Vyborg)

Vibo Valentia S Italy Latin colony 30/1

Vicenza N Italy Lombard League 55/3

Vichy France satellite state of Germany in WW2 132/1

Vicksburg S USA ✕92/5

Victoria state of SE Australia settlement and development 113/1

Victoria W Canada growth 111/1

Videha ancient kingdom of E India 29/4

Vidin W Bulgaria Ottoman Empire 49/1

Vienna (anc. Vindobona Ger. Wien form. Turk. Bec) Austria siege of 48/2

Vienna (mod. Vienne) S France Roman Empire 30/3; archbishopric 26/1

Vientiane Laos trading centre 71/2

Vietnam 1945-75 war 148/3; unification of north and south 141/1; economy 150/1. See also North Vietnam, South Vietnam, Indo-China

Viipuri (Sw. Viborg Russ. Vyborg) SE Finland captured by Russia 132/1

Vijaya (mod. Binh Dinh) S Indo-China capital of Champa Kingdom 51/2

Vikletice N Czechoslovakia burial site 14/2

Vila Nova de São Pedro C Portugal early settlement 14/2

Vilcaconga Peru ✕Pizarro/Inca 68/2

Vilcashuamán Peru ✕Pizarro/Inca 68/2

Villalón N Spain medieval fair 59/2

Villaviciosa Spain ✕81/5

Vilna (Pol. Wilno Russ. Vilno Lith. Vilnius) Lithuania/Poland WW1 119/3; Polish seizure 129/2

Vimeiro Portugal ✕90/1

Viminacium Yugoslavia Roman Empire 24/2

Vinča E Yugoslavia early settlement 14/2

Vincennes C USA fur station 94/1

Vindobona (Eng. Vienna Ger. Wien) Austria Roman Empire 24/2

Viracocha Inca emperor 62T

Virginia state of E USA colony 67/3; Civil War 93/5; Depression 131/2; population 111/5, 145/1

Virginia City W USA mining site 94/1

Virgin Islands W Indies British and Danish settlement 66/4; British colony 79/1; Danish islands acquired by US 111/4 (inset); 139/1 (inset)

Viroconium (mod. Wroxeter) England Roman Empire 30/3

Visby Gotland, E Sweden Hanseatic city 59/2

Visé Belgium medieval fair 58/1

Visigoths Germanic invaders of Europe 32/1, 2; 34/1, 2

Vitebsk W Russia Hanseatic trade 59/2; industry 147/1

Vitoria N Spain ✕90/1

Vittorio Veneto N Italy WW1 ✕119/3

Vivarium S Italy bishopric 27/2

Vizagapatam district of E India ceded to Britain 87/3

Vlaanderen (Flanders)

Vladikavkaz (1931-91 Ordzhonikidze except 1944-54 Dzaudzhikau) Caucasus acquired by Russia 85/1; 1905 Revolution 120/1

Vladimir C Russia early city of Vladimir-Suzdal 45/2; bishopric 38/2; 1905 Revolution 120/1

Vladimir (now Vladimir-Volynskiy Pol. Włozimierz Lat. Lodomeria) W Russia early city of Vladimir-Volynsk 45/2

Vladimir-Suzdal early principality of C Russia 45/2

Vladimir-Volynsk early principality of W Russia 45/2

Vladivostok Russ. Far East on Trans-Siberian railway 127/4, 5; industry 147/1

Vlorë (Valona, Avlona, Avlonya)

Vogelherd S Germany Palaeolithic art 5/3

Volaterrae (mod. Volterra) C Italy Etruscan city 19/4

Volci C Italy Etruscan city 19/4

Volga Bulgars early people of C Russia 44/1, 3; 45/2

Volga-Ural Oilfield Siberia 147/1

Volgograd (between 1925-61 Stalingrad early Tsaritsyn) C Russia industry 147/1

Volhynia region of W Ukraine acquired by Lithuania 56/2

Vologda C Russia city of Muscovy 85/1

Volsci Italic tribe of C Italy 30/1

Volsinii (a/c Velsuna med. Urbs Vetus mod. Orvieto) C Italy Etruscan city 19/4

Volterra (Volaterrae)

Volturno S Italy ✕114/3

Volubilis Morocco Mithraic site 26/1

Volynyanye E Slav tribe of W Russia 44/1

Vorarlberg district of 17C Germany 79/1

Voronezh C Russia founded 85/1; 1905 Revolution 120/1; WW2 133/2

Voroshilovgrad (Lugansk)

Voroshilovsk (Stavropol)

Vouillé W France ✕35/2

Vyatichi early tribe of C Russia 44/1

Vyatka C Russia 1905 Revolution 120/1

Vyatka Territory C Russia 45/2

Vyazma W Russia acquired by Muscovy 85/1

Vyborg (Finn. Viipuri Swed. Viborg) NW Russia 85/1

Wadai early state of C Africa 60/1

Wadan (Fr. Ouadane) W Africa trans-Saharan trade 60-61

Wagram Austria ✕91/1

Wagrians Slav tribe of C Europe 54/1, 2

Wahoo Swamp SE USA ✕95/2

Wahran (Oran)

Waitangi Treaty New Zealand 112/2

Waitara N Island, New Zealand first Taranaki war 112/3

Waiwai Indian tribe of S America 63/1

Wajak Java site of early man 3/3

Wakayama city and prefecture of C Japan 126/1, 2

Wakefield N England Industrial Revolution 98/1

Wake Island C Pacific annexed by US 111/4; attacked by Japanese in WW2 134/1; US base 149/1 (inset)

Walata (Fr. Oualata) W Africa trans-Saharan trade 60-61

Wales (Lat. Cambria Wel. Cymru) Scandinavian settlement 37/1; Black Death 57/1; English control 53/6, 7, 73/4; Reformation 75/1; Civil War 76/4; Industrial Revolution 98/1

Wallachia (Turk. Eflâk) region of Romania under Hungarian suzerainty 56/2; under Ottoman control 49/1; occupied by Russia 91/1, 116/1; part of Romania 116/1

Walla Walla NW USA ✕94/2

Wallis and Futuna Islands C Pacific French colony 139/1 (inset)

Walloons French-speaking people of S Belgium 115/1

Walton N England Industrial Revolution 98/1

Walvis Bay SW Africa occupied by British 103/3

Wandewash SE India ✕87/2

Wanfohsiu W China Buddhist site 27/1

Wanganui N Island, New Zealand 112/3

Wantage S England Industrial Revolution 98/1

Warau Indian tribe of S America 63/1

Wargla (Fr. Ouargla) Algeria trade 58/3

Warnabi Slav tribe of C Europe 54/1

Warrau hunting tribe of N Venezuela 63/1

Warsaw (Pol. Warszawa Ger. Warschau) C Poland Grand Duchy under French protection 91/1; WW1 119/3; WW2 132-3

Warsaw Pact 137/3

Washington E USA 93/5

Washington state of NW USA Depression 130/2; population 111/5, 145/1

Washita C USA ✕95/2

Washshukanni city of Mitanni 21/1

Waterford S Ireland Scandinavian settlement 37/1; Henry II 53/6

Waterloo Belgium ✕90/1

Wat Phu S Thailand Hindu-Buddhist temple 51/2

Wattignies N France ✕89/2

Wearmouth N England monastery 38/3

Weeden Island SE USA site 62/4

Wei N China warring state 28/1

Weichou N China T'ang prefecture 50/1

Wei-fang NE China Shang city 8/4

Weihaiwei N China treaty port 101/2, 107/4

Welford C England Industrial Revolution 98/1

Wellington N Island, New Zealand 112/3

Wels S Germany ✕55/1

Welshpool N Wales Industrial Revolution 98/1

Wenchow E China treaty port 107/4

Wenden (now Latv. Cēsis) NW Russia occupied by Teutonic Knights 54/1

Wendover S England Industrial Revolution 98/1

Wereroa New Zealand ✕112/3

Weris E Belgium megalithic tomb 15/3

Wessex early kingdom of S England 35/3; conversion to Christianity 38/3

West Bank (of Jordan) 141/3

West Bengal province of India 105/5

West Coast S Island, New Zealand gold rush 112/2

Western Australia settlement and development 112/5, 113/1

Western Sahara (Spanish Sahara)

Western Samoa S Pacific German colony 101/2; independence 139/1 (inset)

Western Trail C USA cattle trail 94/1

West Indies Spanish colonial trade 66/1; European settlement 66/4, 86/1. See also Caribbean

West Irian (form. Dutch New Guinea now Irian Jaya) ceded to Indonesia 139/2

West Kennet S England megalithic tomb 14/3

Westland county of S Island, New Zealand founded 112/2

Westminster S England Civil War 76/4